VOTING

VOTING

A Study of Opinion Formation in a Presidential Campaign

BERNARD R. BERELSON

PAUL F. LAZARSFELD

WILLIAM N. McPHEE

THE UNIVERSITY OF CHICAGO PRESS ☒

CHICAGO & LONDON

THE UNIVERSITY OF CHICAGO PRESS, CHICAGO 60637

The University of Chicago Press, Ltd., London

Library of Congress Catalog Card Number: 54-11205
80 79 78 77 76   11 10 9 8 7

To RUTH

—*B. R. B.*

⊠ INTRODUCTION

This is a book about voting—how people come to vote as they do. It deals with such matters as the voters' perception of politics, their reaction to the issues, their attention to the mass media, their influence on one another's political preferences, the role of class and religious affiliations in politics, and the institutional leadership of the local community.

While the study is not intended as an investigation of only one election or of only one community, it is based on a single case—how a thousand citizens living in Elmira, New York, made up their minds in the 1948 election between President Truman and Governor Dewey. This study is part of a series of similar investigations in different elections from 1940 to 1952 all aimed at the same objective: better understanding of the processes of democratic elections.

Yet that is by no means the only aim or product of such studies. One cannot study politics without learning a good deal about recent history, about American community organization, about ethnic and class antagonisms, about small-group processes, about attitude change, about decision-making in general. Observers of the social sciences often comment on the difficulty of carrying out experiments with human beings. But, in a way, society provides its own experimental situations, and elections in the Western world are a typical example. Under varying conditions a great diversity of people make comparable choices. Analysis of the process by which voters come to select one or the other candidate can illuminate human preferences in general. If we add to this consideration the obvious political importance of elections, then it should be regarded as fortunate that we now have available an increasing number of election studies of a fairly standardized type.

In this type of study, first of all, the information is obtained directly from the voters themselves in detailed interviews (in our sample, for example, several hundred items of information are available for each person). Second, and more important, the data are obtained in *repeated* interviews with the *same* voters as their preferences develop over time. Since the people who are interviewed repeatedly form a kind of fixed *panel* of respondents, this particular method of studying opinion development and change among the same people, over time, has come to be called the "panel" method.

The main purpose of this method is to analyze a developing process. In advance of the study the investigator tries to anticipate the psychological and social elements that might play a role in the final decision. The necessary information is collected from interview to interview, through the campaign and past the election. The analytical task then consists in relating preceding attitudes, expectations, personal contacts, group affiliations, and similar data to the final decision. For example, what kinds of experiences are characteristic for the people who change their vote intention from one interview to the next? Who are such people? What is the effect of contact with the parties, the mass media, certain organizations, or one's friends and family? The core of panel analysis consists in relating earlier experiences or attitudes to later changes in the respondent's vote intention.

The success of any interpretation depends upon the variety and the subtlety of the questions that are asked prior to any actual change. This leads to considerable pressure to introduce variables that are not typically included in a public opinion poll. Once so many items of information are available, they can also be used in cross-sectional analysis of the more traditional survey type, where they are particularly valuable because of the sheer wealth of data accumulated in successive panel-interview waves with the same people. But the major effort is devoted to analyses through time. In fact, such study of short-term changes can be extended to encompass the longer-term dynamics of the four-year period between elections and eventually to the decade or more of a typical political era.

RESEARCH CONTINUITY

The first major study of "votes in the making" during a campaign, with data collected and analyzed by such a panel method of repeated interviews, was made in the Roosevelt-Willkie election of 1940 in Erie County, Ohio. It was published under the title, *The People's Choice*. The potential contributions of the panel method to the analysis of opinion formation were set forth in the Introduction to that volume and in the Preface to the second edition.

Since *The People's Choice*, similar studies have been carried out on the presidential elections of 1944, 1948, and 1952; on congressional elections in 1950; and on two general elections in Britain in 1950 and 1951. A summary of the results from these studies is contained in Appendix A. This accumulation of findings provides an initial collection of raw materials that invite replication, systematization, and generalization.

It is important to see the present study, then, as one phase in a cumulative enterprise. Since the total field of electorate behavior in a presidential campaign is so extensive, any one study must concentrate on a few central subjects. In the progression from one study to the next, certain topics tentatively analyzed in an earlier effort are brought more into focus in a later. *The People's Choice*, for example, concentrated upon the role of newspapers and radio in the campaign. Their surface effects were not impressive. But the study concluded with sharp recognition of the importance of the voters' personal influence on one another and pointed up the unsolved problem of the role of political issues in the campaign. The present book gives particular attention to these two topics. In the case of personal influence, what was earlier a matter of conjecture is now elaborated and documented; in the case of issues, what was a puzzle is now beginning to be clarified.

In this same fashion the present study is linked to future efforts in this field. Just as *Voting* represents an advance over *The People's Choice*, so subsequent analyses will improve on this one. Continuity with past findings leads into continuity with future research tasks. Certain aspects of the research plan that appeared simple at the beginning of this study now appear as major problems; and topics hardly noticed before turn out to deserve high priority. For example, the present study includes material on the institutions of the community—labor unions, formal organizations, political parties—but at only a few points is it possible really to show the links between the efforts of the various institutions and the decisions of the voters themselves. Here a new task looms for the next study. Another new direction is indicated by comparative data. A series of small panel studies conducted during the 1950 congressional elections in various districts of the country (and now being analyzed) will show that such topics as the role of issues or the influence of specific pressures are best studied by comparing situations in which they vary. Congressional elections also have the advantage, from the research point of view, that the candidates are different from one place to the next but the parties remain the same. A still further step in the right direction will be made when panel studies are set up in local elections where voters choose among nonpartisan candidates and unstructured referenda, and hence where previous allegiances are reduced to a minimum.

ORGANIZATION OF THE BOOK

The book develops two major themes—loosely called the "social" and the "political." With reference to the first, it is a study of the formation of preferences. The book contains a social and psychological analysis of the ways individuals and groups make a "choice" in a matter not of immediate personal knowledge or, often, of directly appreciated effects. With reference to the second theme, this is a study of the behavior of the electorate in a free democratic society. The theory and values of democracy make certain assumptions about, or state certain requirements for, the democratic voter— his political interest, participation, principles, information, discussion, rationality. This study reports on the actual behavior of one sample of democratic citizens in a major election. Thus, confrontation of democratic theory with democratic practice is the second implied theme that runs throughout the book.

This double emphasis is expressed in the organization of the volume. Part I presents two preliminary chapters (1) describing the community of Elmira and recalling the events of 1948 and (2) presenting background data on political interest and trends in our sample of respondents. Then the two central sections of the book (Parts II and III) ask five parallel questions about the *social* aspects of voting (chaps. 3–7) and about its *political* aspects (chaps. 8–12):

First is the question of what *organizations* or *institutions* are directly or indirectly involved in political campaigns and what their immediate effects are on rank-and-file voting. Chapter 3 answers with respect to labor unions and community organizations generally; chapter 8, with respect to the local political parties.

Next is raised the question of the major *differentiations* among the citizens that are relevant to voting. Of all ways in which the members of a community differ from one another, which seem most directly related to vote? Chapter 4 takes up the differentiation by social strata and groups within the community; chapter 9, the differentiation by political beliefs.

Then there arises the question: What is the *perception* of such differences—if they are perceived at all—by the voters? Here we deal not only with the psychological question of misperception but with the normative consequences of the citizen's perception of "how things are done around here." Chapter 5 analyzes the perception of group voting traditions; chapter 10, the perception of ideological stands by the candidates on issues of the day.

Then follow questions of the *transmission processes* by which information is circulated in a community and preferences developed. Chapter 6 takes up this question with regard to the family and personal associations and the face-to-face discussion within them; chapter 11, with regard to the analogous matter of the party campaigns in the mass media.

The last analyses in each section deal with what might be called the *dynamics* that result from a campaign involving the foregoing processes. The consequences are in part recurrent phases of typical cycles—as with the case of polarization between social groups and other campaign effects on social groups treated in chapter 7. But, in part, effects are particular to the conditions of a given campaign—as with some elements in the Democratic rally of 1948 treated in chapter 12.

Finally, the concluding section of interpretation (Part IV) echoes the same dichotomy. Chapter 13 presents some social-psychological speculations suggested by the data, and chapter 14 reviews some implications of the study for the values and the theory of a democratic political system.

TECHNICAL NOTE

Our sample was drawn from a single community because we wanted detailed, intensive knowledge of a particular set of political and social conditions. We selected Elmira, New York, as an accessible urban community, not too small and not too large, with a relatively heterogeneous population in an area not too rigid in its political beliefs—but nevertheless "abnormally" for one party in the "normal" sectional tradition of the United States.

For practical considerations we had to choose between more respondents or more waves of interviews, and we chose the former. *The People's Choice* had seven interviews with a panel of six hundred; in this study we have four interviews with a panel originally of about one thousand.

Our data were collected from a probability sample based upon the random selection of dwelling units within the community, as described in Appendix C. The number of respondents interviewed in each of the four waves is as follows: June (4–16), 1,029; August (19–September 9), 881; October (16–31), 814; and November (3–23), 944. Every effort was made, up to four callbacks, to secure interviews with members of the sample, but for various reasons this was not always possible. The overlap in interviews and the character of the "mortality" of lost cases are discussed in Appendix C, along with other statistical considerations. Because of such mortality, the existence of "Don't know" responses, and similar reasons, the number of cases in charts and tables do not usually total to the above figures.

The data are presented in three kinds of tabulations. First, there are the usual tabulations from cross-sectional surveys that relate two or more variables or simply present the incidence of a variable. Second, there are trend tabulations on changes in attitude or behavior from one interview to another. Third, there are "panel" tabulations that present the turnover in variables at two or more points in time for the same people.

Such formal statistical techniques as significance tests and confidence intervals have not been used. The fact that all the basic data are presented makes possible any further analyses that others may care to do. In most instances the estimates in which we are interested can be examined by simple tests of significance; many of the differences are large and consistent enough to obviate the necessity of formal tests. Many of our hypotheses have been suggested by the data themselves, so that significance tests can at best show that the hypotheses are strongly enough suggested by these data to justify testing them on new bodies of data. While we approached the study with certain questions in mind, we did not always have clear-cut hypotheses so well established as to justify confining our work to testing them or to measuring their unspecified parameters.

What we are interested in is a "total" picture of the central decision in voting—how and why people come to favor this candidate rather than that one. Measured against this ultimate objective, our study must be considered tentative and contributory. This does not imply that what we report here is not true for the Elmira sample: we believe that it is. But Elmira is one place, 1948 is one point in time, and the total is one set of conditions. Our conclusions need further testing in other places, times, and conditions. We place considerable importance upon the reappearance of similar results in several studies; for this reason we have compiled in Appendix A generalizations from other studies similar to ours. In the long run the validity of our results must be determined by independent studies by different observers under various circumstances, and by the deductions made from them that survive the tests of future experience.

Because of the sheer number of questionnaire items used in the analysis, it has not been feasible to quote question wordings and index components in detail in the text. It is hoped that the general idea is indicated by the text and the tabulation notations; the full questionnaires and indexes appear in Appendix B.

☒ ACKNOWLEDGMENTS

A number of people participated in this study at one or another stage in its development, and we are deeply indebted to them for valuable contributions at various points throughout the planning, the field work, and the analysis.

Contributing authors: John P. Dean and Edward Suchman.

Research associates: Thelma Anderson, Helen Dinerman, J. Gordon Hall, Harris Huey, Philip McCarthy, and Robin Williams.

Contributing analysts: Dick H. Baxter, Hazel Gaudet Erskine, Sylvia Gilliam, David Gleicher, Charles Y. Glock, David Gold, Helmut Guttenberg, Richard Hamilton, Norman Kaplan, Carol Kazin, Bernard Levenson, Alan Meyer, and Alice Kitt Rossi.

Community-study field staff: John P. Dean, director; Roger Baldwin, Jessie Cohen, Leila Calhoun Deasy, Mildred Essick, Irving Fowler, Martin T. Keavin, and Duncan MacIntyre.

Administrative committee: Elmo C. Wilson, chairman; Bernard Berelson, Leo Bogart, Carolyn Crucius, John P. Dean, J. Gordon Hall, Oscar Katz, Paul Lazarsfeld, Edward Suchman, Frank N. Trager, and David Wallace.

In addition, several graduate students have contributed to the study, especially Guido Crocetti, Norman Friedman, Henry Senft, William Spinrad, Mayone Stycos, Wagner Thielens, and Charles Wright. The complications of tabulating, a difficult task in a study of this kind, were handled with promptness and care by Fred Meier, Fred Brunswik, and Pytor Aptakan. Finally, we are indebted to Nina Mills, Margaret Peirce, Catherine Morley, Ruby Taylor Gustafson, Robert Witt, and Nelson Glover for their conscientious secretarial assistance.

The study was supported by grants or other contributions from the Anti-Defamation League; Carnegie Corporation; The University of Chicago; Columbia Broadcasting System; Council for Research in the Social Sciences and the Bureau of Applied Social Research of

Columbia University; Cornell University; *Elmira Star-Gazette;* Elmo Roper, Inc.; The Ford Foundation; International Public Opinion Research, Inc.; National Opinion Research Center; Readers' Digest Association; Rockefeller Foundation; Standard Oil Company (N.J.); and Time Inc.

⊠ TABLE OF CONTENTS

PART I. THE SETTING

PART II. SOCIAL PROCESSES

1 THE SOCIAL AND HISTORICAL BACKGROUND
Elmira and the 1948 Election

Counterparts of our test community are found throughout the industrial Northeast and other parts of the United States. In upstate New York or downstate Illinois, outside Boston or Detroit or Cleveland, there are small cities or middle-sized towns that fall between the village and rural area, on the one hand, and the metropolis, on the other. Such towns are familiar to Americans; they are often termed the "grass roots" of the nation. Yet a student of politics in France or Britain might be puzzled about what manner of places they are, where Protestant factory workers often vote for the "right" and devout Catholics for the "left" and where whole communities vote for (or with) regional traditions whose origins most of them have forgotten.

The same is true for our test year: 1948 is "only yesterday" to the literate citizen today, and so is the New Deal and Fair Deal era, of which the 1948 election was the latest—perhaps the last—rally. Yet the political events of that time, in both the broad and the narrow senses, are not so familiar that they are immediately called forth out of memory. Many Americans today have forgotten that the 1948 election was the first in a quarter-century with more than two "major" parties in contention[1] or that in 1947 and in the opening months of 1948 it was still proper to treat the Soviet Union as a respected, recently friendly ally.

While it is therefore necessary to remind ourselves what com-

1. Despite that fact, this report is essentially limited to the Republican and Democratic vote. The Dixiecrats were not in the Elmira picture, of course, and the (Wallace) Progressive party received only five votes in our November sample of 644 voters and 944 people (and a similar trace in the official count).

3

munities like Elmira and recent years like 1948 were actually like, we wish at the same time to stress that this report is *not* intended as a study of a community or of recent American political history. Quite the opposite, for we should like, ultimately, to have our conclusions independent of the specific time-and-place bounds imposed on them. This is *not* an anthropological or sociological investigation of a community, and, while one could argue that such a study (in the Lynd or the Warner tradition) would enrich our understanding of an activity like politics, the purposes would not be the same as those of this study. Nor is this a current-history survey, as worth while as are the current studies of that type (e.g., in the work of Louis Bean, Samuel Lubell, and Louis Harris). We are, instead, interested in just what the title of the volume states, namely, voting, and we seek to identify, formulate, and test some generalizations on that subject.

But generalizations are based upon particular instances, and the long-term aim for generality must be served by specificity now. Generalizations in the future will depend heavily on replication and comparison in different times and places, and it is an ultimate advantage to pin down each study to a distinct—and not necessarily "typical"—context.[2] This chapter describes the place and the time of this study—the community of Elmira and the events of 1948.

THE COMMUNITY[3]

Elmira, New York, is thirty-five miles southwest of Ithaca and eight miles north of the New York–Pennsylvania border. It covers seven and a half square miles in the broad valley of the Chemung River, is surrounded on three sides by rolling wooded hills, and is situated in the heart of a rather poor agricultural region. Miles from any community of comparable size and facilities, Elmira occupies a unique position in this section of New York State and is sometimes called "Queen City of the Southern Tier."

To anyone who has motored through the middle-sized cities of the

2. It may be, in fact, that national samples for such studies (as used in 1944 and 1952) gain in generality at the cost of blurring specifics. For example, the degree of social differentiation in politics is blurred by nation-wide averaging of data representing quite different patterns of cleavage, e.g., sectional with ethnic and class.

3. This section was prepared by John P. Dean and edited by the authors.

Northeast and Middle West, this "Queen City" label might be puzzling. Elmira in 1948 was an ordinary bustling industrial community and looked it. Railroad tracks run northward and southward through the city, and the Chemung River flows eastward through the middle of town, dividing the North Side from the South Side.

Warehouses, freight depots, and railroad yards cluster in the northeastern section of the town, and factories dot the fringes to the north, east, and south. The downtown section, an area six or eight blocks square that front on the river's north bank, is undistinguished, even drab, and so are the working-class residential areas to the north and east of it. Trailing east from the business section are several blocks of Elmira's "skid row," and several blocks away, at the extreme eastern edge of Elmira's North Side, semirural slum dwellings line the road for a quarter of a mile. The area a few blocks north and slightly east of the business section is the "patch," so named because the early Irish settlers of the area formed a "patch" of Irish from County Cork, a "patch" from County Clare, and so on. As the Irish became middle class and moved to more desirable sections, Italians and then Negroes moved in.

Moving west from the Patch, the residential climate becomes first respectable, then substantial, then fashionable—culminating in the elite residences of Strathmont Park. West Elmira is the area of new construction for fashionable families wanting to live in the "nice part of town."

The South Side of town is residential and industrial, mostly lower-middle and working class. This was not always so. A wide, old, shaded street that begins at the south bank of the river and ends at the southern tip of town is lined for several blocks with huge frame mansions, built in the gingerbread style of the 1880's and 1890's, that formerly were elite homes but now are boarding- and rooming-houses.

Elmira Heights, just north of the city proper, houses the bulk of Elmira's Polish and Ukrainian populations as well as certain large industries. It has a one-street business district and block after block of middle-sized frame houses with small, neat lawns. On a hill just west of the Heights, the big brick state reformatory for boys is located, and near by is Woodlawn Cemetery, where Mark Twain is buried. (He lived on a farm just outside Elmira during the late

1870's and early 1880's, at the time he wrote *Tom Sawyer*. The city's leading hotel is named for him.)

Elmira is near one of America's great summer "play" areas, the Finger Lakes region. Apart from that, recreational facilities are few and simple. There is the usual country club for the social elite and subelite, and for the average Elmiran there are an amusement park, a public golf course, a public outdoor swimming pool, an indoor pool at the YMCA, and a fair number of public parks and play areas scattered over the city. The neighboring hills provide the proper up- and downdrafts, and Elmira claims to be "the gliding capital of the world." Elmira is an eager baseball town with a Class A minor-league team. There are five movie theaters, an art gallery, and a public library.

In short, Elmira is not much different in most respects from other industrial cities of comparable size in its region. It is "an ordinary American town."

Criteria for Selection

Elmira was not a haphazard choice. The main criteria by which the town was selected were the following (in addition to reasonable accessibility from Cornell University, which conducted a further study of the community after this one): (*a*) moderate size; (*b*) independence from a metropolitan district but not isolated; (*c*) reasonable economic and social stability; (*d*) good communication media and a normal educational and cultural environment; (*e*) balanced industrial and labor situation; (*f*) typical ethnic composition; and (*g*) reasonable political party balance. The sixteen cities of New York State between 25,000 and 100,000 were reviewed on these criteria, and Elmira was chosen.

How well did Elmira meet the criteria?

a) *Size.*—The 1940 census gives the population of the city of Elmira as 45,106, with a total of 63,228 for the entire urban area. (The urban area includes the incorporated villages of Elmira Heights, Wellsburg, and Horseheads and the unincorporated towns of Elmira, Horseheads, Ashland, Southport, and Big Flats.) In 1948 the Elmira Association of Commerce estimated the city's population at 52,000 and the urban area at 76,000.

b) *Independence from metropolitan district.*—Elmira is clearly an "independent" urban community, yet it is not isolated. It is the seat of Chemung County, it has a small suburban area of its own, and it contains enough industry to give it reasonable economic self-sufficiency for a city of its size. It is a railroad center, with four trunk lines (Erie; Delaware, Lackawanna and Western; Pennsylvania; and Lehigh Valley) that offer passenger and freight connections with all parts of the country. Four important state highways converge at Elmira, and the Chemung County Airport is serviced by two national airlines and one state airline. Bus lines connect the city to various near-by points, and thirty-one over-the-road trucking companies serve it.

c) Social and economic stability.—Elmira in 1948 was neither a wartime boom town nor a "recession" town. It was an old community, originally settled in 1783; it had experienced steady economic and population growth ever since, with no startling ups or downs in the recent past. During the depression Elmira suffered a population decline (about 5 per cent in the decade between 1930 and 1940). But a new company, Remington Rand, moved in and helped take up some of the slack in the city's economic base. The record shows a steady economic expansion, with little boom and bust.

d) Communication media and educational environment.—Elmira has two daily papers and a Sunday paper, all three owned and operated by the Gannett Press. In addition, Elmira receives the New York daily and Sunday papers and the Syracuse, Binghamton, and Buffalo papers. There are two local radio stations, one owned and operated by the newspapers and the other independent. The American Federation of Labor Trades and Labor Assembly puts out a small semimonthly newspaper, and the Association of Commerce publishes a monthly business journal.

Elmira's education system serves the usual primary and secondary schooling needs. In 1948 Elmira had twenty-two schools, two of them large public high schools and one a small Catholic high school. There is a small women's college in Elmira, with about three hundred and fifty to four hundred students.

e) Industrial and labor situation.—Elmira is not a one-industry or one-company town or a town where one or two labor unions predominate. It has considerable industrial diversity: variation in size of plants, mixed local and absentee ownership, and differences in products, industrial processes, and working conditions. And it has a wide range in size and structure of labor unions.

Altogether, Elmira had about seventy-five industries in 1948. They varied in size from a few employees to more than 5,000, and they manufactured a variety of products, from Coca-Cola bottles to structural steel for bridges. There were twenty plants employing 100 people or more. The largest companies were Remington Rand, producing office equipment and employing 4,500–5,000 people; the absentee-owned Eclipse Machine Division, Bendix Corporation, producing automobile and aircraft parts and employing about 2,000; the Thatcher Manufacturing Company, a locally owned industry that produced glass containers and employed about 1,300 people; and the locally owned American La France Foamite Corporation, manufacturing fire-fighting equipment and employing about 1,000 people. Other important industries were the American Bridge Company, locally known as "the bridge works," a subsidiary of United States Steel, employing about 650 people; the Elmira Foundry of General Electric, employing 900–1,000; Kennedy Valve Manufacturing Company, a local industry manufacturing valves and hydrants, employing about 600; Moore Business Forms, an absentee-owned company producing salesbooks and other business forms, employing about 400; Harding Brothers, Inc., a local plant manufacturing machine tools, employing about 350; Artistic Card Company, a locally owned greeting-card company, employing about 350; Ward La France, a locally owned truck-manufacturing plant, employing about 275; the utilities—New York Telephone Company and New York State Electric and Gas Corporation—each employing between 200 and 500; and the four railroad lines previously mentioned.

In 1948 approximately 86 per cent of Elmira workers eligible for unionization belonged to unions. But Elmira could not be called a "labor town." With two or three exceptions, the unions were old, well established, settled down, and nonmilitant. Until 1947, when the International Association of Machinists local at Remington Rand struck for ten weeks, there had not been a major strike in Elmira since the 1920's. The AF of L building trades were solidly intrenched, and so were the printing trades, with locals at the newspaper and at Moore Business Forms. They, together with the railroad brotherhoods, represented the more conservative wing of Elmira labor. At the other extreme, at least in terms of the position of its international, was the United Electrical Workers local at the Elmira Foundry of General Electric. Somewhere in the middle were the city's two biggest locals—the IAM (machinists) at Remington Rand and the United Automobile Workers, CIO, at Bendix-Eclipse. There were many other unions in Elmira—Teamsters, Office Employees, Ironworkers, Bartenders, Street Railway Employees, State, County, and Municipal Workers—but in numbers, economic strength, and political action the most important were the building trades, the printing trades, the railroad brotherhoods, IAM, UAW, and UE.

f) Ethnic composition.—Elmira had the usual representation of ethnic minorities, with no unusual proportion from any one group. Elmira's Negroes were about 2–3 per cent of the population, and there was about the same proportion of Jews. There were Irish-American and Italian-American groups, and smaller Polish, German, and Russian Ukrainian groups; in 1940 the total foreign-born from all these nationality groups was about 7 per cent.

The foreign-extraction groups had exerted liberal political influences in Elmira, partly because of the working-class character of the major immigration waves and partly because some of the groups, notably the Germans and the Jews, brought liberal European ideologies with them. The first group, in point of time as well as influence on the city, were the Irish, who arrived among the first settlers in 1783 and continued to come especially in the second quarter of the nineteenth century. From 1848 until close to the end of the nineteenth century, groups of political refugees of various European nationalities who came in large numbers to the United States also came to Elmira: Germans and Jews following the revolutionary upheaval of 1848; another wave of Germans following the Franco-Prussian War of 1870; Poles and Ukrainians escaping czarist rule in the 1880's. And during this period came the first group of Negroes on the "Underground Railroad." The expanding Erie Railroad brought Elmira's last big foreign group, the Italians, who began to arrive during the 1890's.

g) Political party balance.—Although upstate New York is heavily Republican by tradition, and Elmira is no exception, the Democratic party has made a better showing there in the past few elections than in most other cities considered for study. In the preceding presidential election, 1944, the Democrats cast about 40 per cent of the Elmira vote.

In sum, Elmira appeared to satisfy the major criteria laid down for the study of voting in a "normal" American community. While there is no such thing as a "normal" American community that can represent, say, New York City, Tuscaloosa, Topeka, and Walla Walla at the same time, nevertheless Elmira contains a sufficiently heterogeneous sample of people and conditions to assure a realistic test of the generalizations advanced in this book.

THE PERIOD

Now let us turn to the *time* location or historical boundaries of the study. In retrospect it is "obvious" that the Truman era was a transitional political period, a time of more or less unstable fluctuation between the parties with lingering resemblance to the Roosevelt era of the 1930's yet foreshadowing the Eisenhower era of the 1950's. At least it is easy to see this "transitional" quality now. But, at the time, the 1948 election almost became the eclipse of Truman and the decisive launching of something quite different—what we would now be calling the "Dewey era"!

Also in retrospect, the Truman administration will be remembered for its international policies and for the emergence of foreign affairs as the dominant concern and issue of the times. It is easy for the historian to assume that this was the will of the electorate in 1948. But, as we shall see, 1948 was a year in which the vote turned on *domestic* concerns of a socioeconomic character. A Republican administration from 1948 to 1952 might have had to do much the same things in foreign affairs as the Democrats. But the fact remains that the slim margin of votes that legitimized the historic Truman policy of containment of Russia through international alliances was gained on the basis of domestic issues affecting labor, consumers, and farmers.

As a final paradox, the 1948 election will always be seen as a great political success for President Truman—which it was—and a parallel defeat for Governor Dewey. Yet, again, what happened afterward colors our perception of what happened then. For no matter how warm the regard of Americans for President Truman in future years, or how cool to Governor Dewey, more or less the opposite was the case at the time of the 1948 campaign. Dewey was respected as an efficient governmental administrator, and Truman was often disrespected as a "well-meaning man out of his depth."

Our own data warn us, then, against too easy a use of hindsight generalizations. But, at the same time, the data do demand background explanation of three main features of the historical period in which the study was made. One has to do with politics itself, the second with international developments, and the third with the United States economy.

As for American politics of the period, after a decade and a half of Democratic rule, the New Deal party lost both houses of Congress in 1946. President Truman as chief executive was at the center of constant controversy. By midsummer 1948 the "left" in the North had deserted him for Wallace's third party (which, while small nationally, took 13.5 per cent of the vote in New York City); some middle-of-the-road Democrats had tried to draft Eisenhower just prior to the conventions; and, in response to Truman's civil rights program, the "right" in the South threatened to desert on the issue and subsequently did, to form the States Rights (Dixiecrat) party that carried thirty-nine electoral votes in the South. The farm vote for the New Deal of the 1930's had returned to the Republicans. The "New Deal coalition" seemed finally to be realizing what had threatened it since 1938—it was falling apart into the pieces from which it had originally been put together.

In contrast, the Republicans were united on the surface and had a wealth of candidates (Taft, Vandenberg, Stassen) from whom they chose Governor Dewey of New York, who had run a fairly close race against Roosevelt in 1944. In addition to the signs of victory inherent in their earlier winning of Congress, the Republicans' candidate (but not the party) was carrying all the reputable polls. Typical of informed belief toward the end of the campaign was this news statement: "Presidential candidate Thomas E. Dewey rested on his oars last week, riding the groundswell of pro-Republican sentiment." Dewey campaigned for six weeks to Truman's eight; traveled 16,000 miles to Truman's 22,000; gave 170 speeches and talks to Truman's 271. While the voters seemed to enjoy President Truman's more vigorous and down-to-earth campaign, it was generally considered a losing gesture. The political situation in mid-1948, in short, provided a near-perfect picture of the decline and fall of a ruling party in favor of a refreshed and confident opposition.

So much for unstable political conditions in the second half of 1948. Preceding and overshadowing them in late 1947 and the first half of 1948 (and continuing in some degree through the campaign) were important instabilities abroad. The period of 1947–48 was the turning point in postwar relations between the U.S.S.R. and the United States. Merely to mention some of the names and dates is to recall the period. On February 25, 1948, a Communist coup gained control of Czechoslovakia. April 18 in Italy and May 10 in Korea were dates of critical elections matching East and West points of view. On June 24 the famous Berlin blockade and airlift was begun. East-West negotiations began thereafter, but they generally failed. The Cominform denounced Tito of Yugoslavia in early summer, but the Chinese Communists took Mukden as the Nationalist forces rapidly collapsed in late fall.

It was an uneasy period for the United States, and responses had already begun. A five-nation Western pact was signed in Brussels in March. President Truman approved the European Recovery Program bill in April, and a bipartisan resolution favoring United States support for a European alliance passed on June 11. On June 19 the first peacetime conscription bill in United States history was passed. And the great domestic Communist hunt began, with Whittaker Chambers making his famous "pumpkin-papers" disclosures against Alger Hiss. While voters were somewhat more hopeful about Dewey's than Truman's ability to curb the Russians, both were firmly committed to do so. And, with Eisenhower refraining and MacArthur rebuffed, it was ambiguous who had an "answer" to foreign affairs. Moreover, the steady succession of foreign incidents seemed to pause in the latter half of the year, long enough for domestic events—such as rapidly rising prices and Truman's defense of labor against "that terrible Republican Eightieth Congress"—to reclaim attention.

One important fact about the 1946–48 era was the political pregnancy of the domestic economy. News references are brief but symptomatic. John L. Lewis was in and out of the headlines (e.g., he was fined for contempt of court arising out of a mine strike). On

May 25 General Motors signed a contract providing for "the third round of wage increases." In midsummer—in fact, announced in his acceptance speech—President Truman called back the Eightieth Congress to deal with high prices. In Elmira, as in many other American communities, a long and painful strike occurred in 1947. President Truman never tired of drumming at the new Republican Taft-Hartley Act regulating labor unions. The act itself was a consequence and a further precipitant of labor-management disputes that, along with parallel price-control quarrels, dominated domestic political news in the first years after World War II.

Productive capacity and purchasing power had been expanded during the war but had been artificially restricted from the civilian market. The economy of the country was now reaching new heights. It may seem curious that labor and management, consumers and farmers, tenants and landlords, should have many conflicts in a time of rapidly expanding prosperity for all of them, but the change was so rapid as to produce many dislocations in the years preceding and including 1948.

As the federally imposed limits on wages and prices began to break, and the first, second, and third "rounds" of strikes succeeded each other in the news, it was inevitable that the struggles led to Washington, itself deadlocked with a Democratic President and a Republican Congress. The latter won most of the economic skirmishes in 1947 and early 1948—cutting the budget, forcing the abandonment of price controls, and passing the Taft-Hartley labor bill. Yet in these economic moves affecting labor and consumers (and especially farmers), the Republicans provided weapons used against them with telling effect in the 1948 campaign.

As if parodying its beginnings in an economic collapse by ending in a boom, the New Deal movement again won a major election—and once again made far-reaching international moves—in a period of domestic quarrels that were the aftermath of economic change.

2 THE POLITICAL BACKGROUND
Voting Trend and Political Interest

Just as the presidential campaign has a social and historical background, so does it have a political background. In a general sense, the remainder of this book is devoted to an analysis of the determinants and the process of the vote decision. Here, however, we must introduce properties of the voting criterion itself, namely, certain features of party preferences, on the one hand, and political participation and interest, on the other. If political attitudes are composed of direction (i.e., pro and con, left and right, Democratic and Republican) and of intensity (i.e., how strongly one feels about an issue), then this chapter contains a description of trends in direction and levels of intensity of opinion about the election, as preparation for the later analysis.

TREND AND PATTERN OF PARTY PREFERENCE

The Stability of Votes

The Republicans made substantial gains in Elmira from 1944 to June, 1948, lost ground during the campaign, and ended up on election day just where they were in 1944 (Chart I). The timing of such gains and losses is crucial. An election is partly a race against time as well as against the opposition. What matters is who is ahead on election day. If Elmira is representative, Dewey's lead seemed sufficient to have won as late as two weeks before election day. And, assuming that the Republicans were sensing the Truman trend and would have taken strong steps against it, Dewey may have won a few weeks after election day.

In contrast to some European practices, American political campaigns are arbitrarily designated "slices" of time out of a historical process, and election day is the terminal point for the wavering

14

of voters. History can hang not only on a candidate's timing, as in the unusual 1948 case, but also on the timing of issues and events during the period. For example, the tensions attending the Berlin blockade raised fears of war, and rising prices increased sentiment for price control (Table 1). Less than one-third of the respondents

CHART I

THE REPUBLICANS GAINED BETWEEN CAMPAIGNS, LOST
DURING THE CAMPAIGN, AND ENDED UP EVEN*

PERCENTAGE REPUBLICAN OF TWO-PARTY VOTE (OR INTENTION)

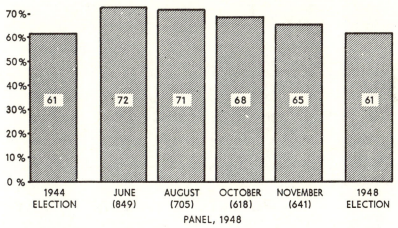

PANEL, 1948

* These figures include all cases available at the specified interview. The distribution of votes does not change more than 2 percentage points if the cases are restricted only to those respondents interviewed in all four waves, thus eliminating the possible effect of mortality. A total of 181 of an additional 238 cases, designated by the sampling plan but not interviewed in June or thereafter in the panel, were found in a November follow-up to be disproportionately Democratic. Had they been included, the "unofficial" figures above would be about 2 points less Republican (and thus nearer the official returns), but presumably the trend would have been similar. See Appendix C.

shifted from one side to the other, but they shifted overwhelmingly in the direction "imposed" by the course of events. The timing of these "natural" events seemed to contribute to Dewey's high point in June and to Truman's rally in November—beyond the generating effect of party propaganda itself (though, of course, the propaganda exploited the events).

Yet, unstable political year as it was compared to such election years as 1924 or 1944, the trends that make all the difference historically are relatively small statistically. Votes are much more stable, as expressions of preference, than opinions on issues. The gross and the net changes in vote, from interview to interview, are much less than the corresponding shift on the issues (Table 2). Whereas the turnover in Table 1 is 32 per cent and 28 per cent, in Table 2 it is 11 per cent, 4 per cent, and 5 per cent. In all repetitive measures of political (or, for that matter, other) preferences, people shift

TABLE 1

TURNOVER IN OPINION DURING THE CAMPAIGN
REVEALS THE EFFECT OF EXTERNAL EVENTS

(Only Respondents with Opinions Both Times)

JUNE	OCTOBER (PER CENT)			JUNE	AUGUST (PER CENT)		
	Expect War within Ten Years	Do Not	Total		For Price Control	Against Price Control	Total
Expect war in ten years*.	32	8	40	For price control*......	38	4	42
Do not......	24	36	60	Against price control....	24	34	58
Total...	56	44	100 (604)	Total....	62	38	100 (782)

* The actual wordings for this and subsequent questions are given in Appendix B.

TABLE 2

TURNOVER IN VOTE DURING THE CAMPAIGN
IS NOT PARTICULARLY HIGH

(Only Respondents with Positions Both Times*)

JUNE	AUGUST (PER CENT)			AUGUST	OCTOBER (PER CENT)			OCTOBER	NOVEMBER (PER CENT)		
	Rep.	Dem.	Total		Rep.	Dem.	Total		Rep.	Dem.	Total
Rep......	67	6	73	Rep....	68	3	71	Rep....	66	4	70
Dem.....	5	22	27	Dem...	1	28	29	Dem...	1	29	30
Total..	72	28	100 (641)	Total.	69	31	100 (543)	Total.	67	33	100 (552)

* The slight discrepancies in marginal percentages for the same interview wave are due to differential mortality in combinations of them (see Appendix C).

back and forth to a greater or lesser extent. By measures of either gross turnover or net trend, vote intentions were more stable than subsidiary opinions in 1948 Elmira. They were less subject to manipulation by the circumstances of the moment and presumably more deeply rooted in the voters' personal predispositions and social surroundings.

In some senses, votes and opinions on issues are not comparable at all in stability. For example, if votes are considered as "average" or summary expressions of a multitude of smaller judgments moving in different directions, then obviously the average is more stable than the parts. Moreover, votes undoubtedly move on larger time scales than current-issue opinions. For many people, votes are not

CHART II

Most Voters Remained Constant throughout the Campaign;
Those Shifting between Parties Ended Up Democratic

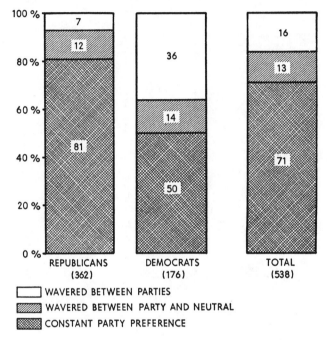

WAVERED BETWEEN PARTIES
WAVERED BETWEEN PARTY AND NEUTRAL
CONSTANT PARTY PREFERENCE

perceived as decisions to be made in each specific election. For them, voting traditions are not changed much more often than careers are chosen, religions drifted into or away from, or tastes revised.

Something like a long-term "standing decision," in V. O. Key's term, seemed to be the case, especially among the Republican voters of Republican Elmira in Republican upstate New York. Most of those who eventually voted Republican had been that way all along without any change during the campaign. Even half of the unstable Democratic minority in the town had been constant during the 1948 campaign (Chart II). (Yet voters who were in both camps during

the campaign were more likely to vote Democratic on election day—
or, rather, eventual Democrats were more likely to have been in
the other party at some point.)

It follows that the time of final decision, that point after which
the voter does not change his intention, occurred *prior* to the campaign for most voters—and thus no "real decision" was made *in* the

CHART III

The Time of Final Decision Was Much Earlier for
Republican Voters than for Democrats

TIME OF FINAL DECISION

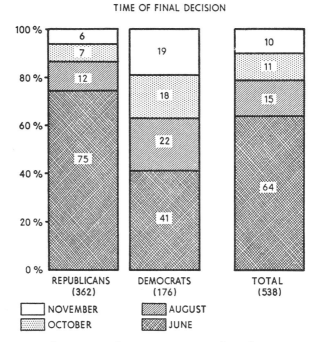

campaign in the sense of waiting to consider alternatives. Again,
this was especially the pattern among the socially supported, traditional Republican majority in Elmira (Chart III).

In making later decisions, the Democrats of Elmira showed greater
signs of instability, the reasons for which we shall examine in some
detail later in the volume. For the moment, however, the differences
between the two parties (in what was an unstable year for the
Democrats) should not obscure the fact that about two-thirds of
those who voted in November had *not* shifted position at all—had

not so much as wavered to a neutral viewpoint from June (*before* the conventions) to November. Votes do not change easily, at least during a campaign.

Constants and Changers

What kinds of votes do change? The people who change most *during* a campaign are the people who changed most *between* campaigns. Among 1948 voters those who intended in June to vote as they had in 1944 were remarkably stable; fully 96 per cent of them (both parties) carried through in November as intended in June. Moreover, of those who were undecided in June, three-fourths returned to their former party. But those supporting a different party in June, 1948, from that supported in the 1944 election were the least stable of all: almost 40 per cent of them returned to their former position. Political preferences are highly self-maintaining; when they start to change, the influences making them what they were reassert themselves and press for a "return to normalcy." How this operates will be touched upon at many points in this volume.

More generally, changers of vote are characterized not only by inconsistencies in the past but by inconsistencies in their present position on subsidiary political matters. It is the people with "cross-pressured" opinions on the issues or candidates or parties—that is, opinions or views simultaneously supporting different sides—who are more likely to be unstable in their voting position during the campaign (see Chart IV).[1] Accepting one stand by a given party but not another, or identifying with a given party but rejecting its stand on a given issue—such "contradictions" weaken the voter's stability. Quite reasonably, if he has a foot in each camp, he is more likely to move between them—or to the midway position of indecision.

How do people get into inconsistent and unstable positions? In part they do so because of conflicting currents in the particular historical situation and the almost inherent contradictions of any two-party sytem in a complex, pluralistic society. But for many voters such inconsistency of opinion, and the resultant fringe of instability

1. In the preparation of this book a distinction was made between charts of central and of supplementary importance. The latter expand, modify, refine, or otherwise elaborate the findings of the former.

The central charts appear here in somewhat larger size and with titles; the supplementary charts appear in reduced form and without titles.

surrounding the solid core of more stable American votes, arises simply from not caring much one way or the other about the election. Stability in vote is characteristic of those interested in politics and instability of those not particularly interested. Since the bulk of each party's votes move only sluggishly if at all, the short-term change that "decides" close elections is disproportionately located among those closer to the border line of disinterest (see Chart V).

CHART IV

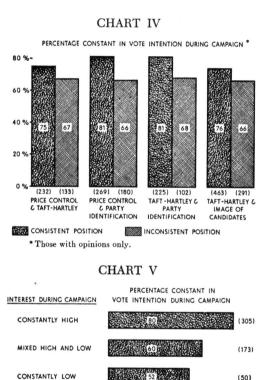

PERCENTAGE CONSTANT IN VOTE INTENTION DURING CAMPAIGN *

	(232) (133)	(269) (180)	(225) (102)	(463) (291)
	75 67	81 66	81 68	76 66
	PRICE CONTROL & TAFT-HARTLEY	PRICE CONTROL & PARTY IDENTIFICATION	TAFT-HARTLEY & PARTY IDENTIFICATION	TAFT-HARTLEY & IMAGE OF CANDIDATES

▓ CONSISTENT POSITION   ▓ INCONSISTENT POSITION

* Those with opinions only.

CHART V

PERCENTAGE CONSTANT IN
INTEREST DURING CAMPAIGN   VOTE INTENTION DURING CAMPAIGN

CONSTANTLY HIGH	80	(305)
MIXED HIGH AND LOW	60	(173)
CONSTANTLY LOW	52	(50)

To summarize some properties of voting changes: first, they are often reversals of earlier attempts to change; second, they are associated with analogous inconsistencies in supporting attitudes at the given time; and, third, they are more likely to occur among those who do not really care about the election.

Changes in Degree

But there is a certain relativity implied in any discussion of the rigidity or fluidity of political preferences. To this point change has meant a shift from one party to undecided or to the other party.

Yet changes can occur *within* a single party preference—in the intensity or extremity with which the preference is held. Instability and fluidity are found within votes if they are considered microscopically. This can be explained as follows.

Elmirans were asked whether they planned to vote at all; if so, for which party; and, finally, how strongly they felt about their choice. These questions can be used to make a primitive kind of scale with five "steps," from extreme Republicans to extreme Democrats. At certain points we shall abandon the arbitrary "cutting points" used in our political system (Democrat–neutral–Republican) and instead deal with these finer gradations within party preferences. One then finds more frequent "molecular" changes within the arbitrary party lines. In fact, if we assume that these finer gradations better represent the reality of American opinion, it then becomes an empirical question how our political system takes a quasi-continuous range of preferences and manages to "squeeze" it into alternatives to which people can answer only "Yes" or "No." For example, how are those near the center polarized apart?

The campaign helps polarize people in this way, at the expense of moderation. There were more voters who strongly supported their candidate at the close of the campaign than at the start and fewer who supported him moderately, especially among the Republicans. But more also came to take a neutral position (Chart VI). The tendency of the campaign is to divide a more or less continuous range of variation into three camps—the extreme left, the extreme right, and the "extreme center" of total withdrawal.

Now, what does voting change at this more molecular level look like? The type of turnover table presented earlier for those with definite vote intentions can now be presented for this more differentiated measure of vote position. All the cases available in the first three interviews can be shown "turning over" between June and August and between August and October (Table 3). The people who stayed constant are along the shaded diagonal; the farther from this diagonal, the greater the change (down toward the Democrats, up toward the Republicans). Outright conversions to the opposite party are located within the dotted-line boxes at the two corners farthest from the diagonal. It immediately becomes apparent that most of the movement is near the diagonal and not in the conversion categories.

Even when these finer gradations are established, more than half the voters stay in the same category. And this stability increases during the active campaign period as compared to the nominating period. Moreover, most of the change takes place in small steps: the only appreciable amount of conversion in the campaign is movement from a moderate position in one party across the nonvoting

CHART VI

THE CAMPAIGN INCREASES THE STRONGS AND NEUTRALS AND DECREASES THE MODERATES, ESPECIALLY AMONG REPUBLICANS*

PERCENTAGE (OF THOSE INTERVIEWED IN ALL THREE WAVES)

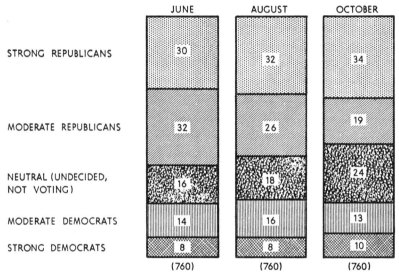

	JUNE	AUGUST	OCTOBER
STRONG REPUBLICANS	30	32	34
MODERATE REPUBLICANS	32	26	19
NEUTRAL (UNDECIDED, NOT VOTING)	16	18	24
MODERATE DEMOCRATS	14	16	13
STRONG DEMOCRATS	8	8	10
	(760)	(760)	(760)

* If only those voters with vote intention are taken into account, the proportion with "strong" feelings for their candidate rises from 45 per cent in June to 49 per cent in August and 57 per cent in October. The increase in the neutral category is mainly a rise in nonvoting, not indecision.

gap into a similarly moderate position on the other side (see Chart VII). The history of ordinary political campaigns presumably consists of small shifts back and forth that decide elections when they cross the arbitrary cut-off points used in counting ballots officially.

In summary, then, the ordinary campaign is characterized by numerous shifts over short "distances" of the political spectrum. But a molecular analysis of the many small movements that go on inside Democratic and Republican votes is not pursued here. For most of the remainder of our analysis, we take the politician's viewpoint that a vote is a vote, and we deal with Republicans and Democrats

TABLE 3

VOTING TRENDS ARE MADE UP OF A LARGE NUMBER OF SMALL SHIFTS

	Strong Republican	Moderate Republican	Neutral	Moderate Democrat	Strong Democrat	
			August			
June:						
Strong Republican.......	145	52	20	7	2	226
Moderate Republican....	83	102	32	23	5	245
Neutral................	10	24	63	17	6	120
Moderate Democrat......	2	13	16	59	18	108
Strong Democrat........	1	8	5	16	31	61
	241	199	136	122	62	760
			October			
August:						
Strong Republican.......	181	31	23	4	2	241
Moderate Republican....	64	93	31	8	3	199
Neutral................	8	14	102	9	3	136
Moderate Democrat......	0	5	19	72	26	122
Strong Democrat........	1	0	8	9	44	62
	254	143	183	102	78	760

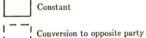 Constant

Conversion to opposite party

CHART VII

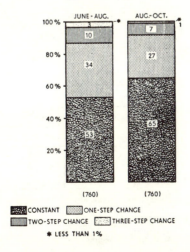

JUNE - AUG.   AUG.-OCT.

(760)   (760)

CONSTANT   ONE-STEP CHANGE
TWO-STEP CHANGE   THREE-STEP CHANGE
✱ LESS THAN 1%

rather than with their modifications. But it is helpful to recognize at the outset that gradations of political preferences are involved in all the changes we shall document later. The votes which we and the official canvass count represent gross segments arbitrarily cut out of a more or less continous spectrum.[2]

INTEREST IN THE ELECTION

The other consideration useful as introduction to the analysis to follow is participation and interest. The democratic citizen is supposed to be interested in public affairs, but even during a presidential campaign—presumably the high point of political intensity—not every citizen is interested. How do we measure interest? Actually, almost all measures of political involvement and participation are highly correlated with one another and, for analytical purposes, interchangeable. Accordingly, we use here the simplest measure, a direct question asking: "How much interest would you say you have in this year's election—a great deal, quite a lot, not very much, none at all?" Only about one-third of Elmirans, by their own claim, were "greatly" interested in the election; another third were moderately interested; and the final third were not interested at all. More important, however, are the preconditions for political interest.

Correlates of Political Interest

Two sets of characteristics—one social, one political—are associated with interest in the election.

2. Microscopic movements of votes could be analyzed by means of the following scheme that provides for all the combinations—stable or shifting—that can occur.

TIME II

		SD	MD	N	MR	SR
	SD	dk	dw	dn	dc	dc
	MD	ds	dk	dn	dc	dc
TIME I	N	ad	ad	nk	ar	ar
	MR	rc	rc	rn	rk	rs
	SR	rc	rc	rn	rw	rk

dk, nk, rk : Constant Democratic, neutral, Republican, respectively
dw, rw   : Weakening in intensity
ds, rs   : Strengthening in intensity
dc, rc   : Converted to opposition
dn, rn   : Neutralized
ad, ar   : Activated from neutral

In the first place, political interest is found in conjunction with some social positions and not others, and especially with high educational status. Better-educated people have more political interest than the less educated (57 per cent of college people had a "great deal" of interest in June as compared to 23 per cent of those with grade school or less); men have more than women (36 per cent to 28 per cent); the older have more than the younger (35 per cent for those over forty-five as against 21 per cent for those under twenty-five); and the upper socioeconomic status (SES) levels have more than the lower (48 per cent to 24 per cent).

Both social stimulation and social obligation appear to be at the root of interest, that is, factors making people both "want" and "have" to be interested. The social environment rewards people when they live up to the requirements imposed upon "their kind of people," whether with respect to etiquette or appearance or morality or politics; and it punishes them, however subtly, when they do not. For example, the better educated are supposed to know more about politics, and they have been trained to take part in civic activity. In the same way, politics is "a man's game"; women have been eligible for participation for only a generation and are thus newcomers to the political scene. The wealthy are alert to political effects upon their interests, and the older people have been around longer, have developed more involvement in political affairs, and have fewer of the romantic distractions that youth finds more attractive. It is the older, well-educated, well-off man who has most political interest in the community.

On the political side, two factors affect degree of interest in the election. The first is a feeling of potency about affecting political affairs at all (see Chart VIII). The more that people feel they can influence public matters, the more politically interested they are. The conviction that things *can* be affected is needed to give people the energy to care. Indeed, it may be such subjective feelings of potency that are responsible for the (alleged) decrease in political interest during the past century or so. The citizen may now feel much less capable of influencing "big government" than was his ancestor, who was "closer" to his governors.

The second set of political factors that affects interest is partisanship itself. The more strongly the voter favors or opposes parties and candidates, the more interested he is in the election (Chart IX).

This is not a tautology; there *are* citizens with high interest in politics but without strong feelings favoring one or the other side of a controversy. Indeed, this interested neutral is precisely the image of the "ideal" political man who exists in some hopeful theories and most civic books. But the conclusion of recent work on attitude measurement is that intensity of involvement and extremity of

CHART VIII

PERCENTAGE WITH "GREAT DEAL" OF INTEREST (JUNE)

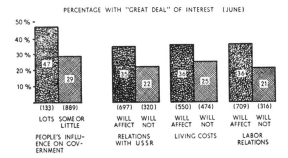

(133)	(889)	(697)	(320)	(550)	(474)	(709)	(316)
LOTS	SOME OR LITTLE	WILL AFFECT	WILL NOT	WILL AFFECT	WILL NOT	WILL AFFECT	WILL NOT
PEOPLE'S INFLU-ENCE ON GOV-ERNMENT		RELATIONS WITH USSR		LIVING COSTS		LABOR RELATIONS	

ELECTION'S INFLUENCE ON ISSUES*

* Respondents were asked how much influence they thought people like themselves had on government and how much it would matter for various issues which candidate became President (see Appendix B for exact wordings). This finding is not affected by the omission of the "Don't know" responses.

CHART IX

THE MORE PARTISANSHIP, THE MORE INTEREST

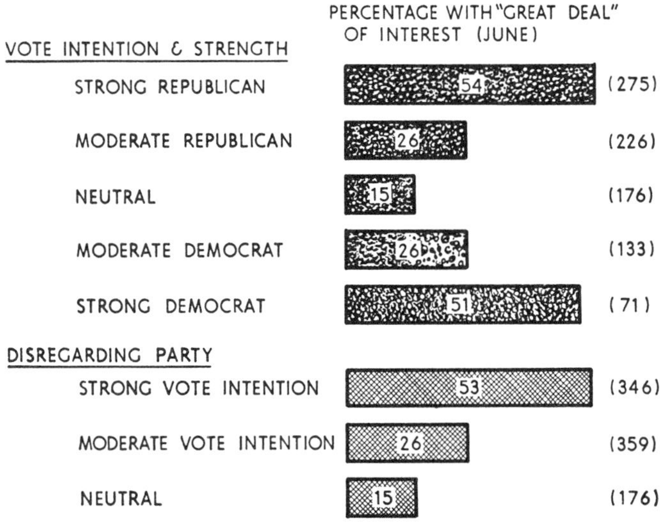

PERCENTAGE WITH "GREAT DEAL" OF INTEREST (JUNE)

VOTE INTENTION & STRENGTH

STRONG REPUBLICAN	54	(275)
MODERATE REPUBLICAN	26	(226)
NEUTRAL	15	(176)
MODERATE DEMOCRAT	26	(133)
STRONG DEMOCRAT	51	(71)

DISREGARDING PARTY

STRONG VOTE INTENTION	53	(346)
MODERATE VOTE INTENTION	26	(359)
NEUTRAL	15	(176)

attitudes are highly correlated. The classic "independent voter" of high interest but low partisanship is a deviant case.

Since partisanship increases political interest, anything that weakens partisan feelings decreases interest. Such is the effect of attitudinal "cross-pressures": people whose attitudes on specific issues are consistent with their vote intention have greater interest than those whose specific attitudes do not correspond with their vote intention. Republicans who disagreed with Truman's position had more interest in the election than Republicans who found some virtue in Truman's stand—and conversely for the Democrats. The "watering-down" of partisanship lowers the respondent's degree of interest; why remain so interested when there is some right on both sides anyway and hence less reason for investment in the outcome? A situation in black and white generates more interest than one in gray (see Table 4). And vice versa: the less interest, the less partisanship.

TABLE 4

	PERCENTAGE WITH "GREAT DEAL" OF INTEREST	
	Republicans	Democrats
Agree with Truman on two or three out of three issues*	39 (208)	37 (150)
Agree with Truman on one or none..................	46 (232)	21 (34)

* The issues were price control, Taft-Hartley, and public housing.

As the campaign proceeds, the relative importance of social as against political factors in interest changes. The correlation of interest with, for example, education or sex remains constant or becomes weaker, whereas the correlation with, for example, strength of feeling about the candidate increases. The difference in proportions highly interested between the more and less educated or between men and women declines during the campaign, but the difference between the strongly and moderately partisan increases considerably. To some extent this is probably the equivalent of comparing a dynamic with a static relationship. The social correlates do not change during the campaign, but feelings of partisanship do—and the increase in intensity of support for a candidate is accompanied by an increase in interest toward the entire political situation (see

Table 5). This shift in emphasis may be what we mean when we speak of the difference between the "heat" of campaign interest and ordinary attention to politics. It must represent, for some people at least, a change from the "disinterested interest" of a socially

TABLE 5

Month	DIFFERENCE IN PERCENTAGE POINTS OF THOSE WITH "GREAT" INTEREST*		
	Between More and Less Educated	Between Men and Women	Between Strongly and Moderately Partisan
June..........	14	9	18
October.......	11	2	37

* This table entry, the difference in percentage points, is here used as a simple index of trend in correlation from June to October. The greater the difference, the more correlation in the given month. For example, in June the percentage with "great interest" was 9 points higher for men than women. By October, the sexes were about the same (a difference of only 2 points).

trained and obligated citizen to the "interested interest" of a political partisan.[3]

Trend in Interest during Campaign

Yet the over-all level of interest in the election did not change during the campaign. A third (31 per cent) were "greatly" interested in June, a third (34 per cent) in August, and a third (34 per cent) in October. In ordinary surveys the constancy of the trend

3. The greater influence of the political factor over the social one is revealed in the following cross-tabulations. In June, strength of feeling is more important than sex in determining interest, but not much (45 per cent to 34 per cent for the off-diagonal cases). By October the difference has increased sharply (59 per cent to 18 per cent)—and, incidentally, the sex difference has disappeared.

Strength of Feeling about Candidate	PERCENTAGE WITH "GREAT DEAL" OF INTEREST					
	June		August		October	
	Men	Women	Men	Women	Men	Women
Feel strongly..........	45	45	51	58	52	59
Do not..............	34	22	30	22	18	18
Total no. of cases..	(143)	(144)	(147)	(156)	(164)	(164)
	(145)	(208)	(143)	(178)	(94)	(150)

in interest might suggest that it is highly rigid and unresponsive to influence. Actually, "turnover" analysis reveals the opposite to be the fact. It was not the *same* third who were interested at the different times. There were compensating changes in degree of interest, with nearly half the respondents moving in one or the other direction (Table 6). This instability reveals a rather fragile involvement.

TABLE 6

THERE ARE MARKED CHANGES IN INTEREST
DURING THE CAMPAIGN

	PER CENT	
	June–August	August–October
No change.................	52	60
Constant great..........	18	22
Constant moderate......	16	18
Constant none..........	18	20
Change...................	48	40
Increase...............	27	18
Decrease...............	21	22
Total no. of cases.....	881	760

Given the instability of political interest, the political campaigner is placed in much the same position as an advertiser trying to maintain equally fragile consumer preferences. He must continue advertising with great fury just to "keep even" with his losses to a multitude of competing interests.

Although the over-all political interest of the community did not appear to shift during the campaign, again the question of change is relative. "Interest" may not be estimated by the respondents against an absolute scale. Reports of subjective interest probably involve comparisons, conscious or not, with what is expected or what is "normal" or what other people are thought to be doing at the particular time. Thus it might take *more* interest, in an absolute sense, to be "moderately" interested in October than "greatly" interested in June. And there is some indication of this. Although subjective expressions of interest by the sample did not change, behavioral manifestations of interest, like political discussion with one's associates, did change under external pressures. Early in the campaign, discussion correlated more highly with interest than it did at the end (Chart X). The relationship is steeper in June and flatter in October, when almost everyone discussed the campaign.

As the base of political interest, then, there may be a shift during a campaign from sole reliance on internal concern to greater influence from external stimuli, when politics is "in season." Certain long-

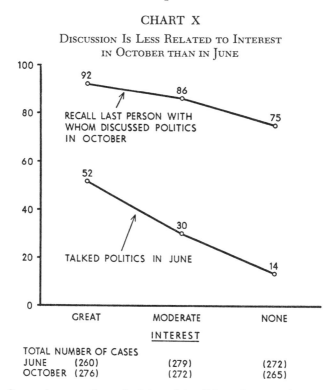

CHART X

DISCUSSION IS LESS RELATED TO INTEREST
IN OCTOBER THAN IN JUNE

time determinants of good citizenship (like education) seem to be supplanted or overlaid by the temporary stimulation of partisanship during the campaign. And such shifts can happen without at the same time any gross increase in the number of people who report that they really care about politics.

Thus, political interest has a high turnover and "fragility" for most Americans, educated or not. In a country in which few are "interested" but many "participate," the campaign develops a substantial degree of participation without any net or cumulative change in the total amount of more deeply internalized interest in politics per se.

Interest and Turnout

Interest is not without its effects upon a variety of behavioral factors—discussion, exposure to campaign communications, doing something to get one's candidate elected, actual turnout at the polls. But interest is by no means equivalent to such participation, and particularly not to turnout—the crucial act of making one's preference official.

CHART XI

MORE PEOPLE VOTE THAN FOLLOW THE CAMPAIGN*

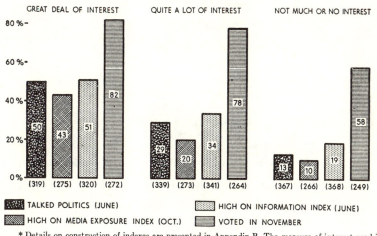

* Details on construction of indexes are presented in Appendix B. The measure of interest used is for the given month in each case (and for October for vote).

Although the over-all level of interest remains constant during the campaign and although certain manifestations (like discussion) increase, the intention to vote *falls* as the campaign goes on—84 per cent intend to vote in August, 79 per cent in October, and 72 per cent actually vote in November.[4] Fewer people vote than intend to only a few days before.

Moreover, the kind of self-generated discussion, eagerness for communication exposure, and sought-out information that distinguish the "responsible citizen" (as customarily defined) are characteristic only of the minority of highly interested people. Yet, in Elmira, the majority of people on every interest level actually vote. This leaves

4. That is, as time goes on, fewer people say they will vote, and, of these, even fewer actually do in November. Questions were not comparable in June, but June data compared to August express the same trend.

a "gap" between genuine welcoming of the debate, on the one hand, and eventual giving in to pressures or duties to vote, on the other (Chart XI).

It is often a mistake to give purely political explanations for non-participation (e.g., to consider failure to vote a politically motivated "choice" or "protest"). Nonvoting is related to persistent social con-

CHART XII

<small>OCTOBER DEMOCRATS ARE LESS LIKELY TO VOTE
THAN OCTOBER REPUBLICANS*</small>

PERCENTAGE NOT VOTING

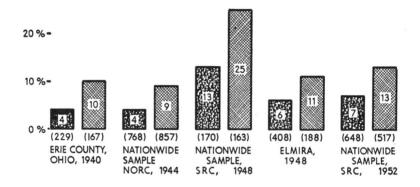

OCTOBER VOTE INTENTION

REPUBLICAN   DEMOCRATIC

* See Appendix A for full description of these studies. The Harris-Roper study in 1952 found that when an index was made of likelihood of voting, about three times as many Democrats as Republicans who were classified as likely voters failed to vote on election day, but the data are not comparable to those above.

ditions having little to do with the candidates or the issues of the moment. For example, because Democrats are on the average less well educated and less involved with dominant groups in the society than Republicans, they vote less on election day. That is, people who intend to vote Democratic in late October are less likely to carry out that intention than people who intend to vote Republican. This was true not only in Elmira in 1948 but in every such study from 1940 on (Chart XII). The Democrats do not mobilize as much of their support as do the Republicans, more likely for social reasons (lower participation of underdog groups in all public activities) than for political ones.

Through most of the following analysis the focus of attention will be on the Republican/Democratic ratio, with less regard to the effects (like those of Chart XII) of participation and interest on the final outcome. But, with regard to the latter, the essential background facts are that real involvement in politics is characteristic of only the minority who are subject to special social stimulation and/or especially see political consequences. But with the temporary campaign excitement and increase in partisanship—the products of external stimulation—in the end the majority take some part in the discussion and even more register their preferences on election day.

SUMMARY

As a summary, here and in subsequent chapters, we list the main points on which the data contribute some evidence.

Trend and Pattern of Voting

1. Turnover in opinion on campaign issues reflects the influence of the events of the time, and the outcome rests in part on timing.

2. Turnover in vote during the campaign is not so great as turnover in opinion on subsidiary issues.

3. Most voters remain constant in their vote intention from June to election day.

4. The time of final decision on vote was earlier for Republicans than for Democrats.

5. The people who change most during a campaign also change most between campaigns.

6. People who change their vote intention are more likely to be subject to cross-pressures in their position on subsidiary political matters.

7. People who change their vote intention are less interested in the election than the constants.

8. Partisanship in political support increases during the campaign.

9. Voting trends during the campaign are made up of a large number of small shifts over short distances of the political continuum.

10. Most conversion in vote during the campaign is composed of movement between moderate positions on the two sides.

Interest in the Election

11. Only about one-third of the voters were "greatly" interested in the election.

12. Better-educated, better-off, older men have more political interest than their counterparts.

13. People who think that they can have some effect upon governmental policy or that governmental policy can have some effect on events are more likely to be interested than those who do not think so.

14. The greater the partisanship, the greater the interest.

15. The less cross-pressures between vote and opinion on the issues, the greater the interest.

16. As the campaign goes on, political factors come to influence interest more than social factors.

17. Although there is little net change in interest during the campaign, there is a considerable amount of gross turnover.

18. Although the voters' estimate of their political interest does not change on the average during the campaign, certain types of behavior that manifest political interest (e.g., political discussion) do increase, as external stimulation becomes more important.

19. More people actually vote on election day than are initially interested in the election or than previously express their interest in political activity.

20. Intended Democrats vote less than intended Republicans under contemporary conditions of socioeconomic backing for the two parties.

Part II ☐
Social Processes ☒

3 SOCIAL INSTITUTIONS

*The Political Role of Labor Unions
and Other Organizations*[1]

The individual's vote is the product of a number of social conditions or influences: his socioeconomic and ethnic affiliations, his family tradition, his personal associations, his attitudes on the issues of the day, his membership in formal organizations. We turn first to this last consideration.

And, although we give some attention to other organizations in the community, we shall concentrate upon the political role of perhaps the most important organization from this standpoint—the labor union. Many assumptions have been made, and not without polemics, about the political activities of unions. Whatever they may be on the national scene or in the large cities, we are able to present a picture of what they amount to in a town like Elmira. Let us start with a review of what the unions themselves did about the 1948 election and then go to an analysis of the political behavior of the members themselves.

THE POLITICAL ACTIVITY OF LABOR UNIONS

Before the Wagner Act, unions were too small and too insecure to act as major pressure groups, even in their own direct interest. Samuel Gompers, founder of the American Federation of Labor, had defined labor's proper role in politics as active but nonpartisan: "Elect your friends and defeat your enemies." But the New Deal gave unions unprecedented legal protection, new strength in numbers, and the beginning of a new outlook on the position of labor in politics and government. During the war the Congress of Indus-

1. This chapter was originally written by John P. Dean and Edward Suchman and was edited for this volume by the authors.

trial Organizations organized its Political Action Committee on a national, state, and local basis, and, by 1948, all the major labor organizations had well-organized political action programs at the top level. The railroad brotherhoods had long employed legislative representatives. John L. Lewis was a political lobby in himself. The CIO-PAC had been operating for several years. And the AF of L had recently organized Labor's League for Political Education. On the national level, then, labor had political machinery; in Truman and Barkley it had candidates friendly to labor; and in the recently enacted Taft-Hartley Act it had a strong issue. The stage was apparently set for the emergence of a genuine grass-roots "labor vote" in the same sense as the familiar "farm vote." What happened in Elmira?

The Thirty-ninth District, of which Elmira was a center, was not a good area for testing the full battery of labor's political action techniques. The district is so solidly Republican that the AF of L's Labor League for Political Education and the CIO's Political Action Committee sent neither money nor trained men to try to influence the election there. But by the very absence of such national professional efforts Elmira was a good testing ground for *local* political action by labor—an area where the whole effort must be local or not at all. The success or failure of such local activities can profoundly influence the organization of labor's political action efforts in the future.

Now it is unrealistic to speak in over-all terms of the political activity of "labor" in the 1948 elections in Elmira. The city's sixty-one unions varied from large industrial locals with keen factional conflict at relatively well-attended meetings to staid craft locals that drew to their meetings a scant ten or twenty of their several hundred members. Their political activity took two forms—collective efforts and individual efforts of particular unions.

Collective Efforts

Two efforts were made—one growing out of dissatisfaction with the other—to form a united political front for Elmira labor. The first was the formation of the Labor Legislative Conference and the second the formation of the Labor Education League. Neither was effective.

The Labor Legislative Conference.—In December, 1947, some CIO unions (e.g., United Automobile Workers, United Electrical Workers), several International Association of Machinists' locals, two Railroad Brotherhood lodges, and a number of small AF of L locals organized the Labor Legislative Conference. Its purpose was highly specific: to defeat the Republican incumbent from the Thirty-ninth Congressional District. It was *not* organized to debate national issues or work for a presidential candidate. By May, 1948, the Conference seemed fairly well established and was holding regular monthly meetings.

The first rift appeared when a resolution supporting Henry Wallace for President was suggested by a delegate from a local whose international union was dominated by left-wing elements. The resolution was withdrawn without a vote when the overwhelming negative sentiment became apparent. But the episode was enough to frighten a Conference majority, over left-wing protest, into adopting an anti-Communist clause in the rules. It also inspired four strongly anti-Communist delegates to undertake a private investigation of the Wallace supporters in the Conference. The results of this investigation led to a show of strength within the Conference—at which certain confidential "evidence" could not be presented—and as a consequence the minority, representing a number of important unions, withdrew from the Conference in mid-May, depleting its treasury and drastically reducing its prestige.

The specific goal was thus lost in ideological conflict. The Conference might have failed because of a number of policy or personality reasons. But such potential obstacles never had time to arise. Before they could, the Conference's inexperienced delegates had demonstrated their inability to control a minority faction that wanted to introduce an irrelevant but highly explosive national issue into an organization designed to further an immediate, local, clearly defined objective.

The Labor Education League.—Late in June the delegates who bolted the Conference formed a new organization, the Labor Education League. By then much time had been lost, and, in addition, some unions had been frightened away from "political action" by their experience in the Conference. Only about one-fifth of Elmira's unions named delegates, and only half of them appeared at the typical meeting. The meetings themselves bogged down in the absence of leaders who could plan and manage the League's activities. In the end, the delegates decided to hold a public rally against the Taft-Hartley Act in late October, featuring a speaker of national prominence. Of all proposals made in connection with the rally, only one (appeals to other union leaders) was carried out. The rally was a failure. Between 7:00 and 7:30 P.M. on October 28 Attorney-General Tom Clark addressed about a hundred and fifty persons scattered over the park area. After Clark spoke, the locally indorsed candidates were introduced. The meeting then ended, and so did the activities of the Labor Education League.

Meetings of the Labor Education League were characterized by absence of strong and forceful personalities, inability of officers to plan the meetings or to formulate objectives clearly, unawareness of the techniques of effective political action, and ineffectiveness in getting delegates to work on the program. In effect, the League was little more than a forum for expressing sentiments against the Taft-Hartley Act. However, recurrent charges against Taft-Hartley undoubtedly did make solid enemies for the law among delegates who had previously known little about it.

Individual Efforts

Yet, in 1948 most Elmira labor leaders believed that some political activity by labor unions was desirable, even essential. Their international unions hammered away at this theme at conventions, through newspapers, magazines, pamphlets, and letters and in person. But the local leaders needed trained men from the state or national organizations to help plan and co-ordinate their political efforts, and, since this heavily Republican area was regarded as nearly hopeless, the help was not forthcoming.

There were other obstacles to effective political action. First was the conviction of most labor leaders in Elmira that political activity by unions should be "nonpartisan." The local leaders agreed unanimously that the incumbent from the Thirty-ninth District, a Republican, should be defeated because he voted for the Taft-Hartley Act. But many union men were themselves registered Republicans (Chart XIII); in fact, there were as many registered Republicans as Democrats among labor leaders in Elmira! For labor to team up with the

Democratic party organization would immediately have antagonized important elements in Elmira's unions. It would also have violated deeply rooted beliefs among most local union leaders about the undesirability of "coercive" techniques.

CHART XIII

THE ENROLMENT OF LABOR LEADERS IN GREATER ELMIRA
ACCORDING TO THEIR PARTY OF CHOICE IN THE
1948 REGISTRATION

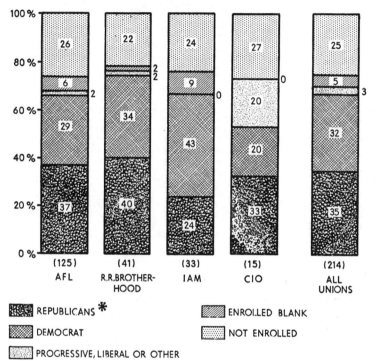

* Some labor leaders who were Democrats may have registered Republican in order to vote in the Republican primary against Republican incumbents they considered antilabor.

A second major obstacle was the fact that political activity never sprang from that most compelling of all motives for a local labor leader—an articulate rank-and-file need. All the pressure came from the international (outside) unions, and much of that was impersonal. Under the circumstances it is remarkable that Elmira's unions engaged in much political activity at all. Jurisdictional division within and between AF of L and CIO was a third factor that interfered with co-ordinated union activity in Elmira. The fourth, and perhaps most basic, obstacle to political effectiveness was simply the inexperience of local union leaders in political activity.

Despite all these problems, however, there was some political activity by labor unions in Elmira (Table 7). Between a half and two-thirds of the locals engaged in something that could be called "po-

TABLE 7

POLITICAL ACTIVITY BY LABOR UNIONS IN ELMIRA

UNION	No. OF LOCALS	APPROXIMATE MEMBERSHIP	No. OF LOCALS INFORMATION RECEIVED FROM	No. OF LOCALS THAT HAD ANY POLITICAL ACTIVITY			
				As an Organization	At Meetings	To Reach Members at Home	At Place of Work
AF of L unions....	*45*	4,000–5,000	*30*	*15*	*18*	*8*	*4*
Building Trades.	10	900	10	7	8	1	0
Printing Trades.	4	300	3	2	1	2	2
Glass Blowers ..	3	1,000	1	1	0	0	0
Teamsters......	1	500	1	0	0	0	0
Iron Workers...	2	600	2	1	1	1	0
Others.........	25	1,000	13	4	8	4	2
CIO-UE.........	1	1,000	1	1	1	1	1
CIO-UAW.......	1	1,200	1	1	1	1	1
IAM............	4	4,000–5,000	2	1	2	1	1
Railroad Brotherhoods.........	10	1,000	10	1	6	7	4
Total........	61	11,000	44	18	28	18	11

litical action," even if it was only an exhortation to "get out and vote." Here are the activities of the major Elmira unions:

United Automobile Workers, CIO.—The local UAW-CIO was a young union of twelve hundred members, founded in 1944 in a hard-fought drive using outside CIO organizers. Of all the Elmira unions, it might have been expected to develop the most effective political action program. The international union strongly encouraged political action and had evolved techniques that it was trying to activate on the local level.

But in 1948 the local UAW leadership was shot through with factional conflict. A conservative group of leaders was in the ascendancy, and, for them, political action meant personal fence-building within the local to secure newly won positions. They had little time or interest for political affairs in the larger community. The local president was briefly a delegate to the Labor Education League but resigned because he was "too busy."

The recently defeated "outs" talked loudly of their conflict with the leadership, called them "power hungry," and deplored their failure to co-operate with the international union in setting up a vigorous political action program for the local. But, like most locals, the UAW had the problem of low rank-and-file attendance at regular union meetings. This chronic condition, together with lack of political interest among the top local leaders, limited the UAW's political efforts to such perfunctory activities as distributing some literature at plant gates, hanging Truman-Barkley posters in the union office, and providing its platform for a speech by a Democratic candidate for Congress who was a member of the IAM.

United Electrical Workers, CIO.—Despite political sophistication among its top leaders, the United Electrical Workers local did less to get out the vote than any Elmira unions, except perhaps the building trades locals. Two key officials concentrated their main efforts on dredging up community support for Wallace: first through the abortive Labor Legislative Conference and then through a Labor Committee for Wallace, organized by the two UE officers and an AF of L typographer.

The UEW local indorsed no candidate, again because of the Wallace issue. The handful of articulate Wallace supporters in the union decided not to force the Wallace issue on the floor of the meeting, fearing it would "split the local wide open." At the same time these leaders wanted to avoid a formal rejection of Wallace by the members. They compromised by persuading the local to adopt the international union's official stand that had been worked out to avoid repudiation of Wallace on the part of the locals: individual union members were free to support the Progressive party, as union members, without formal censure from the local.

With the Wallace problem settled, there was no further political discussion at UE membership meetings except for occasional reports by legislative representatives in Albany and Washington. Through the local's shop newspaper, union officers reminded members to register and vote.

International Association of Machinists (IAM).—This union was feeling the effects of a long strike held in the summer of 1947. The strike was not a success for the union, and it precipitated a radical change in top leadership. In addition, mass layoffs during the campaign period increased the tension. At the time of the campaign the insecure new leaders were struggling with internal union problems that left little time for political activity. They were engaged in a jurisdictional dispute with the CIO United Electrical Workers involving representation for electricians in a plant in Syracuse. They were building barriers against a feared "raid" at the Elmira plant by the CIO United Automobile Workers. They were constantly explaining and defending to opposition factions within the local a post-strike contract that was the weakest negotiated in years. And they were working to keep up the union's membership in the face of the severe 1948 layoffs. The president of this local was highly interested in local and national politics, but he was almost completely prevented by these other considerations from engaging in political activity. And, in general, other IAM leaders did not favor political action on the part of labor: "I don't go for the fact that labor controls votes and has powers of persuasion. If the men are like me, they'll vote as they please."

In spite of these problems, and the constant problem of rank-and-file apathy, the IAM did sponsor a political program of sorts. The locals indorsed candidates; sent press releases to the papers; formed a committee that recruited volunteers to pass out literature at plant gates and carry placards at the labor rally; sent active delegates to the Labor Education League, one of whom was elected president; and heard talks from the Democratic candidate for Congress.

Railroad Brotherhoods.—Rank-and-file members of the Railroad Brotherhoods in Elmira showed little enthusiasm for political activity by the union. During the campaign there was rarely any political discussion on the floor of the meetings, either by officers or by rank-and-file members. No political speakers were brought in to acquaint members with the issues or to urge them to register and vote. At numerous meetings some political communication from Washington or Albany was read, but Brotherhood members were not politically contacted at home by the lodges. No one came around to remind them to register or persuade them to vote for friends of labor. Only two local Brotherhoods supported the Labor Education League, and then only to the extent of sending "observers" and listening politely to their reports at lodge meetings. Most lodge leaders supported such nonpartisan techniques as distributing voting records or posting notices to encourage members to register and vote, but none went any further. Many leaders contacted in this study still felt that "unions shouldn't mess in politics."

American Federation of Labor.—Political apathy characterized both leaders and members of most Elmira AF of L unions in 1948. Rank-and-file participation in union affairs was low, and the same men continued in office year after year, simply because others were not willing to take responsibility. Generally, political literature was not distributed at meetings, and politics was not discussed; most of the unions had rules in their constitutions barring political discussion or limiting it to "nonpartisan" discussion. Once every two or three months the legislative agent for the Central Trades and Labor Assembly spoke on politics and discussed legislation pending in Albany and Washington. During the campaign he injected into his regular reports criticisms of the Eightieth Congress and the congressman from the Thirty-ninth District.

At home, AF of L union members received monthly magazines from their international unions that contained articles dealing with the issues, the need for political activity, or political activity by labor in other areas. Union members were not contacted by canvassers or in any way personally reminded to register and vote.

Two key AF of L men, the secretary and the president of the Central Trades and Labor Assembly, were solidly behind the Labor Education League and were active delegates. The *Elmira Labor Review*, sent to all members of AF of L unions affiliated with the Central Trades and Labor Assembly, criticized the Eightieth Congress, attacked the Thirty-ninth District's representative, and printed information on the activities of the Labor Education League.

Among AF of L unions the printing trades unions had the most politically active leadership and the building trades unions the least active. For the most part, AF of L leadership in Elmira was of the old Gompers school:

> Defeat your enemies and elect your friends. . . . Never tell the members how to vote. . . . It's still America, let's keep it that way. . . . Nobody at the top can tell us at the bottom what to do.

Mind our own business. . . . Let the people vote individually. . . . As labor leaders we should keep out of politics.

I'm a man, and I think I've got the right to think as I please . . . and as long as I live up to union rules it's nobody's business how I vote. . . . I tell 'em that right in my own local and in the State Council.

Political activity by local unions in Elmira in 1948, then, was limited. Aside from occasional attempts to get dollar contributions to a political action organization, locals did little but talk, distribute literature, and send delegates to the Labor Education League (and the latter merely removed political action another step from rank and file). Political discussion at union meetings was ineffective because of low attendance. Beyond this, the union member's vote was left to the local party organizations, his individual initiative, or political apathy.

To sum up, the major reasons for labor's ineffectiveness were not hard to find: (1) apparently wrong assumptions by the leaders about what constitutes effective political action; (2) ideological differences and jurisdictional rivalries between and within various locals that prevented effective co-operation toward a specific common goal; (3) the inadequacy for political purposes of traditional channels of communication between labor leadership and rank and file; (4) lack of the time, money, and experience essential to developing new organizational forms for effective political action; and (5) a tradition of political individualism that inhibited concerted action lest that seem partisan or dictatorial.

THE POLITICS OF UNION MEMBERS

So far as the unions themselves were concerned, then, little was done to influence the votes of members. But that does not necessarily mean that union members (or their families) responded to the campaign just like their fellows. Let us turn now to an analysis of the politics of union members.

To start with, union members among wage-earners vote more Democratic than nonmembers. In each occupational category *non-* union members and their families vote Republican about half again as much as union members (see Chart XIV). Nor is this simply a reflection of different class status; in each broad socioeconomic category (and in more detailed classification too, for that matter) union members are more Democratic (see Chart XV). In fact, no matter what additional characteristic is controlled—education, age, class identification, religion, father's occupation or father's vote, even satisfaction with job or with management—union people are

CHART XIV

PERCENTAGE REPUBLICAN OF TWO-PARTY VOTE

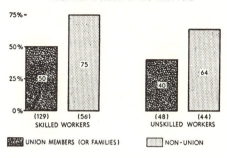

CHART XV

PERCENTAGE REPUBLICAN OF TWO-PARTY VOTE

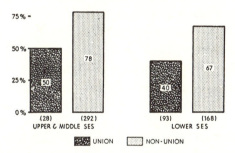

consistently more Democratic than nonunion people of the same kind. In addition, they "feel more strongly" for the Democratic candidate. Presumably the union affiliation helps to bring out the class disposition in the heat of a political campaign. In any event, union membership (by self or family breadwinner) is associated with Democratic support.[2]

2. The "union vote" was not of a piece. CIO voters seemed more Democratic than IAM, and they in turn than AF of L. Partly this reflects job status and partly the political traditions of the different unions—and maybe, even, organizational activity, to a slight extent:

Members of:	Percentage Republican of Two-Party Vote
CIO	33 (15)
IAM (machinists)	38 (48)
AF of L	50 (48)

And the more committed to one's own union or to the union idea in general, the more Democratic the vote among union workers. People who included their union among the groups important to them are more likely to vote Democratic (61 per cent) than those members to whom the union is not particularly important (53 per cent). And union members who think unions are doing a fine job are more Democratic (79 per cent) than those who think unions do more good than harm (66 per cent) or more harm than good (39 per cent).

The Effect of Union Contacts[3]

Thus while union workers are clearly more Democratic than nonunion, still it is hard to attribute the difference to the political activity of the unions themselves. How, then, does a political ideology get transmitted to the members of a substantially nonpolitical organization? A worker's voting behavior is influenced by the pressures of the environment in which he works; the extent to which he is influenced by such stimuli depends on the amount of his exposure to that environment; and the amount of such exposure depends upon his interaction with others in the environment. In this way an individual comes to learn what is considered "appropriate" by the participants in that environment. Rather than direct communication from leaders to followers, this is an indirect process that might be called "social absorption." We shall later analyze in detail the political role of one's friends and co-workers; here let us note the results of the process within a formal organization.

The more interaction with other union members (in the single-plant IAM local where these data were secured), the more Demo-

3. Many data presented in this section were made available to this study by William F. Whyte, Lois R. Dean, and Stephen A. Richardson, who in 1950 sent a mail questionnaire to a sample of 800 workers in a large business-machine manufacturing plant, under the auspices of the New York State School of Industrial and Labor Relations, Cornell University. They received 343 returns. All union members in the plant are affiliated with the International Association of Machinists. Since this return is too low to permit even crude estimates of absolute proportions in the plant, the data are intended only for comparative analysis within the sample of repliers.

cratic the vote (Chart XVI). Just as union members tend to be Democratic, the more "unionized" they are, the more Democratic they come to be. Interaction and time have their effect in indirectly transmitting the political mores of the group—more effect, probably, than formal and direct methods.

This tendency is also demonstrated by the workers' associations at the plant. The more the workers associate with co-workers after working hours, the more Democratic they vote. Again, the common

CHART XVI

THE MORE INTERACTION WITHIN THE UNION BY ITS MEMBERS
THE MORE DEMOCRATIC THE VOTE

PERCENTAGE REPUBLICAN OF TWO-PARTY VOTE

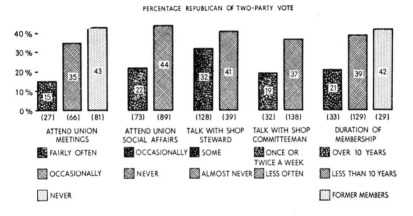

political viewpoint is intensified through personal interaction—and particularly for women, who, generally less interested in politics than men, are more amenable to such personal influence (see Chart XVII).

A crude index of integration in the plant was formed of three characteristics—social interaction with fellow-workers, length of service in the plant, and job satisfaction. Although the number of cases is small, it does appear that plant integration produces Democratic votes among *non*union members like that of members. Whether union members feel themselves a part of the plant or not makes no real difference in these data. But, for *non*members, such interaction seems to be a substitute for union membership, and integrated nonmembers vote about as Democratic as union members. Feeling like a worker leads to voting like one, union or not (see Chart XVIII).

In sum, union membership is associated with Democratic voting, less through organized or official pressure than through the interaction that the union environment leads to. And, the more "union-

CHART XVII

PERCENTAGE REPUBLICAN OF TWO-PARTY VOTE

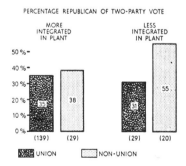

ized" the member—or the more integrated in the plant the nonmember—the stronger the predispositional leaning to the Democrats is expressed.

CHART XVIII

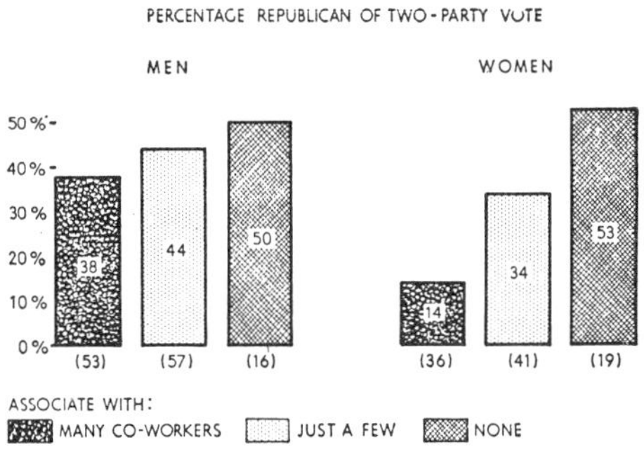

PERCENTAGE REPUBLICAN OF TWO-PARTY VOTE

POLITICS AND OTHER FORMAL ORGANIZATIONS

Although the labor union is probably the most important organization in Elmira from the standpoint of politics, it is not the only relevant one. The voter's decision may be affected by his membership in various organizations in the community—organizations that, for the most part, have nothing directly to do with politics. Slightly over half of the main panel belonged to one or more such organizations, distributed widely by type: lodge (40 per cent of the joiners), social (31 per cent), religious (27 per cent), economic (22 per cent), patriotic (14 per cent), service (11 per cent), civic (11 per cent), sports (7 per cent), cultural (4 per cent), and political (4 per cent). And the story of the political role of such organizations is almost identical with that for labor unions, though in lesser degree throughout.

Even less than unions did other organizations engage directly in political activity. A mail questionnaire to over one hundred community organizations, interviews with leaders and members of the main organizations, and participation in the open meetings of several organizations in Elmira revealed almost no organized activity or indeed any relation to the political campaign. Here are some examples:

B'nai B'rith.—Had a talk on politics by members of the Republican, Democratic, and Progressive parties.

American Legion.—Urged members to register and vote regardless of candidate. Campaign activity limited to a nonpartisan get-out-the-vote drive.

Business and Professional Women.—One nonpartisan speaker. Made a strong effort to get women to exercise their right to vote and to urge others to do so, regardless of personal preference for candidates.

Sorosis.—Reminded members to register and vote.

Rotary.—Reports in meetings of both the Republican and the Democratic conventions by Rotarians who had attended.

But this does not mean, any more than in the case of unions, that organizations do not matter in politics. In the first place, despite the overt nonpolitical character of organizations, people still manage to belong to those congenial to their own political position, largely because of homogeneity in class and religion. Of those who thought that most of their organization's members would vote Republican, 88 per cent intended to vote Republican (in August); for those in "predominantly Democratic" organizations the figure was only 23 per cent and for the "split" organizations, 69 per cent. And people who attend organizational meetings more frequently are more likely to correspond to the perceived vote of their organizations in their own vote (90 per cent to 85 per cent for Republican organizations; 100 per cent to 83 per cent for Democratic).

Again, as with unions, the central effect of organizations is apparently to help "bring out" the latent tendency of social characteristics and express them in partisanship. His memberships help to determine *which* of the individual's loyalties, experiences, affiliations, and attitudes will be brought into play in making political decisions. In Elmira, just as membership in labor unions intensifies the effect of occupation for lower SES people, membership in community organizations reinforces slightly the effect of social status in that

CHART XIX

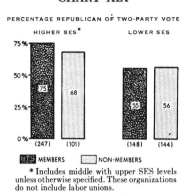

PERCENTAGE REPUBLICAN OF TWO-PARTY VOTE

*Includes middle with upper SES levels unless otherwise specified. These organizations do not include labor unions.

community for the middle and upper class (see Chart XIX). And the more organizations people belong to in this Republican community, the more Republican they are: the range is from 62 per cent among nonmembers to 79 per cent among people who belong to four or more organizations. Similarly, officers are more Republican than members (74 per cent to 63 per cent). Finally, organizational membership favors the Republicans only in the case of the less interested. Those highly interested in the election vote the same whether they join or not (76 per cent to 75 per cent Republican); but the less interested who belong to organizations show a difference on the Republican side (64 per cent to 54 per cent).[4]

The situation for other organizations, then, is very like that for unions: the organizations as such do little in the way of intentional

4. The same is true for turnout at the polls: organizational membership makes a greater difference in voting for those who (otherwise) care least about politics.

political activity, yet membership does have an effect simply by bringing together people of like social position and interests.

SUMMARY

Political Activities of Labor Unions

21. Two collective efforts of Elmira unions in 1948 were ineffective, and individual unions engaged in political activity only perfunctorily.

22. Among the reasons for the small amount of forceful political activity by Elmira labor unions were these: (*a*) partisan splits among the labor leaders themselves; (*b*) no articulate rank-and-file expression favoring political activity; (*c*) jurisdictional conflicts; (*d*) political inexperience of the leaders; and (*e*) labor's tradition of political individualism.

Politics of Union Members

23. Union members vote more Democratic than nonmembers (of the same occupation, class, education, age, religion, or selected attitude).

24. The more that union members are committed to unionism, in general or in particular, the more Democratic their vote.

25. The more interaction with other union members (within a single plant), the more Democratic the vote, especially among (less interested) women.

26. Integration in a plant seems to make nonunion workers more Democratic but has less (additional) effect on those already union members.

Politics and Other Formal Organizations

27. Other organizations in the community engaged in political activity even less than unions.

28. People belong to organizations (perceived to be) congenial to their own political position.

29. Organizational membership brings out latent political predispositions, e.g., the Republican vote in the middle classes.

30. The effects of organizational membership are greater for those less interested.

4 SOCIAL DIFFERENTIATION
Socioeconomic and Ethnic Status

The relation of group memberships and identifications to political choice is central to the problem of consensus and cleavage in a political democracy. If the "community interest" were in actuality the basis for political decison in our society, that would not necessarily mean that all men would have to agree: some could be right and others wrong, or some logical and others illogical, or some perceptive and other unperceptive. However, in that case, we could assume that political differences would distribute themselves at random throughout the society, that is, that they would not be correlated with basic social groupings. But they are.

In contemporary America, political events and social differentiation have combined to produce three major types of political cleavage: (1) occupational, income, and status cleavages; (2) religious racial, and ethnic cleavages; and (3) regional and urban-rural cleavages.[1] For the large majority of the population political experience is organized around major social identifications, associations, and memberships. One's own private political convictions are not so private or so much one's own as they may seem—or as one might wish them to be. In political affairs of the mid-twentieth century the kinds of social experience most persistently underlying political choices are those centering on class, ethnic, and ecological differences. Such social bases of political traditions are the subject matter of the present chapter.

1. By virtue of the design of this *community* study, this factor of place of residence was not included. However, occasional comparisons with other regions or the country as a whole are made, and the influence of the Republican predominance in Elmira is evident at many points.

SOCIOECONOMIC STATUS

In our discussion of social differentiation in politics, the place to start is the "obvious" place: the effect of differing socioeconomic status upon political attitudes. If there is one social characteristic that is generally admitted to affect opinion on public affairs, at least since 1932, this is it. Although voting along socioeconomic lines is generally recognized as characteristic of this country since the depression of the 1930's, it is much older than that—as old, in fact, as the Republic itself.

Class Affiliation

Socioeconomic status—as measured here by an index composed of the breadwinner's occupation, education, and interviewer's rating —is directly related to the final vote decision (Chart XX). The

CHART XX*

SOCIOECONOMIC STATUS INDEX DIFFERENTIATES VOTE

PERCENTAGE REPUBLICAN OF TWO-PARTY VOTE

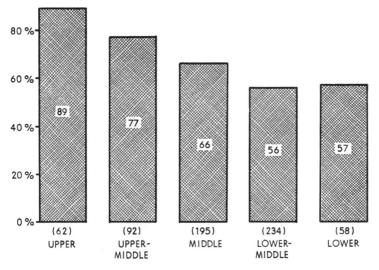

SES INDEX**

* As explained in the Introduction, the sample sizes reported in the text are almost never equal to the total sample. As an illustration of how these deductions inevitably occur, the original sample of 1,029 cases is distributed as follows in Chart XX: represented in the chart, 641; nonvoters in November, 261; November mortality, 85; refused to tell vote, 37; minor party (Wallace), 5 cases.

** For details on the construction of this and subsequent indexes see Appendix B.

higher the socioeconomic status (SES), the more Republican the vote; put crudely, richer people vote Republican more than poorer people.

Class Identification

Nor is this relationship by any means limited to the so-called objective measures of socioeconomic status. It also appears when socioeconomic status is measured in terms of the respondent's own

CHART XXI

SUBJECTIVE CLASS IDENTIFICATION DIFFERENTIATES VOTE
IN ADDITION TO OBJECTIVE SOCIOECONOMIC STATUS

PERCENTAGE REPUBLICAN OF TWO-PARTY VOTE

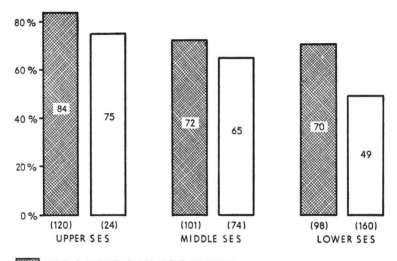

class identification—his own feeling as to the class in which he belongs. With socioeconomic status controlled, class identification exerts an independent influence upon the vote, especially on the lower socioeconomic status level (Chart XXI).

"Class-consciousness"

Since the norms of the general community are more favorable to middle-class and business groups, it is more likely that they will achieve political solidarity than the working class, especially in this small-town environment. Particularly in towns like Elmira, the development of a "class-conscious" vote is inhibited by the status of the dominant community ideology centered in the middle class and its rural forebears. As a result the workers show less political solidarity and more political ambivalence. In 1948 Elmira the business, professional, and white-collar groups supported the Republicans fully 75 per cent; the workers split their vote almost fifty-fifty. There is a more cohesive business vote than labor vote. Were this not the case generally, the closeness of the Republican-Democratic vote in this country would not exist because of the strong numerical majority held by wage workers over salaried employees and independent entrepreneurs and professionals. The working class splits its vote more than does the business class.[2]

This fact can be explained in at least two ways. On the one hand, the workers could have a class-conscious ideology but be split on which party expresses it better. On the other hand, the workers could be themselves split on the matter of ideology itself, especially in a middle-class community like Elmira. The latter seems to be the case. There is little class-consciousness among workers in Elmira and hence no great tendency toward uniform political action.

Now this matter of ideology is not easy to gauge in a few survey questions. What would class-consciousness mean in a town like Elmira? Presumably it would be manifested by such elements as these: response to verbal symbols like "big business" (negative) and "labor" (positive); a conviction that existing institutions are managed in disregard of the workers' rights and interests; a feeling of solidarity with other workers that would express itself in a desire to associate with them in leisure-time and other private activities; and, finally, the desire for a political movement specifically dedicated

2. An important circumstance making for greater political harmony within the business group is simply their greater rate of political activity within the community. They belong to more organizations than the labor group, they talk politics more, and they are looked to more for political advice. They not only reassure themselves through such activities; they also set a political "tone" for the entire community. And they were in positions to do so: about 80 per cent of the occupational elite of the community were Republicans and about 75 per cent of the officers of clubs and organizations.

to the interest of the working class. Accordingly a number of questions were devised to see whether workers consider themselves a special group in the population by such criteria. At least by this test there is little class-consciousness in Elmira. While there are some differences between the workers and other occupations on these items, they are slight (except in the case of attitudes toward labor unions). Workers do not particularly distrust social institutions, or feel unduly handicapped by their social position, or show interest in their own rather than other groups, or have deviant ambitions for their children, or advocate a political party for labor. At

TABLE 8*

ELMIRA WORKERS DISPLAY LITTLE INDICATION OF
WORKING-CLASS-CONSCIOUSNESS
(Per Cent)

THEORETICAL MANIFESTATIONS OF WORKING-CLASS-CONSCIOUSNESS	BREADWINNER'S OCCUPATION		
	Business, Profession, Self-employed	White Collar	Labor
Reactions to symbols:			
Favorable to "billion-dollar corporations"	74	85	75
Favorable to "labor unions"	44	53	66
Images of social institutions:			
Believe "most city governments make the welfare of all citizens their main concern"	63	60	50
Believe most successful people have "gotten ahead" because of "ability"	86	88	74
Styles of life:			
Prefer clubs whose members are "all of my own class"	34	36	41
Like to read or hear stories about			
... "working people"	79	86	80
... "business people"	74	70	55
If son were a lawyer, would like him to work "for himself," "in private law firm," or "for business corporation" (instead of for "labor union" or "government")	95	90	82
If son were a doctor, would like him to be "specialist with private practice" or "head of private hospital" (instead of "head of government medical service")	96	96	92
Political militancy:			
Believe "it would be good for country if labor unions had a political party of their own"	8	7	13
Total no. of cases	171	106	340

* These data were obtained from a mail survey conducted after the election; about 75 per cent of our original sample responded. The questions appear in Appendix B.

bottom, the working class is loyal to the dominant middle-class ideology symbolized by the "American way of life" (Table 8).[3]

Yet the political history of the last twenty years in this country reveals a number of actual and potential clashes between economic interests of the different classes. What this seems to mean in Elmira is that the workers are in an ambivalent position in which their political values are derived from the dominant culture at the same time that their interest in social prestige and economic security is to some extent blocked by the interests of the dominant groups. American cultural values and actual life-experience are mutually reinforcing for upper and middle classes in the society, and accordingly they exhibit a high degree of political consensus. But cultural values and life-experience are often in contradiction for the workers, and accordingly they are more ambivalent and, as we shall see, more unstable in their political support. It takes a depression or a heated political campaign directly aimed at economic interest to bring out their "class vote" sharply against the norms of the "larger community."

Political Generations

The relationship between socioeconomic status (SES) and vote is partly a function of the political conditions under which each generation comes of age. The younger generation raised in the New Deal era showed a high tendency to vote along the socio-economic class lines associated with the Roosevelt elections (Chart XXII).[4] Their elders, introduced to politics in the Republican 1920's,

3. What is more, the analysis of interrelations among these opinions reveals that the few signs of working-class alienation from middle-class norms do not tend to come from the same people. There are only a handful of "radical" workers in Elmira (and some of them seem to represent more of a personality deviation). Worker complaints against "the system" are isolated and individualized, not diffused within a core group of class-conscious workers.

4. In addition, there is a suggestion in the Elmira data that younger people resolve the cross-pressure of religion and class status more in favor of the latter. Younger Catholics of the business and white-collar group are more Republican than older Catholics; and younger Protestants of the union labor group are more Democratic than older Protestants. The data:

AGE	PERCENTAGE REPUBLICAN OF TWO-PARTY VOTE	
	Business and White-Collar Catholics	Union Labor Protestants
Up to 44............	48 (48)	48 (65)
45 and over.........	32 (31)	70 (59)

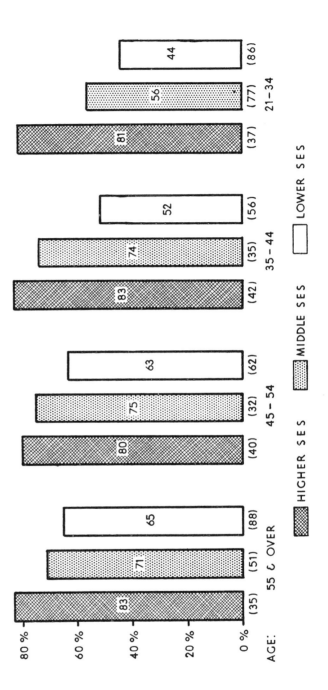

CHART XXII

AGE DIFFERENCES INDICATE A TREND TOWARD GREATER
CLASS VOTING IN THE NEW DEAL GENERATION

PERCENTAGE REPUBLICAN OF TWO-PARTY VOTE

HIGHER SES   MIDDLE SES   LOWER SES

are not so far apart on class lines. Acceptance of the political norms current at the time of political initiation does not stop there; it tends to perpetuate itself through succeeding elections. Recognizing that young voters of the 1930's and later were more Democratic than their elders, many observers concluded that young "liberals" would grow up into old "conservatives." But a whole "political generation" may have been developing for whom the socioeconomic problems of their youth served as bases for permanent political norms—a semipermanent generation that would later bulge the ranks of the Democrats in certain age groups much as the crop of postwar babies is bulging different grades in school as they grow up. Presumably an age generation can be transformed by political events and social conditions into a political generation based on class considerations—a generation that retains its allegiances and norms while succeeding generations are moving in another direction.[5] In addition, in a community like Elmira there is no difference by age at the higher socioeconomic status levels, but at the middle and lower levels there is a tendency for people to become more Republican as they grow older—as the political climate of the community "rubs off" on them.

MINORITY RELIGIOUS AND ETHNIC STATUS[6]

Now let us turn to another basic differentiation within the electorate. The United States has been characterized by many political observers as a nation composed of blocs of minority voters. While the history of American politics attests to the general ineffectiveness

5. Just as age has a revealing relationship to vote when associated with SES, so does sex. As indicated by a measure like interest, women are less politicized than men—they follow the vote of their SES level less than men, on both extremes. High SES men are more Republican than high SES women; low SES men are more Democratic than low SES women. The data:

SES	PERCENTAGE REPUBLICAN OF TWO-PARTY VOTE	
	Men	Women
High	88 (75)	76 (79)
Middle	64 (75)	67 (120)
Low	51 (145)	61 (147)

6. Some material in this section was originally prepared by Edward Suchman and was edited for this volume by the authors.

of minority political parties, it also demonstrates the importance of the minority social vote—an electorate composed of so-called "hyphenated Americans." Racial, religious, and ethnic groups have demonstrated a unity in their voting allegiance that has led some observers to assign them a place of increasing importance in determining the outcome of elections. For example, Samuel Lubell, in *The Future of American Politics,* concludes that "for the immediate future the prospects point to an intensification of 'League of Nations'

CHART XXIII

THE MINORITIES AND THE "MAJORITY" VOTE DIFFERENTLY*

PERCENTAGE REPUBLICAN OF TWO-PARTY VOTE

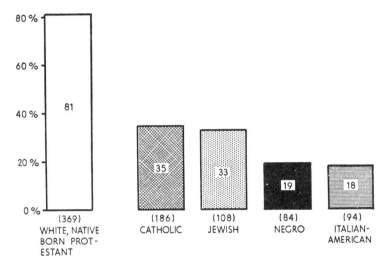

* Studies by the Cornell group on intergroup relations in three other geographically scattered cities strongly support these findings. In three predominantly Democratic communities—Steubenville, Ohio; Bakersfield, California; and Savannah, Georgia—the minority group votes more strongly Democratic:

	Percentage Republican of Two-Party Vote
Steubenville, Ohio:	
Catholic	10 (71)
Italian-American	11 (58)
Jewish	23 (54)
White, native-born Protestant	55 (133)
Bakersfield, Calif.:	
Mexican-American	8 (37)
Negro	16 (140)
White, native-born Protestant	41 (180)
Savannah, Ga.:	
Negro	12 (102)
White, native-born Protestant	30 (104)

Regardless of the geographical section—and even in the South—minority groups are more Democratic than the "majority" members of the community.

politics. . . . Virtually none of the underdog groups has obtained the full recognition of its numbers" (p. 79). Politicians have always been concerned with organizing the "Negro vote" or the "Jewish vote" or the "Italian vote." Such minority voters are quite numerous, especially in crucial metropolitan areas; they offer a common characteristic to which the politician can appeal; and they possess the internal cohesion, and often organization, essential for delivering a solid bloc vote.

A basic difference in political support within the electorate exists between the white native-born Protestant voters, representing the "majority" group in American society, on the one hand, and a number of racial, ethnic, and religious minority groups, on the other (Chart XXIII).

Now it is generally recognized that such minority groups are tied to the Democratic machine in the big cities, where they constitute a large segment of the party's support. But Elmira is a small upstate town with little machine politics and not a great deal of organized minority activity.[7] Even in this small, quiet community

7. The minority groups under study here differ somewhat in the extent to which they constitute meaningful "community groups" in Elmira. Only the Negroes and the Jews have associational and organizational ties. The Catholics and the foreign-born do not form noticeably separate community groups within the town. The Negroes form the most distinctive separate community, with their own social and welfare organizations, an active NAACP chapter, a Negro church, Negro leadership, and a strong sense of being a group set apart from the majority community. The Jewish group was next clear cut in its own in-group organization, with its own Jewish center, recognized Jewish leaders, and a feeling of minority-group membership. Both the Italian-American group and the Catholic group were rather closely integrated into the main stream of community life and neither viewed itself, nor was either viewed by the majority group, as a separate community. For this reason, the Catholics and the ethnic groups serve as examples of demographic voting based upon membership in a common population class with strong *informal* relations, whereas the Negroes and the Jews are examples of more organized groups based upon membership in a physically separated as well as a psychological and social community.

The original sample of the Elmira community contained 297 Catholics, but only 48 foreign-born, 15 Jews, and 17 Negroes. There was an additional group of 224 second-generation Americans (at least one parent foreign-born). A postelection survey, conducted as part of a larger study of intergroup relations in Elmira by the Social Science Research Center of Cornell University, included cross-sectional samples of Jews, Negroes, and Italian-Americans—150 in each group—and this augmented sample permits a comparison of the final vote decision of these minority groups with the votes of the "majority group." (While the Italian-Americans are also Catholic, the Catholic group includes only a minority who are of Italian descent. The results presented are based upon two independent samples of Italian-Americans and Catholics.)

there is a sharp differential in vote between minority ethnic groups and "pure Americans." Even here the election can be clearly seen as a contest between the minority groups and the dominant majority—the former supporting the Democrats and the latter the Republicans. Let us analyze first the Catholic group and then review the situation for the other minority groups.

The Catholic Vote[8]

The relation between votes and socioeconomic status is, after all, "reasonable" in view of the acknowledged relationship between politics and economic problems. In aiding or retarding unionism, in levying taxes upon incomes and profits, in distributing public aid, in financing social security—in these and countless other ways the government participates in what is called "class legislation." No wonder, then, that different classes vote differently.

But what of Catholicism? At first glance it seems to have no direct connection with American politics in 1948. The political issues indirectly involving Catholics were such matters as United States relations with Spain, the Vatican envoy, and the treatment of parochial schools under proposed federal aid to education. These were not salient in the 1948 campaign. Yet Catholics in the Republican community of Elmira voted Republican less than half as much as the Protestants.

To some extent, of course, this tendency reflects a historical identification. The Democratic party in New York State has been traditionally associated with the Catholics (Tammany Hall, Al Smith, Jim Farley, Ed Flynn, *et al.*), and national party leaders have been Catholics, particularly the chairmen of the Democratic National Committee over the last twenty-five years. In addition, there is a long-term connection between the party and the church stemming from the great immigration waves of the nineteenth century. But such considerations do not account for *contemporary* Catholic allegiance to the Democrats.

Independent of Other Factors

Now, in the first place, the Catholic vote is not simply a spurious reflection of other demographic factors. For example, Catholics are

8. For a fuller treatment of the Catholic vote in Elmira see David Gold, "The Influence of Religious Affiliation on Voting Behavior" (Ph.D. dissertation, Department of Sociology, University of Chicago, 1953).

on a lower (average) income level than Protestants, and this condition is sometimes thought to be responsible for the apparent correlation between religion and political attitudes. However, the correlation in Elmira is genuine. No matter what demographic variable is controlled, the relationship between Catholic affiliation and party preference significantly remains (Chart XXIV). Not only that, but

CHART XXIV

REGARDLESS OF WHAT OTHER DEMOGRAPHIC FACTORS ARE TAKEN
INTO ACCOUNT, THERE IS A BASIC DIFFERENCE IN VOTE
BETWEEN CATHOLICS AND PROTESTANTS

PERCENTAGE REPUBLICAN OF TWO-PARTY VOTE

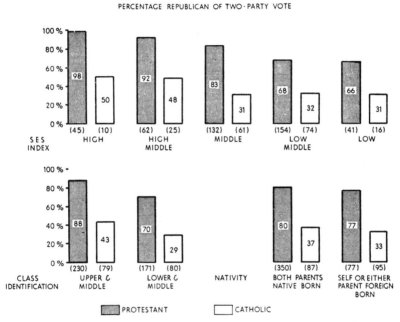

the religious affiliation (and the ethnic differences it represents) appears to be a stronger influence upon vote than any other single factor. For example, on each socioeconomic status level about half as many Catholics vote Republican as Protestants. Catholics of high status vote more Democratic than do Protestants of low status; thus Catholic affiliation is stronger than socioeconomic status in determining vote. In Elmira the Catholics have almost achieved the socioeconomic position of the Protestants, but this has not basically deflected their vote from the Democratic candidate.

Here, then, we find a condition not anticipated nor endorsed by classical political theorists: a nonpolitical, associative factor with strong influence upon the electoral decision. Regardless of other demographic characteristics—and despite democratic claims, protestations, or theories to the contrary—there is a strong "religious vote" in this country.

CHART XXV

RELIGIOUS AFFILIATION IS AS STRONG AN INFLUENCE UPON
VOTE AS "LIBERALISM-CONSERVATISM"

PERCENTAGE REPUBLICAN OF TWO-PARTY VOTE

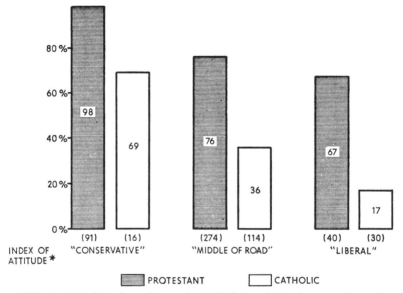

* This classification is based upon the respondents' attitudes toward big business corporations, unions, and price control. For details see Appendix B.

Independent of Attitudes

And, still more, ideological or attitudinal position on the issues is no more powerful an influence than religion. An index of "liberalism," based on socioeconomic issues of the time, illustrates the matter. Conservative Catholics—that is, those who agree in substance with the Republican position on big business, unions, and price control—are no more Republican than liberal Protestants (Chart XXV). At each step of this liberalism-conservatism score

Catholics are much more Democratic than Protestants. In this respect vote is as much conditioned by who one is as by what one believes.

Catholics and "Catholics"

The importance of religious affiliation in affecting political decision can be tested still further. To this point we have dealt simply with the report that one "belongs" to a religion; but there is belonging and belonging. If religious affiliation is operative, it should be even stronger among the more deeply religious or among those more intimately connected with the church. And that is so. The longer Catholics have lived in Elmira (i.e., the longer they have been associated with their co-religionists in this institution), the more Democratic do they vote (Chart XXVI). Similarly, the longer Protestants have lived in Elmira, the more Republican they become, probably in response to the predominantly Republican climate of opinion in the town. But Catholics become more Democratic despite the prevailing opinion climate, illustrating to some extent their group isolation, at least as far as politics is concerned. And the more intimately Catholic they feel, as indicated by their assertion that their religious group is among their "most important" identifications, the more Democratic they vote. (The fact that this is not so for the Protestants suggests the lack of a particular religious orientation to their vote.)[9]

Thus, the more intensely religious status is felt or the more pervasive its influence, the more powerful its effect upon vote. (This effect, incidentally, derives from in-group association and mutual reinforcement—in ways we shall analyze later—rather than from direct suggestion or pressure. Close observation of political activity among formal Catholic organizations, including the local church,

---

9. This is also reflected in the greater family solidarity of the lower-educated Catholic household, as expressed in intrafamily discussion of politics. The data:

PERCENTAGE WHO	AMONG THOSE WITH SOME HIGH SCHOOL OR LESS	
	Catholic	Protestant
Last discussed politics with family member (June) . .	33 (32)	7 (72)
Last discussed politics with family member (October) .	50 (94)	43 (221)

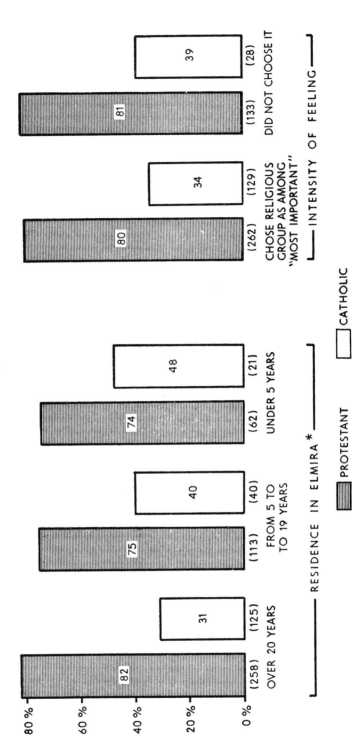

CHART XXVI

THE CLOSER THE RELIGIOUS AFFILIATION, THE
STRONGER ITS EFFECT UPON VOTE

PERCENTAGE REPUBLICAN OF TWO-PARTY VOTE

PROTESTANT   CATHOLIC

—— RESIDENCE IN ELMIRA * ——   —— INTENSITY OF FEELING ——

OVER 20 YEARS   FROM 5 TO   UNDER 5 YEARS   CHOSE RELIGIOUS   DID NOT CHOOSE IT
                 TO 19 YEARS   GROUP AS AMONG
                                                      "MOST IMPORTANT"

(258) 82   (113) 75   (62) 74   (262) 80   (133) 81
(125) 31   (40) 40   (21) 48   (129) 34   (28) 39

80 %
60 %
40 %
20 %
0 %

* This finding is not essentially affected by an age control. Note similar data for other minority groups on p. 72.

failed to reveal any attempt to "deliver" the Catholic vote. The result derived from informal social relations, not formal institutional pressure.)

Religion and Political Involvement

Actually the effect of religious affiliation depends also upon the voter's involvement in politics. The more deeply Catholics are involved, the less effect religion as such has upon their vote. It was the politically *uninterested* Catholics who followed religious affiliation

CHART XXVII

PERCENTAGE REPUBLICAN OF TWO-PARTY VOTE

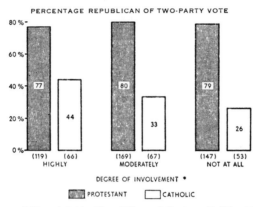

DEGREE OF INVOLVEMENT *

PROTESTANT   CATHOLIC

*This result holds with an SES control. See Appendix B for this index of involvement in politics.

most frequently in determining their vote. The more involved Catholics had certain political considerations on which to base their decision as to how to vote; the less involved simply followed the lead of the religious group (see Chart XXVII).

Long-Term Age Trend

With all this, 1948 marked a weakening of the Catholic vote in Elmira. In 1940 and again in 1944 about 85 per cent of Elmira Catholics claimed to have voted Democratic, and in 1948 this proportion had fallen to about 65 per cent. The likelihood of a trend away from the Democratic party on the part of Catholics is further suggested by the vote of different age groups. Political observers generally seem to believe that younger people—out of greater "liberalism"—have been more Democratic in recent years. But this is a complicated matter. The younger Protestants do vote more Democratic, but the younger Catholics vote more Republican (Chart XXVIII). Thus the younger generation of Catholics voted

CHART XXVIII

THE RELIGIOUS DIFFERENCE IS GREATEST AMONG THE OLDER
PEOPLE AND LEAST AMONG THE YOUNGER

PERCENTAGE REPUBLICAN OF TWO-PARTY VOTE

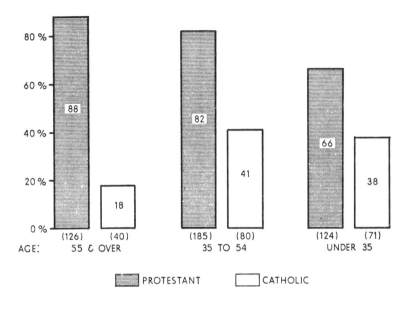

less by religion than their elders, and in time this may diminish the difference between the two religious groups. The largest difference between Protestants and Catholics exists among the older people (70 percentage points); among the middle-aged this difference has fallen to about 40 percentage points and among the younger people to less than 30. The succession of generations seems to be softening the religious difference.

To recapitulate, here is a social characteristic that is not directly involved in political issues but nevertheless makes a big difference in vote. Catholics vote differently from Protestants, and this difference is not simply a function of differing demographic or ideological positions. Regardless of socioeconomic status level or age or even political attitude, Catholics vote more Democratic than do Protestants. And the more closely they are bound to their religion, the more Democratic they are.

Other Minorities

What about the other minority groups in Elmira? In most respects the story is the same. As we have noted, Italians, Negroes, and Jews voted heavily Democratic in Elmira in 1948—82 per cent of the Italian-Americans, 81 per cent of the Negroes, and 67 of the Jews. And, as in the case of the Catholics, the vote for Truman is not

CHART XXIX

PERCENTAGE REPUBLICAN OF TWO-PARTY VOTE

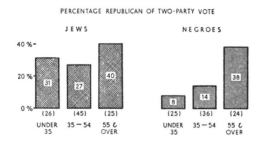

particularly affected by differences in socioeconomic status. Even among the highest-income Jewish voters the ratio of Truman to Dewey voters is about three to one. There is little variance by socioeconomic status level within the Negro group, and on each socioeconomic status level the Italians are more Democratic than the nonethnic native-born.

Contrary to the tendency among Catholics, however, the younger Negroes and Jews supported the Democrats even more strongly than their elders. Thus the educated youth may serve as the standard-bearers of these more newly active minorities, just as youth led the disintegration of older cleavages between Catholics and Protestants. In any case, the younger generation in these minority groups is more Democratic than the younger generation of Catholics (see Chart XXIX).

But in the case of psychological identification and social interaction with the group, these minorities are the same as the Catholics—the more closely the members identified with their minority group, the stronger their Democratic vote (Chart XXX). Regardless of the particular measure, those minority members who feel close to their own group (or who feel hostile to the out-group) are more likely to express the group's political preference (i.e., vote Democratic) than their fellows.

Minority voting patterns are closely linked to the social and psychological forces that determine intergroup relations in the

CHART XXX

The Closer the Minority Group Affiliation, the Stronger the Democratic Vote*

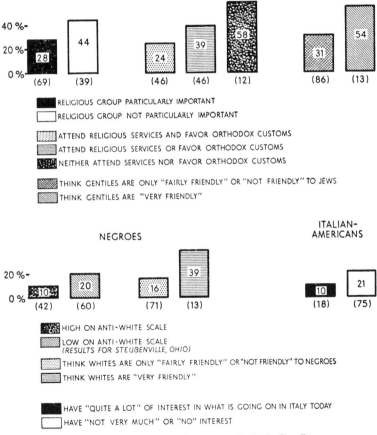

PERCENTAGE REPUBLICAN OF TWO-PARTY VOTE

JEWS

RELIGIOUS GROUP PARTICULARLY IMPORTANT
RELIGIOUS GROUP NOT PARTICULARLY IMPORTANT

ATTEND RELIGIOUS SERVICES AND FAVOR ORTHODOX CUSTOMS
ATTEND RELIGIOUS SERVICES OR FAVOR ORTHODOX CUSTOMS
NEITHER ATTEND SERVICES NOR FAVOR ORTHODOX CUSTOMS

THINK GENTILES ARE ONLY "FAIRLY FRIENDLY" OR "NOT FRIENDLY" TO JEWS
THINK GENTILES ARE "VERY FRIENDLY"

NEGROES

ITALIAN-AMERICANS

HIGH ON ANTI-WHITE SCALE
LOW ON ANTI-WHITE SCALE
(RESULTS FOR STEUBENVILLE, OHIO)
THINK WHITES ARE ONLY "FAIRLY FRIENDLY" OR "NOT FRIENDLY" TO NEGROES
THINK WHITES ARE "VERY FRIENDLY"

HAVE "QUITE A LOT" OF INTEREST IN WHAT IS GOING ON IN ITALY TODAY
HAVE "NOT VERY MUCH" OR "NO" INTEREST

*Most of these data were provided by supplementary studies by the Cornell group.

United States today. In the political arena, as in other spheres of community life, the intergroup tension present in most American communities results in a difference of opinion between the members of minority and "majority" groups. This division of political support is expected behavior on the part of both groups. During an election campaign it becomes an overtly expressed and openly recognized political alignment, reinforced by the stereotyped expectations of both sides. Different voting patterns become one of the prevailing practices of the community—"the way we do things around here."

THE SOCIAL TRANSMISSION OF POLITICAL CHOICES

In Elmira, then, it is the socioeconomic classes, on the one hand, and the religious and ethnic groups, on the other, that serve as the social carriers of political traditions. In the country at large, to these two kinds of differentiation in the population is added the ecological division of region or size of community (e.g., the metropolitan area as against the small town). In contrast, there are only minor differences in voting between men and women or between young and old or, indeed, on any other characteristic.

Why do certain characteristics make a difference and not others? Why is there not a distinctive women's vote or a sharp cleavage along age lines or, for that matter, a more or less random dispersal of the votes of individuals? In part this is a matter of timing, that is, of the historical period in which our study happens to be made. But, if a number of such studies had been made over the entire span of the two-party system, it is likely that most of them would have found similar differences in voting by class, ethnic, and ecological blocs of the American population. Why are such bases of political cleavage so persistent?

Explanations of a political character are prominent; for example, the explanation that such people have group interests in common and represent convenient blocs for political appeal and mobilization. Thus, in simplified terms, Jews vote Democratic "because" of Roosevelt's interventionist stand against Hitler; Negroes, "because" of the relief and welfare program of the New Deal; and both "because" of civil rights legislation. Less understood, however, are the social conditions that contribute to the success of such political mobilization—and, more importantly, to its persistence. Voting blocs are often perpetuated so long after group needs and political alternatives have changed that it is unrealistic to speak of active, contemporary "interests" being involved in more than a few of the voting differences between groups that exist in the country at a given time. Why do the others persist with such force?

There appear to be three ways in which social relations contribute to the maintenance of political differences.

First, there is the necessary condition of an economic division of labor or a physical separation or a social differentiation in the population such that people of unlike characteristics are affected in different ways by a single political policy. In other words, it is necessary to have a social basis for a political interest. It would be difficult in contemporary America, for example, to maintain strong voting differences by sex, because there are few policy issues persisting over a period of time that affect men and women differently. *Differentiation* is a condition for disagreement.

Second, a necessary condition for the persistence of political differences is their *transmission* to succeeding generations. Parents and children sharing the same characteristics provide a condition of continuity in which political choices can be taught, however subtly and unconsciously, by the one to the other. Some such transmission is necessary so that voting traditions do not die out. This presumably is a reason why youth movements in politics are often less stable or persistent than other bases of voting traditions that can more easily be transmitted from generation to generation. Similarly, a political movement based on the special interests of old age (e.g., pensions) has difficulty in maintaining itself because of the necessary absence of a generational tie. *Transmission* is a condition for persistence.

Finally, given the origin of a voting difference in one generation and the transmittibility of it to the next, another condition is necessary for it to survive in the succeeding generation. Members of the social groups involved must be substantially more in contact with one another, socially and physically, than they are with opposing groups. This condition will be analyzed in some detail in chapter 6, where we will try to show how political traditions are maintained through marriage and through living and working with socially alike, and hence politically like-minded, people. *Contact* is a condition for consensus.

In sum, the conditions underlying persistent voting cleavages seem to be (1) initial social differentiation such that the consequences of political policy are materially or symbolically different for different groups; (2) conditions of transmittibility from generation to generation; and (3) conditions of physical and social proximity providing for continued in-group contact in succeeding generations. In contemporary America these conditions are best met in *class*, in *ethnic*, and in *ecological* divisions of the population. They continue to provide, then, the most durable social bases for political cleavage.

SUMMARY

Socioeconomic Status

31. Higher socioeconomic status groups vote more Republican than lower.

32. Class identification affects vote in addition to objective class status: voters identifying with the middle and upper class vote more Republican than those identifying with the working or lower class.

33. White-collar and business groups have greater political solidarity, as indicated by uniform party preference, than workers.

34. Workers are not particularly class-conscious.

35. Age differences reveal greater class voting in the younger groups raised in the New Deal era—suggesting the development of a "political generation."

    and (*a*) Young Catholics and Protestants are more likely than older voters to resolve the cross-pressure between religion and class in favor of class.

36. Women, less politicized than men, follow the class tendency in voting less than men in the current era.

Ethnic Status

37. White native-born Protestants vote Republican more than minority ethnic groups—specifically, Catholics, Italian-Americans, Jews, and Negroes.

38. Catholics vote more Democratic than Protestants regardless of class status or class identification or national origin.

39. Catholics vote more Democratic than Protestants regardless of the "liberalism" or "conservatism" of their attitudes on political issues.

40. Catholics closely identified with their religion vote Democratic more than Catholics not so identified.

41. Catholics personally involved in political affairs follow the religious lead in voting less than Catholics not so involved.

42. The difference between Catholics and Protestants in voting is strongest among older people; young Catholics are more Republican than their elders, and young Protestants more Democratic.

43. The Democratic vote of Italian-Americans, Jews, and Negroes is not eliminated by class controls.

44. Contrary to the case with Catholics, younger members of the currently active minorities, Jews and Negroes, are more Democratic than their elders.

45. As in the case of Catholics, the more closely members of minorities identify with their ethnic group, the more Democratic their vote.

5 SOCIAL PERCEPTION

Group Voting Norms

The preceding chapter has shown what group differences in voting exist; succeeding chapters will show how they are maintained. Growing out of the former consideration and introductory to the latter, however, is the question: What do Elmirans know about the political structure of their community? How do they perceive group support in politics? From social-psychological theory and research we can assume that the perception of emotion-charged reality is not always clear and direct. Any reasonably complete picture of voting must take into account not only how groups in the community vote but also how people *perceive* groups as voting. Again we shall deal primarily with the important socioeconomic and ethnic strata.

WHO VOTES FOR WHOM?

In the June interview the respondents were asked about the support given to the parties by various groups in the community: "Do you think most —— around here would be more likely to vote for the Republican, Democratic, or Wallace third party?" Included in this question were five socioeconomic and occupational groups (factory workers, poor people, farmers, college people, rich people) and three ethnic groups (Negroes, Catholics, Jews).[1] How is the voter's perception of group support related to political preference and what effect does it have?

First, on the average, over one-third of the electorate did not

1. In addition, the list included one political group—Communists. A third of the respondents did not know how they would vote, and almost 90 per cent of the rest thought they would vote for the Wallace third party.

77

know, or rather did not think they knew, how certain groups were going to vote. The "Don't know" response for the nine groups ranged from 21 per cent (for poor people and farmers) to 42 per cent (for college people—a less stereotyped group).

However, the majority who did respond generally recognized that groups did vote as blocs. Respondents could have answered that the group under consideration did not vote as a bloc, but this denial ranged only from less than 1 per cent (for the Communists) to 16 per cent (for the Catholics) and 13 per cent (for college people).

CHART XXXI*

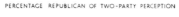
PERCENTAGE REPUBLICAN OF TWO-PARTY PERCEPTION

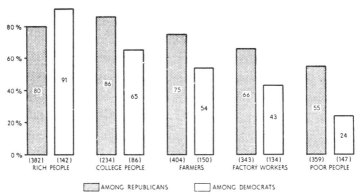

*The bar represents perception of the vote of the group in question by Republican and Democrats.

The others ranged between 5 and 8 per cent. Among those who did not say "Don't know," then, there was general acknowledgment of a group-oriented political cleavage within the community and relatively little attempt to ignore it, deny it, or explain it away.

But the major point has to do with political preference, for the vote of the respondents has its effect upon the perception of several groups. Take those of a socioeconomic character first. By and large, the reality of the political situation shows through; the rank order of the groups is about the same as perceived by both sides. The upper socioeconomic status groups are seen as more Republican by members of both parties—as, in fact, they were. But, in every case except one, Republicans inclined to perceive these groups as voting more Republican than did Democrats. In general, partisans

managed perceptually to "pull" such social groups their own way
(see Chart XXXI).

The one exception is "rich people"; Democrats are more likely
to assign them to the Republicans than the latter are to claim them!
Political parties are reluctant to appear as defenders of the rich—
and opponents are eager to attach that label. This is also reflected
in the respondents' conceptions of which party "would do the best
job" for each of the classes—the upper, the middle, the working, and

CHART XXXII

WITH ONE EXCEPTION, VOTERS THINK THEIR OWN PARTY WILL
DO THE BEST JOB FOR THE WHOLE COMMUNITY

PERCENTAGE WHO THOUGHT THE REPUBLICANS WOULD DO "BEST JOB"
FOR INDICATED CLASS (OF THOSE WITH OPINIONS)

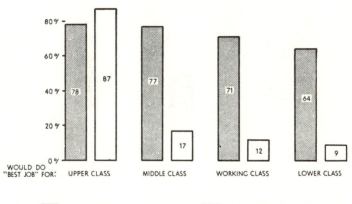

the lower. Again, except for this one case, there is high conformity
between vote and the respondents' assertion of who will do the
best job for the various classes (Chart XXXII). Republicans say
that the Republicans will be best for everybody, and the Democrats
say that the Democrats will be, except for the "upper class." Democrats overwhelmingly think that the Republicans are good only for
the upper classes, but the Republicans predominantly believe that
their party is best for everybody.

Class-consciousness, then, emerges only with respect to the
negative image of the "upper-class"–Republican connection for
Democratic voters. Otherwise, rather than acknowledge that they
support their own party because it is to their own interest to do so

(i.e., because it is the party of their class), the respondents tend to believe or to rationalize that their party is good for the whole community. Thus the class basis for vote, which clearly exists, is not overtly admitted. To a large extent, this is probably due to the requirements of the "American creed" that rejects the notion of serving class interests through political action. Even the one exception fits this to a degree; if popular democratic ideology allows *any* class distinction to be made, it is that which differentiates between a party's serving "the people" and "the upper classes."

In the case of ethnic groups—Catholics, Negroes, and Jews—the picture is not so clear. Fewer respondents knew how they would

CHART XXXIII

PERCENTAGE REPUBLICAN OF TWO-PARTY PERCEPTION

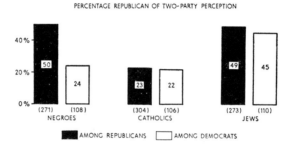

vote, on the average, than for the socioeconomic groups; and there was a greater discrepancy between perceived vote and actual vote. In Elmira about a third of the Catholics and the Jews and a fifth of the Negroes voted Republican; the respondents with opinions overrated the Republican vote of Jews and underrated that of Catholics. Presumably the Jews were perceived more as an economic group (they are high in Elmira) than as a religious or an ethnic minority. Perceptions of Catholics may not yet reflect the emerging trend away from the Democrats in that group. Only in the case of Negroes was there a differential perception between Republicans and Democrats (see Chart XXXIII).

POLITICAL PERCEPTION AND SOCIAL DISTANCE

Now perception is affected not solely by political position but also by social position of both the socioeconomic and the ethnic varieties. Not all members of the community are equidistant from the perceived groups whose political support was asked about.

The degree of social proximity—that implies a certain direct knowledge of the perceived group—affects perception of group support.

In general, the closer the voter is in socioeconomic position to the perceived groups, the more likely he is to see them as voting his own way (Chart XXXIV). And this holds whether proximity is indicated by objective status (e.g., occupation or socioeconomic status level) or by subjective designation (e.g., identification with class). Thus Republican *workers* perceived "factory workers" as voting for Dewey more frequently than the Republicans of *white-collar* occupation or above; and Democratic workers see them as voting for Truman more frequently than white-collar Democrats. Perception by respondents of different class identifications is similar. Again, with "poor people" there is a steady progression by socioeconomic status level and by class identification within each party. The closer the voter is to a group socially, the more he "pulls" the group into a similar proximity politically. This proximity factor operates even at a historical distance: Elmirans who were born on a farm—and thus have some subjective identification with farm people if not actual ties through relatives and friends—are more likely to see farmers as voting for their own party, regardless of which it was.[2]

There are two conditions—one subjective, the other objective—that presumably combine to explain this consistent patterning of perception. The first is the psychological indulgence received from the belief that people close to one's self are behaving like one's self, that is, that "people like you" conform to your own judgment. In

2. Here, again, the reality of the situation comes through. In Chart XXXIV, in addition to the effect of social position, Democrats are more likely to claim poor people and Republicans are more likely to claim farmers (and, in Elmira, factory workers). There is also a correlation between friendship patterns and class identification. Within each broad class stratum the individual's conception of the class he belongs to is related to the political preferences (and hence inferentially, the class status) of the majority of his friends.

MAJORITY OF FRIENDS	PERCENTAGE CONSIDERING THEMSELVES AS "UPPER" OR "MIDDLE" CLASS	
	White Collar and Above	Skilled Worker and Below
Republican..........	76 (184)	45 (206)
Democratic..........	50 (54)	27 (105)

CHART XXXIV

The Closer the Voters Are (or Feel) to the Perceived Groups, the More Likely They Are To "Pull" Them in Their Own Political Direction

PERCENTAGE WHO PERCEIVE THE GROUP AS VOTING
THEIR OWN WAY (OF TWO-PARTY PERCEPTION)

HOW FACTORY WORKERS WILL VOTE, AS SEEN BY:

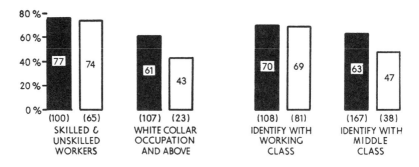

HOW POOR PEOPLE WILL VOTE, AS SEEN BY:

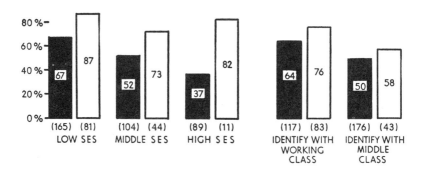

HOW FARMERS WILL VOTE, AS SEEN BY:

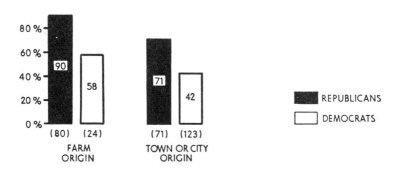

other words, the voters subjectively create a favorable personal environment by assigning to their own party the groups "closest" to themselves.

The second is the simple fact that people are more likely to associate with people like themselves—alike in political complexion as well as social position. For example, Republican workers associate with other Republican workers, and, when they are asked how workers are going to vote, they are likely to assign their own political position to the entire group. Thus union members with Republican co-workers perceive that their union is strongly Republican (91 per cent of thirty-four cases), and those with Democratic co-workers perceive that it is Democratic (84 per cent of thirty-eight cases)—and this regardless of the union (AF of L or CIO). The complexion of the small primary group is assigned to the larger formal organization.[3]

Political perception is also related to ethnic hostility or group prejudice—a condition that has little "real" connection with politics.

Our interviews contained a few questions intended to get at the respondent's attitudes toward the three ethnic groups for whom we have perception data, that is, the Negroes, the Catholics, and the Jews. It turns out that prejudiced voters are more likely to assign these groups to the *other* party—that is, perceptually to "push" them out of one's own political camp (Chart XXXV). If the ethnic

---

3. At the same time there was a tendency in specific unions to underestimate the Republican vote of the union, probably because of the general image of the Democrat-union tieup. In each case there were more Republican votes in the union than perceptions of Republican votes:

UNION	PERCENTAGE REPUBLICAN (MEMBERS OF EACH UNION ONLY)	
	Say They Will Vote	Think Union Will Vote
AF of L and independents	47 (73)	29 (103)
CIO	33 (15)	24 (25)
Remington Rand local	34 (32)	15 (54)

Here may be a nice instance of what sociologists have called "pluralistic ignorance"—a code thought to be accepted by "everyone," though, in fact, it is not (like the attitude of some southerners toward the Negro). However, the correct answer was that most members would vote Democratic, and in this sense the perception is largely accurate.

group is rejected on social or personal grounds, it is also rejected politically; and thus hostility is generalized to another sphere of activity. It is precisely this kind of condition that can seriously disturb the "community interest"—where social groups take political positions primarily on the ground that disapproved groups have taken the contrary position.

CHART XXXV

Ethnic Hostility Affects Political Perception by "Pushing" the Ethnic Group Away from One's Own Position*

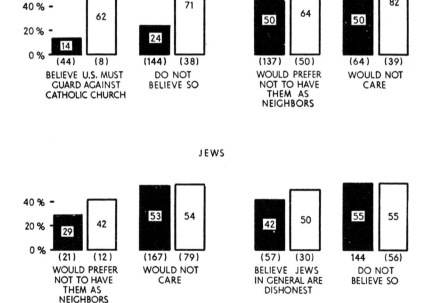

PERCENTAGE WHO PERCEIVED THE GROUP AS VOTING THEIR OWN WAY (OF TWO-PARTY PERCEPTION)

* This relationship is not confirmed by all the questions dealing with ethnic hostility. Since we were unable to construct a firm measure of ethnic hostility, this result should be accepted with caution.

Within these groups the awareness among minority-group members of how their own group votes is positively related to their
own vote. Whichever the direction of the influence—whether the

CHART XXXVI

MEMBERS OF ETHNIC GROUPS SEE THEIR OWN
GROUPS AS VOTING THEIR WAY

PERCENTAGE REPUBLICAN OF TWO-PARTY PERCEPTION OF OWN GROUP

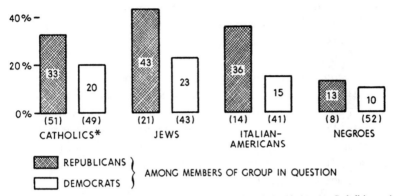

* This is the case despite the tendency of Catholics to deny the relationship between Catholicism and
vote. Only 9 per cent of the Protestants said that the Catholics would not vote as a bloc as compared to 30
per cent of the Catholics. Similarly, of the forty-three Republican Catholics who perceived most Catholics
as Democrats, only one stated that his religion had nothing to do with his vote when queried about the
"discrepancy."

individual's vote is cast in conformity with the group or the group
is seen as a projection of the individual's preference—there is an
association between the respondent's vote and his perception of the
predominant vote of his own minority group (Chart XXXVI). Republican Catholics see Catholics as voting more Republican than
Democratic Catholics; and the same is true of Jews' perception of
the Jewish vote, Negroes' of the Negro vote, and so on.

PSYCHOLOGICAL AND SOCIAL FUNCTIONS

What are some consequences of such perception of the political
position of social groups? For the individual, perceptual distortion
probably has the effect of relieving tension. Here, in the broadest
terms, the data fit the finding of experimental psychology: what

people notice in the external world is partly determined by their needs. People like to be reassured that they are right, in politics as in other matters, and, as a result, in this case they overrate the tendency of approved groups to vote their own way.

But psychological theory is not so clear with respect to our results on the effect of social proximity. If a man is closer to a certain group, he might know it better or he might have an even greater desire to feel that the group agrees with him. On this point the data support the latter position. And, in the case of ethnic hostility, the data refine the notion of need as the basis of perceptual distortion: not only does political perception probably serve needs for social support but perhaps also it serves certain needs or tensions for aggression against the "outsiders."

Perceptual distortion has its consequences for the society, too. First, it must make political systems more workable by making individual decisions easier. If everyone saw the true complexity of politics and no one could make up his mind, no government would be possible. Intentional or not, when the individual exaggerates the differences between social groups, he can more readily come to a decision. It is often more important *that* a decision is made than *which* decision is made.

Second, this bias must mean that actual cleavage within the community is deepened by the voter's perception of it. Differences in perception are a product of social stratification, and they reinforce it. Perceptual distortion increases the objective differences between "we" and "they." And that can make for a negative effect if carried to an extreme, as in some European countries in recent years. This makes for a unidimensional or monolithic distinction between the good people and the bad people (in religion, in status, in culture, *and* in politics), and it is a danger to a pluralistically organized democracy.

Finally, another possible result of such perception is heightened political stability. Individuals are less likely to shift from one allegiance to another when their initial allegiances are made "clearer" by perceptual distortion. From one point of view, this makes for a lack of flexibility in the system; but, from another, it conserves political integrity and makes progress (or movement) appropriately gradual.

SUMMARY

46. About one-third of the electorate does not profess to know how major socioeconomic and ethnic groups will vote.

47. Of those with opinions, very few deny the existence of bloc voting; and, in general, people are correct in their estimates.

48. Partisans tend to "pull" the support of socioeconomic groups in favor of their own party.

49. Republicans think their party would be better for the whole community, and Democrats think their party would be better for everyone except the rich.

50. The closer the voter is to the perceived groups in socioeconomic status, the more likely he is to perceive them as voting his way.

51. People hostile to religious and ethnic minorities are more likely to assign them to the opposition parties.

52. Members of religious and ethnic groups tend to see their own groups as voting their own way.

6 SOCIAL PROCESS
Small Groups and Political Discussion

The social differences politically relevant and politically perceived in Elmira were described in the two preceding chapters. Now we inquire more closely into the ways they are transmitted and maintained through small groups—the political role of family, friends, and co-workers. We dealt, so to speak, with the social *what;* now we deal with the *how* and *why.*

This chapter consists of two parts. First we present material on political homogeneity in primary groups and then material on political discussion within them. The first describes the political situation in families and among personal associates; the second tells, at least to some extent, how it got that way.

I. POLITICAL HOMOGENEITY IN PRIMARY GROUPS

THE FAMILY AND VOTE

How does a vote start with each new generation of citizens? Where should we look for the roots of political belief?

The "Hereditary Vote"

We should look first where we find the roots of personality, of religious and ethical values, of general cultural tastes—within the parental family. The family's influence upon vote begins long before the individual reaches voting age. A "hereditary vote"—the influence of the political tradition of one generation upon the political conviction of the next—is suggested by the association between the respondents and their fathers (Chart XXXVII). The association is particularly strong among the younger voters—four out of five with Republican fathers voted Republican in 1948, and two out of three

88

with Democratic fathers voted Democratic even in this Republican town. In other words, about 75 per cent of the first voters in the community sided with their fathers in their political choice.[1] And a high proportion of the total group, regardless of age, continue the political partisanship of their fathers in later life, though, as we shall see in chapter 7, the processes of persistence are more com-

CHART XXXVII

Parental Political Traditions Are Visible in the Vote but Especially among the Young Voters

PERCENTAGE REPUBLICAN OF TWO-PARTY VOTE

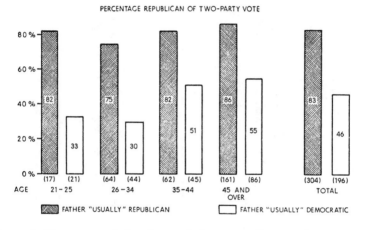

plicated. The parental family, and the constellation of social and psychological forces expressed through and around it, initiates a political disposition that with proper reinforcement carries through life.

This "inheritance" of political position is naturally maintained by the several characteristics held in common by family members; that is, it operates within the broad factors of socioeconomic status and religion that distinguish both parents and children (Chart XXXVIII). Where these associations or loyalties are in conflict, the father's traditional vote is modified, though a noticeable influence

1. Some of the correlation, of course, must be a projection of present convictions into the memory of the father's past vote, but this ambiguity in recollection should be at a minimum among the youngest voters, most of whom are still living with or near their parents. Among them the correlation of own and father's vote is the highest of all.

still persists. Where father's vote and social position are reinforcing, the children's vote is quite predictable. (This interplay of parental traditions and contemporary influences within religions and classes is discussed in more detail in the following chapter.)

The modification of parental loyalty by the child's social status is

CHART XXXVIII

THE EFFECT OF FATHER'S VOTE PERSISTS IN DIFFERENT
CLASS AND RELIGIOUS GROUPS

PERCENTAGE REPUBLICAN OF TWO-PARTY VOTE

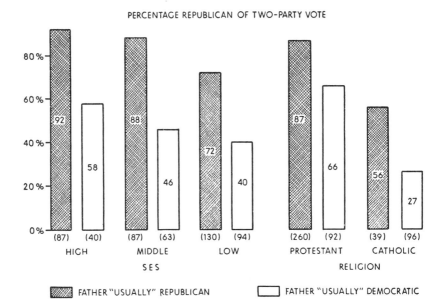

FATHER "USUALLY" REPUBLICAN   FATHER "USUALLY" DEMOCRATIC

revealed in intergenerational mobility. The children who have "moved up" in the world are more likely to vote Republican than those who have remained roughly in their father's social strata (Chart XXXIX). The comparative social status of the son or daughter is a qualifying factor to the father's political tradition.

Conversely, most of the deviants in class voting can be explained in terms of father's traditional vote. About two-thirds of upper socioeconomic-status Democrats and lower socioeconomic-status Republicans were voting in line with their fathers.

How does this political continuity between parent and child come

Bases of Generational Stability

about? Two conditions stand out: the first is a quality of the young voters; the second, a quality of the families in which they are brought up.

Contributing to the young voter's conformity with the parental tradition is his lack of involvement in politics. There is a belief in

CHART XXXIX

THE CHILD'S CORRESPONDENCE WITH THE FATHER'S VOTE IS
AFFECTED BY HIS RELATIVE STATUS IN THE WORLD

PERCENTAGE REPUBLICAN OF TWO-PARTY VOTE

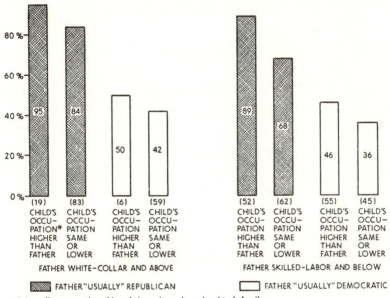

* Actually, occupation of breadwinner in son's or daughter's family.

this country that youth is politically radical; closer to the truth is the proposition that young people do not care much about politics. True, there are some indications that the young people carry the seeds of political deviation from traditional voting patterns; that is, they are more idealistic, more independent (or at least inconsistent), in their opinions. But in the end they do not carry through: they do not pay much attention to political materials, they tend not to vote, they are less likely to care if the opposition wins, and—this is the payoff—they fail to carry through deviant voting intentions (Table 9). Thus the age group most expected to "revolt" from tradition is least likely to go through with it in practice. And, because of that, here is an important link in the transmission of part of the

TABLE 9

MANY YOUNG VOTERS CARRY THE SEEDS OF DEVIATION BUT IN PRACTICE ARE STILL ONLY SUPERFICIALLY INVOLVED IN POLITICS

HYPOTHESIZED CHARACTERISTICS OF YOUNGER VOTERS, WITH EXAMPLES	PERCENTAGES BY AGE			
	21–25	26–34	35–54	55 and Older
More idealistic: Think election outcome will affect relations with Russia	79	73	65	62
More inconsistent with party label: Voted opposite own opinion on Taft-Hartley and/or price control (those with opinions on both)	76	61	54	46
Political interest is only newly arrived: Say they are more interested in this election than last one	80	62	61	55
Interest not strongly reinforced: Did not give high attention to campaign in mass media	73	62	59	59
*Lack of real commitment:** After election, percentage of Dewey voters who were "satisfied" with Truman victory	37	36	27	16
Good intentions not carried through: Among those who said they would vote for one of the two major parties in August *failed* to do so in November	46	22	8	16
Among those who said in August they would vote opposite of parental tradition failed to carry it out in November (i.e., failed to vote or returned to parent's party)	56	47	16	23
Total no. of cases	18–130	36–242	56–387	35–270

* Data from supplementary mail sample conducted as part of the Cornell studies of intergroup relations. Undecided voters included unless otherwise stated.

political heritage, from generation to generation—and an element of stability in the political system.

The second condition contributing to generational stability is this: about 90 per cent of those adult family members living together in the same house who had made up their minds agreed on their voting intentions in late October; all relationships within the immediate family had about the same level of agreement. Here is primary group solidarity of a high order. In the end many American families vote *as a unit*, making joint decisions in voting as in spending parts of the common family income. Indeed, it would not be inappropriate to consider the family as the primary unit of voting analysis, just as for some problems in economics the household or the spending unit is taken as the basis of study. There would be advantages to understanding voting decisions in this way—as the joint pooling of experience, information, and partisanship by several members of the primary and extended family into the crystallization or change of family voting traditions.

The young voter is brought up, then, in a one-sided political atmosphere. In addition, as we shall see in the following section, such homogeneity extends beyond the family to the whole circle of people with whom the youth associates as he comes to political age —his family's friends as well as his own. For example, because of social similarities, the youth is likely to marry within his political tradition. To the extent that parents bring up their children in a "one-party" climate of opinion like that provided by the primary-group homogeneity of middle-aged Elmirans, that environment provides strong pressures toward the perpetuation of political uniformities from one generation to the next. Just as young people learn from their elders, say, the religion and the table manners appropriate to their situation, so do they learn the appropriate political beliefs. His environment does not provide the young adult with clear political alternatives on a more or less random basis but rather a "natural selection" of the "correct way of life" as applied to politics. As he comes to voting age, the young voter's political consciousness is no *tabula rasa* on which various interests can contend; it is pre-shaped in particular political directions, as it is in other ways. And this process of socializing the ongoing generation in political matters, informal and nonpurposive as it is, provides an element of generational stability in the American political system.

PERSONAL ASSOCIATIONS AND VOTE

In addition to his family, the voter lives his day-to-day life largely in the company of his friends and his co-workers. This study collected information on the political preferences of three of the respondent's closest friends and three of his closest co-workers. With the family, they make up the primary social groups whose members mold each other's political opinions as well as other behavior.

In passing, we might remark that this view of friends and co-workers as "groups" within which the voter is a "member" is the customary but not entirely appropriate image. Actually, friends and co-workers serve less as closed cliques than as *contact points* through whom the individual is connected to whole networks of social relations that affect political behavior. The networks are organized in major socioeconomic and ethnic blocs, and at their center are the main institutions of the community and its ultimate leadership. Thus, one's personal associations are not distinct entities from class and ethnic strata but rather connect the individual to others in such strata. Data on the voter's friends and co-workers reveal how he is "hooked into" the larger community and hence partly indicate which social interests are more likely to influence him in his political choices.

Political Character of the Personal Environment

By and large, the voter is tied into a network of personal associations that is both homogeneous and congenial. Republican voters are more likely to have Republican friends and co-workers, and Democratic voters are more likely to have Democratic (Chart XL). The homogeneity is slightly greater for friends, since the voters can choose them more freely than co-workers, but for both groups the agreement within small clusters of personal associates is high—and higher for Republicans in this particular community. Only about one in five Republicans has a Democrat among his immediate associates, and about two in five Democrats have a Republican. For the community as a whole the proportion with associates from the *other* party is about 25 per cent. In a democracy the individual is expected to have available to him, not only in formal channels of communication but in informal channels of personal contact, a rich variety of experience, a diversity of information, a competition of ideas, and a maximum number of choices. Yet for this the individual is partly dependent on the accumulated information, aggregate experience, and collective judgment of his friends and co-workers (and that larger community to which he is connected through them). Most voters, and especially those of the majority party,

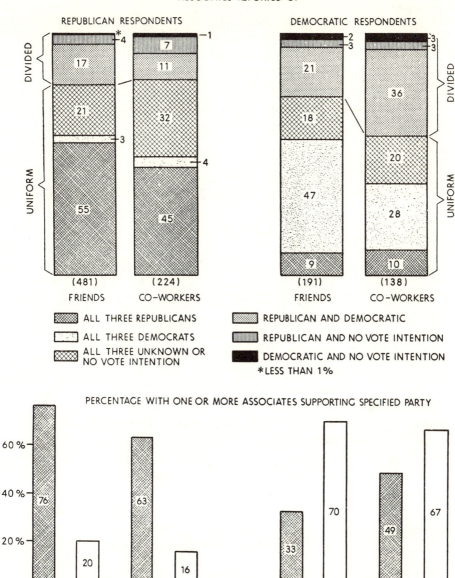

CHART XL

THE PERSONAL ENVIRONMENT IS POLITICALLY HOMOGENEOUS

ASSOCIATES REPORTED BY

REPUBLICAN RESPONDENTS   DEMOCRATIC RESPONDENTS

DIVIDED

UNIFORM

*
4
17
21
3
55
(481)
FRIENDS

—1
7
11
32
—4
45
(224)
CO-WORKERS

—2
—3
21
18
47
9
(191)
FRIENDS

3
3
36
20
28
10
(138)
CO-WORKERS

DIVIDED

UNIFORM

ALL THREE REPUBLICANS   REPUBLICAN AND DEMOCRATIC

ALL THREE DEMOCRATS   REPUBLICAN AND NO VOTE INTENTION

ALL THREE UNKNOWN OR NO VOTE INTENTION   DEMOCRATIC AND NO VOTE INTENTION

*LESS THAN 1%

PERCENTAGE WITH ONE OR MORE ASSOCIATES SUPPORTING SPECIFIED PARTY

60%

40%

20%

0%

76
20
FRIENDS
63
16
CO-WORKERS
REPUBLICANS

33
70
FRIENDS
49
67
CO-WORKERS
DEMOCRATS

ONE OR MORE REPUBLICAN ASSOCIATE

ONE OR MORE DEMOCRATIC ASSOCIATE

carry on these personal associations in what approaches a political monopoly.[2]

Moreover, the political complexion of one's friends is related to one's own social position. Those predisposed toward a Democratic vote (e.g., working-class people and Catholics) are more likely to have Democratic friends; and conversely for those predisposed Republican (see Chart XLI). Here, again, the general complexion of the Republican community is apparent, but the differential between groups is too. Friends transmit the predispositional tendencies of

CHART XLI*

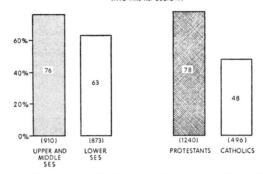

* Questions about friends and co-workers were asked in August.

class and religion; in a sense, such predispositions *are* mainly the accumulated influence of like-positioned and hence like-minded associates on each other.

The political homogeneity of personal associations increases as the voter grows older and settles more and more into his life-pattern (Chart XLII). Only half of the young *first* voters are in agreement with all three of their close friends, and almost 30 per cent disagree with two or all three of them. The young people just coming to voting age are establishing new families and finding their way into

2. The effect of the politics of one's friends is also clear between elections. Those 1944 Republicans with a majority of Republican friends stayed Republican (98 per cent); those 1944 Democrats with a majority of Democratic friends stayed Democratic, even in Elmira (91 per cent). But those in conflict between their earlier allegiance and their current friendships divided, in effect, with the community (i.e., 63 per cent Republican). A campaign catches some individuals in a personal environment contradictory to their own voting tradition and produces a kind of political exchange of social captives.

new jobs, new neighborhoods, and new associations that provide opportunities for political inconsistences and conflicts. Their elders —and this means those from age thirty-five on—come to fall into agreeable associations through the very process of living in jobs, communities, organizations. Thus political homogeneity of the pri-

CHART XLII

POLITICAL HOMOGENEITY INCREASES WITH AGE*

PERCENTAGE (OF THOSE WHO KNOW VOTE INTENTION OF ALL THREE)

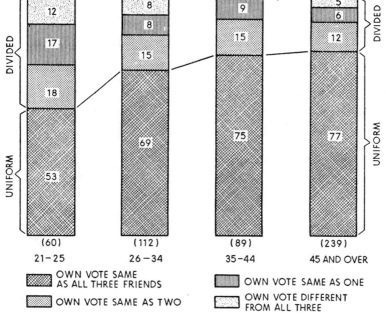

* This result holds for each party separately.

mary environment, high to start with, becomes even higher with the passage of time.

Friends, Co-workers, and Voting

The data can be rearranged to show the harmony between one's own vote and the vote of his associates in a different sense—the respondent's vote as a *consequence* of the preferences of his associates. Again eliminating the "Don't know's" and the unknowns, we find an agreement in over 85 per cent of the extreme cases; and, when the political complexion of friends and co-workers is divided, the distribution of the respondents' votes reflects the nature of the division (see Chart XLIII).

More than that, friends and co-workers also affect the strength of conviction with which the vote preference is held. It is voters with homogeneous and agreeable associates who believe strongly in the rightness of their candidate and party (Chart XLIV). Those with friends in both camps are less sure of their vote. Thus, the

CHART XLIII

PERCENTAGE REPUBLICAN OF RESPONDENT'S VOTE INTENTION
(TWO PARTY)

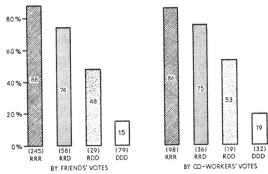

(RRR MEANS ALL THREE REPUBLICAN, RRD MEANS TWO REPUBLICAN AND
ONE DEMOCRATIC, AND SO ON)

political conviction of the individual is closely bound to the political character of his personal relations—or at least his perception of their political complexion. A sense of security about one's judgment seems to be a function of the congeniality of the personal environment; here, as elsewhere in the realm of political attitudes and behavior, the private political conscience of the citizen rests upon a near-by group norm represented by the people around him. Without their full support it is not easy to hold strong political attitudes, and relatively few people do.

Friends, the Community, and Breakage in the Vote

Finally, what of the inevitable discords between the small cluster of personal associates with whom the individual voter lives and the larger community in which he lives? It is customary to say that what matters for the voter is the social environment *close* to him; and so it does. When the primary group of friends or co-workers

CHART XLIV

The Voter's Strength of Conviction Is Related to the Political Homogeneity of His Associates

RESPONDENT'S VOTE INTENTION AND STRENGTH (AUGUST)

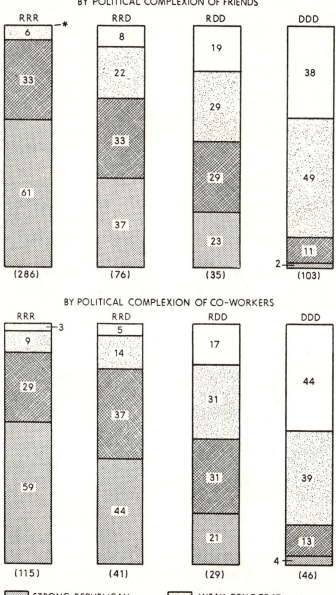

BY POLITICAL COMPLEXION OF FRIENDS

| RRR | RRD | RDD | DDD |

RRR —*
6
33
61
(286)

RRD
8
22
33
37
(76)

RDD
19
29
29
23
(35)

DDD
38
49
11
2—
(103)

BY POLITICAL COMPLEXION OF CO-WORKERS

RRR —3
9
29
59
(115)

RRD
5
14
37
44
(41)

RDD
17
31
31
21
(29)

DDD
44
39
13
4—
(46)

▨ STRONG REPUBLICAN   ▧ WEAK DEMOCRAT

▨ WEAK REPUBLICAN   ☐ STRONG DEMOCRAT

* Less than 1 per cent.

is united in political opinion, then the respondent's vote is firm. When Democratic primary groups are "solid," the party vote is not significantly lower than for "solid" Republican groups (i.e., each side loses only about 12 or 15 per cent in deviations). The strong community majority for the Republicans has little effect because it has little access to persons within homogeneous Democratic groups.

But when the primary environment is internally *divided* the effect of the distant community can be seen. Then the Republicans get a higher proportion of the vote. If friends and co-workers are divided two-to-one Republican, the vote goes about three-fourths Republican; but, if they are two-to-one Democratic, the vote goes only about half Democratic. It is as though the average vote in *mixed* primary groups was moved some distance to the Republican side. The impact of the larger community is thus most evident among voters with discordant or disagreeing primary groups. When the voter's close associates do not provide him with a single, clear political direction—when instead they offer an alternative—then wider associations in the surrounding community reinforce one position over the other.

The same effect can be seen within each socioeconomic status and religious category. With supporting friends entirely of the "right" party (the traditional party of the stratum), each of the subgroups is 90 per cent "solid" in vote. But, in almost every intermediate case, the Republican-disposed category with a mixed group of friends retains a stronger vote for its party than its Democratic counterpart. Protestants with one Democratic friend (of three) "lose" only 15 per cent of their vote to the Democrats, but Catholics with one Republican friend "lose" 36 per cent of theirs (see Chart XLV).

In general, then, the Republicans get more than their random share of the adjustment to a conflicting environment, because of the pervasive Republican atmosphere of Elmira that thus tends to perpetuate itself. The surrounding majority gets the benefit of the operation of cross-pressures. One might call this the "breakage" effect, borrowing a term from horse-racing circles. In the parimutuel system people bet against and influence one another. But, when the result is settled in round sums, the odd pennies left over—the breakage—go to the track or to the state in the background. In our case the breakage in small-group adjustment goes to the Republican community. At any one moment the breakage may be trivial, as it is at the track; but over a period of time it is considerable. For example, the heavier Republican vote of older people in Elmira may

CHART XLV

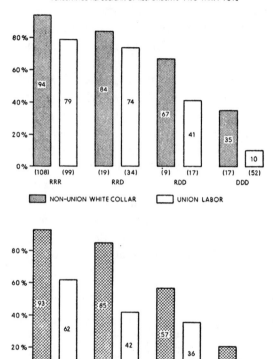
PERCENTAGE REPUBLICAN OF RESPONDENTS' TWO-PARTY VOTE

be the result of just such attrition from the give-and-take of primary groups. With advancing age, a steady toll is taken of former Democrats in the Republican community.

II. The Nature of Political Discussion

The social environment of the typical voter, then, is politically homogeneous. How does it get that way and how is it kept that way? One answer is "through political discussion."[3] Where is such discussion carried on? Between whom? About what?

Political Discussion with Family and Associates

Naturally, a major locale for the discussion of politics in Elmira is the home, but it varies with the extent to which politics is "in season." Whereas only 15 per cent of the discussants named another family member as the person with whom they had last discussed politics in June, this figure became 52 per cent in October, at the height of the campaign. Of those naming someone "among the people you know and associate with to whom you would be most likely to go" to discuss a question connected with the campaign, about 27 per cent named a family member.

The most strongly family-oriented in political discussion are married women, who look to their husbands as the primary source of political materials, particularly when politics is not in the forefront of attention (Chart XLVI). The men discuss politics with their wives—that is, they *tell* them—but they do not particularly respect them. On the side of the wives there is trust; on the side of the husbands, apparently, there is the need to reply or to guide.

Among personal associations *outside* the family, who talks politics with whom? The broad answer is that people mostly discuss politics with other people like themselves—"like" in such characters as

3. In October about 83 per cent of the respondents recalled a recent political discussion.

In his doctoral dissertation based on Elmira data, "Interpersonal Contact and Exposure to Mass Media during a Presidential Campaign" (Faculty of Political Science, Columbia University, 1951), Dick H. Baxter analyzed about fifty intensive interviews conducted in September in order to identify the reasons people give for *not* discussing politics. Following is a list of the reasons identified and illustrative quotations:

Feelings of political deficiency: "I don't talk it over with my friends or anybody. I don't know enough to talk it over with anybody."

Limited accessibility: "I don't get the opportunity too much. Being a widow, I don't go to many parties and the like."

Disagreement with associates: "All my neighbors are Democrats, so there's no use talking with them about it."

Other interests: "We don't talk politics. We all have children, and that's what we talk about."

No time: "I'd like to discuss politics with the employees, but I just don't have time. We're too shorthanded."

Unwillingness to talk politics in business situations: "I don't talk politics at the store because it's bad for business."

Tensions and unpleasantness associated with political dicussion: "I've seen arguments, and it's not worth it. Through the years I've seen different arguments, and it is just not worth it."

social position, age, occupation, and attitude. To a large extent, political discussion follows the composition of friendship groups. Those respondents with Republican friends tend to talk with Republicans and, again with a little loss on the "breakage," the same

CHART XLVI

MARRIED WOMEN REPORT THAT THEY DISCUSS POLITICS WITHIN THE FAMILY MORE THAN MEN DO, ESPECIALLY IN QUIET TIMES

MARRIED COUPLES
(NON-DISCUSSANTS ELIMINATED)

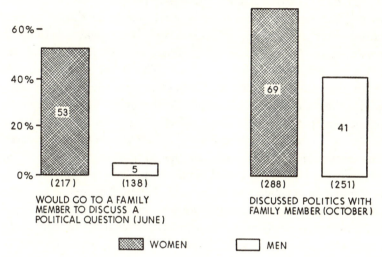

60% –

40% –

20% –

0% –

| (217) | (138) | | (288) | (251) |

WOULD GO TO A FAMILY MEMBER TO DISCUSS A POLITICAL QUESTION (JUNE)

DISCUSSED POLITICS WITH FAMILY MEMBER (OCTOBER)

▨ WOMEN   ☐ MEN

goes for Democrats (see Chart XLVII). This suggests that political discussion is carried on *within* groups rather than *between* them. Let us now document this in somewhat more detail.

CHART XLVII

LAST DISCUSSED POLITICS
WITH A REPUBLICAN

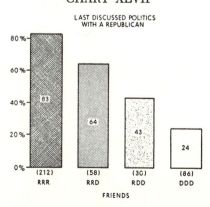

80% –
60% –
40% –
20% –
0% –

| (212) | (58) | (30) | (86) |
| RRR | RRD | RDD | DDD |

FRIENDS

First, people of different ages tend to go to other people of about the same age for discussion of the campaign (Chart XLVIIIA). The relative social ease of intra- rather than intergenerational communication is thus expressed in the sphere of politics. At the same time, however, the deviation is upward: youth seems to have much more respect for their elders' opinions than the elders do for youth's.

Next—and more relevant politically—is the tendency to discuss politics with people of a similar occupational status (Chart XLVIIIB). Professional and managerial people are more likely to go to other professional and managerial people for discussion, and skilled workers to other skilled workers. Here, again, patterns of personal association, of likes with likes, are expressed in political terms, though with some exceptions. The lower occupations are much more likely to look to the higher occupations for political advice than the other way around. For example, 34 per cent of the skilled workers name a professional or managerial person, whereas only 8 per cent of the latter name a skilled worker. To some extent this pattern is probably attributable to the heavily Republican environment of Elmira; but to some extent, too, it is probably due to the greater prestige and status of the "better" occupations and to their stronger power position in the community (which is thus open to reinforcement). At any rate, political interchange among occupational groups in the form of respected personal discussion was by no means bidirectional in Elmira. To a large extent occupational groups talked to themselves, and, for the rest, the lower occupations looked to the higher.[4]

4. A sidelight on occupational patterns of political talk is provided by data on the initiation of discussion. Respondents reporting a recent political talk in June were asked: "How did the discussion start? Did the other person ask your views?" The people who talked with equal or higher occupations were more likely to have *started* the discussion themselves than those who talked with lower occupations. In the latter case the person having the lower occupation seemed to be asking the person "above" him about politics.

Discussion Initiated	Talked with Person from Higher or Equal Occupation	Talked with Person from Lower Occupation
By self..................	21%	12%
By other person..........	35	51
By both................	44	37
Total no. of cases....	159	35

CHART XLVIII

In Political Discussions Outside the Family, People Talk to People of Like Characteristics*

(SHADING INDICATES DISCUSSANT SAME AS RESPONDENT)

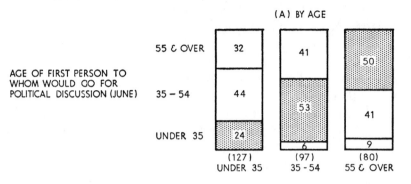

(A) BY AGE

AGE OF FIRST PERSON TO WHOM WOULD GO FOR POLITICAL DISCUSSION (JUNE)

55 & OVER

35 – 54

UNDER 35

(127) UNDER 35 · (97) 35 - 54 · (80) 55 & OVER

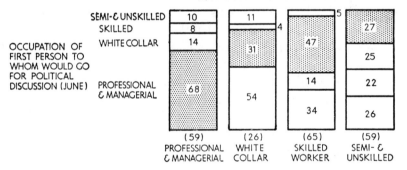

(B) BY OCCUPATION (OF BREADWINNER)

OCCUPATION OF FIRST PERSON TO WHOM WOULD GO FOR POLITICAL DISCUSSION (JUNE)

SEMI-& UNSKILLED
SKILLED
WHITE COLLAR
PROFESSIONAL & MANAGERIAL

(59) PROFESSIONAL & MANAGERIAL · (26) WHITE COLLAR · (65) SKILLED WORKER · (59) SEMI- & UNSKILLED

(C) BY VOTE INTENTION

VOTE INTENTION OF LAST PERSON WITH WHOM DIS- CUSSED POLITICS (OCTOBER)

DEMOCRAT

REPUBLICAN

(157) REPUBLICANS · (77) DEMOCRATS

*Data include only extra-family discussions. If intra-family discussions are included, the correlations of course become more marked.

And all this adds up to a concentration of discussion among people of the same political preference (Chart XLVIIIC). Although the preponderance of Republicans in Elmira does affect them, Democrats still manage to concentrate most of their discussion among congenial people—and the Republicans do so to a greater extent.

At the height of the campaign, then, political discussion on the grass-roots level apparently consists more of the exchange of mutually agreeable remarks than of controversial ones. The process of clarifying and modifying views with opponents that is assumed to constitute the give-and-take of informal political debate throughout the community is not predominant during the presidential campaign. There is a tendency against intergenerational or interoccupational or interparty discussion. There is some talk across social categories but more within them.

This is further reinforced by the respondents' own recollections, at the end of the campaign, of *what* was talked about in their most recent political discussions. In about a third of the cases the discussion centers about topics that do not directly involve political preferences—such as predictions about victory in the election, exchange of information, or neutral observation about the conduct of the campaign. In the remainder of the cases mutual agreement between the discussants outnumbers disagreement ten to one: about 63 per cent amount to reinforcing exchanges about common positions on the candidates or the issues, and only 6 per cent involve some degree of argument between the discussants. Lowell was not far wrong:

> To a great extent, people hear what they want to hear and see what they want to see. They associate by preference with people who think as they do, enter freely into conversation with them, and avoid with others topics that are controversial, irritating, or unpleasant. This is not less true of what they read. To most people that which runs counter to their ideas is disagreeable, and sought only from a sense of duty.[5]

Thus there is relatively little political exchange among the electorate in the sense of open differences of views. This is true not only in the heat of the campaign, but early, too, when personal investment in the election is not so great. About 70 per cent of the "most recent" political talks in June were reported to be agreeable in

5. A. Lawrence Lowell, *Public Opinion in War and Peace,* p. 47.

nature, and only about 20 per cent involved disagreement (the remainder were "Don't knows").

The degree of agreement correlates slightly with the relationship between the discussants (see Chart XLIX). The respondent was slightly more likely to agree with someone higher on the occupation-al scale and to disagree with someone lower; and he was more likely to agree if he initiated the discussion or participated in its initiation.[6]

CHART XLIX

PERCENTAGE AGREEING IN MOST RECENT TALK (JUNE)

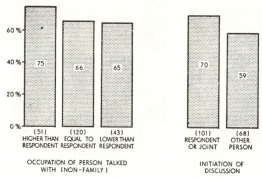

OCCUPATION OF PERSON TALKED WITH (NON-FAMILY)

INITIATION OF DISCUSSION

Finally, the political complexion of friends does not affect every-one equally. Strangely enough, the friendship pattern is more in-fluential in the case of those voters who talk politics *less*. This is not simply a question of their low interest, for the lower the interest the less one votes consistently with his friends (Chart L). One ex-planation is that after the period at which friends' preferences were measured (August), those *within* our sample who talked most actively influenced their friends *outside* the sample to adjust to them more often than did the passive nontalkers. The former active dis-

6. This deals with matters within the confines of the election campaign. It may be that discussion is much more open, more given to genuine interchange and disagreement, at other times. The data, while far from conclusive, do indi-cate that at least the respondents *think* that there is more disagreement in their personal discussions of politics. About 20 per cent report such disagreement with "a few" of their close friends, 15 per cent with "some" of them, and (only) 2 per cent with "most." Thus a total of from 35 to 40 per cent believe that they have some degree of disagreement in their own circles, although much less disagreement seems to come to the surface in actual discussions dur-ing the campaign. The people who report more disagreement with their fel-lows are the more interested, the better educated, and the more active discus-sants.

cussants are able in some part to act *on* their environment; the latter passive people are more likely to be submissive *to* that environment.

CHART L

Voters Who Talk Politics Least Agree
with Their Friends the Most

PERCENTAGE VOTING WITH MAJORITY OF FRIENDS

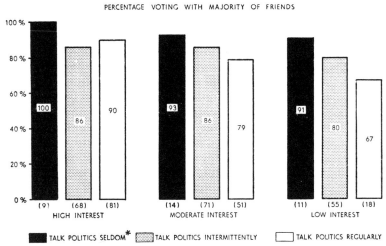

TALK POLITICS SELDOM*   TALK POLITICS INTERMITTENTLY   TALK POLITICS REGULARLY

*This simple index combines June and October discussion questions. See Appendix B.

On the whole, however, because of the channeling of political contacts through congenial personal associations outside as well as inside the family, discussionable disagreements on politics are not widespread within the community. Most of the political talk that went on in the living-rooms of Elmira, over the back fences, at the bars, on the job, and in similar places—the everyday, informal, grass-roots discussion of public affairs that serves as a base of democratic judgment—involved the exchange of mutually agreeable points of view. Political controversy is a good deal more prevalent in the content of the mass media than in the content of private conversations about public affairs. Certainly the first of Lindsay's two processes was the more important:

One gets an impression sometimes as though there were always two processes going on in politics—on the one hand the process of collective enthusiasm at party meetings (or the subtler and perhaps more poisonous, if calmer, process of producing self-complacency when men of the same political persuasion deplore in common the folly and knavery of their political opponents), and on the other hand a great process of discussion between men who do not agree but do discuss their disagreement.[7]

The "Opinion Leaders"

However, political discussion is not all of a piece. As Bryce puts it: "Opinion does not merely grow; it is also made. There is not merely the passive class of person; there is the active class, who occupy themselves primarily with public affairs, who aspire to create and lead opinion."[8] Given such specialists, the political genius of the citizenry may reside less in how well they can judge public policy than in how well they can judge the people who advise them how to judge policy. And herein lies the importance of a notion that in *The People's Choice* we termed "opinion leadership." To whom do the rank-and-file voters typically "delegate" the main burden of political discussion in the community? That may be as important a question as how much the rank and file themselves discuss the matter or expose themselves directly to the national debate. When the electorate "consults with itself," *who* is actually consulted?

For leadership in political discussion people mainly turn to others like themselves. The banker and mayor and union officer may be "opinion leaders" in a distant sense, but ordinary voters listen to near-by influencers. For this reason, one might properly speak less of leaders than of a complex web of opinion-leading relationships. It is true that one can single out those individuals who are more likely than others to be at the center of several such relationships and call them "opinion leaders," as we do in this analysis.[9]

7. A. D. Lindsay, *Essentials of Democracy,* p. 36.

8. James Bryce, *American Commonwealth,* II, 256.

9. For our purposes the opinion leader is defined in this way: In the June interview respondents were asked: "Compared with the people you know, are you more or less likely than any of them to be asked your views about politics?" The next question was: "Have you talked politics with anyone recently?" All those people who (1) answered "More" to the first question *or* (2) answered "Same" to the first question *and* "Yes" to the second were defined as opinion leaders—a total of 23 per cent of the sample.

This simple classificatory device is derived from a series of research experiences regarding opinion leaders. Following up the Erie County study, one of the authors made a study in which opinion leaders were selected in a twofold way. On the one hand, they stated themselves whether they had been

But when it is found also that the people so singled out as leaders report, in turn, that they *seek advice* on politics more than others (52 per cent to 43 per cent), we are reminded again that in practice there must be unending circuits of leadership relationships running through the community, like a nerve system through the body.

What kind of people were more active than others in such circuits of rank-and-file leadership? Three qualities distinguish these informal leaders, much as they do leaders generally. The first is a particular *interest and competence* in the sphere of discussion for which they lead (Chart LI).

This greater personal competence in the particular subject matter is coupled closely to greater *interaction through more strategic social locations*. The competence of the leader and his contact with followers go together like Shaw's temptation and opportunity (Chart LII).

These matters facilitating informal leadership—first, greater interest and competence and, second, greater social activity or opportunity—are understandable enough. But failure to understand a third quality of effective leaders in political discussion is at the root of many mistaken ideas, for example, that "prominent men" lead political opinion. Actually, opinion leaders are found in all strata of society. The disproportion in party support in Elmira did not affect the incidence of opinion leadership; there are relatively the same number in the Democratic party as the Republican. There are no concentrations of opinion leadership in different age groups or socioeconomic levels. Occupationally there is a balanced distribution between the white-collar and blue-collar segments of the community (see Chart LIII). What, then, is the distinctiveness of these informal leaders?

Actually, it seems to be a delicate matter of being distinctive

---

singled out for advice. On the other hand, a check was made to see whether the alleged advice-seeker actually confirmed the event. As a result of careful analysis it appeared that "self-designation" could be used as a workable index for the type of personal influence we have in mind here (for details see Elihu Katz, Paul F. Lazarsfeld, *et. al., Personal Influence* [Glencoe, Ill.: Free Press, 1954]). The problem still remains to arrive at this self-designation in a simple way. Again the preceding studies indicate that a combination of two questions seems sufficient for a *rough* classification. The one should be a general rating as to how the respondent judges his importance as an adviser in a specific field. The second question should check whether he has actually had a pertinent recent contact.

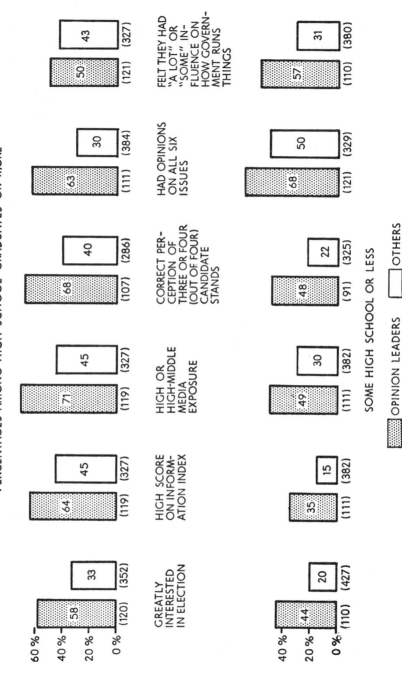

CHART LI

OPINION LEADERS ARE MORE INTERESTED IN
AND INFORMED ABOUT THE SUBJECT

PERCENTAGES AMONG HIGH SCHOOL GRADUATES OR MORE

SOME HIGH SCHOOL OR LESS

OPINION LEADERS   OTHERS

without being *too* distinctive. Occupationally, there is the same suggestion of an upward tendency in the process of opinion leadership that appeared in the data on personal discussion of politics. On each side of the broad occupational dichotomy between white-collar and blue-collar workers, the upper occupational group within each pair provided more opinion leaders than the lower. One inference

CHART LII

OPINION LEADERS ARE MORE ACTIVE
AND MORE STRATEGICALLY LOCATED

PERCENTAGE AMONG THOSE WITH GREAT INTEREST

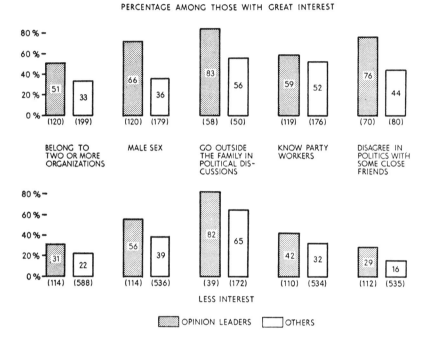

is that white-collar people look more to professional and managerial people as their opinion leaders and that the semi- and unskilled workers similarly look to the skilled workers.

This same general point is supported by the fact that within each socioeconomic status level the opinion leader was somewhat more likely to come from the better-educated members of the group. The difference was not so much as to put him out of touch with the group, but it was enough perhaps to win respect. Thus, while the opinion leader appeared throughout the society, he was presumably

selected out by his fellows or himself within each group because
of a (slightly) "higher" qualification (see Chart LIV).

This tendency for the opinion leader to be like everyone else,
only slightly more so, is also reflected in his political attitudes. Within each party the opinion leader is more likely to support his own
party's position on the two basic issues of the campaign. For ex-

CHART LIII

PERCENTAGE WHO ARE OPINION LEADERS

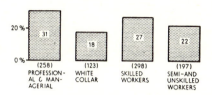

BREADWINNER'S OCCUPATION

CHART LIV*

AVERAGE YEARS OF EDUCATION

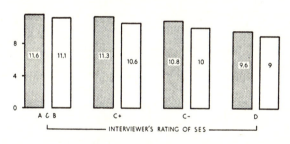

*Since our general SES index includes education, we use here the simple
interviewer's rating of SES (A high, D low). See Appendix B.

ample, the Republican opinion leaders favor the Taft-Hartley Law
more than the other Republicans, and Democratic leaders oppose
it more than other Democrats (see Chart LV).

Thus the leaders represent or symbolize the given group's norms
in the particular sphere—the *given* group's norms, say, labor's and
not business', and in the *particular* sphere, say, voting, not running
the community's welfare movement or baseball team. Those men
can better lead who are traveling the same road as their followers
but are a little ahead.

Such critical individuals at the junction points in networks of personal influence manifest in modern society a Jeffersonian image of the ideal grass-roots leader. That is, they are likely to be active in routine social life, competent in politics, but yet so thoroughly ordinary citizens that they are in fact models or prototypes for the others whom they inform, argue with, and influence in politics. If something like this is the actual case in the factories, farms, and neighborhoods of today, then the political wisdom of an apolitical

CHART LV

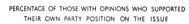

PERCENTAGE OF THOSE WITH OPINIONS WHO SUPPORTED
THEIR OWN PARTY POSITION ON THE ISSUE

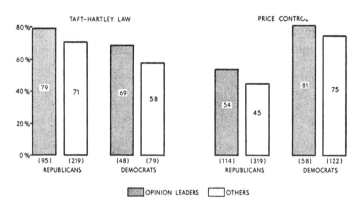

people may consist of an ability to judge among the especially competent and trusted people around them, as well as the theoretically desirable but practically difficult capacity to judge the distant national debate. In the nature of the case, everyone cannot understand and evaluate everything. The "opinion leader" relationship is a useful instrument in democratic life.

THE SOCIAL GROUP AND THE POLITICAL SYSTEM

Underlying the influence of the social group is the ambiguity of political stimuli. The individualistic tradition of thinking about politics, as typically expressed in democratic theory, implies that it is possible and reasonably convenient for the voter to see clearcut alternatives: to judge the differences between candidates, weigh the relevance of the issues to his own needs, and then rightly or wrongly "decide" what to do. The scheme implied in this tradition of thinking about politics requires a reasonably clear political choice that can be responded to directly by the individual, but this is not always, or even usually, the case.

Suppose we think of two polar types of modern elections. An unusual type of election (e.g., 1936) presents a clear-cut and easily understood program that had major consequences for a large number of voters, that was highlighted by dramatic events, and that was symbolized by a magnetic candidate. At the opposite pole there is an election period (e.g., 1948) in which voters can find no clear programs, no simple picture of what is at stake, no visible consequences win or lose for the average citizen, no appealing and dramatic candidates—in short, a thoroughly ordinary period against the backdrop of reasonably stable times during which the citizen would prefer to be left undisturbed in the normal pursuit of job and family activities.

In situations of high ambiguity, according to the evidence of psychological experiments, two kinds of behavior occur that we have encountered in this political analysis. First, with no clear directives from stimuli outside themselves, people are likely to fall back on directive forces within themselves. This means that voters are likely to fall back on early allegiances, experiences, values, and norms—for example, those associated with being raised as a member of the working class or a minority group. Second, voters are likely to be especially vulnerable to less relevant influences than direct political stimuli. If voters cannot test the appropriateness of their decisions by reference to political consequences, then they are especially likely to be influenced by other, nonpolitical facts—for example, what trusted people around them are doing. As a result, old interests and traditions of class and minority blocs are brought to bear upon the determination of today's vote. In this process the principal agencies are not Machiavellian manipulators, as is commonly supposed when bloc votes are delivered at the polls, but the ordinary family, friends, co-workers, and fellow organization members with whom we are all surrounded. In short, the influences to which voters are most susceptible are opinions of trusted people expressed to one another.

SUMMARY

Political Homogeneity in Primary Groups: The Family

53. The political tradition of the parent is reflected in the party choice of present voters, and especially young voters.

54. This relationship between the generations is best maintained when in harmony with class or religious voting traditions.

55. Children who have achieved upward social mobility over their parents vote more Republican.

56. High generational stability is maintained particularly because young people are raised in a politically homogeneous environment and because they are only superficially involved in politics at the time of first voting when the generational influence is strongest.

57. There is a high degree of agreement (upward of 90 per cent) on political preference within the family.

Political Homogeneity in Primary Groups: Personal Associations

58. The personal environment outside the family is also politically homogeneous: voters are likely to have friends and co-workers of the same political preference.

    and (*a*) Such homogeneity is slightly higher for friends (who are self-chosen) than for "closest" co-workers.

59. Voters predisposed to the Republican position by class or religion have more Republican friends, and the same with Democrats.

60. Political homogeneity among friends increases with age.

61. The more homogeneous the personal associates, the stronger the conviction in support of a candidate.

62. When the voter's immediate personal environment is split in political preference, he is more likely to vote in line with the majority of the larger community (the breakage effect).

The Nature of Political Discussion: Discussion
  with Family and Associates

63. Much political talk is centered in the family; and married women report discussing politics in the family more than married men, especially in quiet times.

64. Most political discussion goes on among people of like characteristics—like in friendship, in age (although young people look more to older people than the opposite), in occupation (although

lower groups look more to upper groups than the opposite), and in political preference itself (although the political minority looks more to the majority).

65. Political discussions are made up much more of mutual agreement than of disagreement.

> *and* (*a*) Voters are more likely to agree with someone of higher occupational status than themselves;
>
> (*b*) Voters are more likely to agree if they have initiated the discussion themselves;
>
> (*c*) Voters think they generally disagree with their associates more than they actually do in particular campaign discussions.

66. Voters who talk politics the least are most likely to agree in vote with their friends.

The Nature of Political Discussion: The Opinion Leaders

67. Opinion leaders are characterized by (1) greater interest and competence in politics; (2) greater activity in more strategic social locations; and (3) closer representativeness of those they influence.

> *and* (*a*) Within broad strata, opinion leaders are slightly higher in occupational and educational status than others.

68. Opinion leaders support their own party position more strongly on the subsidiary issues than do others.

7 SOCIAL EFFECTS OF THE CAMPAIGN
Personal Influence and Political Polarization

What changes do these social processes produce when they are set in motion by the modern campaign of a presidential election? Answers can be given in different degrees of complexity—differing with the social unit under consideration and with the time unit involved. The former can range from small-scale, "molecular" interaction between individual voters—people talking about the election in face-to-face contact—to the large-scale, gross voting patterns of whole blocs of the population. The latter can range from generational shifts in politics to changes between elections and finally to changes during or in the campaign itself.

Let us turn first to the changes occasioned within social units, going from the smaller to the larger.

I. VOTING CHANGES BY SOCIAL UNITS

Face-to-Face Discussion

A good starting point for analyzing social influences in voting change is the pattern of political discussion reported in the preceding chapter. Since who talks politics with whom makes a lot of

CHART LVI

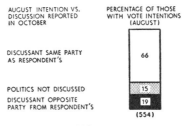

AUGUST INTENTION VS. DISCUSSION REPORTED IN OCTOBER	PERCENTAGE OF THOSE WITH VOTE INTENTIONS (AUGUST)
DISCUSSANT SAME PARTY AS RESPONDENT'S	66
POLITICS NOT DISCUSSED	15
DISCUSSANT OPPOSITE PARTY FROM RESPONDENT'S	19
	(554)

118

difference in vote changes, earlier data are recapitulated here (in slightly different form). This distribution suggests that static or no-change results would characterize the large majority, because they talk to people of preferences identical to their own (see Chart LVI). Some potential for change or for instability is evident. About 19 per cent talked most recently in October with a person of the

CHART LVII

VOTING CHANGES ARE PROPORTIONATE
TO THE TYPE OF DISCUSSION REPORTED

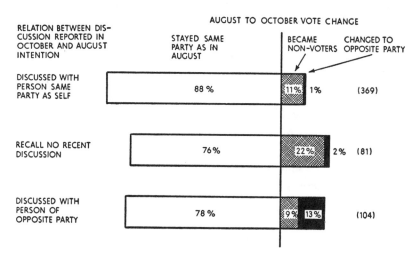

party opposite their own August preference, and another 15 per cent of the intended voters engaged in no political discussions, that is, they must have been talking with indifferent people who customarily do not include politics in their conversation.

Now, what happens when discussion of the latter, nonreinforcing kinds goes on over the several months of a political campaign? For example, does argumentation among opposites strengthen each participant in the conviction that he is right? Quite the reverse seems to be the result. Those who discuss politics with the opposition are more likely than others subsequently to take on that opposite preference in their own voting (Chart LVII). And those who do not talk politics are more likely to be unstable in general, often by adopting the neutrality or apathy of their social surroundings.

In each case the pattern of change resembles the pattern of discussion. The results are important to repeat: Those who talk with compatible persons remain most firm in their prior convictions; those who cannot recall any discussion of politics in their groups are unstable generally, often receding into nonvoting or neutrality; and those in contact with opposition preferences show it by their heavy rate of defection to that opposition. The general result is that the chances of changing to a new preference are a function of participation in political discussions with those holding that preference (and the chances of *no* really firm or stable preference are greatest among those not discussing politics). This is an elementary effect from which many larger campaign phenomena will be seen to follow.

Primary Groups

Let us move from face-to-face discussion by individual voters up one step in social organization to the primary groups of family, friends, and co-workers. As already indicated, most political discussion is carried on along lines set by existing groups and long-standing relationships. Whether the individual discusses politics with those of the same or different preferences depends on the distribution of preferences among his intimate social associates. (Hence, in turn, the discussion among all members of these small groups has consequences for the end distribution of votes in the group as a whole. For our respondents are not the only ones being influenced; they in turn influence the others with whom they are in close contact.)

It is not surprising to find, then, that *changes* in vote are related to the political color of such intimate groups as the family household (Chart LVIII). While there are occasional deviations, individual members of a family adjust their views toward each others'. Results are less clear cut for friendship groups. Those who claim they "don't know" friends' votes change most. But those with compatible friends change the least, as usual (Chart LIX). And, finally, the same is true in the case of co-workers (as their votes were reported by employed voters). Again any heterogeneity of preferences in these work groups, whether it is co-workers of opposing views or simply the absence of *any* positive political support from compatible co-workers, is associated with voting changes among the respondents (Chart LX).

While there are some variations in these charts, the total weight

CHART LVIII

VOTING CHANGE DEPENDS UPON THE DISTRIBUTION
OF FAMILY PREFERENCES

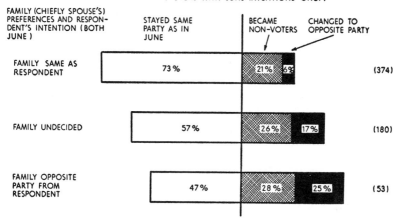

of the evidence is clear. Those with compatible associates are stable,
the others unstable. As a consequence, the already high homogeneity of small groups maintains itself and even builds up still

CHART LIX

VOTING CHANGE DEPENDS UPON THE DISTRIBUTION
OF FRIENDS' PREFERENCES*

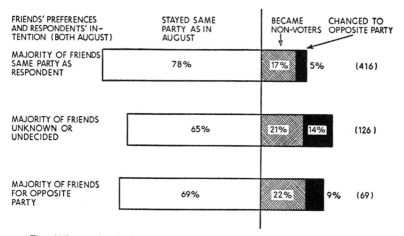

*The middle group is probably (1) unstable for other reasons, e.g., low interest, and (2) actually ex-
posed to fairly heterogeneous associates.

further. We know from the preceding chapter that little of this effective discussion is real "debate" or "argument." Instead, many of these people might be said to be learning from each other; still others are probably taking over the judgments of respected intimates as better informed than their own; still others are no doubt stimulating one another toward freshly emergent viewpoints; certainly many are calling each other's attention to common interests;

CHART LX

VOTING CHANGE DEPENDS UPON THE DISTRIBUTION
OF CO-WORKERS' PREFERENCES

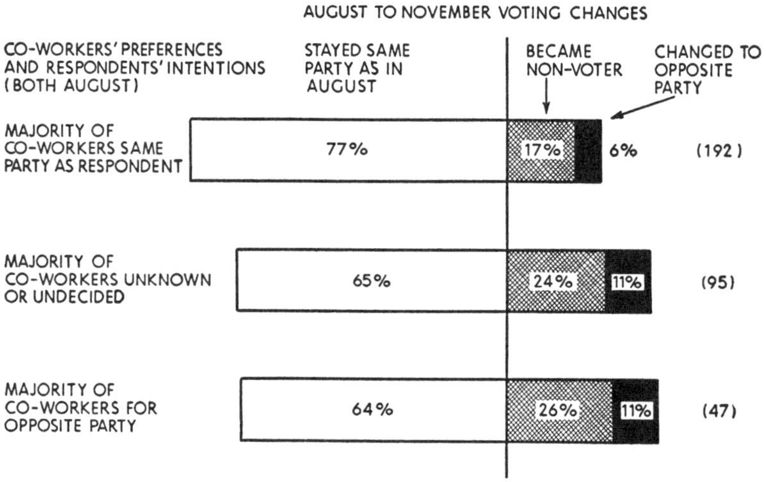

AUGUST TO NOVEMBER VOTING CHANGES

and in total all are adjusting small discords of a temporary sort in otherwise compatible and enduring relationships.

Whatever the psychological mechanisms, the social and political consequence is much the same: the development of homogeneous political preferences within small groups and along lines of close social ties connecting them. During a campaign political preferences are "contagious" over the range of personal contacts.

Social Strata

The further consequences of political discussion and of the attendant increase in political homogeneity of small groups depend upon the ways that discussants and primary groups are connected in the larger community. For a small-group circle is seldom a closed circle, and friends are responsive to other friends in chains running through thousands of people. But not without end; limits must be reached. All the analysis that has gone before makes us believe there are "discontinuities" in the patterns of close social contacts in Elmira, and therefore discontinuites are to be expected in the way that votes change in different parts of the community. In other words, there is not just "one" community of continuously connected groups and therefore of uniform political discussion in Elmira but a number of only partly integrated subcommunities. Patterns of social discussion, therefore typical voting changes in a campaign, may be more or less continuous within but are *dis*continuous between different segments of the community (e.g., between the "old stock" and "new stock" religio-ethnic groups).[1] Thus different consequences follow for individuals holding the same political preferences in different social locations in the community.

For example, what is it like to be one of the few Republicans in the Catholic ethnic groups of Elmira? Until recent years it has meant voting against the traditions of one's parents, holding preferences different from the majority of the people with whom one went to parochial school, expressing views contrary to those of the people with whom one currently maintains contacts through common church or nationality-group activities, and evaluating political matters contrary to the judgment of trusted intimates with whom one is continuously in contact. For a given individual, of course, none of these may be the case; but for one hundred such Catholic Republicans in Elmira, the *chances* of social support and reinforcing

1. The tendency for discussion to go on *within* rather than across social strata is again demonstrated in the following comparison of the respondents' vote with the vote of people with whom they are in contact in social aggregates:

	PERCENTAGE REPUBLICAN (TWO-PARTY) AMONG:			
	Protestants		Catholics	
	Nonunion White Collar	Union Labor	Nonunion White Collar	Union Labor
Respondents themselves (October)	94	60	50	25
Recent discussants reported by them (October)	87	59	64	27
All friends they reported (August)	86	64	56	39
Total no. of cases	(125–398)	(107–316)	(44–132)	(55–161)

The voting distribution among respondents is similar in each social category to that of the discussants and friends of these respondents, i.e., they are friends for each other.

discussion in compatible primary groups, down through the years, would be low. The stability of such Catholic Republican votes, then, should be correspondingly low.

For example, during the midsummer convention period when Elmirans began to discuss politics again, Catholic Republicans (temporarily swollen in number) proved less firm in their convictions (Chart LXI). More of them defected to the opposition, in

CHART LXI

THE PREVAILING VOTE IN A SOCIAL STRATUM IS STABLE; THE
MINORITY OR DEVIANT VOTE, UNSTABLE: RELIGION*

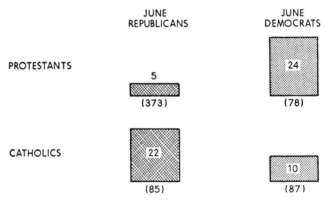

PERCENTAGE (TWO-PARTY) OF DEFECTORS TO
OPPOSITE PARTY IN AUGUST, AMONG:

	JUNE REPUBLICANS	JUNE DEMOCRATS
PROTESTANTS	5 (373)	24 (78)
CATHOLICS	22 (85)	10 (87)

*For simplicity we omit the neutral cases. If included, they only strengthen the argument, since they decide disproportionately for the "prevailing" or "proper" vote in the group.

little more than a month's time, than within the traditional Democratic majority. We will see later that the campaign intensified this tendency for the minority to take on the preferences of the majority.

Read either from left to right or from top to bottom, this chart provides valuable information. Among Catholics, defection is more frequent if the respondent was originally Republican; among Protestants, defection is greater if he was a Democrat. It is the political *minority* in each religious stratum that has the more unstable vote intention. Comparison of Democrats and Republicans yields essentially the same results. Because Catholics are more "natural" Democrats, it is the Protestant Democrats who show the greater defection; among the Republicans it is the Catholics who are unstable. Along the diagonal of normal correlation (Protestant-Republican and Catholic-Democratic) the vote is stable. But the *off-diagonal*, deviant votes are unstable. Generalized, the rule is: The "proper" vote intention for a given stratum is more stable.

This applies to union-labor and nonunion white-collar workers, where the Democratic vote is more proper for labor and the Republican vote for the white-collar group. Again the "proper" vote has fewer defectors and is more stable (Chart LXII). (An apparent

CHART LXII

THE PREVAILING VOTE IN A SOCIAL STRATUM IS STABLE; THE
MINORITY OR DEVIANT VOTE, UNSTABLE: OCCUPATION

PERCENTAGE (TWO-PARTY) OF DEFECTORS TO
OPPOSITE PARTY IN AUGUST, AMONG:

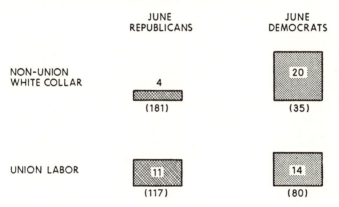

	JUNE REPUBLICANS	JUNE DEMOCRATS
NON-UNION WHITE COLLAR	4 (181)	20 (35)
UNION LABOR	11 (117)	14 (80)

exception merely confirms the rule: At this point in the campaign, June to August, both parties were equally unstable among union-labor members of Elmira. But it was hard to say at that time what was the "prevailing" preference in the union shops of Elmira; traditionally Democratic labor showed a temporary *Republican* majority! With no clear minority or majority, both sides were equally unstable. Later we shall see the old majority become dominant.)

With respect to the more clear-out instances, previous studies have found this result for a variety of strata. In *The People's Choice* an index of political predisposition (IPP) was formed to combine all such findings. One can take all the strata in which, let us say, Democratic vote intention is the prevailing one (e.g., Catholic, labor, urban, etc.). An individual can then be scored according to the number of social strata to which he belongs in which a Democratic vote intention is "proper." In this way, an index (IPP) score can be developed that ranks people according to how strongly their demographic location predisposes them to receive social influences or otherwise be inclined to vote for one or the other of the major parties. At the start, then, the higher the IPP score, the stronger the vote intention for one party. And thereafter, stability of vote for that given party is greater the higher the demographic predisposition in its favor.

The stability of a preference, then, varies with the chances of social support for it. And the chances of social support for given political choices, in turn, vary with the distribution of such preferences in the particular segment of the community. Within a given group, then, the political majority holds the informal social pressures to *stay* a majority.

Naturally, "interests" and questions of political alternatives and many other factors are involved in these figures. Yet out of the ebb and flow of various forces can be abstracted a constant element—the chronic instability of preferences among people whose social location gives them smaller chances of compatible political support and discussion. This can produce an important consequence.

Paradoxical as it may seem, the minority preference in a given group is influenced to stay a minority partly because it *is* a minority. The circumstances that produce an unequal distribution of political preferences within a group also produce an unintended means of maintaining the inequality—namely, unequal chances for social support of unpopular versus popular views in the group.

In fact, in many instances exchanges of preferences seem to follow a rough rule of near-proportionality to the existing (and past) distribution of social influences in groups and subcommunities. This can be shown statistically to have "conservative" consequences. One-sided distributions of social attitudes can develop *sui generis* powers of maintaining themselves over and beyond any good "reason" for that persistence arising external to the group.[2]

2. An example illustrates the arithmetic of this result. Take a group of 100 people with 80 holding a preference and 20 not holding it. Suppose the subsequent rates of change were exactly proportionate to the chances of each type

With no external disturbance, exchanges of preferences can easily fall into this stability-maintaining type. Our results document a process whose consequences can be aggregate persistence (despite individual turnover) of *one-sided* distributions of social attitudes, prejudices, tastes, and habits. It is a process that can lead to individual changes that, in the aggregate, do not modify group distributions. The latter must come from *external* influences. "Social politics" is, in pure or undisturbed form, conservative politics.

Overlapping Strata and the Total Community

Finally, can we extend this analysis—that went from simple personal discussion to small groups and then to larger strata of the community—to the total community?[3] In many respects, a community of

---

being matched in social discussion with a randomly chosen friend holding the opposite view. Then the majority would lose at only one-fourth the rate of the minority, say, 10 per cent versus 40 per cent defection from each. This would seem discouraging to individual proponents of the unpopular view and satisfying to the stable popular majority, but, in fact, each would have exchanged the same *number* (i.e., 8 adherents) with the other. Thus they would remain the *same* in size.

3. Cyclical swings of the total community that look like a departure from 50-50 [⌐ _ _ _ _] 50 may actually consist of an approach among opposition groups toward 50-50—toward greater heterogeneity [_ _ _ ⌐ _ _ _ _] 50 within opposition groups.

Such a cyclical swing often implies a loss of consensus and a heightening of discord among groups in the political minority. Not only is this true for broad social categories (e.g., when a Republican swing splits away deviants from formerly Democratic groups such as the Catholics and union labor) but it can also be shown to increase the amount of deviation in intimate social groups, like Democratic family or friendship groups in an extreme situation like the Republican peak in June, 1948. (November data are shown for contrast.)

THOSE WHO REPORTED:	PERCENTAGE OF RESPONDENTS VOTING "OPPOSITE" GROUPS IN QUESTION	
	Republican Peak (June)	Partial Democratic Readjustment (November)
Republican families.....................	8 (297)	12 (241)
Democratic families.....................	24 (106)	20 (81)
Republican friends......................	14 (384)	16 (324)
Democratic friends......................	35 (147)	25 (110)

One result of a cyclical swing, in an electorate composed of social groups in a state of more or less counterbalanced polarization, is that the swing sets up the

the size of Elmira is not so meaningful a unit for the analysis of voting changes as the individual, the primary group, or social strata, since it is a combination of them.

We shall not extend this analysis to the voting changes of the community as a whole. But let us see how the community is bound together in one respect. This requires that we consider change and instability among those people who provide a linkage between otherwise divergent political and social parts of Elmira—joint members of politically opposed but socially overlapping strata. For example, take the occupational and ethnic combinations of white-collar Catholics and union-labor Protestants.

As we have seen, family and friendship formation and social discussion generally take place among people who are *alike* socially in the politically relevant respects (e.g., class and religion). But not always. When memberships in two strata overlap, small-group formations and social discussion spread among people alike in some respects but not in other important ways. Therefore, when a campaign starts, associates may find themselves on opposite sides politically. Even after the group adjustments of many years, such members of overlapping strata in Elmira still had some contact with

---

very conditions that can lead to its correction. For if the swing has not gone so far as completely to break up the norms of the opposition social groups, they have a rather considerable potential to control their deviants (who chiefly made up the swing) and attract them back again. This was in fact the case in 1948. Those who, during the Republican swing from 1944 to June, 1948, had changed parties in such a way as to come into disharmony with primary groups or traditions of larger strata tended to change back again disproportionately:

JUNE POSITION (OF RESPONDENTS WHO HAD CHANGED BE- TWEEN ELECTIONS)	PERCENTAGE NOVEMBER VOTE			
	Voted Same as June Inten- tion	Failed To Vote	Voted Opposite June Inten- tion	TOTALS
Harmony with family...................	69	2	29	100 (45)
Disharmony...........................	38	8	54	100 (13)
Harmony with friends.................	76	8	16	100 (49)
Disharmony (respondent, June; friends, August).............................	32	5	63	100 (19)
Harmony with religion................	70	7	23	100 (53)
Disharmony...........................	47	8	45	100 (47)
Harmony with occupation.............	63	8	29	100 (48)
Disharmony...........................	52	9	39	100 (54)

political opposites, more so than their fellows in homogeneous surroundings (see Chart LXIII).

CHART LXIII

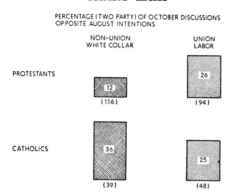

PERCENTAGE (TWO PARTY) OF OCTOBER DISCUSSIONS OPPOSITE AUGUST INTENTIONS

As a consequence, members of social strata with opposed prevailing vote are unstable in their vote intention. This can be clearly seen in Chart LXIV (which partly extends what was said in connection with Chart LXI and partly gives this new result). In the upper-right-hand corner and in the lower-left-hand corner there are examples of how a strong political predisposition, indexed here by religion and occupation, makes for great stability of the "proper" vote.

The height of each bar indicates instability, since it represents the proportion who change their vote intention to the opposite party. Line by line, one can compare the rate of defection for June Democrats and June Republicans in various demographic strata. But our interest here is focused on the two groups in the center, in which an index of political predisposition on the two strata would be near zero (because the pressure coming from the religious affiliation cancels, so to speak, that coming from the occupational). In the right-center sector and the left-center sector the proportion of defectors reveals significant instability for *both* parties (with religion the stronger determinant of change than class, incidentally).

Whatever the members of overlapping but politically incompatible strata do, they are potentially on the unpopular side in *some* social category. By no means would all or most voters who are members of such cross-pressured social combinations realize that they were in this "predicament." But in a probabilistic sense, with respect to the chances of being influenced by others, all of them are in a vulnerable position in some social stratum of the community to which they belong, with respect to their political preferences.

CHART LXIV

CROSS-PRESSURED VOTERS MORE NEARLY APPROACH
EQUAL RATES OF EXCHANGE

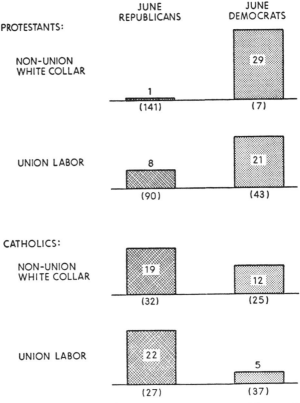

PERCENTAGE (TWO-PARTY) OF DEFECTORS TO
OPPOSITE PARTY IN AUGUST, AMONG:

This ambivalent situation becomes even more evident when we consider the "time of decision" of such people as an index of stability (early decision) or instability (later change). Cross-pressured voters continue to change until later in the campaign (Chart LXV). Incidentally, these data bear directly on the earlier point that it is molecular social interaction more than, say, distant group interests or symbolic identification that most affects the stability or instability of group voting distributions. For nominal conflicts between social categories like religion and class are associated less with delay than primary-group discords, and the more so the more intimate the discordant groups involved.

In one sense, the "cross-pressured" people are simply members of separate social groups within which preference distributions are

CHART LXV

CROSS-PRESSURED VOTERS MAKE LATER DECISIONS, AND
THE MORE SO THE MORE INTIMATE THE CONFLICTS

PERCENTAGE OF VOTERS WHO MADE LATE DECISIONS (FINAL VOTE NOT
DECIDED UNTIL OCTOBER INTERVIEW OR LATER)

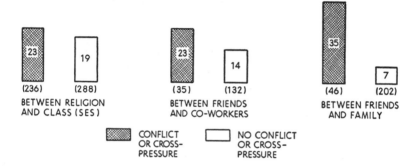

more nearly equal. Hence, their chances of receiving social support for either preference are more nearly equal. No doubt this is the way they themselves feel their position.

Yet, viewing them from the point of view of the total community, they are *in between* the great voting blocs. They make up the social bridges between otherwise distinct and separated political subcommunities. Yet actually, such people, by being subject to the influence upon social minorities of *different* majorities, have more "freedom of choice" as to which group they will side with. They have no more freedom of choice on paper, so to speak, but their social location gives them more in practice. But this freedom—which helps give the community a certain flexibility of political change—is purchased only at the price of high turnover or individual instability. Towns like Elmira are *not* one community but many divergent ones, and

those who are in the position of bridging almost unbridgeable sociological gaps are inevitably ambivalent and politically unstable.

II. VOTING CHANGES BY TIME UNITS

The first half of this chapter has considered increasingly large
social units, from two-person discussions to small groups to networks of them running into large social blocs of the community.

In this section we shall examine how the changes we found are
modified when we follow people over larger time units than just
the month or two elapsing between interviews made in the political campaign. Our main analytical device will again be the "de-
fector" rates—change to the opposition. We shall start with the
largest time unit, political change beween generations, and then
work through interelection changes and finally to intracampaign
changes themselves.

Time will play a twofold role in the following discussion. On the
one hand, it brings about changes in the life-cycle of our respondents. They grow up, they marry, they leave the parental home, they
go through a sequence of occupational and other social experiences.
The longer a time span we consider, the more elements must we
take into account in the interpretation of our findings. We shall
turn first to the life-cycle or generational aspect. Yet time also plays
a quite different role, connected not with the people themselves but
to the tides of political activities as they impinge upon all people, in
whatever stage they are, owing to the workings of the political
system. To this we will turn later in this chapter.[4]

Generational Turnover

The relatively high stability of group voting patterns over generations (i.e., the aggregate similarity in the distribution of parental
votes to the distribution of offspring's votes in the same social strata)
is only in part accounted for by the perpetuation of *identical* votes
from parent to child. Granting the importance of such "hereditary

4. A third aspect of time can be considered—what might be called the "historical aspect." A man in a given phase of his cycle and in a given moment of
the institutional political cycle might still behave differently in 1948 compared
to 1928, because the general historical context is different now or was different
when the man was a youngster. The social psychologist, the political scientist,
and the historian, respectively, stress each of these three aspects of the time factor.

voting," nevertheless there is some turnover between parents' and children's votes. Such turnover would substantially reduce the original voting cleavages along social lines if the changes were *random or equal* for all preferences in a group. The Catholic-Protestant

CHART LXVI

DEFECTION FROM THE MINORITY POSITION CONTINUES OVER A GENER-
ATION: CATHOLIC REPUBLICAN AND PROTESTANT DEMO-
CRATIC TRADITIONS ARE UNSTABLE

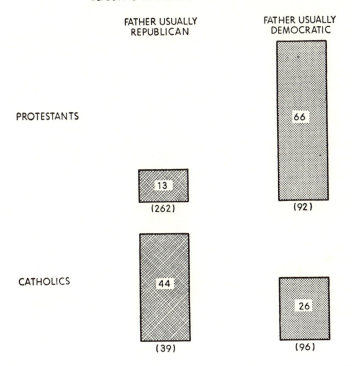

PERCENTAGE (TWO-PARTY) OF RESPONDENTS
DEFECTING TO PARTY OPPOSITE PARENTS

cleavage of the 1920's and before, for example, would have been reduced much more quickly than it has been.

But what happens in point of fact is that unequal rates of change, between popular versus unpopular preferences in the group, occur between generations (Chart LXVI). For example, consider the change of votes between parents and children among Catholics. Catholics with Republican fathers more often had become Democrats in November, 1948, despite the Republican atmosphere of the larger community; and fewer of the Democratic majority of parents had "lost" their children to the Republicans. (When parents' politics were indeterminate, the children went Democratic two to one in this Catholic subcommunity.) Within the Protestant group the figures are reversed, and here the minority preference (Democratic) fares even more poorly. Many of the children of Democratic Protestants had gone over to the Republicans by 1948, but only a few of the Protestants with Republican fathers had made the reverse change. (And, again, when parents' politics were indeterminate, children were Republican two to one in the Protestant subcommunity.)[5]

Thus the general rule in twenty-five-year exchanges between generations is much the same as that for the one-month changes we examined earlier: the smaller the number of people in the group holding the preference initially and thus the smaller their chances of social support within the group, the greater their subsequent change to the opposition.

But by no means need this eliminate the unpopular preference entirely. Equilibrium points are reached such that the greater *rate* of loss from the minority equals in *amount* the numbers needed to replace small rates of erosion from the majority, pending an outside influence (e.g., wars, depressions). Lack of support and instability for the unpopular view is a self-maintaining rather than a self-eliminating phenomenon under most conditions.

What would happen if the processes we have outlined went on undisturbed for long periods of time? Imagine a continual turnover

---

5. The turnover of parents and children by occupations reveals the same patterns underneath the secular trends. Here are the full data:

FATHER	UNION LABOR				NONUNION WHITE COLLAR			
	Percentage Respondents			Total No. of Cases	Percentage Respondents			Total No. of Cases
	Rep.	Nei-ther	Dem.		Rep.	Nei-ther	Dem.	
Republican......	43*	30	27†	102	81*	15	4†	144
Neither.........	25	35	40	80	50	32	20	56
Democrat.......	22†	34	44*	109	41†	24	35*	80

* Same party as father.
† Opposite party from father.

of preferences, with the political majority exchanging with the political minority inside a group by the differential rates needed to maintain that majority. Then a curious result would be the outcome. The initial distribution bequeathed to children of the group by their parents would survive, but only as a statistical equilibrium. The individual political loyalty of each child to each parent would

CHART LXVII

Votes Are Compatible with Present Rather than Past Families

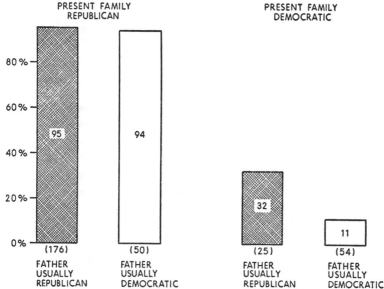

PERCENTAGE REPUBLICAN OF TWO-PARTY VOTE

PRESENT FAMILY REPUBLICAN

PRESENT FAMILY DEMOCRATIC

80%
60%
40%
20%
0%

95
(176)
FATHER USUALLY REPUBLICAN

94
(50)
FATHER USUALLY DEMOCRATIC

32
(25)
FATHER USUALLY REPUBLICAN

11
(54)
FATHER USUALLY DEMOCRATIC

be sacrificed to *contemporary* influence. This is illustrated by what happens when marriage in these groups matches people of different parental traditions. Voting is adjusted in the contemporary group at the expense of parents (Chart LXVII).[6]

How does it come about that we find considerable constancy of

6. Note the effect in Chart LXVII analogous to our "breakage" discussion in chap. 6. Comparing the two center bar graphs, in which parental-family and present-family preferences are opposed and must be adjusted, the Republican side fares better in the Republican community. While 32 per cent of those with Republican fathers hold out against Democratic spouses, only 6 per cent (100–94) of those with Democratic fathers hold out against Republican spouses. Context shows its effect, again, where there is discord and need for adjustment.

vote between parents and children when, at the same time, there is a slow deterioration of personal and direct parental influence on politics in the course of the life-cycle of the new generation? The answer is that religious and socioeconomic status (SES) groups remain more or less constant from one generation to the next, and

CHART LXVIII

WITHIN HOMOGENEOUS SOCIAL STRATA, PARENTAL TRADITIONS ARE
SHARED COLLECTIVELY RATHER THAN INDIVIDUALLY

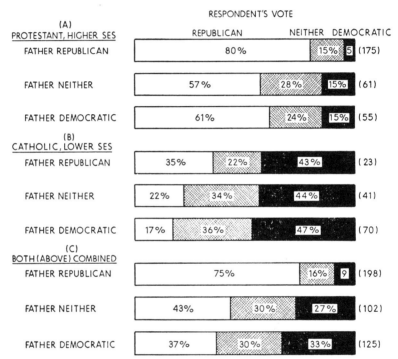

equilibrium states within them link the vote of the two generations for the whole community, even if there is no exact parent-child association *within* any specific social stratum.

If parental traditions were gone (by, say, age thirty-five), and the children were entirely influencing each other, still *chance* alone would, at a given time, find the majority in the same preference position as their fathers. Since the one-sided starting distribution in the group would have strong self-maintaining properties, the children might be "disloyal" individually, but they would never entirely escape the parental heritage collectively. For example, the relationship between child and parent within homogeneous groups (high SES Protestants and low SES Catholics) is *not* very high (Chart LXVIII). Among the lower SES Catholics, for example, the relationship between individual father's and individual child's vote nearly disappears. There is a *common* group distribution *regardless* of individual and parental starting points. Among high SES Protestants, the same is found with only the exception that Republican parental traditions have survived in the Republican community somewhat better than average.

In part (*C*) of Chart LXVIII the data from parts (*A*) and (*B*) are combined. This is done merely to show that, as one takes more heterogeneous groupings and eventually the community, there is a quite marked correlation of parents' and children's votes more because they share the same social locations than because, through life, the father has "determined" the child's vote.

Thus, while there are exceptions, the tendency is for people's votes in time to become independent of parent's preferences in the *individual* case but to remain closely proportionate to the aggregate parents' preferences *as a social group*. After the parent's starting point, the distribution of the offspring's preferences tends to parallel the distribution of influences to which they are exposed. But since these "influences" are each other's preferences, the distribution of them more or less parallels the parental traditions of years and years before! A political tradition is a class and religious (i.e., a social) heritage as well as a purely family inheritance.

It would be foolhardy to push further, with only these simple assumptions and memory-distorted data, into the complex realm of "survivals" of group voting traditions in American politics. But at the least the question is raised: What is transmitted between generations—chiefly identical preferences from father to son that never wear off or chiefly the start of a collective tradition that the offspring enforce on each other in an equilibrium-like process of exchanging preferences? Not only do preferences, prejudices, and habits probably change back and forth between generations more than one might expect, but the question of persistences and survivals probably turns in many cases less on the identity of individual opinions from one time to the next than on the sluggishness of change in *collective* distributions of preferences (i.e., "traditions") in social groups.

Interelection Turnover

Shifts in voting between generations, then, are dependent upon and consequences of social location, social support, and social control. Let us examine the same process over the shorter time span

CHART LXIX

GROUP MEMBERS UNAWARE OF THEIR SOCIOPOLITICAL
SURROUNDINGS ARE MOST UNSTABLE

PERCENTAGE REPUBLICAN OF TWO-PARTY VOTE

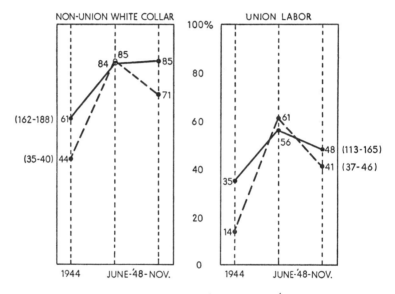

————TWO-PARTY VOTERS WHO KNOW (SOME) FRIENDS' POLITICS (AUGUST)
— — TWO-PARTY VOTERS WHO DO NOT KNOW (ANY) FRIENDS' POLITICS

between elections (e.g., between 1944 and June, 1948). A special example highlights this condition, and it is worth digressing briefly to examine the analogy between it and later conclusions.

If political discussion is central to voting changes, then the situation should be different for people who do *not* discuss politics much at all and almost never between elections. For example, about one-fifth of our sample did not know the politics of any of their three closest friends in August. Such people have so little political content in their normal social interaction that what little they do learn about politics is largely independent of their social surroundings most of the time. Therefore they are more likely than their fellows to be "blown about" by the political winds of the times, in a way especially independent of their social surroundings. And this was the case for people in both occupational groups who were not discussing politics enough by August to know their friends' preferences. In the fluctuations of vote between the 1944 and 1948 elections, they fluctuated most of all (Chart LXIX). They moved with the "trend of the times" the most; they were more Democratic in the Democratic election of 1944, more Republican at the Republican peak of June, 1948, and more Democratic again on election day. Those least bound politically into social groups most followed the secular trend regardless of group affiliation.

While it is true that there are many other elements not equal here, notably the interest and partisanship that go with knowing friends' politics, this is exactly the point: people who practically never discuss politics with one another do not maintain those qualities (like interest) which lead to stability of the preferences that characterize the social surroundings and group interests. Interestingly, those with politically colored acquaintanceships and those without them behave similarly in following the secular trend between campaigns. But when campaign discussion begins again, occupational affiliations make a difference for those who *know* their friends' politics but not for the others, who continue to follow the secular trend irrespective of groups.

Now this comparison must be an analogy to the condition in which most Americans find themselves, alternating virtually no discussion of politics *between* campaigns with considerable talk about it *during* campaigns. During the no-discussion period, then, one expects relaxation of social controls and thus of the one-sidedness of preferences within social groups.

Yet people of all kinds continue to read much the same newspapers and hear much the same radio and television comments on political news. Thus there is continued influence from outside stimuli *equal* across all groups. This leads to much the same secular trend between campaigns on the part of all types of voters, without regard to majority/minority social influences. That was the case between 1944 and June, 1948, for religious groups. The rate of defection to the opposition was about the same for a given party among both Catholics and Protestants (Chart LXX).

The picture is complicated somewhat by a between-election secular trend to the Republicans during the most difficult Truman period.

CHART LXX

DEFECTION RATIOS HAVE LESS RELATION TO GROUP DISTRIBUTIONS
BETWEEN CAMPAIGNS THAN DURING CAMPAIGNS: RELIGION

PERCENTAGE (TWO PARTY) OF DEFECTORS TO PARTY
OPPOSITE PREFERENCE AT PRIOR TIME

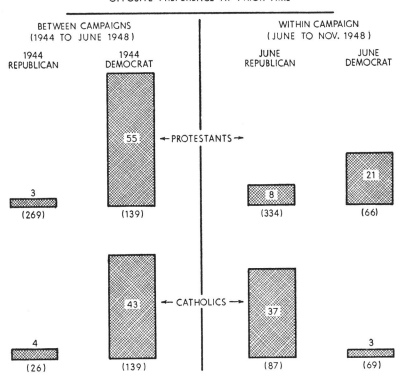

But it can be seen that the secular trend is manifested in the changes among Catholics and Protestants in a not too disproportionate way. That is, the *between*-election responses were relatively independent of the majority/minority distributions in the two groups. Our earlier rules are nearly suspended between elections.

The same general phenomenon is apparent in comparisons of

defection rates (between versus within campaigns) among union-labor families and nonunion white-collar families (Chart LXXI).

CHART LXXI

DEFECTION RATIOS HAVE LESS RELATION TO GROUP DISTRIBUTIONS
BETWEEN CAMPAIGNS THAN DURING CAMPAIGNS: CLASS

PERCENTAGE (TWO-PARTY) OF DEFECTORS TO PARTY
OPPOSITE PREFERENCE AT PRIOR TIME

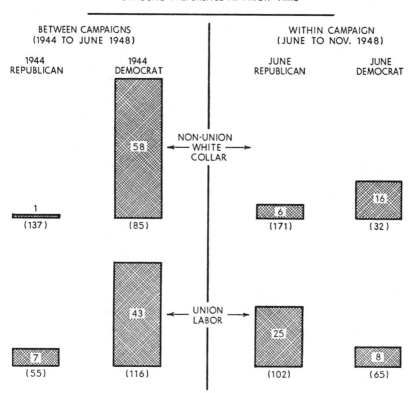

Again we see the tendency for *between*-campaign exchanges to move more with the political winds of the moment (e.g., as reflected in the mass media) and less with the distribution of social forces in the social group (as they do *in* the campaign).

Because of the relaxation of social controls between campaigns, the "traffic flow" of party exchanges during that period is composed of people going *away* from the norms of their social groups more than during the campaign itself (Chart LXXII). This chart in essence reproduces the conclusions of the two previous charts in different form, to show that the between-campaign period of low discussion is the one of greater deviation away from group traditions

CHART LXXII

THE CHANGE "TRAFFIC" BETWEEN CAMPAIGNS WAS CONTRARY TO GROUP NORMS MORE THAN THE CHANGE DURING THE CAMPAIGN

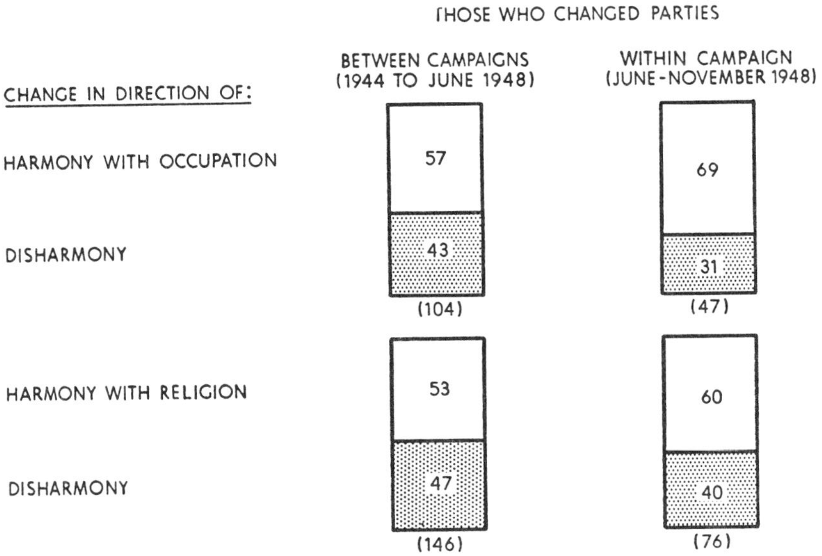

THOSE WHO CHANGED PARTIES

CHANGE IN DIRECTION OF:	BETWEEN CAMPAIGNS (1944 TO JUNE 1948)	WITHIN CAMPAIGN (JUNE - NOVEMBER 1948)
HARMONY WITH OCCUPATION	57	69
DISHARMONY	43	31
	(104)	(47)
HARMONY WITH RELIGION	53	60
DISHARMONY	47	40
	(146)	(76)

(despite statistical regression problems that complicate the result). If members of a social group do not share their preferences through discussion, the group majority can easily erode away. And if the holders of unpopular views in the group keep quiet—provided that there are external forces working for both sides—they should find their ranks mysteriously growing.

In any event, there is a clear-cut condition when social controls over political preferences are relaxed, namely, when people do not talk about them!

Intracampaign Turnover

The campaign itself, then, is a period of reassertion of social discussion and thence of influence on the deviant political minorities in social groups. The pattern of change goes from a uniform manifestation of the secular trend across all groups back to the *un-equal* majority-minority pattern that we had earlier associated with unequal distribution of social influence in such blocs. The heat of discussion brings "majority rule" with a vengeance; but how?

In Charts LXX and LXXI, for example, we have seen that from 16 to 37 per cent of the two--party vote among group minorities defected to the majority; but the defection in the reverse direction (from the group's popular to unpopular views) was only from 3 to 8 per cent.

That is, the popular viewpoint in the group fares *much better* in campaign turnover, and the traditional minority *much worse*, than would be expected if change were directly proportionate to the potential influence of sheer numbers of opposition people alone. The change in some groups is so disproportionate that there is a rapid build-up of the majority in numbers. During the campaign, then, the force of the majority seems greatly exaggerated. Actually, most of the campaign buildup of the majority is composed of previous defectors "returning home." Why is this, and what are its consequences?

No doubt the campaign provides arguments in such a way that certain influences in a given group are more effective than counter-influences. Truman certainly "strengthened the hand" of Democrats, while Dewey failed to help the Republicans in the union-labor shops of Elmira in 1948.

In addition, while the numerical size of different preferences in a group may fluctuate temporarily, there is a very strong carry-over of the effects of past influences and past habits into present discussions. Thus, half the Catholics of Elmira may have toyed with the idea of a Republican vote in June. But the undercurrents of feeling and discussion within Catholic circles must have carried a great deal of ambivalence about the Republicans as well as deeper Democratic sympathy than current intentions alone would indicate. Discussion probably intensified the ambivalence. Old loyalties, often recessive during a period of little thought on the matter, become "re-emergent" when a number of like people begin talking of the matter in like manner. The return of such people rebuilds the majority.

Finally, there must be a curious kind of "multiplicative" effect of group discussion of a subject at a *very high rate* of interaction. For example, in simple pair conversations taking place only infrequently, members of the minority have a chance to run into compatible people in proportion to their number in the group. And they can more easily forget infrequent opposing influences of low intensity. But as the campaign raises this to three-person, four-person and more discussions, in a group or in rapid succession of contacts, with rapidly cumulating impact, then the chances of the minority of finding compatible *groups*, or receiving compatible reinforcement in *successive* contacts, become less than proportionate to their numbers in the total category. There can easily be an effect, arithmetical as well as social-psychological, not unlike that when the majority "gangs up" on the minority.

As these forces combined in the Truman rally of 1948, former New Deal groups (Catholic and union labor) displayed a renewed solidarity within the traditional Democratic majority and a marked breakdown of the deviant Republican tendencies that had prevailed between elections.

At the same time there is a limit beyond which the majority simply cannot regain its deviants. When a majority already has overwhelming dominance, it becomes all the harder to persuade additional members of the minority to its position. This appears to be the case with both Protestants and white-collar people in shifts from August to election day. After all, the holdouts at that point are just that—holdouts. The system seems to reach a point of diminishing returns for the majority group; too much input is required for the increment in support.

In less one-sided communities than Elmira this diminishing-returns point would be less important. Yet even in Elmira (as in Erie County in 1940) the over-all effect was a growing divergence of the major social segments of the community—a rebuilding of homogeneity within and of polarization between social groups on political matters. Not only did union labor respond to the Democratic campaign; Truman directly appealed to them. But also the Catholic social groups of Elmira worked themselves back toward their traditional Democratic norms, with scarcely a breath of religion entering the campaign overtly (Chart LXXIII). This general social phenomenon—increasing polarization *between* dissimilar peo-

CHART LXXIII

The Campaign Increases Homogeneity within and Polarization between Occupational and Religious Groups

PERCENTAGE REPUBLICAN OF TWO-PARTY VOTE (OR INTENTION)

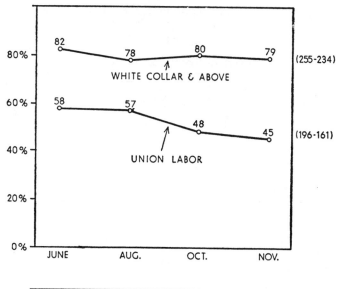

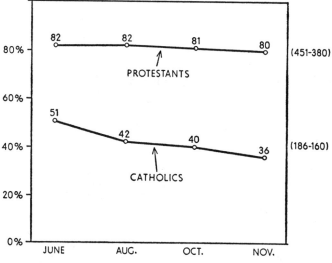

ple and increasing homogeneity *within* similar ones—may well be a typical result detectable underneath the specific content of every hard-fought, much-discussed propaganda battle.

Moreover, if a hiatus on social discussion and thus relaxation of social controls *between* such campaigns is equally typical as the campaign build-up, one might find a kind of "pulsation" of the

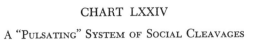

CHART LXXIV

A "Pulsating" System of Social Cleavages

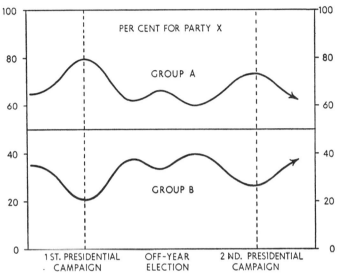

system of social cleavages in voting during a given era. Between major presidential campaigns majorities in social groups would tend to erode away; during campaigns they would tend to build up rapidly and to restore themselves (Chart LXXIV).[7]

7. One is reminded by such data of a historic puzzle in American politics, whereby the political majority nationally tends to lose ground in the less-heated, less-discussed "off-year" congressional elections. While political explanations are usually given to account for this, it would be interesting to test whether, for periods in which the political majority was compounded out of well-established and stable *social* majorities (e.g., in the 1920's and again in the late 1930's and early 1940's), this "off-year" phenomenon could not be accounted for in part by the reasoning of this chapter. That is, in stable times, social majorities in self-contained communities should recede in off-year elections—producing a net loss for the party having the most such groups on its side—and then rebuild again in heated presidential elections. A test of this will be made by one of the authors in connection with analysis of a study of the 1950 election.

The theory is, then, that unusually high rates of interaction, permitting rapid cumulation of successive influences or simultaneous multiple-person influence on an individual, rebuild majorities in social groups beyond the specific political reasons involved. Alternation of high with low rates of such influence must produce a "pulsating" system of greater and lesser social differentiation in politics, accompanying greater and lesser social discussion of politics over recurrent phases of the (in this case, four-year) cycle.[8]

The social analysis of political votes, then, arrives back at the starting point. The solid foundations of American political parties are in distinctive social groups that not only have "interests" involved but have sufficient social differentiation from other groups, sufficient continuity between generations, and sufficient closed or in-group contact in successive generations to transform these initial *political* interests into persistent and durable *social* traditions. It is the re-emergence of these traditions, as much as fresh political developments, that characterizes a modern presidential election campaign.

SUMMARY

I. Voting Changes by Social Units

69. Voting changes within the campaign are affected by the partisan character of political discussion engaged in (e.g., the more

---

8. The proviso hardly needs to be added that all this might happen if "other things are equal." However, they are seldom if ever so, and what we have here is less a description of any one four-year period than a manner of reasoning about what could be abstracted out of many of them.

The foregoing chapter presented, in necessarily compressed and simplified form, some of the elements from which a rather systematic treatment of the relations between face-to-face influences and statistical voting changes in large blocs of the population might be worked out. That is, a number of the findings and conclusions concerning *larger* blocs of the population can perhaps be shown, with the aid of simplifying assumptions, to be logically or mathematically coherent with the analogous data and reasoning about face-to-face discussions in small groups. Most of the tabulations in the chapter were in fact suggested by (in some cases more strictly deduced from) current efforts to work out such a systematic treatment of related empirical generalizations being carried on by staff members of the Bureau of Applied Social Research. The technical reader will note similar data or ideas elaborated mathematically in the papers of Nicolas Rashevsky, Theodore Anderson, and James Coleman in Paul F. Lazarsfeld (ed.), *Mathematical Thinking in the Social Sciences* (Glencoe, Ill.: Free Press, 1954).

talk with members of the opposition party, the more likely a change in vote to that party).

70. Voting change is correlated with the political preference of family members.

71. Voting change is correlated with opposite political preferences or the absence of known preferences of one's friends.

72. Voting change is correlated with opposite political preferences or the absence of known preferences of one's co-workers.

73. Within social strata with unambiguous political preferences the political majority is more stable than the political minority.

74. Changes in the vote of the total community reflect shifts in the balance of opposed groups (e.g., the collapse of preferences in some groups toward the center and their subsequent rebuilding under conditions of intensive discussion during the campaign).

75. People under cross-pressures (e.g., between class and religion) change their vote during the campaign more than people in homogeneous circumstances.

>   *and:* (a) The rates of change for cross-pressured voters are more nearly equal for members of the majority and minority parties.

76. People under cross-pressures (between class and religion, between friends and co-workers, between friends and family) come to their final vote decision later than people in homogeneous circumstances.

>   *and:* (a) The more intimate the conflict (as between family and friends), the later the decision.

II. Voting Changes by Time Units

77. Voting change between generations is affected by the political traditions of social strata: among Catholics, Republican fathers "lose" more of their children's votes to the opposition; among Protestants, Democratic fathers "lose" more (and similarly for occupational groups).

78. Votes are more alike in the present than the past family.

79. Between generations—and especially in homogeneous social strata—a group tradition in voting survives more easily than individual father-to-son identities of preference.

80. People who do not discuss politics much are relatively unstable in their voting.

    and: (*a*) People who do not discuss politics much are more likely to follow the secular trend irrespective of groups.

81. Deviation from group norms in voting (for religious and class groups) is stronger between campaigns than during campaigns.

82. Strong majorities (e.g., in Elmira, the Republicans among Protestants and white-collar occupations) reach a point of diminishing returns in regaining support from small minorities of deviants.

83. The campaign increases homogeneity within and polarization between religious groups and occupational groups.

84. Alternating periods of high versus low discussion of politics probably produce a "pulsation" in the degree of political polarization between social groups.

Part III

Political Processes

8 POLITICAL INSTITUTIONS

Parties in the Local Community[1]

Political parties were formed to implement the objectives of interest groups, and gradually they became an essential political institution. Democratic theorists assign a prime responsibility to the political party for initiatory and guidance functions in the electoral processes analyzed in this study. Accordingly, we turn to the political party first as an organization in the community and later as a subjective concept in the minds of voters.

Fortunately, we can observe the local parties from the viewpoints of both the organization and the voters. As a joint endeavor of this study and a larger study of community intergroup relations, a senior staff member lived in Elmira during and beyond the 1948 campaign period, interviewing party leaders, observing party activities, polling precinct workers, and collecting pertinent materials. At the same time data were collected from our panel sample on such matters as contact or acquaintance with party workers. These joint observations form the basis of our inquiry into the nature of contemporary party organizations and their role in the election processes of the local community.

The image of the local political party is perhaps stereotyped in some quarters as a band of enthusiastic, articulate, self-interested, powerful political activists in the community, selected by party members or winning out through factional struggles. According to the idealistic assumption, a corps of dedicated protagonists draw together to work for the party cause within the formal organization, and others support it by their own independent actions. From such

1. Most of this chapter was originally written by John P. Dean and Edward Suchman and was edited for this volume by the authors.

153

loyal partisans emerge public-spirited leaders to give guidance to the selection of party candidates, to articulate the party program, and to propound it before the people. That may be the ideal image. Actually, in a community like Elmira, what are the political parties and what do they do?

PARTY FUNDS AND LEADERSHIP

Before examining the levels of party leadership in the local community—and as background for the description of party activities—let us review the matter of party funds. Where does the money come from, and what is it used for? For money is often the most tangible sign of power.

Party Funds

First of all, the money does not mainly come from the small contributions of the ordinary membership and voting supporters of the party. It may be "their" party, but it is run on someone else's contributions—the contributions of a relatively few large donors. In all, about $11,400 was contributed to the Republican County Committee by 187 donors and about $3,000 to the Democratic Committee by 65 donors; the Republicans had three times as many contributors and over three times as much money. About half the total contributions came from only 11 per cent of the donors— those who gave over $100 each. At the other end of the scale over half of the contributors accounted for only about 15 per cent of the funds, in donations of $25 or less.

Who gives the funds? The parties are elected by dispersed citizens at large, but they are financed by concentrated centers of power with direct stakes in the election. In Elmira in 1948 the power centers lay within local business and local government (officeholders), and the Republicans had the support of both (Chart LXXV). The Democrats received only odd crumbs from these sources; their support, such as it was, came disproportionately from groups marginal to the local business and local government hierarchies and from outside the community (i.e., the state committee).

The contributions of officeholders—and even of tavern-keepers— are understandable in ordinary political terms. But what sort of

CHART LXXV

Local Power Centers Supported One Party; Marginal Groups, the Other

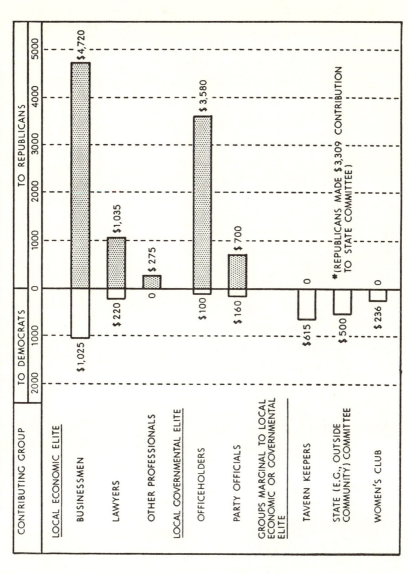

CONTRIBUTING GROUP	TO DEMOCRATS				TO REPUBLICANS				
	2000	1000	0		1000	2000	3000	4000	5000
LOCAL ECONOMIC ELITE									
BUSINESSMEN		$1,025							$4,720
LAWYERS		$220			$1,035				
OTHER PROFESSIONALS			0	$275					
LOCAL GOVERNMENTAL ELITE									
OFFICEHOLDERS			$100					$3,580	
PARTY OFFICIALS			$160	$700					
GROUPS MARGINAL TO LOCAL ECONOMIC OR GOVERNMENTAL ELITE									
TAVERN KEEPERS		$615		0					
STATE (E.G., OUTSIDE COMMUNITY) COMMITTEE		$500							
WOMEN'S CLUB		$236	0						

*(REPUBLICANS MADE $3,309 CONTRIBUTION TO STATE COMMITTEE)

return on their generous contributions do the influential business leaders expect from the party they support?

In thinking of the local level of politics, most business leaders seem to view their political contributions to the Republican party as part of the cost of doing business or as investments that indirectly or ultimately will earn a fair return, rather than as gifts that would be "paid back" in favors. And, in terms of national politics, the

TABLE 10*

MOST OF THE CASH WENT INTO THE PRECINCTS

PURPOSE OF EXPENDITURE	PERCENTAGE EXPENDITURE BY	
	Republicans	Democrats
Election districts (e.g., work on election day)	36.6	37.6
Canvass	33.1	0.0
Rent and maintenance	12.3	3.9
Advertising and printing	10.8	28.8
Telephone, telegraph, office supplies, and postage	2.0	6.1
Clerical work at headquarters	4.8	3.8
Payments to party workers for car hire and other	0.0	11.0
Dinner, band for rally, and assistance to candidate	0.0	8.6
Miscellaneous	0.4	0.2
Total expenses	100.0	100.0
Contribution to state committee	$ 3,309.00	†
Total expenditures	$10,198.23	$3,443.45

* Source: Official statements of campaign receipts, expenditures, and contributions as required by the election law of the state of New York. The Democratic figures came from a typewritten report before it was sent to Albany, and the Republican figures came from the notarized report. Period of time covered by Republican report, August 13–November 4; by Democratic report, September 24–November 20.

† Received $500 *from* state committee.

contributions imply agreement on such concepts as "less government in business," "lower taxes," and "less labor racketeering." In other words, contributions are expected to redound to the welfare of the business community by promoting what that group stands for. In this question of money, then, we find one of the ideological elements of the local party situation. Those who give money may have had more ideological conviction or stake than those who receive and spend it; and most gifts carry more ideological content than most votes.

What are the funds used for? In the case of the Republicans, most of the funds went into precinct work, canvassing, and maintenance of party headquarters; in the case of the Democrats, most of the money was spent for precinct and other party work and for publicity (Table 10).

Party Leadership among the Ins: The Republicans

This takes us into the local party structure. Let us start at the top of the local organization, with the formal political leadership of the community. And since Elmira was a "Republican town" let us start with the Republican leadership.

Given that this is the party of the business and white-collar segments of the community, we might expect that the Republican leadership would be recruited from and be representative of the leadership of the business community. We might expect that during the New Deal era Elmira's business entrepreneurs, corporation executives, bankers, professional men, and social leaders would have thrown up, from among their own ranks, a leadership for the local Republican party on a par in socioeconomic power and skill at least with the leadership provided by the same groups for corporation boards, city-club and country-club directorates, the Junior League, etc.

The core of local economic leadership rested in the hands of a few men on the boards of the leading business banks and among the directors and officers of several locally owned industries of long standing. The interlocking directorships of these concerns single out about a dozen community leaders known to be highly influential in community life and conspicuous among the members of its most exclusive elite. The dozen or so "old-guard" families have participated at one time or another in the key decisions regarding the founding and conduct of the nonsectarian hospital, the organization of the Community Chest, the activities of the Chamber of Commerce, and the affairs of the social elite.

Surrounding the old-guard group is an inner circle of forty or fifty families that are linked with the old guard and with one another in joint memberships in local business enterprise or on boards of elite social agencies. They hold memberships in the city club and country club, and their daughters are usually members of the Junior League.

Overlapping this inner circle is a third group of families headed by executives of absentee-owned industry located in Elmira. More recently arrived in town and more likely to be transferred elsewhere, such families appear less integrated into community life and less participant in decisions affecting community destiny, but nevertheless they are economically powerful.

Then, finally, there are the numerous other businessmen of the community who for the most part identify their interests with the core of leadership outlined above.

To what extent does this business and social hierarchy of the community overlap with the political hierarchy of the Republican party? Elmira's Republican mayor was president of a leading dry-goods concern; one Republican councilman was a local business executive; the Republican corporation counsel was a member of a leading law firm; and a few other minor part-time Republican offices were staffed by businessmen. But with these few exceptions (almost none of which involved really powerful members of the old guard or inner circle) the business hierarchy did not provide active leadership for the political party of their choice. Business was "above" such things.

When the economic leaders made themselves felt politically, it was not so much by active participation as by financial support and various kinds of influence behind the scenes. Few influential business leaders take part in the activities of local government, preferring either by conscious delegation or by default to leave these matters "to the politicians."

Especially was default of leadership noticeable among executives of the absentee-owned corporations. Ten of the twenty Elmira businesses employing more than a hundred people were absentee-owned. The executives of locally owned businesses contributed heavily to the Republican treasury, but *not one* of the executives of the absentee-owned firms contributed to the local Republican party. Two gave something to the Democrats, and the other executives abstained entirely, solemn testimony perhaps to the indifference or studied avoidance by such corporations of alliances in the local political community.

Hence business support for the Republican party came from the wings rather than the center of the stage. Out of this situation, what leadership emerged to guide the day-to-day activities of the GOP?

One of the leaders to whom the reins of the local party were turned over, the county chairman, was a former druggist, apparently nominated to the post of county clerk as a reward for his party efforts. Like him, the vice-chairman (a woman) held a political job, that of city clerk. Also of modest background, she seemed to enjoy the status that accompanied party leadership on the local level. Together, these two leaders handled the patronage of the local Republican party, the paid-for party work, and the hundred and one other day-to-day duties essential during the campaign.

How did these probably competent but certainly not representative leaders emerge to make decisions in behalf of, for example, eight members of the old guard who gave $1,775 to the Republicans locally in 1948, twenty-nine members of the inner circle who gave $1,920, and sixty-three other local business owners or executives who gave $2,620? What common ground could these patronage holders have—as "leaders" supposedly have with the led—with, for example, one long-time heavy contributor who was a member of a wealthy family, corporation lawyer, honorary board chairman of a major corporation, president of two Elmira corporations, and director of six other firms?

The answer to the puzzle of the nonrepresentative leadership of business in politics seems to lie in a kind of *intermediary* leadership —a delegation of power from the financially contributing elite to a politically active mediary who, after building the current party organization himself, in turn delegated active, day-to-day leadership to the above lieutenants who have the time and the patronage incentive to carry on. This intermediary, a successful insurance man now among the influential business leaders of the town, had apparently come from a reasonably modest background. Perhaps at first less of a business leader delegated to go "down" into the political arena, he was instead probably helped by politics to go "up" into the economic hierarchy. His firm now carries a substantial portion of the insurance placed by local government units. Good politics and good business contributed to each other.

Thus we find a curious kind of political leadership for the dominant business and white-collar community of Elmira. There can be no question where much of the social and economic power behind the Elmira Republican party resides. But this power is defaulted by some and delegated by others through a system of intermediary leadership to routine "political" job-holders who, despite their competence at specialized duties such as patronage and canvassing, do not provide the segments of the community that support them with decision-making, policy-formulating "leadership" in either the ideological or the material spheres. To this extent, the local Republican community was deprived, as the great debate neared and discussion began, of direct and visible leadership of a representative kind on the local scene.

Party Leadership among the Outs: The Democrats

But perhaps the crucial matter in a democracy is the kind of local leadership the *opposition* has. When a party is in power in the community, as the Republicans have been in Elmira since 1936, its potential leadership for election activities is not really tested. It can win without them. But if the political system of the community is to resist oligarchical tendencies, to be adaptable and flexible under changing conditions, and to provide for full discussion and debate, then presumably fresh and energetic leadership must emerge from the opposition.

But where, for a party out of political power in the community for a dozen years and representing minorities, workers, and marginal groups always out of power in the community socially and economically—where can Elmira's Democratic leadership come from? The "outs" have almost no leverage with the local business leadership as far as favors go, either direct or indirect, and therefore they have little pulling power with the energetic young businessmen they need to help run the party.

The most capable young men interested in Democratic politics in Elmira were among the least active. Several young lawyers participated from time to time, an executive in a local department store took an occasional hand as master of ceremonies for Democratic dinners, the president of a local milk company held the post of party treasurer. These men could have given leadership to the ailing Democratic party in Elmira, but the thanklessness of party work, the pressure of other duties, the "unpopularity" of the minority party, and the small likelihood of concrete rewards for party activity left them somewhat lackadaisical and peripheral to the party. In short, business—either young or old—was not a fruitful source of Democratic leadership.

Another main source of leadership that the Republicans tapped was also closed, by and large, to the Democrats—the patronage job-holders. In November, 1948, the Republicans enjoyed a wide lead in the patronage competition. They controlled the city government, the county government, the majority of the towns, and the state; their Democratic rivals controlled only the distant federal government. None of the local Democratic party officials in 1948 held public office (as contrasted with all four of the leading Republican party officials). Except for some of the lesser committeemen and inspectors, the Democratic party in 1948 had its base almost entirely outside the local government structure. Patronage, the very base on which Democratic city machines are built, was shut off to a party also denied the support of the main business community.

The Democrats did have one strong base of support, not available to the Republicans, from which some of its leadership could have been recruited—the "underdog" groups in the community, for example, minorities and workers. As we shall see, a good many of its precinct workers did come from such sources, particularly from the Irish Catholics and from the union-labor shops in town. But the more visible these groups are as underdogs in the larger community, the less likely they are to emerge as "front" leaders. If underprivileged strata (and other marginal groups such as the tavern-keepers who supported the Democrats) are truly underdogs, as they are in Elmira, it is difficult for them to provide effective community-wide leadership.

Who, then, could the Democrats fall back on for leadership? They had only (1) those who would work as a labor of love or (2) some old-timers still around from the days when being a Democrat paid off. In most cases, the two motives were synonymous, and, added together, they produced an "old faithful" type of leadership. The man who headed the Democratic party, sometimes called the Democratic "boss," was a politician by descent; an uncle of his was a former mayor. A number of veterans from the political wars of earlier days were still around. Two tavern-keepers and the bartender at the Elks Club were still active in their respective wards, even though one of them was in his seventies. An old party war horse who was secretary of the Democratic County Committee, 1920–29, and chairman, 1929–42, was one of the best-informed men in Chemung County on political matters. The old-timer still most active in party work was chairman of the Democratic county organization at this time—seventy-seven years old, for forty years a loyal Democratic worker in his ward and district. The fact is that the Democrats had to fall back for leadership on six men in their seventies, and on one of them to fill the local party's highest office.

Here, then, is "old-time" political leadership with a vengeance. But not old-time organization politics to go with it; for it was all these tired, old political veterans could do to keep the rusty parts of their Democratic "machine" from falling apart. In more than a decade out of power, and to some extent in a generation of changing conditions since the "good old days," no one had felt it worth while to grasp control of a defeated minority party from these tiring hands. Thus in 1948 the Democrats of Elmira had, not the vigorous spokesmen of a self-renewing opposition, but a leadership surviving from the defeats of the past—a leadership of nostalgia (as Samuel Lubell termed it in *The Future of American Politics*).

It comes to this. The Democrats without new leadership and the Republicans without representative leadership—each party was led, in a sense, by intermediaries. Its leaders merely connected it with the real centers of power behind each party. The Republican organization was built in the 1930's on a foundation of business support, and today its leader is an intermediary between the business leadership and the party workers. The Democratic organization —what survives of it—was built on past political spoils in the wards and precincts of the old days. Its leaders can be thought of as "intermediaries" too, ghostly representatives of the Democrats' old centers of power in the city halls, ward headquarters, saloons, and street corners of the first quarter of the century. In each case, it might be said, the leaders were links between the party and the centers of power at the time its organization was built.

The leaders in both parties were capable and devoted workers trained by years of practical experience in party politics. But however capable they were in providing leadership for the day-to-day activities of the local parties, they did not provide firsthand policy-making or direct responsibility for articulate debate on the political issues that most deeply concerned the principal interests in the community, nor did they see such tasks as their affair. Measured against such criteria for adequate leadership, the Elmira parties fail to provide the community with the kind of local guidance that might be expected in a decision process that brought nearly three-quarters of its citizens to the polls.

PARTY WORKERS—PROFESSIONAL AND AMATEUR

A good deal of the parties' funds are expended through the party workers, and a good deal of the parties' activities are carried on through them. Who were they? What did they do? What was their impact on the citizenry at large?

Who They Are

Both parties acquire their workers by rather haphazard procedures. If a vacancy for committeeman occurs, the party leaders cast about among the other party workers in a district for an appropriate person. If one is found that seems to fit the bill, his name will appear on the primary ballot. Often it turns out to be a relative or close friend of one of the other workers who has helped the party before. After all, the extra dollars that come in for party work represent a real bonus to persons of modest income, and the word gets around.

Over against the pressure of party workers to corral the party jobs for friends or relatives is the party leaders' attempt to get only hard workers for party posts. The result is a potpourri of many different types of people, and few generalizations can be made about them. The Republicans, because of their system of a committee-man and a committeewoman for each election district, were more evenly divided as to sex than the Democratic workers, who were nearly four-fifths men. And, for the most part, the Democratic workers were younger than the Republican workers.

Judging from names (Kelly, O'Leary, O'Brien, Kerny, Costello, Holleran), nearly two-fifths of the Democratic workers were of

Irish extraction; among the Republicans, the Irish numbered only one out of every nine or ten. Each party had eight or nine from the Italian, Ukrainian, and Polish groups, and each had one Jewish committeeman. Both parties drew over a tenth of their workers from among the retired or widowed, a tendency especially noticeable among the women workers. Republican committeemen were drawn more from the white-collar classes, with only about one-quarter from the factory or other blue-collar groups. The Democrats drew half their party workers from this latter source: fourteen worked at "the Rand," eleven were "with the Lackawanna" (Delaware, Lackawanna and Western Railroad), and the others were scattered among the other "shops" in the city.

It was not possible in this study to make a systematic typology of party workers. But it may be worth giving a rough, impressionistic classification of the workers according to the major interests that appeared to the field staff to explain their presence in party work. Among the range and variety of persons drawn into political work, a discerning observer might see the following types:

The officeholders.—Among the Republicans only, a third of the male committeemen (or their wives) held local governmental posts, and many of the others had patronage incentives of one kind or another.

The old party war horses.—Both parties could count among both their men and their women workers some old-timers who had been around since the days of torchlight parades. Some of the women had first become active in the suffragette movement and had been interested and active in politics ever since.

The odd-dollar workers.—The $35.00–$70.00 received by Republican committeemen, the $10.00 or so received by the Democrats, and the $60.00 that both Democratic and Republican election inspectors took in represented welcome extra income during inflationary times. The eagerness with which some of the workers clung to their committee posts long after they had ceased to be active or energetic workers for the party was a source of distress to the leadership of both parties.

Relatives of party leaders.—If one's spouse or near-relative is active and busy in politics at certain times of the year, one is himself more likely to become interested and active. And there is a better chance that his name will come to the attention of the leaders when they are casting about for someone to fill a committee vacancy.

The ethnic aides.—Each party tried to be careful to have a few workers from the various ethnic groups, like the Polish, the Italian, the Ukrainian, the Jewish, and the Negro. The more self-contained, culturally isolated, or localized the groups, the more important it was to have party workers among them to help get out the vote.

The professional neighborers.—Women who have lived for years in one neighborhood, kept track of the comings and goings of the residents, and made scores of acquaintances who impart the latest gossip seem to make good party workers. For them, making the canvass is a social event that renews these contacts and fills in the gaps in their store of local news.

The status aspirants.—Both parties, but especially the Democrats, appeared to number among their young workers a few "eager beavers" of modest background who thrived on the prestige they received from a party post, the chance to call local party leaders by their first names, and the opportunity to shake the hand of an occasional congressman or senator. They were usually interested in what the party might be able to do for them.

The coasters.—Each party also had an undistinguished group of party workers whose enthusiasm for party work had dwindled but who managed to keep their names on the list and to receive their payments for party "work."

The fill-ins.—Both parties had occasional difficulty in finding an interested person to fill a vacancy. To have a full complement of workers, and in hope of getting new persons interested, people were occasionally taken on "for the time being." The Democrats never were able to fill some of their committeeman posts in 1948, a symptom of their diminished leverage in politics.

The young actives.—In both parties there are a few persons (e.g., wives of professional or businessmen) who appear to be active out of a sense of civic duty and a desire to be a responsible citizen.

Of all these types, perhaps only the last is in politics because of a genuine interest in the ideological position, platform, candidates, or campaign issues of the party they worked for. The workers' stand on political issues appeared to be more the product than the cause of their affiliation.

The professional party workers were hardly a political elite, active in the business of policy-making and power allocation. Nor were large numbers of them representative citizen-members either; certainly they were not chosen by their friends and neighbors to look after local affairs of their parties. At worst, some were merely hangers-on, picking up crumbs, or gregarious busybodies being exploited for political ends not their own. At best, and more fairly, most were the usual collection of cheerful part-time workers that any organization picks up, for love or for money, to perform the thankless tasks for which its leaders have little time, its members little interest, and its treasury little money. Not outstanding leaders or even representative voters in many cases—and in many respects playing roles marginal to both leaders and voters—nevertheless they were the people who made up the visible, tangible political parties of the community.

What They Do

On the Republican side the party workers carried on a quite accurate canvass of the vote, ward by ward. Despite the fact that the canvass provided partly a form of payment for party workers who simply turned in old or borrowed records, it played at least a potentially positive role in the election. Intended as a guide to party efforts (e.g., to locate the voters who needed help to get to the polls), it served also as a form of party intelligence. The Republicans knew from their party canvass records, for example, that as usual they had more than 60 per cent of the vote in the area, that their local candidates and local patronage were not endangered, that as usual certain wards were more of a problem than others, etc. And, despite the delinquencies of party workers and often incomplete, outdated records that served for current information, the Republican canvass was highly accurate (Table 11). The Republicans did not sense the Democratic revival of the closing days of the campaign, but, after all, that did not amount to enough to disturb the local balance of power.

Despite the fact that the Republicans took no large-scale action on the basis of these routine records in 1948, in potential they had a practical, many-purpose intelligence operation under way, and *from* the voters to the leaders. It would have warned the latter in advance of any serious complaints, local uprisings, or radical shifts of voting sentiment. Thus the local party organizations served the

TABLE 11

THE REPUBLICAN CANVASS PROVIDED
ACCURATE INTELLIGENCE

City Ward or Township	Election Results Per Cent for Truman	Republican Canvass Books Per Cent for Truman	Per Cent Canvass Books over or under Election Results
1	24.1	21.8	−2.3
2	52.9	55.8	+2.9
3	35.6	35.8	+0.2
4	53.5	47.7	−5.8
5	51.8	54.9	+3.1
6	63.8	65.5	+1.7
7	53.0	47.4	−5.6
8	49.7	48.3	−1.4
9	35.7	30.4	−5.3
10	34.8	33.2	−1.6
11	37.8	39.7	+1.9
12	38.3	35.2	−3.1
City total	43.9	42.7	−1.2
Horseheads Village	19.5	20.0	+0.5
Elmira Heights	32.6	27.2	−5.4
West Elmira	17.0	15.3	−1.7
Southport	30.8	21.6	−9.2
Townships total	21.5	25.9	−4.4
City and township totals	38.4	35.9	−2.5

important secondary function of information-gathering, keeping the candidates and leaders in touch with the people who intended to vote for them.

Another activity of the party workers was to insure a fair election. In New York State the election inspectors are appointed by the county board of elections from lists of qualified party members submitted by the political parties. In addition, the election commissioners (who supervise registration and certification of election results) are appointed on the recommendation of the major parties. Thus the two major parties effectively control election machinery through their power to nominate the personnel who operate the machinery. And, in fact, appointment to the board of elections is used as a device to reward party workers. In effect, the personnel conducting the elections have a dual responsibility. Selected by their parties, they are responsible both to them and to the local governments that pay their salaries as public employees. But their prime function is to watch each other as representatives of the major parties. Not impartiality but balanced partiality is the safeguard.

PARTY CONTACT WITH THE CITIZENRY

One of the tasks of the party workers is to maintain contact between the party and the people. Another is to affect the outcome of the election by maximizing the vote cast for the party. Let us now look at their performance from the other side—from the citizen's experiences in 1948 as reported in our survey. How effective were the parties in reaching and influencing the citizenry?

By late October about 8 per cent of the respondents reported contact by party workers, in person or by phone, and 19 per cent remembered receiving party literature. With duplication eliminated, about one-quarter of the sample had some contact with one or the other of the parties *up to* the final two weeks or ten days of the campaign.

Not many more voters were acquainted with party workers, whether or not they were contacted in this campaign: slightly less than 40 per cent of the respondents knew a Republican or a Democratic worker.[2] Of them, 17 per cent knew only Republican workers, 7 per cent knew only Democratic workers, and 15 per cent knew both—another indication of what it means to live in a "Republican town." (Only 1 per cent knew someone working for the Wallace third party—or would admit it.) And knowing a party worker did not improve one's chances of being contacted (8 per cent were contacted of those who knew one or more workers personally, and 6 per cent of those who did not).

2. When panel members were asked whom they would go to if they "had some question in connection with the presidential campaign and wanted to discuss it with someone," only 15 per cent of those mentioning someone named a party leader or party committeeman. And when they were asked which of their identifications were important to them, only 18 per cent of all respondents named a political party (as against 65 per cent for a religious group, 45 per cent for a work group or profession, or 42 per cent for a nationality).

Who knows party workers? In the first place, of course, those interested in politics are more likely to be acquainted with party workers, for the obvious reasons (see Chart LXXVI). What may not be so obvious, however, is the significance of this fact for the party system. What it provides is a channel for potential *articulation* be-

CHART LXXVI

PERCENTAGE KNOWING PARTY WORKER

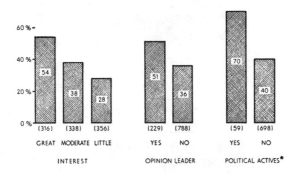

* Actives are the 6 per cent who in June were "doing anything to help your party win. . . ." About one-fourth of the actives did canvassing or committee work for their party.

Political actives are not more likely than the inactive to know only Republican or only Democratic party workers, but they are much more likely to know *both*. Perhaps being politically active brings one in contact with party workers; perhaps knowing party workers stimulates interest and activity. In either case the relationship is clear, and it is perhaps a mark of the two-party system in a town like Elmira where, after all, politics is not deep-cutting. In a community with more basic ideological differences expressed in political affiliation—the multiparty European community or even a large American city where political affairs are more highly organized—political activity would probably correlate with knowing one's own party workers and *not* knowing the opposition. In Elmira there is more of a "unified" aspect to political activities. The data:

Acquaintanceship with Party Workers	Per Cent among Political Actives	Per Cent among Non-actives
Both Republican and Democratic...............	47	13
Only Republican...............................	17	19
Only Democratic..............................	5	8
Neither Republican nor Democratic.............	31	60
Total no. of cases.........................	59	698

tween the leaders and the led—between the professionals and the amateurs. In more detail the internal relationship of a well-ordered political system in a town like Elmira would look like this:

Top party leaders ⇌ Party workers ⇌ Lay enthusiasts ⇌ Grass roots

A break in communication at any one point means a break in the total system. In this instance, at least, the critical point between the professionals and amateurs seemed to be reasonably intact. The

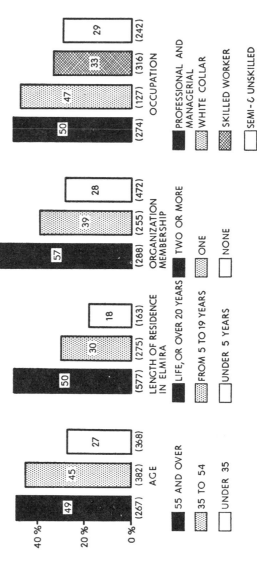

CHART LXXVII

THE MORE INTEGRATED INTO THE COMMUNITY, THE MORE LIKELY ONE IS TO KNOW PARTY WORKERS

PERCENTAGE KNOWING PARTY WORKERS*

AGE
- 55 AND OVER — 49 (267)
- 35 TO 54 — 45 (382)
- UNDER 35 — 27 (368)

LENGTH OF RESIDENCE IN ELMIRA
- LIFE, OR OVER 20 YEARS — 50 (577)
- FROM 5 TO 19 YEARS — 30 (275)
- UNDER 5 YEARS — 18 (163)

ORGANIZATION MEMBERSHIP
- TWO OR MORE — 57 (288)
- ONE — 39 (255)
- NONE — 28 (472)

OCCUPATION
- PROFESSIONAL AND MANAGERIAL — 50 (274)
- WHITE COLLAR — 47 (127)
- SKILLED WORKER — 33 (316)
- SEMI-& UNSKILLED — 29 (242)

40 % 20 % 0 %

* All these differences hold with an interest control. In fact, most of them are stronger than interest.

connection is not 100 per cent, and its effectiveness is unknown (e.g., whether the professional and amateur actives actually respect one another and communicate in both directions). Yet it does seem that the party organizations of Elmira, as innocuous and unrepresentative as they are, are potentially able to bridge the gap between a dozen or two leaders and several thousand party enthusiasts.

Moreover, knowing party workers is a function of a complex of factors that might be termed "community integration" (e.g., acquaintance where it counts). The longer the citizen is around (age and duration of residence in Elmira), the more he circulates in the community (organization membership), the closer he is to the dominant political powers (occupation), and the more likely he is to know party workers (Chart LXXVII). The relationship of these characteristics to political acquaintanceship is marked.

Parties Contact Their Own

Finally, these social ties between party and community are not randomly dispersed; they "make sense" politically. If a citizen knows party workers (especially those who know workers from only one of the parties), the odds are that he will know the "right" ones for his stratum of the population. Wealthy people know Republican workers, lower-income people know more Democrats, etc. (Chart LXXVIII). The parties are "rooted" best within those strata which they most represent politically.

In addition, the parties tend to contact voters predisposed toward their own position (Chart LXXIX). Republicans go after the better-off, the Protestants, the conservatives—indeed, the Republicans themselves. While Democratic contacts necessarily reached many Republican types in this Republican community, they too gave disproportionate attention to their own kind of voters. The pattern is such as to reinforce and activate the (potentially) faithful rather than to convert the opposition or the indifferent.

Parties Mobilize the Vote

This is further demonstrated by the emphasis of party workers themselves upon mobilization rather than conversion as their function. The major types of "problem voters" mentioned as productive targets by experienced district committeemen of both parties were these:

The voters who have to be called for—the aged or feeble or sick and others who would not get to the polls without some special effort on the committeemen's part.

The people who should be reminded—those likely to forget or ignore their opportunity unless the committeeman reminds them once or twice and checks up on them.

CHART LXXVIII

Voters Know More Party Workers on Their Own Side
(Only Those Who Know Workers)

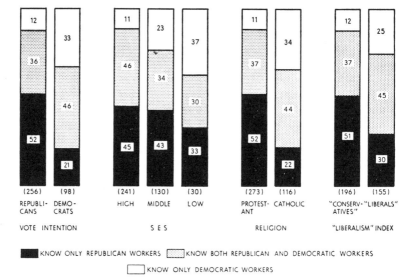

The wives, who must be brought to the polls by husbands who take the family responsibility in such things.

The absentee voters (in Elmira, mainly railroad men), who have to be contacted to make sure they have made proper absentee-ballot arrangements.

The new voters, who have to give evidence of literacy and perhaps be transported to take the literacy test.

The "vote-if-induced" people, who in some districts have come to expect a little extra compensation (in the way of a few dollars or a drink) to exercise their franchise.

Even a cursory inspection of this crude pigeonholing of problem or target voters reveals the basic perspective of the committeeman when he looks at the voter: How shall he classify the voters as to what he has to do with them to mobilize his own strength, not what

CHART LXXIX

THE PARTIES MAINLY CONTACT PEOPLE OF THEIR OWN
POLITICAL PERSUASION

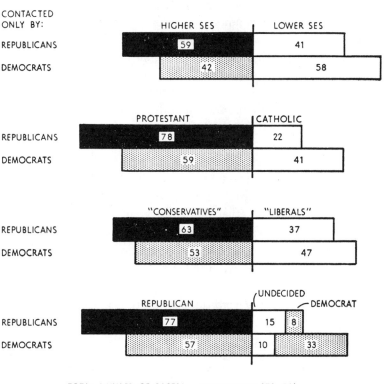

TOTAL NUMBER OF CASES: REPUBLICANS (72–79)
DEMOCRATS (73–76)

he should do to make new converts. His is an administrative rather than a persuasive task.

Reports of the Elmira sample members who were personally contacted confirm this picture. Of sixty-three panel members contacted by the parties who gave information on the purpose of the call, thirty-seven mentioned registration; nineteen listed other miscellaneous purposes, such as routine canvassing; and only seven reported that the party representative tried to convince them how to vote.

Nor, finally, was there much tendency to mix the canvassing work of the official parties with the private and more zealous persuasive efforts that ordinary friends use on each other. Of sixty-three respondents who said that they knew a Republican party worker among their acquaintances but who personally intended in June to vote Democratic, *none* reported receiving any phone calls or visits from this or any other Republican party worker, and only three recalled literature sent them by mail. The same is true for those ninety-nine individuals who knew Democratic party workers among their acquaintances but intended to vote Republican. Of them, *none* was contacted by telephone call or visit; only eleven received mail. Even here, under friendly circumstances where personal contacts would be most likely to be influential, the local political parties did not make the effort of winning over known members of the opposition.

In summary, party contact was selectively directed not toward the joining of political issues in discussion or debate on the level of the individual voter.[3] Rather it was directed toward the agreeable (noncontroversial) exploitation of existing strength. At least in a community like Elmira, the party organization was not effective as a persuasive agent, nor did it function particularly to maximize political discussion and debate within the community.

As for mobilizing the vote directly, party contact *is* effective in

---

3. Acquaintance with party workers relates to political discussion especially when the acquaintances are members of the minority party. On each level of interest, people who know a Democratic worker are more likely to talk politics than those who know only Republicans or neither. Here the context of the larger community again shows through: knowing Republican workers in a town as strongly Republican as Elmira is more of a social fact than a political one. On the other hand, knowing a Democratic worker is reflected in a greater degree of participation in political discussion. The data:

PARTY WORKERS KNOWN	PERCENTAGE WHO TALKED POLITICS RECENTLY (JUNE)	
	Great Interest	Less Interest
Both Republican and Democratic..........	68 (78)	30 (77)
Only Democratic.......................	64 (25)	33 (45)
Only Republican.......................	46 (68)	22 (104)
Neither Republican nor Democratic........	41 (143)	17 (464)

stimulating turnout. But it is less so among the general run of in-terested voters than among the *marginal* voters, as an auxiliary stimulus to those who would not otherwise have been likely to vote (Chart LXXX). It is the group *least* likely to vote that *most* seems to benefit from party contact.[4]

While they thus have some effect, it cannot be said that the local parties "mobilized" the bulk of the vote in Elmira. The citizens, stirred by the national party campaigns and not by the local cam-paigns, mobilized themselves. Among those who intended to vote in August before the party contact, 89 per cent of those subsequent-ly contacted did so, but 81 per cent of those *not* contacted did so also. And among those who in August did not intend to vote, only 33 per cent of the contactees and 25 per cent of the noncontactees actually did turn up at the polls. Party contact makes a difference, but the controlling variable was whether or not—far in advance of that party contact—the person himself wants to vote. The party organization only supplements the efforts of voters themselves, and especially where supplements are needed.

Finally, what about the effect of party contact or acquaintance-ship upon the vote itself? Formal contact, which, as we have seen, is seldom devoted to conversion, has little effect at all of a persuasive nature.

Voters contacted by the party *opposite* to their August vote inten-tion, those contacted by the *same* party they intended to vote for in August, and those contacted by *neither* party all voted equally strongly for their August candidate. Among each group the same proportion (9 per cent) switched to the opposite party in November. *Formal* party contact makes for little change.

4. One exception is the relationship between party contact and length of resi-dence in the town. Those who have lived in Elmira longest (also a category most likely to vote) show the greatest presumed effects of party contact. The data:

By Length of Residence in Elmira	Percentage Not Voting	
	Contacted	Not Contacted
20 years to life..................	12 (113)	23 (327)
5–19 years.....................	23 (52)	34 (164)
Under 5 years.................	32 (35)	35 (83)

One explanation is that party contact has a strong cumulative effect; those on the party lists in well-canvassed districts for long periods of time succumb to the pressures (of their party-worker neighbors) to vote.

CHART LXXX

Party Contact Is Most Effective in Cutting Down the Nonvoters among Those Least Likely To Vote

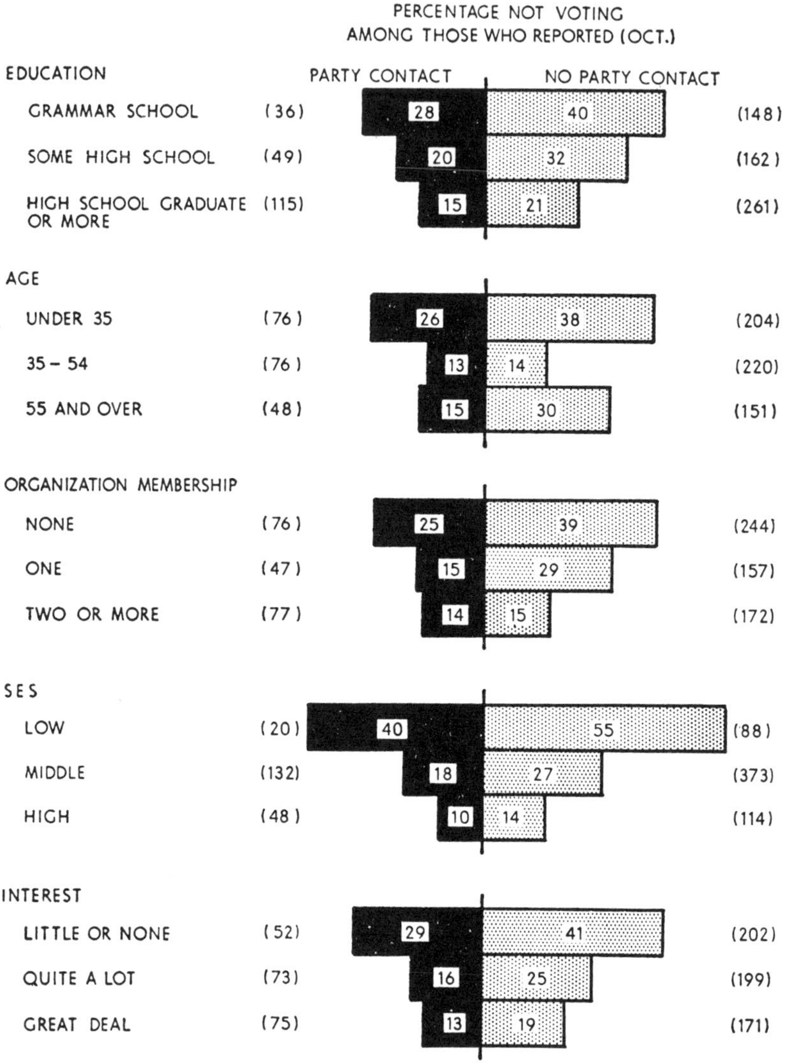

PERCENTAGE NOT VOTING
AMONG THOSE WHO REPORTED (OCT.)

		PARTY CONTACT	NO PARTY CONTACT	
EDUCATION				
GRAMMAR SCHOOL	(36)	28	40	(148)
SOME HIGH SCHOOL	(49)	20	32	(162)
HIGH SCHOOL GRADUATE OR MORE	(115)	15	21	(261)
AGE				
UNDER 35	(76)	26	38	(204)
35 – 54	(76)	13	14	(220)
55 AND OVER	(48)	15	30	(151)
ORGANIZATION MEMBERSHIP				
NONE	(76)	25	39	(244)
ONE	(47)	15	29	(157)
TWO OR MORE	(77)	14	15	(172)
SES				
LOW	(20)	40	55	(88)
MIDDLE	(132)	18	27	(373)
HIGH	(48)	10	14	(114)
INTEREST				
LITTLE OR NONE	(52)	29	41	(202)
QUITE A LOT	(73)	16	25	(199)
GREAT DEAL	(75)	13	19	(171)

But acquaintanceship is something else again. Unlike party contact, *knowing* party workers is a matter that follows social lines within friendly strata where group support for votes can be mustered, and it has persuasive consequences. Not that many people change their vote "because" they knew a party worker. But the Elmira voting changes in 1948 do show an association between

CHART LXXXI

PERCENTAGE OF TWO-PARTY
VOTE OPPOSITE AUGUST INTENTION

| (115) | (123) | (28) |
| FROM BOTH PARTIES | FROM OWN PARTY ONLY | FROM OPPOSITE PARTY ONLY |

└──ACQUAINTED WITH PARTY WORKERS──┘

conversions and knowing party workers of the opposite party (see Chart LXXXI). The patterns of acquaintanceship tie the political organizations into whatever forces (e.g., small groups) are actually converting or maintaining votes. It is less propaganda than informal access.

THE ROLE OF THE PARTY

What function is a local political organization supposed to perform in a national election? Presumably it is supposed to interpret the national party line within the community; to influence people to vote the right way, by reinforcing the faithful, converting the opposition, and activating the indifferent; and to mobilize the vote on election day.

In the ordinary community of Elmira—not unlike towns where millions of "typical" Americans live and vote—the party is not particularly successful at any one of these. The local party leadership operates at an indirect and unrepresentative remove from the voters. The "chosen leadership" is neither chosen by nor does it lead for the bulk of the citizenry; the ward and precinct organizations are not really made up of neighborhood political enthusiasts; and the money to support the party does not come from the rank and file.

The local party may be an organization *for* the voters, but it is not *of* or *by* them.

Of coures it is true that the party organizations provide a means of linkage between political leaders and laymen. Strong social ties exist that potentially subject the parties to appropriate social control. But such close collaboration was in 1948 Elmira more in potential reserve than in day-to-day operation. Compared to other parts of the political system and to the voters themselves, the local party is not particularly effective in influencing or mobilizing the electorate. In Elmira, at least, the parties did not use their roots in the community to provide effective contact between the voters and the distant leaders and ideas they were voting for. Instead, the parties in 1948 Elmira performed auxiliary administrative tasks. The local organizations seemed to function chiefly as small bureaucracies on the edge of the great debate, performing numerous small tasks that make an election possible. What the local parties did *not* do was to guide the political hands of the community—theoretically its central task.

Old-timers in Elmira claim that things used to be different—that the local parties wielded a major political influence around the turn of the century, in the days of torchlight parades, clambakes, picnics, free liquor, and vote-buying. In 1948 there were no political parades or street-corner meetings or sound trucks in Elmira; there were only three public occasions for political persuasion—an outing, a presentation, and a labor rally—and these were perfunctory and less than enthusiastic. Why the shift in the past half-century?

One answer seems to be that social and political developments have taken away from the local party many of its former functions and thus have transformed its character. The job of informing and persuading the voters has been taken over by the mass media, particularly radio and now television. The base of support provided by aiding underprivileged groups (e.g., immigrants or unemployed)— the party's welfare function—has been lost as foreign-extraction groups have been assimilated and as welfare services have been taken over by social and political institutions. The base of local economic support has been weakened by the need of business interests to turn their attention and influence to the national government, where the big decisions affecting them are now made. The tightening of election laws and practices has removed opportunities for corruption and the support based on it. The base of patronage has been cut by the growth of civil service, by the emergence of big government at the federal and the state levels, and by the attractions of full private employment.

Such changes on the American scene in the past half-century have tended in a town like Elmira to move the functions of the local parties toward routine administrative jobs and, probably, toward an atrophy of spirit. At any rate, the 1948 debate bypassed the local political parties. They were not the main participants but the subsidiary entourages in such recent electoral struggles—not the potent powers behind the votes, as they perhaps once were, but only appendages to those powers.

As the American party system matures, there is less need for cajoling or herding voters into the party. And, as party points of view become ingrained in whole strata of the population, partisans can effectively teach them to each other—and to their children—without as much help as before. And, finally, the mass media of communication permit the heads of the parties at the state and national levels efficiently to supply millions of the faithful with the constantly adjusting party point of view without the intervening organization.

What does "party" mean? Probably three things: (1) the national party leadership; (2) the local organization; and (3) the symbol in the minds of men. In recent decades, with the growth of big government, the first has become even more prominent and powerful. In an age of mass education and mass communication, the third maintains and increases in importance. But in the small community like Elmira, though not necessarily in the large city, the local organization loses strength.

The party thus has evolved, as have some of our Western religions, on the one hand, into a central institutional leadership and, on the other hand, into essentially a psychological and social phenomenon whose enormous power is chiefly carried in the minds of its members as they respond to distant symbols. An old religious spiritual says, "The big wheel is run by faith, and the little wheel by the grace of God." In contemporary local communities, the big wheel is run by faith, and the little wheel by "the organization."

SUMMARY

Party Funds and Leadership

85. Party funds come primarily from the larger contributions of relatively few donors.

86. Financial support for the Republicans came primarily from the local business and governmental elite; for the Democrats, marginal or outside groups contributed disproportionately.

87. Party funds are spent primarily for precinct work, maintenance of headquarters, and publicity.

88. The business hierarchy in Elmira did not provide direct leadership for the local Republican party.

89. The leadership of the Democratic party was made up of old party stalwarts.

Party Workers—Professional and Amateur

90. Workers for the two parties differed somewhat in personal characteristics; the Democratic party had more younger men, more members of ethnic groups, and more manual workers.

91. Only a minority of party workers seemed motivated by ideological concerns or civic duty.

92. Republican party workers conducted a reliable canvass of the vote, and both parties safeguarded the accuracy of the ballot.

Contact with the Citizenry

93. About one-fourth of the people were contacted by one or the other party by the close of the campaign (more by mail than in person), and less than four in ten knew a party worker personally.

94. Those interested in politics are more likely to know party workers.

95. Those better integrated into the community are more likely to know party workers.

96. Voters are more likely to know workers from their own party.

97. Party workers are more likely to contact people favoring their own side, in attitude or in predisposition.

98. Party contact increases turnout most among the types of people least likely to vote.

but: (*a*) Party contact increases turnout most among people
of long residence in the community.

99. Formal contact is not particularly effective in converting
voters from one party to the other.

but: (*a*) Acquaintance with party workers is correlated with
change in voting.

9 POLITICAL DIFFERENTIATION
Issues in the Campaign

In Elmira, then, "the parties" have their main impact in the attitudes and the perceptions held by the voters. Political ideas associated with the parties are more important locally than the formal organizations themselves. Accordingly, the next step is to review what Republicans and Democrats think about politics—the "pictures in their heads." We start with the issues of the campaign.

The content of political debate is supplied by the issues—statements that allege differences between the contending parties or candidates with reference to such matters as domestic and international policy, the nature of a party's support, or the capabilities of the nominees. In a campaign the issues are articulated by party leaders, and they are the "stuff" in terms of which a democratic political campaign is rationalized, in both senses.

What do we mean by "the role of issues" in an election campaign, and how should one analyze it? At the one extreme there are those who maintain that issues play no real part in a campaign. According to this view, issues are only a window-dressing for the play of self-interest or of blind party loyalty or of indifference. An opposite view holds that issues play the *key* role in the campaign. In this view issues do affect voters in one or another way; they are essential to provide the rationale for the vote; the campaign is based upon them; and it makes all the difference, both in tactical and in historical terms, which issues come to the fore and provide the basis for decision by the electorate.

Views of such generality are both right and wrong. These are too one-dimensional and oversimplified to represent accurately the complexity of the actual situation. Something of each view is ob-

182

viously correct; in such a complicated and diversified matter, how could there not be people who fit almost any description?

But what actually does take place? Over the years the parties and the partisans articulate for the electorate a large number of "issues" of varying content, varying generality, and varying appeal: something for everyone. At the start of any political campaign the individual voter agrees with some issues, disagrees with some, and is indifferent to some. As a result there are potential or actual conflicts over issues within individuals, within social groups and strata, and within parties. Then the campaign goes on, and somehow the combination of internal predispositions and external influences, brought to bear on the content of the campaign (the issues), leads to a decision on election day that one or the other party shall control the presidency for the following four years.

Thus, what starts as a relatively unstructured mass of diverse opinions with countless cleavages within the electorate is finally transformed into, or at least represented by, a single basic cleavage between the two sets of partisans. Out of many small disagreements emerges one big disagreement, and that is "settled" by the election. This process enables the system to work by getting a decision; it reduces the numerous component decisions (or lack of them) to a single one; it settles the election; and it partially disposes of, without necessarily deciding, many of the issues. In this view the political process which finds its climax in the campaign is a system by which disagreements are reduced, simplified, and generalized into one big residual difference of opinion. It is a system for *organizing* disagreements.[1]

To evaluate a political system, then, it is essential to examine the forms of agreement and disagreement—the pattern of consensus and cleavage—in the system at a given time. What is the quantitative balance between the two? For too much of either agreement or disagreement could equally destroy the system of discussion. What is the content of the disagreement? For cleavage over some questions

1. A strikingly similar formulation was used in a different field by Herbert A. Simon, "Birth of an Organization: The Economic Cooperation Administration," *Public Administration Review*, XIII (autumn, 1953), 227–36. "In its formative stages the organization consisted largely of a series of pictures in the minds of different people. These several pictures were far from congruent with each other, and the process of organizing consisted in considerable measure in arriving at a single picture that was held more or less in common" (*ibid.*, p. 227).

would have greater danger than others for the survival of the system itself or greater relevance for the future history of the nation. And what are the sources of cleavage or consensus? For the system can mediate strains and stresses generated by the larger society or merely provide a forum for debating superficial arguments generated within the political system itself.

Position and Style Issues

For a framework within which to discuss this matter, let us distinguish two general sets of political issues: Position issues and Style issues (or "material" and "ideal" issues). The distinction can be characterized thus:

	Position Issues	*Style Issues*
EXAMPLES:	Taxation, labor-management, tariffs, farm prices, freight rates, monopoly, price control, etc.	Prohibition, religious education, civil liberties, UNESCO, immigration, intergroup relations, blue laws, candidates' personalities, governmental corruption, etc.
PRESUMED MOTIVATIONAL APPEAL:	Self-interest of a relatively direct kind	Self-expression of a rather indirect, projective kind
TYPICAL CONTENT:	Matters of money and material power (i.e., economic interests)	Matters of style, taste, way of life (i.e., cultural and personal interests)
TYPICALLY OPPOSED GROUPS:	Classes, geographical sections, industries, and similar economic organizations	Religious and ethnic groups, cities versus country, and similar cultural groups, as well as opposing personality types
TIME DURATION:	Long-range, reference to past; historical	Short-range, reference to present; topical
CONSEQUENCES:	Direct, objective, tangible gains for successful group	Indirect, subjective, symbolic gratifications for successful group

In general, one type of issue refers to the question, "In whose *style* should the government be run?" whereas the other type refers to the question, "In whose *interest* should the government be run?" Position issues cannot as well be "created" by "propaganda" as can Style issues; they are more likely to arise out of socioeconomic conditions. And political parties can only take a stand with reference to them, whereas they can more often "invent" the issues that are associated with Style. Historically, Position issues seem to have such strength because economic conditions call them forth with such cogency (e.g., free western land, silver, the New Deal). Indeed, it may be that Style issues gain the center of the stage only when Position issues are not particularly important, as, for example, with the prohibition issue, which was so much more important in 1928 than in 1932, when there were "more real" issues at stake. But in the broad sweep of political history the Big Issues are those which combine Position and Style aspects, as, for example, slavery in this country or the French Revolution.

BASES OF CONSENSUS

Against this background let us review the amount, the nature, and the sources of consensus between the parties. Even in the heat of a presidential campaign there are only minor disagreements between Republicans and Democrats on a wide range of political considerations.

For example, there is general agreement before the campaign on what the *important issues* of the election are supposed to be. With a remarkable lack of difference—that may be attributed to the impact of common events and of common communication media—Republicans and Democrats named the same measures as most and least important to their own vote decisions (Chart LXXXII). This common focus in conception and evaluation is not to be taken lightly; it carries a distinct value for a democratic community. Consider the alternative—a community or an era in which the partisans disagree not only on the stands they take on various issues but also on *what* political issues are relevant to take stands on. In such cases the partisans hardly join issues at all—they argue past one another—and the political debate languishes. And it is easy to recall situations in which each party develops its own favorite issues without relevance to its opponents. Basic agreement on the issues to be considered is a desirable, if not necessary, basis for political action. Whatever happens later, it is useful for the community to start the discussion with a common agenda. (But we shall see in chapter 11 that the candidates were less inclined than the voters to agree on the agenda.)

Second, there is some correspondence between the partisans in the *criteria* used to judge the candidates. Republicans and Democrats hold similar views about the types of competence required for the presidency, and there is no correlation between desirable experience

CHART LXXXII.

REPUBLICANS AND DEMOCRATS AGREE ON THE RELATIVE IMPORTANCE OF VARIOUS ISSUES

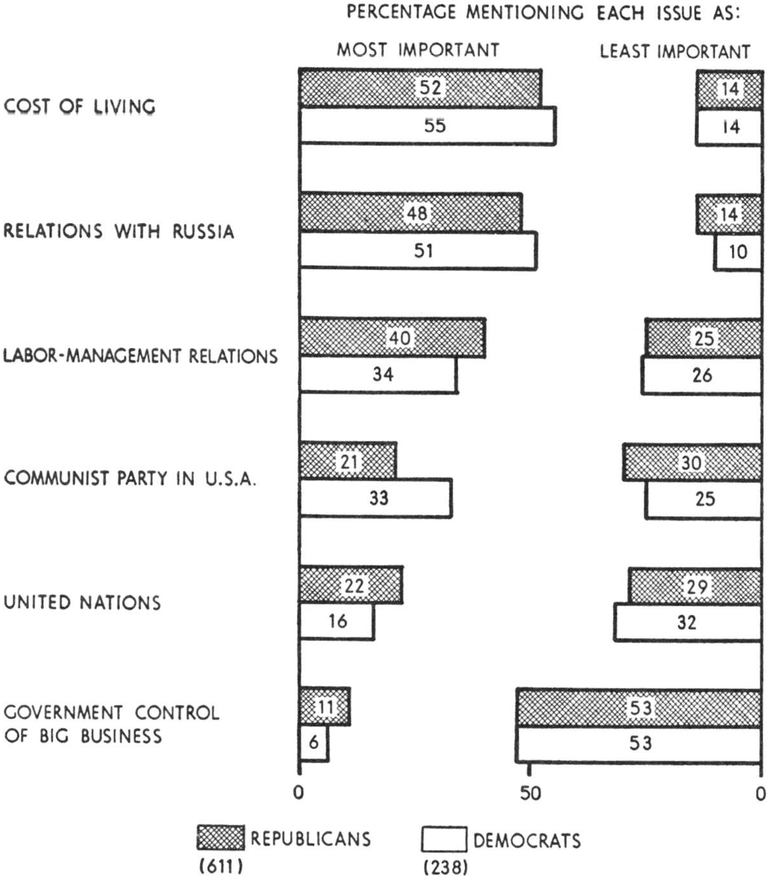

PERCENTAGE MENTIONING EACH ISSUE AS:

MOST IMPORTANT   LEAST IMPORTANT

	Most Important	Least Important
COST OF LIVING	52 / 55	14 / 14
RELATIONS WITH RUSSIA	48 / 51	14 / 10
LABOR-MANAGEMENT RELATIONS	40 / 34	25 / 26
COMMUNIST PARTY IN U.S.A.	21 / 33	30 / 25
UNITED NATIONS	22 / 16	29 / 32
GOVERNMENT CONTROL OF BIG BUSINESS	11 / 6	53 / 53

0   50   0

REPUBLICANS   DEMOCRATS
(611)   (238)

for a President and party preference (Chart LXXXIII). This obviously does not mean that Republicans and Democrats agree on *all* criteria for judgment, but there are many agreements, at least verbally, on the broad political ends to be served.

Third, a common body of *expectations* about major political

events is shared by the partisans. Republicans and Democrats do
not differ in their anticipations of war and depression; equal proportions are pessimistic and optimistic about the broadest events
on which their votes might have some effect (Chart LXXXIV).

CHART LXXXIII

REPUBLICANS AND DEMOCRATS AGREE ON SOME CRITERIA
FOR THE SELECTION OF THE PRESIDENT IN 1948

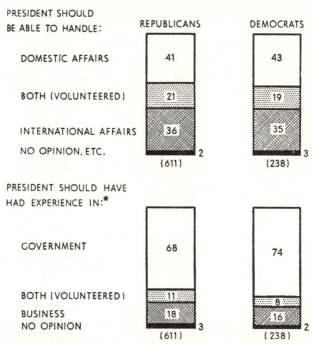

PRESIDENT SHOULD
BE ABLE TO HANDLE:

REPUBLICANS   DEMOCRATS

DOMESTIC AFFAIRS   41   43

BOTH (VOLUNTEERED)   21   19

INTERNATIONAL AFFAIRS 36   35

NO OPINION, ETC.   2   3
                      (611)   (238)

PRESIDENT SHOULD HAVE
HAD EXPERIENCE IN:*

GOVERNMENT   68   74

BOTH (VOLUNTEERED)   11   8

BUSINESS   18   16
NO OPINION   3   2
                      (611)   (238)

* This provides a striking example of how minor issues of Style are not "real" issues at all. In 1948,
when both candidates had backgrounds in government, the parties agreed. In 1940, when one came from
business (Willkie) and one from government (Roosevelt), the parties differed: 69 per cent of the Republicans
in Erie County, Ohio, thought that business experience was more important, and 67 per cent of the Democrats thought that government experience was more important! The "cleavage" of 1940 on this criterion
disappeared with shifting political winds. It was "only politics."

Indeed, pessimism seems to be distributed *across* the parties rather
than concentrated within one; those who expect one of the disasters
tend to expect the other too.

Fourth, there is a similarity in the partisan's conception of *how
much the election matters.* In June, before the actual campaigning
began, the respondents were asked whether they thought "whoever
is elected President this year will affect" relations with Russia, labor-

management relations, and living costs. And they were also asked how much influence they thought "people like you" had on the government. The partisans agree in placing high evaluations upon the policy consequences of this particular election and low evaluations upon their own general political roles (Chart LXXXV). Re-

CHART LXXXIV

REPUBLICANS AND DEMOCRATS HAVE SIMILAR EXPECTATIONS ABOUT THE POLITICAL FUTURE

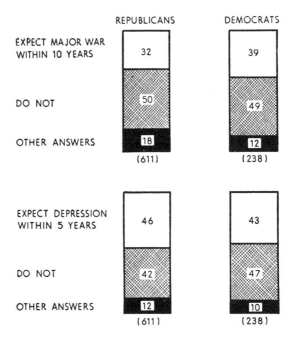

publicans and Democrats may argue very differently about *what* the consequences would be under one outcome rather than the other. But they do agree in substance upon the general kind and amount of "mattering" involved in the election, for example, that the total election would matter a lot but that their own personal votes would matter very little.

Fifth, there is agreement between the parties on *certain political issues* (Chart LXXXVI). True, they do not tend to be the basic issues of the campaign, almost by definition; they are withdrawn from controversy precisely because there is little controversy in them. On some issues—like the Communist spy issue—there is virtual unanimity within the community. On others—like civil rights issues—there is disagreement in the community but not primarily along partisan lines. And such issues were in 1948 likely to be

CHART LXXXV

The Party Supporters Have Similar Conceptions of How Much the Election Would Affect Political Affairs and How Much Influence They Have on the Government

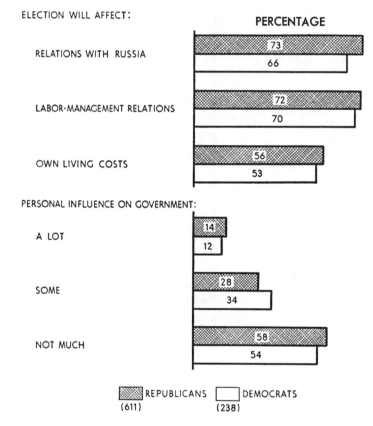

ELECTION WILL AFFECT:

PERCENTAGE

RELATIONS WITH RUSSIA — 73 / 66

LABOR-MANAGEMENT RELATIONS — 72 / 70

OWN LIVING COSTS — 56 / 53

PERSONAL INFLUENCE ON GOVERNMENT:

A LOT — 14 / 12

SOME — 28 / 34

NOT MUCH — 58 / 54

REPUBLICANS (611)   DEMOCRATS (238)

Style issues—matters of taste and self-expression, whether international or domestic. This consensus on Style issues serves as a base on which rests cleavage on Position issues.

As a matter of fact, these two kinds of Style issues—on internationalism and civil rights—are correlated with each other, and this

CHART LXXXVI

On Such Style Issues as Internationalism and Civil Rights, There Is Either General Consensus or Nonpartisan Dispute

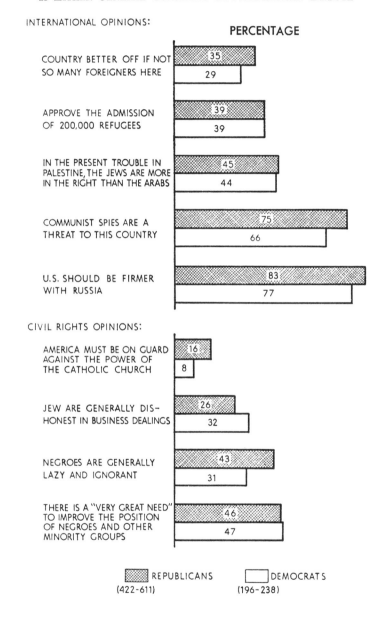

INTERNATIONAL OPINIONS:

PERCENTAGE

COUNTRY BETTER OFF IF NOT SO MANY FOREIGNERS HERE
- 35
- 29

APPROVE THE ADMISSION OF 200,000 REFUGEES
- 39
- 39

IN THE PRESENT TROUBLE IN PALESTINE, THE JEWS ARE MORE IN THE RIGHT THAN THE ARABS
- 45
- 44

COMMUNIST SPIES ARE A THREAT TO THIS COUNTRY
- 75
- 66

U.S. SHOULD BE FIRMER WITH RUSSIA
- 83
- 77

CIVIL RIGHTS OPINIONS:

AMERICA MUST BE ON GUARD AGAINST THE POWER OF THE CATHOLIC CHURCH
- 16
- 8

JEW ARE GENERALLY DIS-HONEST IN BUSINESS DEALINGS
- 26
- 32

NEGROES ARE GENERALLY LAZY AND IGNORANT
- 43
- 31

THERE IS A "VERY GREAT NEED" TO IMPROVE THE POSITION OF NEGROES AND OTHER MINORITY GROUPS
- 46
- 47

REPUBLICANS (422-611)   DEMOCRATS (196-238)

suggests an underlying dimension of ethnocentrism or out-group hostility. Voters who oppose admission of displaced persons, for example, are more likely to be anti-Negro or anti-Jew or anti-Catholic than voters not in opposition; and the same relationship holds in other cases (see Chart LXXXVII). Not only do many of the so-called isolationist and hypernationalist attitudes form a common cluster with some illiberal civil rights opinions, but both sets of attitudes rest partly on certain personality characteristics rather than on political considerations as such. For example, people who feel that they "have to struggle for everything in life" are more

CHART LXXXVII

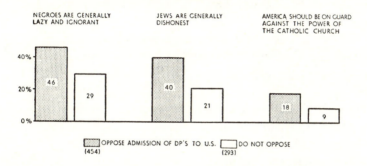

likely than their counterparts to be anti-Semitic (37 to 23 per cent) or antiforeign-born (42 to 25 per cent). Thus it may be that opinions on such Style issues are in good part expressive or symbolic of matters of personal temperament and private experience having little or nothing to do with the realities of the issues or the material interests involved in them. Such political problems are often complex, ambiguous, confusing, difficult to solve; they are "issues of frustration," and they attract opposition from, among others, frustrated personalities found in all parts of the population.

This brings us to the sixth characteristic on which Republicans and Democrats are alike. Many opinions are related to *"personality" factors* (e.g., individual differences in temperament), and it is important to know if such personality differences are correlated with contemporary American political cleavages. One such cluster of personal dispositions, the so-called "authoritarian" or "submissive" orientations toward others, has been under intensive psychological investigation in recent years.[2] In Elmira there are no differences between the parties in answers to a series of key questions from this study. Both parties seem to have their share of whatever anxieties and personality constrictions are tapped by these test items (Chart LXXXVIII). The lack of relationship between such politically irrelevant personality characteristics and vote is not a necessary result, as we know from authoritarian movements in Europe.

Finally, there are the obvious agreements on the *"rules of the game."* Elmirans of both parties appear to unite in the beliefs that politics should not involve physical force, fraud, and the like and that, despite the heat of controversy, the party defeated in elections or legislative struggles should accept the defeat. Indeed, about a quarter of the Republicans in Elmira were even "satisfied" with the outcome of the election! After it was over, Republicans accepted Truman as "their" President, too—behavior obvious enough to a twentieth-century American but probably quite remarkable to an eighteenth-century Yankee or a twentieth-century Iranian.

Here are illustrations, then, of some of the agreements between the partisans. There is consensus on the focus of debate, on some of the criteria by which issues and candidates should be judged, on certain expectations about future events confronting the political system, on the effect of personal and/or collective votes, on some issues, and on the rules by which the election is to be carried out. And at the same time there is equivalent distribution of private

---

2. The idea of an "authoritarian personality" has its origin in a series of studies inaugurated by Max Horkheimer and his associates during the late 1920's. Foreseeing the Hitler danger, they centered on the role of the desire for authority in history and in modern society (Erich Fromm's well-known *Escape from Freedom* was one of a series of ensuing studies). Later on the question was raised whether this attitude can be measured directly. In a collaboration between various psychologists and the Horkheimer group the so-called *F*-scale was developed for this purpose (for details see Adorno *et al.*, *The Authoritarian Personality* [New York: Harper & Bros., 1950]). It is based on a projective principle. A variety of situations are selected which ostensibly have nothing to do with public affairs. Respondents are asked whether in these situations they would favor a permissive or a punitive solution of a problem, implying distrust of other people, concern with their own status or security, etc. The number of nonpermissive reactions is used as an index of "authoritarianism." The *F*-scale, while controversial, has proved useful in a variety of areas. The reader should keep in mind that the questions are not to be taken at their face value. They serve as indicators of an underlying attitude that a respondent might not reveal if the questions referred directly to public affairs.

experiences of a cross-cutting or idiosyncratic kind (e.g., "person-alities" and "personal differences"). What this amounts to, in sum, is nonpartisanship on those matters that set the stage, define the procedures, spell out the agenda, maintain a degree of relevance, limit the range of disagreement, set the judging methods, and as-

CHART LXXXVIII

Republicans and Democrats Do Not Differ
in Selected Personality Test Items

PERCENTAGE AGREEING WITH EACH STATEMENT

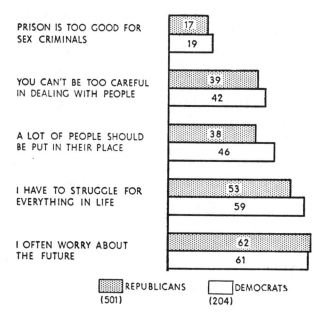

PRISON IS TOO GOOD FOR
SEX CRIMINALS
17
19

YOU CAN'T BE TOO CAREFUL
IN DEALING WITH PEOPLE
39
42

A LOT OF PEOPLE SHOULD
BE PUT IN THEIR PLACE
38
46

I HAVE TO STRUGGLE FOR
EVERYTHING IN LIFE
53
59

I OFTEN WORRY ABOUT
THE FUTURE
62
61

REPUBLICANS   DEMOCRATS
(501)   (204)

sure the acceptance of the decision—in short, on matters that pro-vide a background for organizing the disagreement.

Such organizing agreements, though "needed," are not always built into the system by rational and purposive design. They arise from diverse sources: from the pressure of commonly experienced events and the uniform interpretation given them by the mass media; from objective reality itself; from a myriad of small-scale factors inducing disagreement within but agreement between the lines of larger social organization on which parties are based; from the giant weight of the American cultural and political tradition that blankets all segments of society. From such sources may (or may not) come the elements of consensus that permit a reasonably orderly and peaceable debate on political issues. For a democratic political system to survive as an institution organizing and containing the social struggle, the partisans must hold positions in common as well as in opposition. And in 1948 Elmira they did.

BASES OF CLEAVAGE

What *dis*agreements are thus organized and contained within the broad area of consensus?

Rank-and-file Republicans and Democrats need not disagree on many things to make an election important. Yet without *some* central matters of cleavage, political institutions would have stability, true, but it would be the stability of a monolithic state or the trivial survival of a purely "political" contest irrelevant to the larger society. Neither was the case in 1948; the partisans did disagree on a few real issues.

By Position

The major issues of direct cleavage between Republicans and Democrats in 1948 Elmira were Position issues reflecting differences

CHART LXXXIX

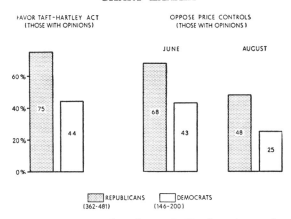

in material interests—namely, the Taft-Hartley Act and price control (see Chart LXXXIX). On these issues there are sizable differences in opinion between the parties—and the differences stem directly from the class bases of party support. As an example take the case of Taft-Hartley, which symbolized in 1948 a conflict in class interests. Though it was clearly identified with a party difference—the authors were Republican, and a Democratic President vetoed it and campaigned vigorously for its repeal—still opinion on it varied as much by social class within political parties as by political preference itself (Chart XC).

Not only that, but the cleavage between the partisans on such

CHART XC

OPINION ON THE POSITION ISSUE OF TAFT-HARTLEY VARIES ABOUT AS MUCH BY SOCIOECONOMIC CLASS AS BY POLITICAL PARTY

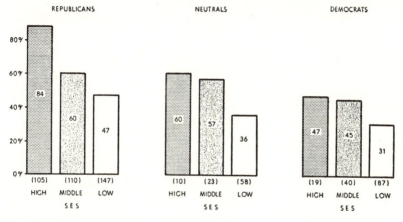

Position issues is greatest among the most partisan. Disagreement between parties is characteristic of those who care most about politics, and agreement or sheer heterogeneity without pattern is characteristic of those who care least. The differential between Republicans and Democrats on price control or on the Taft-Hartley Law is twice as great among those highly interested as against those not interested in political matters (Chart XCI). Republicans and Democrats of the apathetic type differ relatively little in their political opinions; only in the involved voters is there evidence of what might be called an ideological vote. Psychologists might say that the highly involved voters "live on" their differences with the opposition; that is, the very fact of difference provides them with a psychic energy with which they continue to engage themselves politically. And, in reverse, their deeper political engagement no

CHART XCI

The Greater the Political Interest, the Sharper the Party Differences on Major Issues

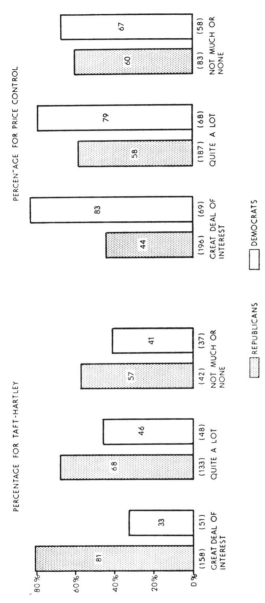

PERCENTAGE FOR TAFT-HARTLEY

PERCENTAGE FOR PRICE CONTROL

GREAT DEAL OF INTEREST (158) 81 / (51) 33

QUITE A LOT (133) 68 / (48) 46

NOT MUCH OR NONE (42) 57 / (37) 41

GREAT DEAL OF INTEREST (196) 44 / (69) 83

QUITE A LOT (187) 58 / (68) 79

NOT MUCH OR NONE (83) 60 / (58) 67

80% 60% 40% 20% 0%

▨ REPUBLICANS   ☐ DEMOCRATS

PERCENTAGE POINTS DIFFERENCE BETWEEN DEMOCRATS AND REPUBLICANS

ON TAFT HARTLEY

GREAT DEAL OF INTEREST 48

QUITE A LOT 22

NOT MUCH OR NONE 16

ON PRICE CONTROLS (AUG)

GREAT DEAL OF INTEREST 59

QUITE A LOT 21

NOT MUCH OR NONE 7

doubt leads them to see and feel differences with the opposition to an unusual degree.

But, whatever the psychological mechanisms, socially and politically the fact is that not all voters are needed to achieve a sharp polarization into two parties; that is carried on by "professional disagreers." These more politically specialized and sophisticated segments of the population are then linked to the remainder of the community socially, as discussed, for example, in chapter 6, in such a way that large numbers of the latter simply "go along" with what is for them a more artificial cleavage.

By Style

Not all the cleavages between the parties in 1948 were on Position issues. We have already seen that there was considerable agreement on Style issues. When such issues come into conflict, it is typically the case that the end is clearly approved and that there is a difference only in deciding which candidate would realize it better or faster. The voters' position on United States relations with the U.S.S.R. illustrates a pattern of this kind. By 1948 the community was nearly unanimous that the United States should be "firmer" with Russia. But there was considerable partisan disagreement over who would better implement this policy (Chart XCII).

In the main, however, the disagreements of 1948 centered on Position issues rather than on Style issues. Yet, why not both?

The answer takes us into important political circumstances of the Roosevelt-Truman era. "Liberalism" on domestic (Position) issues was *not* correlated with "liberalism" on civil rights and international (Style) issues. To the extent that a party organized around one type of issue, it could not easily handle the other. Democrats who could unite on labor legislation were split on civil rights; Republicans who shared a common economic conservatism were split on foreign policy. And had the parties been organized the other way around, on international or civil rights issues, then they probably would have been split on economic or "class" issues of the New Deal type (as was the case in the South).

The dilemma is that the two contemporary axes of liberalism-conservatism, the one economic-class and the other ethnic-international, vary independently of each other. The percentage of

internationally liberal voters within domestically liberal and conservative groups was about the same—42 per cent and 48 per cent.
To know, for example, that someone supported the New Deal on
economic issues provided no indication of his international or civil
rights opinions. Presumably, economic liberalism arises out of the

CHART XCII

Agreement on Ends Is Accompanied by Differences
about Who Would Best Realize Them

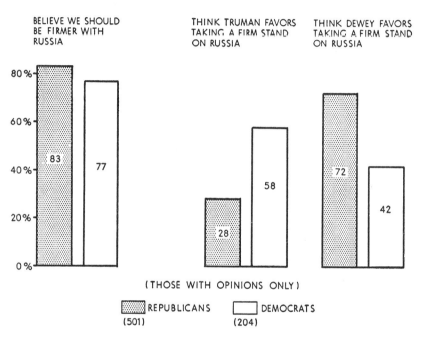

organization of society (e.g., occupational strata), whereas international liberalism derives from regional, ethnic, and educational
traditions—and the two do not particularly go together. And the
vote differed much more by domestic (Position) issues than by
international (Style) issues (Chart XCIII). Historically, this lack
of relationship between domestic and international opinions proved
to be a chronic source of difficulty for Roosevelt and Truman in
rallying materially liberal workers and farmers behind symbolically
liberal programs for civil rights and international relations.

THE RESOLUTION OF DIFFERENCES OVER ISSUES

At any given time, then, some people in one political camp or social group agree with some people in another, and such agreement maintains political discussion and negotiation and compromise and settlement. At the same time political issues are in conflict through-

CHART XCIII

PARTY PREFERENCE VARIES MORE BY POSITION ISSUES THAN STYLE ISSUES

PERCENTAGE REPUBLICAN OF TWO-PARTY VOTE

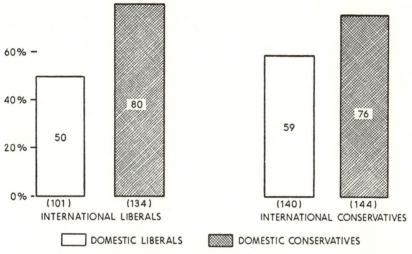

(For index of international liberalism, including questions about need for international president, about the United Nations, about admission of displaced persons, etc., see Appendix B.)

out the community. They are in conflict within the individual, within the party, and within the society. At each level there is the problem of resolving the many differences into a single stand, of resolving a pluralism of opinions into one basic disagreement.

Conflict within the Individual

The major ideological difference between the parties during the Roosevelt-Truman era was that centered on the Position issues symbolized by the New Deal. Yet, with the events leading to and flowing from World War II, questions of international affairs have claimed more and more attention. Just as the Democratic party is associated with socioeconomic measures of a "class" nature from 1932 to 1948, so it became associated with a more internationalist position abroad (and this despite Senator Vandenberg and the bipartisan foreign policy). In the broad sweep of political history this relationship between party positions on domestic and international affairs was still in flux in 1948. But it could probably be maintained that the "more natural" position for Democrats—the position more in harmony with the position of their party leaders—was the "liberal" position both at home and abroad and that the "more natural" position for Republicans was the "conservative" side. This leaves some voters with split opinions—liberal on one set of issues and conservative on the other—in a cross-pressured situation, potentially if not actually. They are attracted to each party by one set of opinions and repelled by another; "attitudinal conflict" may be too strong a term for their experience, but they are inconsistent.

How are such inconsistencies overridden? A few cross-pressured voters act like the proverbial donkey and do not vote at all. Others, however, do make a choice between the parties. How do they manage to do so? One answer is: through the weights or priorities assigned, by the individual himself or by larger events, to the relevant issues.

We attempted to ascertain the weights given to the two sets of issues in two ways. First, we asked respondents what they personally considered important problems (of a list) and classified their answers into domestic and international categories. Second, we asked respondents whether they thought the outcome of the election would affect such problems as relations with the U.S.S.R. or domestic labor-management relations. Using such measures, we find that votes correlate with the side given greater weight (Chart XCIV). For example, take the domestic liberals who are international conservatives. Those who think domestic problems are more important vote less Republican than those who think international problems are more important, and similarly in the case of the election's effect upon policy. And among domestic conservatives who are international liberals, the reverse is the case. In other words, voters with an attitudinal foot in each camp, so to speak, tend to choose the party that corresponds to their own position on those issues to which they assign particular weight.

CHART XCIV

Vote Decision Is Related to Weight Assigned to Issues

PERCENTAGE REPUBLICAN OF TWO-PARTY VOTE

DOMESTIC LIBERALS WHO ARE INTERNATIONAL CONSERVATIVES

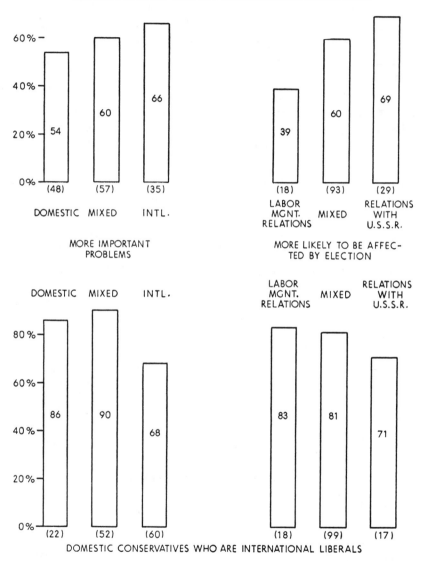

MORE IMPORTANT
PROBLEMS

MORE LIKELY TO BE AFFEC-
TED BY ELECTION

DOMESTIC CONSERVATIVES WHO ARE INTERNATIONAL LIBERALS

The relationship between hierarchical weighting of issues and voting behavior has the character of mutual interaction over time; voting partisanship can determine in the first place how issues are ranked, as well as the reverse. Nevertheless, in 1948, such weighting of issues by voters holding inconsistent views on them had noticeable power to affect subsequent voting changes. Whether the voter in potential conflict (e.g., the man who supported the Democrats' liberal international program but not their liberal domestic economic policies) assigned high importance or effectiveness to one or the other conflicting sphere of issues early in the campaign makes a difference in his voting changes later (Chart XCV).

Let us examine this tabulation more closely as an example of the reduction of several pieces of information into one. All those cross-pressured respondents who assigned more importance to the side of the issues on which they themselves were liberal, that is, domestic liberals who thought domestic problems more important or international liberals who thought international problems more important, are combined in the first group, and similarly throughout the rest of the chart. We thus construct groups of voters cross-pressured on the issues, with liberal or conservative weights attached to them. In every case the shift from June to November follows the assignment of weight. Republicans in June with a "liberal weight" are less Republican on election day than those with a "conservative weight." And Democrats with a liberal weight on importance or effectiveness are less likely to become Republican.

It is difficult to change people's preferences; it is easier to affect the priorities or weights they give to subpreferences bearing on the central decision. A voter may assess the political situation from several standpoints; from one, the Democrats appear better to him and, from another, the Republicans do. His decision is likely to follow the aspect given greater weight by him—with no change in the substance of his own opinions. Thus the voter's feeling about what is critical in the political situation enables him to find a way out of a potential "conflict" over the issues and hence facilitates political integration within the individual.

Within the Party

How a *party* resolves its own conflicts—"how a party makes up its mind"—has been extensively studied by political scientists. Most prominent of the conflict-resolving processes within the parties are nominating conventions, primary elections, and the like. They typically attempt to deal with those matters that crosscut existing lines of party organization. It is an important half-truth that the

CHART XCV

The Weight Assigned to Issues Influences Change in Vote

PERCENTAGE REPUBLICAN OF TWO-PARTY VOTE*

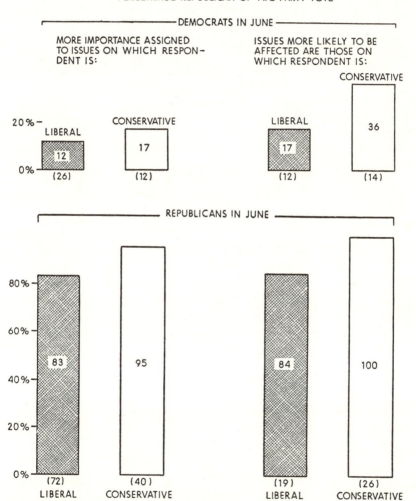

* Among "conflict" or inconsistent cases only, e.g., among domestic-liberal-and-international-conservative and domestic-conservative-and-international-liberal only.

most important issues of the times are settled *within* the majority party. This is true because those issues which do not fit existing lines of party cleavage must be settled within parties, but it is only half-true because other and important issues are already bases of at least official consensus within parties (e.g., New Deal issues) and are thus settled *between* them.[3]

Positions on such matters are often represented by different candidates for nomination. For example, prior to the conventions in

CHART XCVI

VANDENBERG AND TAFT REPRESENTED SPECIAL
VIEWPOINTS; DEWEY, ALL VIEWPOINTS

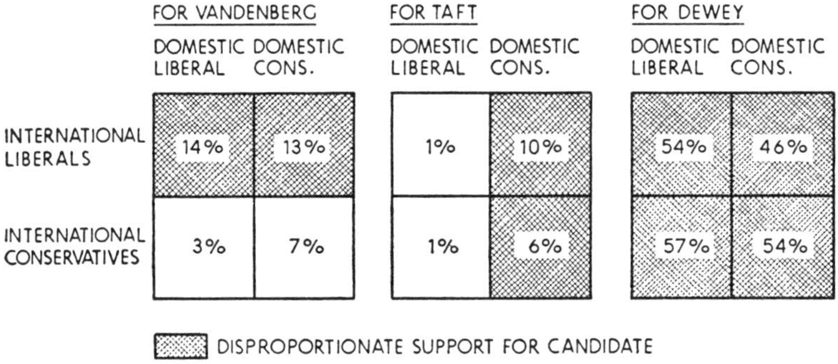

	FOR VANDENBERG		FOR TAFT		FOR DEWEY	
	DOMESTIC LIBERAL	DOMESTIC CONS.	DOMESTIC LIBERAL	DOMESTIC CONS.	DOMESTIC LIBERAL	DOMESTIC CONS.
INTERNATIONAL LIBERALS	14%	13%	1%	10%	54%	46%
INTERNATIONAL CONSERVATIVES	3%	7%	1%	6%	57%	54%

▓ DISPROPORTIONATE SUPPORT FOR CANDIDATE

1948, Vandenberg was the candidate of some international liberals among the Republicans, and Taft was the candidate of some of the domestic conservatives of the party (Chart XCVI). If either man had been nominated, that might have settled party policy for the moment, but there would have been danger of defection or nonsupport among those of opposing views. A typical procedure—both

3. This consensus is less evident among the rank and file. Considerably less than half the voters in Elmira agreed with their own party's position on both Taft-Hartley and price control, the central issues in 1948:

OPINION ON TAFT-HARTLEY AND PRICE CONTROL (AUGUST)	PERCENTAGE (AMONG THOSE WITH OPINIONS ON BOTH ISSUES)		
	Republican	Democratic	Total
Agree with own party on both issues..	41	44	42
On one..........................	42	48	44
On neither........................	17	8	14
Total no. of cases..............	317	132	449

a rational device for settling conflict and also perhaps an unintended result of the mediation and averaging of intraparty discords—is for a party to nominate a candidate "above" such factionalism, whose personal popularity or chances of winning can "unite" the party or whose views are sufficiently ambiguous or unknown to represent all things to all men in the party. Such seemed to be the pattern of support for Dewey among Republicans of all combinations of views in 1948 before the convention. Small-appearing differences are more bearable than large-appearing ones, and what emerges as the middle-of-the-road choice must be that which seems close to all sides.

When such a candidate is nominated, most of the party's intended

CHART XCVII

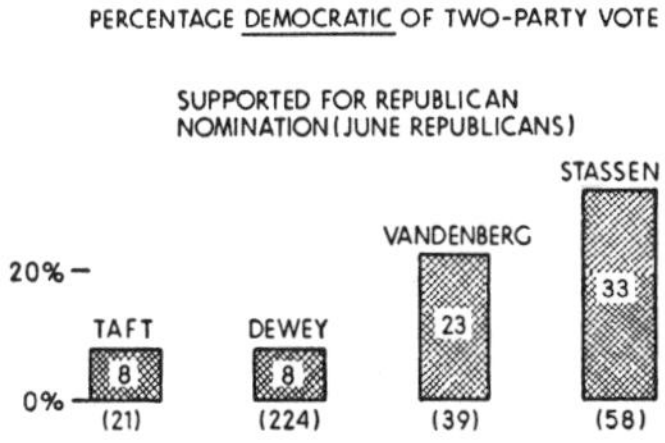

PERCENTAGE DEMOCRATIC OF TWO-PARTY VOTE

SUPPORTED FOR REPUBLICAN
NOMINATION (JUNE REPUBLICANS)

voters accept the decision and stay with their party's choice through the remainder of the campaign (see Chart XCVII). In Elmira only some supporters of the candidates closest to the opposition position were lost to the Republicans—supporters of Vandenberg and Stassen. The Taft men were Republicans first and last. Ideological conflicts within a party are not so much "settled" as they are transcended by the substitution of one candidate and one party cause (i.e., to elect him) in place of many ideologies. It is a false dichotomy to say that Americans vote "for the man rather than the issues." Nevertheless, the grain of truth in this saying lies in the fact that party harmony is partly achieved by by-passing issues on which members cannot agree in the selection of a man on whom they can (best) agree. "Issues are never decided; they are only superseded."

Another device that enables the parties to resolve attitudinal conflict involves the operation of the party system itself. After all, one votes for a party, not an ideology. And it is relatively convenient, when "pulled" this way or that by opposing opinions on the issues, to reaffirm the wisdom of one's earlier decision by voting for the same party one supported before. Voters caught between the partisans in their positions on domestic and international affairs end largely by following their earlier choices. In this Republican community almost all those with a Republican voting history voted Republican, and two-thirds of those with a Democratic voting history voted Democratic.

Finally, the earlier analysis of weights or priorities provides a promising approach to the paradox of how people of so many different viewpoints can unite in one party. First, we see how the seeming "conflicts"—that is, inconsistencies and contradictions—can be resolved in practice by differential weighting of the potency of each. But, more important, in the variation of weights between Democrats and Republicans in the same cross-pressured situation (e.g., when the former give their liberal, the latter their conservative, ideas priority), we have a clue to a basis of unity on issues within a giant contemporary party.

It need not be a unity with regard to the content of the issues, who is for or against what, nor need it necessarily be a unity of the importance of different issues. What unifies a great heterogeneous party is this: On those matters which are important or relevant or salient to particular voters in the same party, they are uniformly against the opposition. One Republican may be most concerned with foreign policy, and on that subject he is against the Democrats. Another Republican may be most concerned with domestic economics, and on that subject he is against the Democrats. Party members need not agree on specific issues; their unity is at a different level. Their unity lies in the fact that on *something* important to each, they share a common position of disagreement with the opposition.

Thus, whether or not there is a blurred, unclear basis of cleavage in the era or whether or not this cleavage between the parties leaves great tangles of inconsistency remaining within each one, there is a solid basis of unity still remaining in each great party. Its members agree on one thing transcending their disagreement: they have, for one reason or another, the *same opposition*.

Within the Society

Finally, there is the central matter of how the political system as a whole handles the resolution of issues. This requires a longer look at the political process than is afforded by our view of a single election alone. Let us try to locate the 1948 campaign in the historical stream of political decision.

The "life-history."—In their course across the political stage viable issues seem to "move" through various phases—from near-unanimous rejection at first through sharp partisan disagreement to near-unanimous acceptance at the end, perhaps a generation later (Chart XCVIII). Issues seem to have a characteristic *life-history*.

Issues are typically introduced by a small vanguard normally toward the left, or experimental, end of the political spectrum, who are often aided by the circumstantial event. If successful, the issue wins its way slowly across the political field. At each point rejection turns to resistance, then to acquiescence, and finally to approval. After the initially "radical" proposal becomes a *fait accompli* through acceptance in practice, it takes its place as a "natural" characteristic of political life, and attention in the political arena turns to new matters. For example, social security had gone through all these phases within the lifetime of 1948 voters.

But what is it that "moves" the issue through various stages of disagreement? Certainly it is not partisan agitation alone. From a long-range viewpoint, many issues of a particular presidential campaign can be seen as topical expressions of underlying historical trends, outgrowths of such great economic and social events as depressions and wars, of evolving changes in the society, of emerging domestic and international power balances. Political parties do not "create" these issues; they only seize upon and articulate them. And, as times change, so does the content of the party position. On economic legislation, for example, the difference between the modern parties in this country is less a fixed ideology—consider what William Howard Taft would think of Robert Taft's housing bill or what Woodrow Wilson would think of Harry Truman's health proposals!—than a fixed *position* of welcome or resistance to a succession of related needs or opportunities for change presented by emerging developments in the society.

Take an example of such movement of the issues over the long run. The case deals with the community's attitude toward labor unions, as reflected by a four-part question. By 1948 labor unions were permanent features of American life, like it or not. More people approved than disapproved of them, except on the extreme

CHART XCVIII

Schematic Diagram of Support for a Proposal

PERCENTAGE "FOR" PROPOSAL (HYPOTHETICAL)
AT EACH POSITION ON POLITICAL SPECTRUM

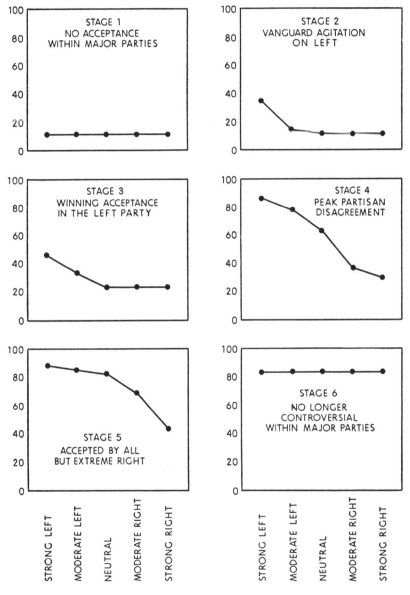

STAGE 1
NO ACCEPTANCE
WITHIN MAJOR PARTIES

STAGE 2
VANGUARD AGITATION
ON LEFT

STAGE 3
WINNING ACCEPTANCE
IN THE LEFT PARTY

STAGE 4
PEAK PARTISAN
DISAGREEMENT

STAGE 5
ACCEPTED BY ALL
BUT EXTREME RIGHT

STAGE 6
NO LONGER
CONTROVERSIAL
WITHIN MAJOR PARTIES

STRONG LEFT MODERATE LEFT NEUTRAL MODERATE RIGHT STRONG RIGHT

STRONG LEFT MODERATE LEFT NEUTRAL MODERATE RIGHT STRONG RIGHT

right. But the warmth of their acceptance diminishes from left to right on the spectrum. The difference between the parties lies less in outright acceptance or rejection of unionism than in differ-

CHART XCIX

ATTITUDES TOWARD LABOR UNIONS ACROSS THE POLITICAL SPECTRUM
REVEAL A STAGE IN THE LIFE-HISTORY OF A POLITICAL ISSUE

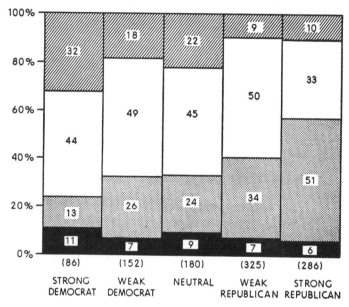

 entical enthusiasm and resistance, varying around the common acceptance of the historic development (Chart XCIX).

The "political gateway."—Thus party dispositions are fixed positions of enthusiasm or resistance taken on either side of an *entry point*—so to speak, a political "gateway"—through which an endless succession of social proposals have passed, are passing, and will pass. The issues are disputed only during the time they remain at the point of legislative or electoral decision, when the issue "hangs in the balance." Before that they are not at the level of popular visibility. After that they are accomplished facts and out of controversy in a historically brief time.

To the extent that the division into two parties is achieved with the aid of issues, the cleavage will turn around those proposals that are near, just approaching or just passing, the critical gateway phase of precarious balance between acceptance or rejection. Thus it is important to know not only what issues are in the political arena during a campaign but what issues are at the most critical phase of partisan disagreement at that point of time.

In 1948 Elmira the picture on economic and social issues looked something like this:

Issues past the gateway or decision phase	Public housing Social security Wagner Act AAA farm program
Issues in the gateway, being decided at the time	Labor relations, and specifically the Taft-Hartley Act Peacetime price and rent controls
Issues not yet in the gateway or decision phase	Compulsory health insurance New (e.g., Brannan) farm plans New controls on corporations

On the first group of issues—those well past the decision point and now "settled" features of the American life—we would expect no sharp party disagreement. And on the last group of political issues —not yet seriously proposed in 1948 by party leaders—we would expect little opinion to exist at all, and what there is of it also to be relatively unrelated to major party lines. If on the former we would expect consensus, on the latter we would expect, to coin a barbarism, "no-sensus." Only on the narrow range of currently active issues in between—specific proposals then hanging in the balance—would we expect sharp party disagreement: dissensus. And so was the case in 1948 Elmira (Chart C).

In sum, to understand the process of cleavage on the issues, one must understand the broader historical trends on which the cleavage is based and of which the campaign issues are topical manifestations. Across these trends, or rather athwart the entry points or gateways through which specific proposals comprising these trends

CHART C

Among Socioeconomic Proposals of the New Deal–Fair Deal Trend, Only Those Currently at the Decision Point Evoke Sharp Partisan Disagreement

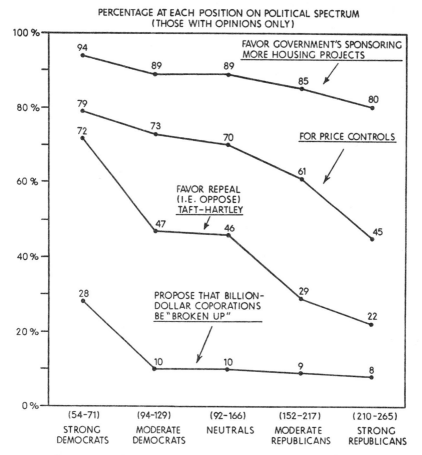

PERCENTAGE AT EACH POSITION ON POLITICAL SPECTRUM
(THOSE WITH OPINIONS ONLY)

FAVOR GOVERNMENT'S SPONSORING MORE HOUSING PROJECTS

FOR PRICE CONTROLS

FAVOR REPEAL (I.E. OPPOSE) TAFT–HARTLEY

PROPOSE THAT BILLION-DOLLAR COPORATIONS BE "BROKEN UP"

| (54–71) | (94–129) | (92–166) | (152–217) | (210–265) |
| STRONG DEMOCRATS | MODERATE DEMOCRATS | NEUTRALS | MODERATE REPUBLICANS | STRONG REPUBLICANS |

enter the stage of decision, the parties are typically arrayed as welcoming enthusiasts or resisting critics.

As events and the needs of the society push such proposals into, through, and beyond the political gateway of decision, party dispositions facilitate or inhibit not so much the final decision as the speed of acceptance. Thus, given this differential speed of accept-ance, there occurs a critical phase in the decision process when the left or welcoming party has already accepted the innovation but the right or resisting party is still opposed. The result is tem-porarily—what in historical perspective seems only a passing mo-ment—a sharp partisan disagreement over the proposal.

Now, as a presidential campaign intrudes in the midst of this historical process, those issues that are at the moment nearest to the critical phases of dispute are most likely to provide the current, topical symbols of the underlying sources of cleavage be-tween leftist and rightist parties in that particular era. These issues must become, then, the subjects of sharpest disagreement between parties and the points of greatest rallying power within each party. They become what the disagreement is about—the content of the debate between polar political positions. In this sense, a sequence of long-range *agreements* representing the "trend of the times" is formed, paradoxically enough, by a sequence of short-range *disagreements* around which parties polarize and elections are in part decided.[4]

SUMMARY[5]

Bases of Consensus

100. Republicans and Democrats agreed on what are the important issues of the campaign.

4. There are of course many qualifications implicit in the oversimplified expo-sition here. For one thing, a "typical" election out of a sequence of similar elec-tions is assumed, as is a clear-cut historical trend underlying these similar elec-tions. For another thing, the whole process of feedback is omitted, by which political innovations—the election outcome itself, in fact—change the character of the trend and the nature of cleavage. For another, the analysis is carried on as though all individual voters decided on the basis of the content of the cam-paign issues. But, despite such limitations, analysis of this kind is desirable, and even necessary, to relate the findings of such surveys to the broader picture of political institutions and movements provided by historical analysis.

5. The assertions of this summary and of other summaries in this volume are of several kinds. Some like Nos. 108, 112, 113, and 117 are hypotheses about general relationships one could test in almost any voting system at any historical time. Others like Nos. 100–107 are quite different assertions about important variables or conditions useful in describing the state of a political system at a given time, conditions in the United States in 1948 being presented here as illus-trations. One would not expect the state to be the same in other systems or in different eras, only that changes or different conditions in these respects would be important because of their (as yet unknown) relationships to end results. Other assertions like No. 118 are simply orientations that do not specify variables or relationships.

101. Republicans and Democrats agreed on some criteria used to judge the candidates.

102. Republicans and Democrats had similar expectations about future political events (specifically, in 1948, war and depression).

103. Republicans and Democrats agreed on how much effect the election would have on certain issues and on how much influence they themselves had on the government.

104. Republicans and Democrats agreed on some political issues —in 1948 on such Style issues as international affairs and civil rights (that are themselves correlated).

105. Republicans and Democrats gave similar answers to selected personality test items.

106. Republicans and Democrats agreed on the rules of the political game, i.e., on procedures for democratic elections.

Bases of Cleavage

107. Republicans and Democrats disagreed on major Position issues—for example, Taft-Hartley and price control in 1948.

> *and:* (*a*) On Position issues such as Taft-Hartley, opinion varied about as much by socioeconomic status as by party.

108. The greater the interest in the election, the sharper the differences between partisans on Position issues like Taft-Hartley and price control.

109. When partisans agree on the ends of political policy (e.g., firmness toward Russia), they disagree on which candidate will better realize the end.

110. Vote in 1948 differed more by the voters' stand on domestic-economic (Position) issues than by international-ethnic (Style) issues.

111. There was no correlation between "liberalism" on domestic-economic (Position) issues and "liberalism" on international-ethnic (Style) issues.

Resolution of Differences

112. The party choice of cross-pressured voters tends to follow the weight assigned to the issues.

113. Shifts in vote among such people also correspond to the weights assigned to the issues.

114. Less than half the voters agreed with their own party's position on major Position issues like Taft-Hartley and price control.

115. The Republicans nominated the candidate most acceptable to all groups within the party.

116. Republicans who before the convention preferred a Republican candidate closer to the Democratic position (e.g., Vandenberg or Stassen) were more likely to vote Democratic on election day.

117. Cross-pressured voters tend to follow their own voting history.

118. The attitude of partisans toward labor unions, from strong Republican to strong Democratic, illustrates the life-history of political issues, i.e., their movement through the political spectrum with different rates of acceptance from left to right.

119. Partisan disagreement on the issues is sharpest for those issues in the "political gateway" at a given time; there is relatively little disagreement on those issues that have passed through the "gateway" or those not yet there.

10 POLITICAL PERCEPTION
The Candidates' Stand on the Issues

As indicated in the first chapter in this section, the modern political party in a town like Elmira has an effective existence more in the minds of the partisans than in the local community's formal political organizations. And, as indicated in the second chapter in this section, this existence is primarily expressed through differences in attitudes toward political issues of the day.

But this is not the only way in which the partisans differentiate themselves. There is also the fact of political perception—how the voter *sees* events in the political world. Specifically, we are concerned here with how voters in 1948 saw the issues of the campaign and what difference that made in their political behavior.

Now this is not simply a nice psychological problem with little relevance for the political situation. The process of political perception can operate to increase cleavage or consensus within the community. It undoubtedly contributes directly to a "real" definition of the differences between the parties, in terms of what might be called their "political norms."

For political beliefs and perceptions have a strongly "normative" quality. They not only state that "this is the way things are," but they also imply that "this is their customary or natural state" and therefore what they "ought" to be. The parties are not only what their leaders do or say; the parties are also what their followers believe they are, expect them to be, and therefore think they should be.

Once again we encounter a brief glimpse of the spiral of cause and effect that constitutes political history—in this case the history of political issues: What the parties do affects what the voters think they are and what the voters think they are affects what they subsequently do. Out of this interaction between subjective perception and objective reality, mutually affecting one another over decades, emerges not only our definition but the reality of a political party's role. The popular image of "what Republicans (or Democrats) are like" helps to define and determine what they "really" are. Today's subjective unreality in the voters' minds affects tomorrow's objective reality in the political arena.

About thirty years ago an analyst of public opinion gained lasting distinction by elaborating the differences between "the world outside and the pictures in our heads." Walter Lippmann discussed what many theorists—philosophers, psychologists, sociologists, political scientists, anthropologists—have noted and documented before and since: subjective perception does not always reflect objective reality accurately. Selective perception—sampling the real world—must be taken into account. The mirror that the mind holds up to nature is often distorted in accordance with the subject's predispositions. The "trickle of messages from the outside is affected by the stored-up images, the preconceptions, and the prejudices which interpret, fill them out, and in their turn powerfully direct the play of our attention, and our vision itself. . . . In the individual person, the limited messages from outside, formed into a pattern of stereotypes, are identified with his own interests as he feels and conceives them."[1] Another student of public opinion put it similarly: "Each looks at, and looks for, the facts and reasons to which his attention points, perceiving little, if at all, those to which his mind is not directed. As a rule, men see what they look for, and observe the things they expect to see."[2]

The world of political reality, even as it involves a presidential campaign and election, is by no means simple or narrow. Nor is it crystal-clear. Over a period of six months, and intensively for six weeks, the electorate is subjected to a wide variety of campaign events. Even if all the political events were unambiguous, there would still be a problem of political perception; but, as it is, the campaign is composed (often deliberately) of ambiguous as well as clear elements.

1. Walter Lippmann, *Public Opinion*, p. 21.
2. A. Lawrence Lowell, *Public Opinion in War and Peace*, p. 22.

PERCEPTION AND VOTING

Just how clear was the objective field to be perceived in 1948? Some propagandists, and some students of propaganda, believe that ambiguity often promotes effectiveness, since each subject is then free to define the matter in terms satisfactory to himself. While a sharply clear statement may win some friends by its very decisive-

TABLE 12

POSITIONS TAKEN BY DEWEY AND TRUMAN ON FOUR
ISSUES DURING THE CAMPAIGN

	Dewey	Truman
Price control	Causes of high prices were war, foreign aid, the administration's discouragement of production, governmental mismanagement Remedies: cut government spending, reduce national debt, increase production No reference to imposition of controls Only one major reference	Republicans would not act against inflation in Eightieth Congress or special session; they rejected the administration's program Called for price controls or anti-inflation measures on several occasions
Taft-Hartley Law	Referred to it as "Labor-Management Relations Act of 1947," never as "Taft-Hartley Law" Made abstract remarks about "labor's freedoms" which would be "zealously guarded and extended" Approved the law in general ("will not retreat from advances made") but left door open for improvements ("where laws affecting labor can be made a better instrument for labor relations . . .")	Made the "shameful" and "vicious" law a major issue; recalled that Republicans passed it over his veto: "It ought to be repealed" Took this position in at least ten major campaign speeches during October
Policy toward U.S.S.R.	Took a strong anti-communism position; linked communism to administration Made this a major issue in about seven campaign speeches	Took an anti-communism position; major references twice
Public housing	Only minor references to need for more housing (Republican platform called for housing financed by private enterprise, with federal "encouragement" when private industry and local government were unable to fill need)	Republicans "killed" Taft-Ellender-Wagner Bill Called for public housing sponsored by government in at least ten major campaign speeches

ness, it may also lose some people for the same reason. Now Truman and Dewey had both been public figures for some time and had taken public stands on many political matters; yet their positions on the issues in the campaign were not equally clear.

In 1948 Truman took a more straightforward and more aggressive position on these issues than Dewey (Table 12). The latter spoke to a large extent on the need for unity, peace, and freedom, while

Truman specified his position *for* price control and public housing and *against* the Taft-Hartley Law. And Truman used quite vigorous language in stating his position, whereas Dewey employed a more lofty rhetoric. Except perhaps for the Russian issue (which became involved with the spy and domestic Communist issue), there can be no question but that, objectively, Dewey's position was more amenable to misperception than Truman's.

And this is reflected in the extent of nonperception of the candidates' stands.[3] On the four issues the proportion of respondents who do not know the candidates' stands average about 10 per cent for Truman and about 25 per cent for Dewey. (This also reflects the fact that Truman's official position brought him before the public on such issues on numerous occasions; but a counterconsideration is that Dewey's position as governor of New York made him especially familiar to Elmirans.)

Perception and Party Preference

More importantly, the voter's perception of where the candidates stand on the issues is not uniformly affected by partisan preference— only selectively so (Chart CI). It is not marked on the central issues of price control and the Taft-Hartley Law. Republicans and Democrats agree that Truman is for price control and against the Taft-Hartley Law and that Dewey is for the Taft-Hartley Law and against price control (although on this last there is by no means a clear perception of where Dewey stood). On public housing (and, as we saw earlier, on the Russian problem) the difference between the parties was greater.

Why should the partisans agree in perception on some issues and disagree on others? For one thing, of course, perception varies with the ambiguity of the situation. The less ambiguous the objective situation (e.g., Truman's position on price control), the less disagreement. But, for another, perception seems to vary with the degree of controversiality of the issues in the community. On price control and the Taft-Hartley Law the respondents with opinions divided about 60–40; on the other two issues (including firmness

3. The questions followed this form: "From what you know, is Truman (Dewey) for the Taft-Hartley Law or against it?" The respondent could say "Don't know" or state that the candidate had not taken any stand on the issue. The perception questions were asked in August, before the campaign proper; replies may have been different in October.

toward Russia), in Elmira the split is about 90–10. In the latter case, then, there is virtual agreement within the community—which means that one side of the issue is considered "right" and the other side "wrong." Hence there is, so to speak, a standard to guide misperception—and each side pulls its own candidate toward the "correct position" and pushes the opponent away from it. On the two

CHART CI

PARTY PREFERENCE DOES NOT PARTICULARLY AFFECT THE
VOTER'S PERCEPTION OF WHERE THE CANDIDATES
STAND ON SOME CAMPAIGN ISSUES

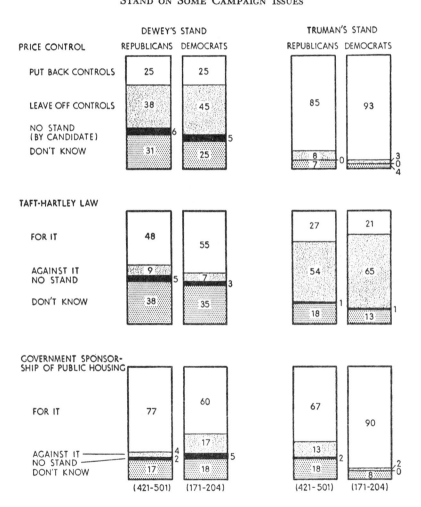

central issues, however, the controversy is too visible to allow a designation of "rightness" for one or the other side, and as a result there is less motive for or gain in misperception. If the voter gets nothing for his misperception (e.g., being "right"), there is less reason for him to engage in it. Deviation or misperception requires a certain degree of ambiguity in the objective situation being perceived, but it also requires a psychic indulgence for the misperceiver. Where this opportunity is not present, perception is likely to be more accurate.

Perception and Own Stand

This suggests that perception of the candidates' stands on issues may be affected by the respondents' own stands on them. The voters can thus manage to increase the consistency within their own political position, or at least the apparent consistency. And this is clearly the case. In almost every instance respondents perceive their candidate's stand on these issues as similar to their own and the opponent's stand as dissimilar—whatever their own position (Chart CII). For example, those Republicans who favor price control perceive Dewey as favoring price control (70 per cent), and few who oppose price control perceive Dewey as favoring controls (14 per cent). And the Republicans who are against controls perceive Truman as favoring them somewhat more than the Republicans who are for them. As with their perception of group support, so with their perception of the issues: the partisans manage to "pull" their own candidate and "push" the opposing candidate with considerable consistency. Overlaying the base of objective observation is the distortion effect—distortion in harmony with political predispositions. As Schumpeter says, "Information and arguments in political matters will 'register' only if they link up with the citizen's preconceived ideas."[4]

At the same time, some voters maintain or increase their perceptual defense on political issues by refusing to acknowledge differences with one's own candidate or similarities to the opposition candidate. Such denial of reality, a defense utilized against uncongenial aspects of the environment, is well documented by case studies and laboratory experiments in the psychological literature

4. Joseph Schumpeter, *Capitalism, Socialism, and Democracy*, p. 263.

CHART CII

The Voters' Own Stands on the Issues Affect Their Perception of the Candidates' Stands*

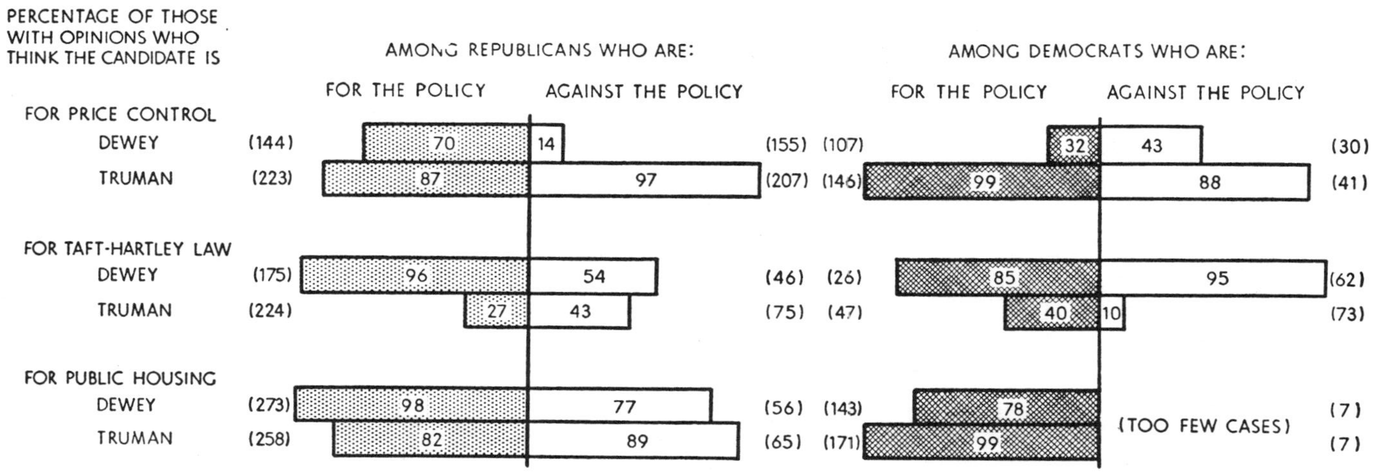

PERCENTAGE OF THOSE
WITH OPINIONS WHO
THINK THE CANDIDATE IS

AMONG REPUBLICANS WHO ARE:

AMONG DEMOCRATS WHO ARE:

FOR THE POLICY   AGAINST THE POLICY   FOR THE POLICY   AGAINST THE POLICY

FOR PRICE CONTROL

DEWEY (144)   70   14 (155)   (107) 32   43 (30)

TRUMAN (223)   87   97 (207)   (146) 99   88 (41)

FOR TAFT-HARTLEY LAW

DEWEY (175)   96   54 (46)   (26) 85   95 (62)

TRUMAN (224)   27   43 (75)   (47) 40   10 (73)

FOR PUBLIC HOUSING

DEWEY (273)   98   77 (56)   (143) 78   (TOO FEW CASES) (7)

TRUMAN (258)   82   89 (65)   (171) 99   (7)

* For simplification and clarity, the "No stand" and the "Don't know" responses have been omitted from this chart. The omission does not affect the point of the data.

of neurosis. Here we have evidence on its operation in the midst
of a political campaign where motivation is less strong.

Take the two major issues of price control and the Taft-Hartley
Law, on which the candidates took relatively clear positions. Objectively, an observer would say that Truman was for and Dewey

CHART CIII

PARTISANS TEND NOT TO PERCEIVE DIFFERENCES WITH THEIR OWN
CANDIDATE OR SIMILARITIES TO THE OPPOSITION CANDIDATE

PERCENTAGE WHO "DON'T KNOW" THEIR OWN CANDIDATE'S STAND

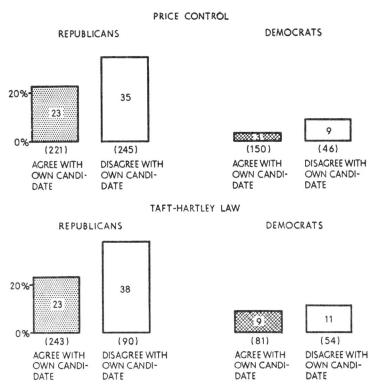

against price control and that Truman was against and Dewey for
the Taft-Hartley Law. Yet, when our respondents are asked where
the candidates stand, a certain proportion of them do not know or
profess not to know. But—and this is the point—the "Don't knows"
are more frequent among partisans who themselves take a different
position from their own candidate or the same position as the
opponent (Chart CIII).

Perception and Strength of Feeling

This tendency to "misperceive" issues in a favorable direction does not operate in a uniform fashion within the electorate. The degree of affect attached to the election, in the form of intensity upon one's vote intention, also influences perception. Those voters who feel strongly about their vote intention perceive political issues differently from those who do not feel so strongly about the matter (Chart CIV). With remarkable consistency within each party, the intensely involved "pull" their own candidate and "push" the opponent more than the less involved. (Incidentally, it is probably not too much to suggest that this "pull" and "push" are equivalent to the psychological defense mechanisms of generalization and exclusion.)

For example, when objectively they are *not* in agreement with their own party, *strong* Republicans and Democrats perceive their candidate's stand on the issues as more in harmony with their own stand than do weak Republicans and Democrats in the same situation. But, by no means is this a general tendency to see everyone in agreement with themselves. When they objectively disagree with the *opposition* candidate, the strong partisans are quickest to perceive that disagreement. The stronger the partisanship, the *greater* the (mis)perception of agreement with one's own side and the *less* the (mis)perception of agreement with the opposition. Presumably, misperception makes for partisanship, and the reverse. Thus, the people strongest for a candidate—the ones most interested in and active for his election, the ones who make up the core of the party support—are the ones who take the least equivocal position on what their party stands for. And, at the same time, those who favor the party position as they see it are more likely to support the candidate strongly.

In the course of the campaign, then, strength of party support influences the perception of political issues. The more intensely one holds a vote position, the more likely he is to see the political environment as favorable to himself, as conforming to his own beliefs. He is less likely to perceive uncongenial and contradictory events or points of view and hence presumably less likely to revise his own original position. In this manner perception can play a major role in the spiraling effect of political reinforcement.

CHART CIV

The Stronger the Political Affiliation, the Greater the Tendency To Perceive Political Issues Favorably to One's Self*

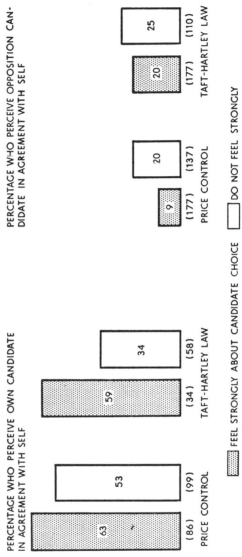

AMONG THOSE OBJECTIVELY IN DISAGREEMENT WITH THE GIVEN CANDIDATE

PERCENTAGE WHO PERCEIVE OPPOSITION CAN-
DIDATE IN AGREEMENT WITH SELF

25 (110)   TAFT-HARTLEY LAW
20 (177)

20 (137)   PRICE CONTROL
9   (177)

PERCENTAGE WHO PERCEIVE OWN CANDIDATE
IN AGREEMENT WITH SELF

34 (58)   TAFT-HARTLEY LAW
59 (34)

53 (99)   PRICE CONTROL
63 (86)

[shaded] FEEL STRONGLY ABOUT CANDIDATE CHOICE   [white] DO NOT FEEL STRONGLY

* Analogous results are obtained for the housing and "firmer with Russia" issues. This same tendency appears in the case of perception of the support given the candidates by various socioeconomic and ethnic groups. In almost every case strong partisans "pull" approved groups more than weak partisans.

Necessarily, such partisanly motivated perception increases the recognized or believed differences between the parties. Strong Republicans and Democrats are farther apart in perception of political issues than weak Republicans and Democrats; they disagree more sharply in their perception of campaign events. Among the strongly partisan, then, the process of perception operates to make the opponent into more of an "enemy" and thus to magnify the potential for political cleavage.

But all this should not be taken to exaggerate the effect of perception (or issues). Regardless of their perception of the issues, important social groups still follow their own voting tradition.[5] An index of agreement was constructed between the position of each respondent and the position he perceived each candidate to be taking. Here again Catholics vote more strongly Democratic regardless of the degree of their ideological agreement with Truman or Dewey (Chart CV). But why does agreement with Dewey make more difference for Catholics, and agreement with Truman for Protestants?

Now when these two indexes of agreement are combined into one, this curious effect of perceived agreement sharpens. If Protestants and Catholics agree with "their own group's" candidate and disagree with the opponent, then the vote is overwhelmingly for one's own candidate; and, if the situation is reversed, so is the vote—though not so strongly (see Chart CVI). But what of those people who agree with both candidates, as perceived, or with neither? The answer is that voters who *disagree* with both candidates' stands on the issues, as they perceive them, end by supporting their group's "proper" candidate (more strongly than those who agree with both). If they disagree with both candidates, they seem to have no alternative. So they remain loyal, "at home." If they *agree* with both, however, they are more likely to try the other side. When the grass is green in *both* yards, it seems a little greener in the other fellow's!

5. Nor was perception related to *changes* in voting. We hypothesized that voters might maintain stability by means of misperception, but there were no differences in the data on voting changes subsequent to the asking of perception questions. If perception questions had been repeated, then one would expect perception to adjust to vote more often than the reverse.

CHART CV

Social Differences in Voting Remain Regardless of Perceived Agreement with Candidates

PERCENTAGE REPUBLICAN OF TWO-PARTY VOTE

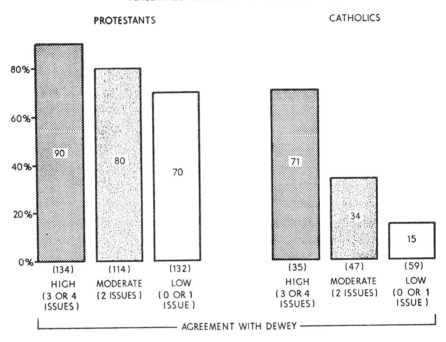

PROTESTANTS — CATHOLICS

AGREEMENT WITH DEWEY

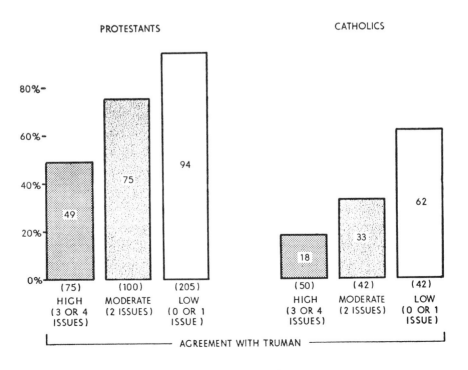

PROTESTANTS — CATHOLICS

AGREEMENT WITH TRUMAN

ACCURACY OF PERCEPTION

The question of "correct" and "incorrect" perception has been implicit in our discussion thus far, since differentiation in perception requires a degree of misperception on the part of some perceivers (assuming a definition of objective reality). But the question has not been given explicit consideration. Without retracing our steps, let us now summarize from this vantage point.

Analysis of the perception that occurs during a presidential campaign requires a definition of what is "correct" perception. In the case of political issues, perceiving the candidates' stands as they

CHART CVI

PROTESTANTS AND CATHOLICS

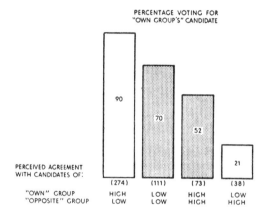

PERCENTAGE VOTING FOR
"OWN GROUP'S" CANDIDATE

PERCEIVED AGREEMENT WITH CANDIDATES OF:	90	70	52	21
	(274)	(111)	(73)	(38)
"OWN" GROUP	HIGH	LOW	HIGH	LOW
"OPPOSITE" GROUP	LOW	LOW	HIGH	HIGH

predominantly appear in the campaign speeches should serve. Since some stands are ambiguous, or at least contain an element of propagandistic vagueness, we use here two stands of Truman and Dewey that are reasonably straightforward and clear—those on the Taft-Hartley Law (with Truman against and Dewey for) and on price control (with Truman for and Dewey against). The index of correct perception on the issues is based upon the number of correct responses given out of the four possible.

In the first place, the amount of correct perception in the community is limited. Only 16 per cent of the respondents know the correct stands of both candidates on both issues, and another 21 per cent know them on three of the four. Over a third of the respondents know only one stand correctly or none at all. And these are crucial issues in the campaign, much discussed in the communication media. Thus, a good deal less than half the political perception in the community is reasonably accurate, by such definitions.[6]

CHART CVII

Several Characteristics Are Associated with Accurate
Perception of the Candidates' Stands on Issues*

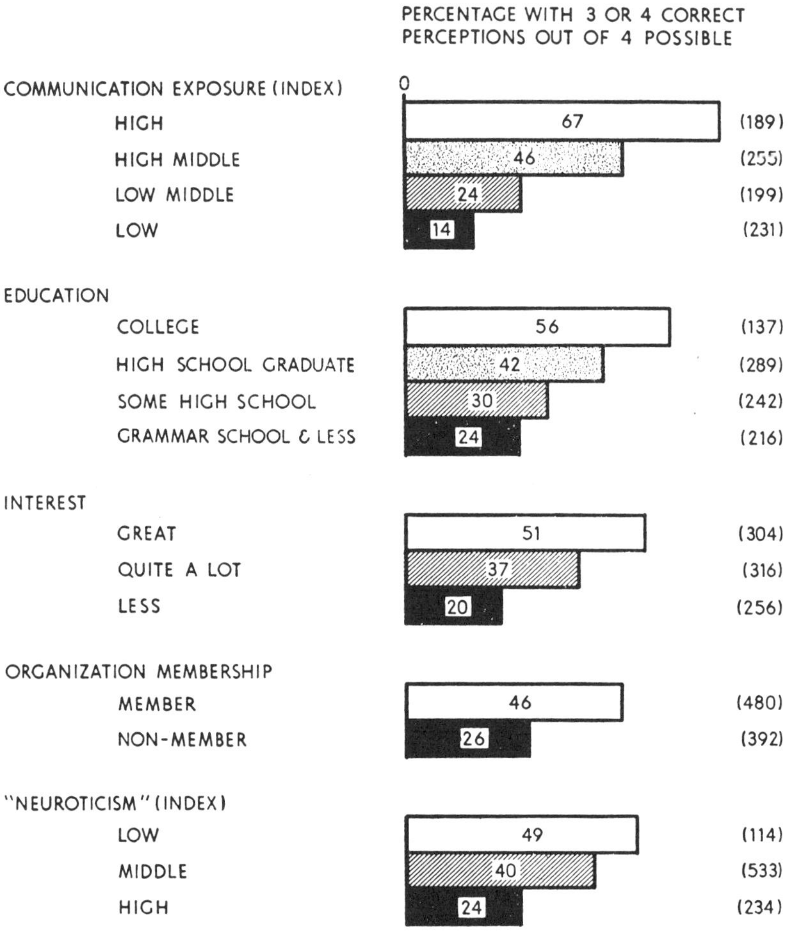

PERCENTAGE WITH 3 OR 4 CORRECT
PERCEPTIONS OUT OF 4 POSSIBLE

COMMUNICATION EXPOSURE (INDEX)

HIGH	67	(189)
HIGH MIDDLE	46	(255)
LOW MIDDLE	24	(199)
LOW	14	(231)

EDUCATION

COLLEGE	56	(137)
HIGH SCHOOL GRADUATE	42	(289)
SOME HIGH SCHOOL	30	(242)
GRAMMAR SCHOOL & LESS	24	(216)

INTEREST

GREAT	51	(304)
QUITE A LOT	37	(316)
LESS	20	(256)

ORGANIZATION MEMBERSHIP

MEMBER	46	(480)
NON-MEMBER	26	(392)

"NEUROTICISM" (INDEX)

LOW	49	(114)
MIDDLE	40	(533)
HIGH	24	(234)

* Each of these characteristics works independently of the others.

But any such arbitrary measure is less useful for its absolute than for its relative value. Who are the people more and less likely

6. To repeat: these figures apply to the early campaign period of August. Similar data for October, at the end of the campaign, would almost certainly raise these estimates.

to perceive political issues correctly? For example, what of attention to the campaign in the press and radio? Do the people who read and listen about politics more than others perceive more correctly, or does selective perception get in the way? It seems that communication exposure clarifies perception probably more than any other factor (Chart CVII). This is an important consideration: the more reading and listening people do on campaign matters, the more

CHART CVIII

PERCENTAGE WITH 3 OR 4 PERCEPTIONS CORRECT

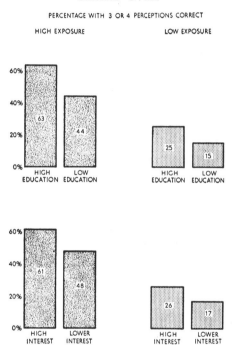

likely they are to come to recognize the positions the candidates take on major issues. It is as though the weight of the media is sufficient to "impose" a certain amount of correct perception, regardless of the barrier presented by the voter's party preference (and despite the fact that those who do most of the reading and listening also feel most strongly for their candidate and are hence more amenable to selective perception). The more that people are *exposed* to political material, the more gets through.

Other characteristics also make for accurate perception. The intellectual training received in the classroom enables the voter to make clearer discriminations in the political arena. And, despite greater affect toward campaign affairs, the interested people manage to maintain a clearer view of the issues (see Chart CVIII). In addition, accuracy of perception is a function of cross-pressures. Voters cross-pressured on class and religion are less accurate than those not so cross-pressured (34 per cent high to 41 per cent); and voters cross-pressured (inconsistent) on price control and Taft-Hartley are less accurate than those not so cross-pressured (42 to 65 per cent). But, of all these factors, the strongest is communication exposure. It is more effectively related to accurate perception of where the candidates stand than either education or interest. Reading and listening must make a difference.

INFERENCES: PSYCHOLOGICAL AND POLITICAL

What are the implications of this perceptual situation? Broadly speaking, there are two sets of conclusions which can be drawn.

The first deals with the psychology of political perception. For perceptual selection must serve a definite psychological function for the individual voter. As in other spheres of activity, so in the political: one function must be to avoid potential stress. The voter must do this, even though unconsciously, by using his perceptual opportunities as a defense or protection against the complexities, contradictions, and problems of the campaign. Indeed, the extent and nature of misperception suggests that the voter may even be aware of the attitudinal cross-pressures to which the campaign subjects him and from which he gains escape through perceptual processes. For the greater his affect toward the election (in terms of strength of feeling toward the candidates), the greater the degree of psychic protection. The voter tends to oversee or to invent what is favorable to himself and to distort or to deny much of what is unfavorable. This must leave him fewer internal conflicts to resolve—with, so to speak, a favorable balance of perception. In any event, the voters manage to use the materials of politics, even of a presidential campaign, for their own psychological protection—for the avoidance of some inconsistencies in their beliefs that otherwise would be manifest.

Then there are certain political implications of the patterning of perception. First, there are in a sense two political campaigns. One is the objective campaign that is carried on in the "real" world, and the other is the campaign that exists in the voter's mind, that is, the "real" campaign as perceived. There is no one-to-one correspondence between them. Given the chance, some voters transform the objective campaign into a subjective one more satisfying to them. The campaign waged by the candidates—even when deliberately unambiguous—is not the one perceived by all the voters, but this does not make it any less "real" for the voters themselves. "If men define situations as real, they are real in their consequences."

Second, there is the meaning of perception for rational political judgment. Here its role must make the voter's political judgment *seem* more rational to him because it maximizes agreement with his own side and maximizes disagreement with the opposition. In other words, perception often operates to make the differences between the parties *appear* greater than they actually may be—and thus to make the voter's decision *appear* more rational (in one sense) than it actually is. In this way, paradoxical though it may seem, misperception contributes to a seeming "rationality" in politics.

Third, perception must reduce or even eliminate certain political cross-pressures before they come to the level of visibility—before they start pressing. If the voter finds himself holding opinions championed by opposing parties, it has been thought that he could do one of two things: remain in this "inconsistent" position (which is, of course, altogether legtimate) or remove the "inconsistency" by changing one opinion to fit the other. But he has another out: he can perceptually select, out of the somewhat ambiguous propaganda of the campaign, those political cues which remove the problem by defining it away. He can "see" that the candidates do not disagree on the issue at hand or that his candidate really agrees with him or that the opponent really disagrees or that he cannot tell where his candidate stands. Just as the process may reduce the voter's level of psychological tension, so may it reduce his political inconsistency.

Finally, this serves to introduce the major political implications of our perceptual material—its implications for the problem of cleavage and consensus in the democratic community. In an earlier section we dealt with this problem in the *evaluation* of political affairs; now we meet it in perception. The over-all effect of political perception is to increase the amount of political consensus *within* the parties and to increase the amount of political cleavage *between* the parties—once again, homogeneity within and polarization between. Both are achieved by something like the mechanisms of generalization, exclusion, and denial—through the perceptual enlargement of the area of agreement with one's own candidate (generalization); through the misperceived rejection of the opponent's position (exclusion); and through the professed lack of knowledge of one's candidate's stand where disagreement is likely (denial).

Let us close this chapter by comparing it briefly with the chapter on the perception of groups. In each case the perceptions are likely to help voters to maintain their own position, without being too much concerned by contradiction. In the social case it is harmony with people; in the present case it is a harmony with ideas. With groups the matter was fairly simple: each respondent is surrounded by a primary group in which the large majority thinks like himself. No wonder, then, that he infers that "everyone" will vote as he does. (Of course, this tendency is tempered by a strong sense of reality; misperception is only superimposed upon it.) In the case of the candidates' stand, the voter gets his information from reading, listening, and discussion. This is subject to *selective* gathering of information, forgetting of disturbing elements, reinterpretation of what the candidate "really" means—all mechanisms familiar in social psychology. Probably, even, social selection reinforces the selective collection of information, as a result of discussion between like-minded people.

In a way, both phenomena can be subsumed under one heading. Voters cannot have contact with the whole world of people and ideas; they must *sample* them. And the sampling is biased. People pick the people and the ideas to suit their personal equilibrium and then project that sample upon the universe. First, selective perception, then misperception, then the strengthening of opinion, and then, in turn, more selective perception. Fortunately, there are realities, competing concerns, and corrosion of existing beliefs that, under normal circumstances, do not permit this process to get far out of bounds.

In sum, then, the actual operation of political perception during a presidential campaign decreases tension in the individual and increases tension in the community—one might almost say, *by* increasing tension in the community. The voters, each in the solitude of his own mind, wish to see the campaign in a favorable way, and they use their perception of where the candidates stand to this end. "Democracy in its original form never seriously faced the problem which arises because the pictures inside people's heads do not automatically correspond with the world outside."[7]

SUMMARY

Perception and Voting

120. Party preference does not particularly affect the voter's perception of where the candidates stand on the issues.

121. The less ambiguous the objective situation, the more agreement in perception between the two sides.

122. Partisans tend to perceive the candidate's stand on the issues as favorable to their own stand. (1) They perceive their candidate's stand as similar to their own and the opponent's stand as dissimilar. (2) They tend *not* to perceive differences with their own candidate or similarities to the opposition candidate.

123. Voters who feel strongly about their choice are more likely to misperceive the candidates' stands on the issues as favorable to their own positions.

124. Social differences in voting are largely maintained regardless of perceived agreement with the candidates.

125. Voters who disagree with both candidates' stands, as perceived, support their own candidate more strongly than those who agree with both.

Accuracy of Perception

126. Only about one-third of the voters are highly accurate in their perception of where the candidates stand on the issues.

127. Accuracy of perception is affected by communication exposure, education, interest, and cross-pressures—with communication exposure probably the strongest influence.

7. Walter Lippmann, *Public Opinion*, p. 21.

11 POLITICAL PROCESSES

The Role of the Mass Media[1]

That communication is characteristic of a democracy both its proponents and its opponents agree. The latter deprecate democracy as a futile "debating society" in which policy and action are constantly obstructed by "mere talk." The advocates give a central place in their theory to the desirability and even the necessity of communication.

As society has outgrown the town meeting, questions have arisen as to how far democratic communication is possible in a mass society. In our society, extension of the political debate far beyond the limits of face-to-face contact is made possible by the existence of the mass media. Newspapers, magazines, radio, and now television are essential for the process of "making the sense of the meeting" when the meeting involves more than fifty million participants.

Seen in this perspective, the familiar question as to whether the mass media "influence" elections is, on the surface, an absurd question. In the first place, it is dubious whether any decisions at all would be possible without some mass device for enabling the leaders to present their proposals to the people. Second, typical debates about the role of the media too often imply a simple, direct "influence"--like a hypodermic stimulus on an inert subject—and that is a naïve formulation of the political effects of mass communications. Third, another common notion—that any influence of the media is somehow suspect, as if "interfering" with the rational deliberations of the voters—implies an autonomously operating electorate. Such an image is also unrealistic.

1. For a more extensive report on this subject see the Baxter dissertation mentioned in chap. 6.

"The electorate cannot be regarded by itself, or in isolation, or as if it were a sovereign which was the beginning and the end, initiating everything and concluding everything. It is a part of a system of discussion."[2] This "system-of-discussion" analogy provides us with a good place to begin our analysis of the mass media in the campaign. For there is a system and it involves the national parties and their candidates to supply the content, the media to transmit it, and the electorate to consume it. We take up each in turn.

WHAT THE CANDIDATES DID

Democratic theorists have always insisted on the need for public debate among political leaders:

> The bystander's only recourse is to insist upon debate. He will not be able, we may assume, to judge the merits of the arguments. But if he does insist upon full freedom of discussion, the advocates are very likely to expose one another. Open debate may lead to no conclusion and throw no light whatever on the problem or its answer, but it will tend to betray the partisan and the advocate. And if it has identified them for the true public, debate will have served its main purpose.[3]

To what extent do the parties engage in genuine discussion and debate of relevant public affairs during a campaign when the whole nation can listen in?

In 1948 the official platforms of the two parties showed more similarities than genuine divergences. The Republicans and Democrats essentially agreed in their platform planks on such subjects as foreign policy, civil rights, communism, housing, veterans, agriculture, and resources. Only on our two major issues was there disagreement: on inflation and price controls, where each party blamed the other for high prices; and on labor, where the Democrats came out for repeal of the Taft-Hartley Law and the Republicans for "a sensible reform of the labor law." Otherwise, it would take close comparative reading for Elmirans to know from the platforms just how the parties differed on major issues.

Actually, American parties put the main burden of argument on their candidates. To what extent did the candidates themselves debate the campaign issues? The forty major speeches made by

2. Ernest Barker, *Reflections on Government*, p. 41.
3. Walter Lippmann, *The Phantom Public*, pp. 113–14.

the two candidates in September and October—seventeen by
Dewey and twenty-three by Truman—covered a wide range of
topics, but there was by no means equivalent emphasis on them
(Chart CIX).

CHART CIX

THE CANDIDATES DID NOT EMPHASIZE THE SAME TOPICS
IN THEIR RADIO SPEECHES**

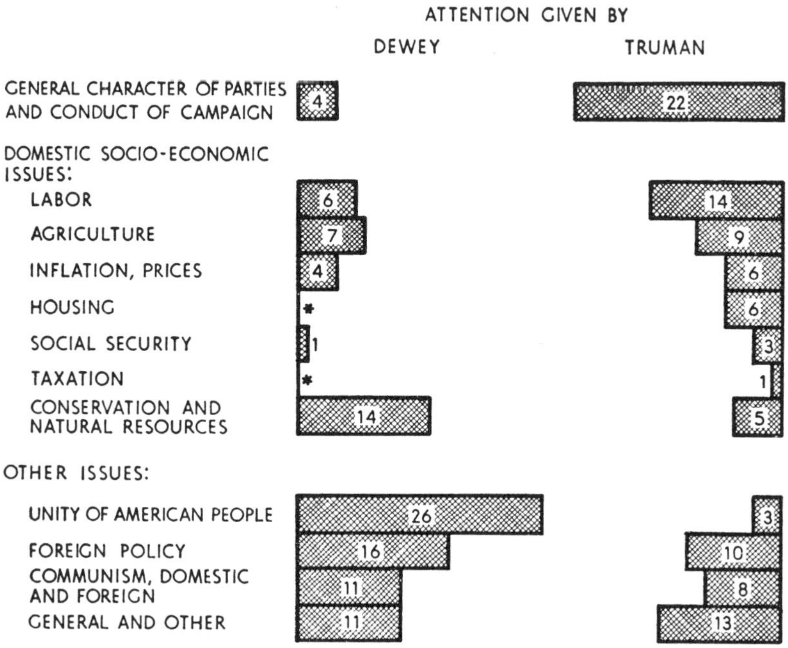

ATTENTION GIVEN BY

DEWEY   TRUMAN

GENERAL CHARACTER OF PARTIES   4   22
AND CONDUCT OF CAMPAIGN

DOMESTIC SOCIO-ECONOMIC
ISSUES:
    LABOR   6   14
    AGRICULTURE   7   9
    INFLATION, PRICES   4   6
    HOUSING   *   6
    SOCIAL SECURITY   1   3
    TAXATION   *   1
    CONSERVATION AND   14   5
    NATURAL RESOURCES

OTHER ISSUES:

    UNITY OF AMERICAN PEOPLE   26   3
    FOREIGN POLICY   16   10
    COMMUNISM, DOMESTIC   11   8
    AND FOREIGN
    GENERAL AND OTHER   11   13

* Less than 1%.
** The speeches were analyzed from text versions appearing in the *New York Times*. Measurements are
in column inches but they can be considered as measures of radio time also.

The opposing candidates tended to "talk past each other,"
almost as though they were participating in two different elections.
In that respect, at least, there was little meeting of the minds or
joining of the issues between Dewey and Truman on some major
topics. Each candidate stressed the matters considered most strategic
and effective in his own propaganda. While Dewey was talking
about unity, foreign affairs, and the Communists (i.e., Style issues),
Truman was talking about the differing character of the Republican

and Democratic parties on socioeconomic matters (i.e., Position issues). Truman devoted almost 80 per cent of his speeches to the discussion of current domestic issues facing the country—labor, price control, farm policy, housing, conservation, social security, taxes, and general party philosophies on such matters (e.g., the New Deal)—whereas Dewey gave less than half his attention to them, and then largely to less controversial matters like conservation. Dewey dwelt to an especially large extent on the noncontroversial desirability and need for "unity" and "faith" in the United States.

This analysis implies that Truman courted but Dewey avoided what might be called genuine debate of truly controversial issues. Truman, in fact, asserted that this was the case. Again and again he claimed the Republicans would not state their position or their differences with him, and a simple index of the degree of genuine debate of this kind bears him out. In his speeches Truman treated the issues or topics of Chart CIX a total of ninety-six times in some substance. In seventy-six of these he explicitly *compared* the party positions, in this sense "debating" the issues in 79 per cent of the instances. For Dewey the corresponding proportion was 30 per cent (twenty-two out of seventy-four). If debate is thus defined as presenting the voters with an explicit choice between differing positions on controversial questions, Dewey generally failed to debate. What Dewey in contrast to Truman was doing can be illustrated as follows:

Dewey

The Republican party is engaged in this campaign for the express purpose of bringing our people closer together so that they can realize their great future and find peace with honor in the world [Des Moines, September 20].

This great campaign to strengthen and unite our country . . . has meaning far beyond our own shores. . . . We will be united. We shall find unity without uniformity [Boston, October 28].

Truman

Of all the fake campaigns, this is tops so far as the Republican candidate is concerned. He has been following me and making speeches about home, mother, unity, and efficiency. He won't talk issues [St. Louis, October 30].

They are afraid to go before the American people on the merits of the policies they believe in. So they try to distract the people's attention with false issues [Boston, October 27].

In short, Truman stressed Position issues of contemporary cleavage; Dewey, Style issues of consensus. Each was no doubt taking what he considered the best political tack. Truman felt his best position was that based on the New Deal–Fair Deal. Dewey seemed to be sure of victory at the time, and he apparently saw no sense either in possibly offending some interest group or in prematurely committing himself to a clear position when he could preserve freedom of action by use of an ambiguous one. Dewey spoke as a "certain winner" who would shortly have to lead a Congress and a nation through difficult problems on which agreement would be needed. Thus the 1948 Dewey campaign may have provided a taste of what "debate" is like in an era when winners are assured and when there is no effective competition and presumably no likely alternative (as, for example, in 1924). Under such conditions, preaching of conciliation may typically prevail over discussion of controversial problems.

WHAT THE LOCAL NEWSPAPERS DID

That was how the discussion was originated by the national parties and leaders and reflected in the national media (primarily the radio). Was something further added by the media at the *local* level or was the national party propaganda simply passed along?

In the local press, newspaper stories on *official* party speeches, meetings, and statements were more frequent and more prominent than the columns, editorials, and occasional news stories originating from nonparty sources; in the sample of items presented for the respondents' recognition in late October, this ratio was about three to one. All the major items (speeches) on the radio were official. Only in the magazines did privately originated items prevail, and they were few. The situation is probably different in the larger cities, but in a small community like Elmira most of the campaign material that comes to people's attention through the mass media derives directly from the official political parties.

However, there is some interpretation added by the press, and, more important, there has to be a considerable amount of *selection and deletion* to meet space limits. Moreover, that the media are primarily transmitting agents, from the parties to the voters, does not mean that they are neutral or inert in such selection. These strategic channels of discussion are largely owned and operated by men closely allied with one of the contending interests in contemporary disputes, namely, business and the business-professional classes. Such ties are not easily evaded in *any* democracy; for example, in state-organized communications systems (like the British Broadcasting Corporation) there is the corresponding problem of safeguarding channels of communication from influence by the incumbent administration. The way in which political information is

CHART CX

PERCENTAGE PRO-DEWEY OF TWO-PARTY ITEMS*

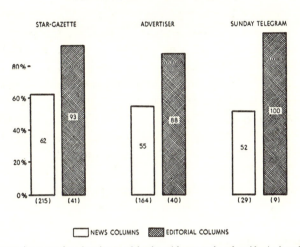

STAR-GAZETTE   ADVERTISER   SUNDAY TELEGRAM

☐ NEWS COLUMNS   ▨ EDITORIAL COLUMNS

* Two-party items are those favoring or originating with one or the other side. An item is a separate news story, article, editorial, column, or cartoon. Note that the *Sunday Telegram* mostly clearly separated editorial position from news selection. The 40 per cent of total items that were nonpartisan are omitted from this chart.

transmitted by agents not neutral to that information presents a major problem to contemporary democracies.

Let us look at its severity in one instance where it might have been great—in the Republican press of a Republican town in what was for the American press generally a "Republican year." Elmira's three newspapers, all published by Frank Gannett, were Republican, and they showed it. In a year when (by customary standards of what constitutes "news") Truman was making at least as much news as his opponent, Elmiran readers had almost a two-to-one better chance to find material favorable to Dewey.

Actually, however, the *news* columns were not particularly biased;

about 40 per cent of the two-party items favored Truman. The partisanship of the newspapers was confined largely to where most newspapermen believe it belongs—on the editorial page and in the signed columns (see Chart CX). Moreover, in the paper there was much nonpartisan reporting and comment. About 40 per cent of the total number of items did not support either side, being accounts of campaign activities, round-up articles by the press services, etc.

WHAT THE ELECTORATE DID

But our main concern is with the electorate itself. How many individuals pay direct attention to the campaign via the mass media? Two answers can be given to this question. If the people themselves define what constitutes paying attention, the claims are modest. In June only 36 per cent and in October 38 per cent claimed to be paying a "great deal of attention to news about the election."

So much for subjective claims of attention; how about somewhat more objective checkups on the matter? Here we find an unexpected result. Far greater numbers, usually more than half, gave some evidence of familiarity with campaign materials. More people showed signs of exposure than claimed to be paying "attention." For example, about a fifth followed the major conventions "very closely" (25 per cent for the Republican, 16 per cent for the Democratic, and 7 per cent for the Progressive), and another two-fifths "fairly closely" (43, 38, and 13 per cent, respectively). When people were asked if they could "remember the last two items (about the election) you read in the newspaper," 50 per cent could name at least one specifically; 55 and 23 per cent could name analogous items on the radio and in magazines; and fully 74 per cent recalled a reasonably specific item from at least one of the three media. When check lists of current news items from these media were shown the voters, the number who "remembered reading about or listening to" the items rose to 67 per cent for newspapers and 77 per cent for any of the three media. Minimum exposure was widely dispersed.

Yet despite this extended degree of "campaign exposure," which is in any case a matter of arbitrary definition, much campaign material "piles up" or overlaps among the few who are interested much more than the minimum. Those who scored high in communication exposure in one connection were more likely to score high in another (Chart CXI). For example, (a) there was an overlap through *time:* people who paid more attention to campaign matters in June were also paying more in October; (b) there was an overlap by *channel:* people who read more campaign material in the newspaper also read more in magazines and listened to more over the radio; and (c) there was an overlap in *events:* people who followed the Republican convention more closely also gave more attention to the Democratic convention. In fact, every one of fifteen cross-tabulations possible in our data between paired measures of political exposure to the mass media was positive. In no case is there a reversal or even the absence of a relationship. Beyond minimum exposure levels, there is a consistent and concentrated audience rather than a random and dispersed one.

This consistent and concentrated exposure is conditioned by many personal and social characteristics—membership in community organizations, education, class, sex, and (crudely) freedom from certain personality disorders. In each case there is a clear relationship to media exposure (Table 13, in which political interest is controlled, since exposure is highly correlated with it). Inferentially, the major determinants of media exposure to political materials appear to be (a) cultural and social awareness as well as civic participation, as represented in our data by organization membership; (b) habituation to dealing with abstractions and related communication skills, as represented by formal education; (c) subjective feeling of investment in social and political power, as represented by socioeconomic status; (d) socially sanctioned responsibility for political affairs, as represented by sex; and (e) freedom from personal maladjustment that allows the individual to focus on public affairs in addition to private concerns, as represented by a (primitive) index of certain kinds of neuroticism. The "joiners," the better-educated, the better-off, the men, the less troubled—these are the people who pay most attention to the political campaign as presented through newspaper, magazines, and radio.

Actually, a large part of the impact of these characteristics upon political exposure might be attributed to the general factor of social pressure. The social contacts in their primary groups channel the better-educated and the better-off toward the political con-

CHART CXI

There Is Considerable Concentration among Various Types
of Communication Exposure to the Campaign*

(A) THROUGH TIME

ATTENTION: JUNE

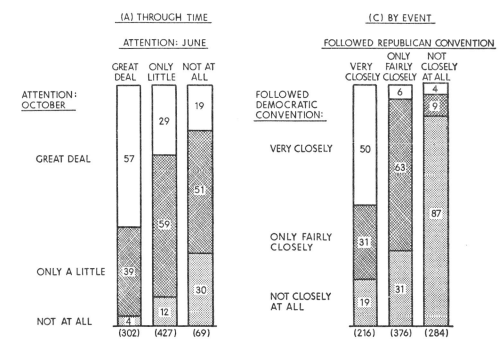

(C) BY EVENT

FOLLOWED REPUBLICAN CONVENTION

(B) BY CHANNEL

PERCENTAGE RECALLING ONE OR MORE ITEMS:

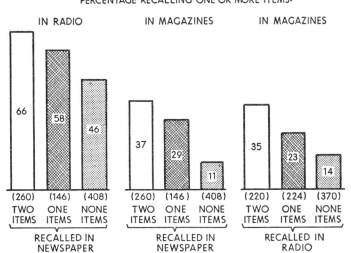

* There is also concentration between media exposure and political discussion. Those "often" discussing politics were 33 per cent
of those high on the index of communication exposure, and only 11 per cent of those middle or low. The heavy overlap in convention
listening may be an interviewing artifact to some extent, since the questions were asked one after the other and since the answer t
the first may have served as a halo for the second.

tent of the media; their fellows expect it of each other, and they have learned to expect it of themselves. Organization members are responding in part to this same sort of stimulation, produced by the very multiplicity of contacts. Men are traditionally and historically expected to know about politics. (Even the so-called "neuroticism"

TABLE 13

WITH INTEREST CONTROLLED,* CERTAIN PERSONAL CHARAC-
TERISTICS ARE RELATED TO THE AMOUNT OF POLITICAL
EXPOSURE TO THE MASS MEDIA

CHARACTERISTICS	PERCENTAGE WITH HIGH OR HIGH-MIDDLE EXPOSURE (ON INDEX)† LEVEL OF INTEREST		
	Great Deal	Quite a Lot	Not Much at All
a) *Organization membership:*			
Belongs to two or more.....	82 (103)	68 (87)	39 (64)
Belongs to one............	72 (71)	57 (74)	34 (68)
Belongs to none...........	62 (100)	47 (112)	24 (126)
b) *Education:*			
College..................	88 (58)	62 (37)	48 (25)
High school..............	71 (166)	60 (171)	30 (152)
Grammar school and less....	56 (48)	45 (62)	25 (81)
c) *Socioeconomic status:*			
Higher..................	79 (167)	63 (120)	39 (105)
Lower...................	60 (108)	52 (153)	25 (154)
d) *Sex:*			
Men....................	72 (122)	60 (124)	38 (110)
Women..................	71 (153)	54 (149)	25 (149)
e) *Neuroticism (index):*			
Low....................	77 (112)	64 (106)	30 (100)
High...................	67 (149)	50 (147)	30 (138)

* Since interest in politics is a mediating variable between these independent sources and the dependent phenomenon of media exposure, controlling interest works against the relationships. Even so, they are clear. Interest itself, of course, correlates highly with exposure: 72–56–31 per cent high or high-middle on the index for those high, moderate, and low in interest respectively.

† The index of communications exposure used in this chapter is made up of two questions: one asking for free-answer recall of recent items seen or heard in the media, the other asking about recognition of sample items presented in a check list. The measure was made in October but is used as an indicator of exposure at any time in the pre-election period (see Appendix B).

index is, among other things, a measure of social rapport, confidence, and trust.) Thus a given citizen's amount of attention to political materials in the mass media must derive in good measure from the amount of stimulation exercised upon him by the social environment—especially by his internalized expectations of how he should behave in this respect, built up by the groups in which he lives.

Such people actively go after political content. But there is another type to whom political content "just comes." They "run across" political content in the media rather than seek it out. For people who pay *general,* nonpolitical attention to newspapers, radios, and magazines tend to see and hear more *political* material, along with everything else (Chart CXII). Thus the very ac-

CHART CXII

THE MORE ATTENTION TO THE MASS MEDIA IN GENERAL, THE MORE
EXPOSURE TO POLITICAL MATERIALS IN PARTICULAR*

PERCENTAGE RECALLING ONE OR MORE POLITICAL
ITEMS IN THE MEDIUM

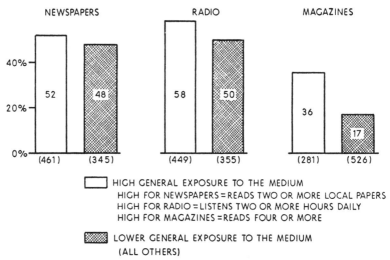

HIGH GENERAL EXPOSURE TO THE MEDIUM
HIGH FOR NEWSPAPERS = READS TWO OR MORE LOCAL PAPERS
HIGH FOR RADIO = LISTENS TWO OR MORE HOURS DAILY
HIGH FOR MAGAZINES = READS FOUR OR MORE

LOWER GENERAL EXPOSURE TO THE MEDIUM
(ALL OTHERS)

* This result holds with an interest control. The questions on general exposure were asked in June.

cessibility of the medium "rubs off" a certain amount of political exposure. It would take almost deliberate action to keep from some exposure to politics under such conditions.

With the appealing devices of mass communications and their widespread use as habit, duty, or pastime, people are exposed to miscellaneous information about a far greater range of things than those in which they are genuinely interested. But, at the same time, they really follow only the few topics that genuinely concern them. On any single subject many "hear" but few "listen." Together, the two types of attention merge in varying degrees and mixtures to make up the audience of the modern mass media on any topic. While only a minority is interested, the majority is accessible. So, campaign exposure seems to be of two different kinds: (1) the heavy exposure of the few really "attending" to the campaign and (2) the moderate exposure of the many "also present."

Now the latter kind of exposure must depend on the sheer volume of campaign material accessible in the media. It is a credit to the agencies of communication (media and parties) that far more Americans participate in politics than are really interested. But there is a limit—reached fairly soon—to what availability without interest can do. Beyond that, only interest based on enduring social involvements can go. The most likely sources of heavy as opposed to superficial communication exposure are in the main independent of and prior to the communications themselves. If minimum or superficial exposure can be "manipulated" externally by such matters as the volume and the accessibility of media materials, the conditions for more concentrated or serious attention lie in the society and individuals themselves.

All this relates to an old argument in connection with communication. There are those who think it "does no good" to make information widely accessible in which people are not basically interested. If this view prevailed, however, perhaps only a minority of Americans would vote, and even fewer would know, even rudimentarily, what they were voting for. On the other hand, there are those who hold the equally unrealistic view that if only Americans could be sufficiently flooded with mass-media propaganda, good citizenship could be "sold" like toothpaste. These views are neither right nor wrong; the effective audience for politics today is a mixture of the minority who have reasons for learning about current political events and the majority who do not but who do learn something—"because it's there."[4]

4. As to *what* people read and listen to, there is a slight tendency for people to see and hear their own side. But this was not particularly strong in Elmira, and each group of partisans paid considerable attention to the opposition. And despite the disproportion in availability, this was about the same for Republicans and Democrats:

READ OR HEARD (OF SAMPLE LIST)	PER CENT	
	Republicans	Democrats
More items favorable to Dewey.	54	43
More items favorable to Truman	46	57
Total no. of items.......	215	94

THE EFFECTS OF POLITICAL EXPOSURE

What were the effects of the candidates' speeches and the media's transmission upon the electorate? Their effect upon the actual distribution of the vote will be taken up in the following chapter on changes in attitudes during the campaign. Here we shall deal with two preliminary effects—upon the intensity of political feelings and upon information about the election.[5]

Effects upon Political Intensity

The more that people read about and listen to the campaign on the mass media, the more interested they become in the election and the more strongly they come to feel about their candidate (Chart CXIII). In every comparison between those higher and lower in media exposure, interest and intensity increase from August to October.

Here is a finding that typifies the spiral effect of mutually influencing variables in complex human situations. "The appetite grows by what it feeds on." Communication exposure affects some of the factors that affect it. Exposure to a campaign obviously cannot lead a person to go back and get a better education so that he can listen more attentively to that campaign. In this sense, the matter is in part predetermined and the limits set. But such distant and independent conditions for attention to political news may not enter into communication behavior in direct or "raw" form. Instead, there are connecting or mediating variables of a more proximate sort, such as the psychological conditions we call by such terms as a "sense of participation," "interest," or "partisanship."[6]

5. The effects described here hold for personal discussion as well as media exposure.

6. In addition, there is such a mutual-effect relationship between media exposure and personal discussion. The more people read politics, the more they talk politics; and, the more they talk, the more they read. For example:

	PERCENTAGE NAMING LAST PERSON WITH WHOM POLITICS DISCUSSED (OCTOBER)*	
	Higher Media Exposure	Lower Media Exposure
Had talked politics in June......	96 (190)	86 (133)
Had not......................	89 (238)	73 (226)

* This holds with an interest control.

In the same way, reading and listening lead to more of the same.

CHART CXIII

The More Media Exposure on the Campaign, the More Political Interest and Strength of Support for the Candidate

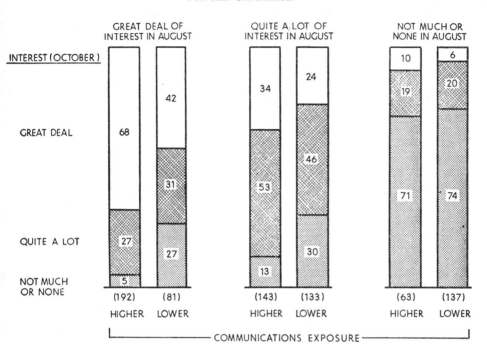

INTEREST (OCTOBER)

GREAT DEAL OF INTEREST IN AUGUST

QUITE A LOT OF INTEREST IN AUGUST

NOT MUCH OR NONE IN AUGUST

GREAT DEAL

QUITE A LOT

NOT MUCH OR NONE

COMMUNICATIONS EXPOSURE

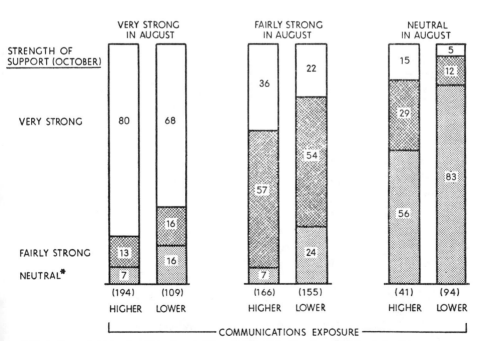

STRENGTH OF SUPPORT (OCTOBER)

VERY STRONG IN AUGUST

FAIRLY STRONG IN AUGUST

NEUTRAL IN AUGUST

VERY STRONG

FAIRLY STRONG

NEUTRAL*

COMMUNICATIONS EXPOSURE

* "Neutral" = undecided or do not intend to vote. "Very strong" = intend to vote and feel strongly for choice.

Such mediating variables are only loosely "fitted" to their more distant and more constant preconditions (like education). Not only does the greater freedom and variability of such mediating conditions increase the range of potential variation in communications exposure but it permits an interaction between the two. Mass-media exposure affects mediating variables like partisanship, interest, and discussion that in turn lead back to mass-media exposure. There is thus the potential for a spiral build-up.

But this process does not, and presumably cannot, go on indefinitely. What limits it? First, there are the basic social and psychological preconditions for communications exposure, like education, that are not subject to manipulation in or by a political campaign. Here is where the electorate "normally" starts in the spiraling development of political exposure and political interest. But those not in at the start have that much less chance to be in at the finish. To them that hath shall be given. . . . Second, there are competing demands that take over attention, especially when the political campaign lacks intensity. And, third, there is probably a built-in check of satiation—a kind of psychological regression effect whereby more and more political exposure at one point becomes too much and the more interest builds up, the harder it becomes to build it further. In these ways the spiral effect of exposure and interest on each other must be "dampened," although not without a campaign build-up of each under favorable circumstances.

As a corollary of such increases in interest and intensity, the people who do more reading and listening are less likely to change parties and more likely to vote (Chart CXIV). Media exposure gets out the vote at the same time that it solidifies preferences. It crystallizes and reinforces more than it converts.

Effect upon Political Information

Now for the second major result of media exposure: the more people read about and listen to the campaign in the mass media, the more likely they are to "know the score"—to know about the issues of the election and to perceive correctly the candidates' stands on the issues (Chart CXV). (By controlling the accuracy of perception of *groups* in June, we attempt to show the increase in information about *issues* and the perception of issues in August

CHART CXIV

THE MORE MEDIA EXPOSURE ON THE CAMPAIGN, THE LESS CHANGE IN PARTY PREFERENCE AND THE MORE TURNOUT

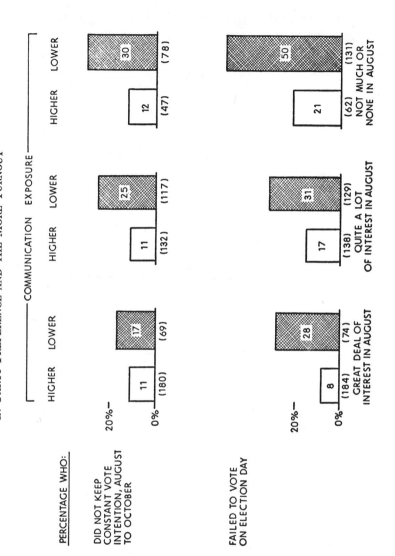

as a genuine consequence of media-exposure habits.) Obviously, a large degree of the voter's knowledge and perception of political reality—of what it is all about, what is being decided, what is at stake—must come primarily from mass-media campaigns and their extensions through personal discussion. In our data media ex-

CHART CXV

Exposure to Mass Communications Clarifies
Political Perception

PERCENTAGE WITH THREE OR MORE ACCURATE PERCEPTIONS
OF ISSUES IN AUGUST

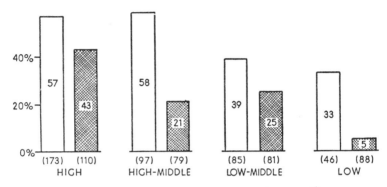

ACCURACY OF PERCEPTION OF GROUPS IN JUNE*

☐ HIGHER EXPOSURE TO CAMPAIGN

▨ LOWER EXPOSURE TO CAMPAIGN

* Perception of how poor people, rich people, Catholics, etc., will vote—asked in June. The index is a simple, cumulative count of correct perceptions.

posure always makes a difference in political information, no matter what other variables are controlled.

Now this effect serves to introduce and illustrate a phenomenon that the 1948 mass-media campaign highlighted. Each voter may have several dozen motives, needs, values, attitudes, and other dispositions which could be brought into play in the election. Yet no one would be able to act if *all* his tendencies came into play at once; much less could an electorate as a whole come to any decision if the thousands of potential cross-currents within it were operative. But, in practice, a relatively few main dispositions came to the fore in a given era—that is, are found relevant to issues in the political gateway of the time—and on them the elections of the time turn.

It is here that the content of mass communications must play a decisive role. It is the role of narrowing down, of focusing, of defining what elections mean, and thus determining on what few dispositions, out of numerous possibilities, the political outcome of the election and the political history of the era will center. How this process worked in 1948 Elmira is analyzed in a continuation of the effects of campaign communication in the following chapter.

SUMMARY

What the Candidates Did

128. The 1948 candidates emphasized different topics in their campaign speeches.

129. The expected loser (Truman) stressed explicit comparisons between the parties (cleavage), but the expected winner dealt in unifying generalities (consensus).

What the Local Newspapers Did

130. The news columns of the Elmira newspapers were not particularly one-sided, but the editorial materials were.

What the Electorate Did

131. There is a concentration of media exposure to the campaign (*a*) by time: the same people tend to read and listen both early and late in the campaign; (*b*) by channel: the same people tend to read *and* listen *and* discuss politics; and (*c*) by events: the same people tend to follow both party conventions.

132. Exposure to the mass media on the campaign is affected by such characteristics as organization membership, formal education, socioeconomic status, sex (men), and personal adjustment.

133. Exposure to *political* materials in the mass media is higher for people who give more *general* attention to the media

    and: (*a*) Hence, there appear to be two kinds of campaign exposure: a minority is attracted by active interest and the majority is exposed by mere accessibility.

134. There is some tendency to read and listen to one's own side.

Effects of Political Exposure

135. The more exposure to the campaign in the mass media, the more interested voters become and the more strongly they come to feel about their candidate.

136. The more exposure to the campaign in the mass media, the less voters change their positions and the more they carry through on election day.

137. The more exposure to the campaign in the mass media, the more correct information the voters have about the campaign and the more correct their perception of where the candidates stand on the issues.

12 POLITICAL EFFECTS
Leave-taking and Return

How does the political campaign affect the voters? The query is not, *"Does* it affect them?" but *"How?"* It is easy to acknowledge that campaign issues and arguments have some effects, but it is not easy to understand and to measure them. Present methods of social science are better adapted to the study of end products than of intervening processes. It is not hard to relate such preconditions as class position or religion or even personal associations to such end products as turnout or party preference. But it is hard to analyze and document the fine sequences of events that intervene between them. *How* is a harder question to answer than *what.*

Such effects can take place over various periods of time. There probably are occasional dramatic conversions of almost simultaneous effect, when voters are convinced by a single speech to give their vote to a candidate. On the other hand, there are influences as subtle and pervasive as the slow movement of social learning itself, as, for example, when a whole new generation of voters was "brought up" on New Deal ideas. Here we shall deal with effects in middle range, over the period of a five-month campaign. An effect of the campaign was to draw out, or revive, or activate latent predispositions. This is one thing campaigns are intended to do by the people who conduct them. How did it happen in 1948 Elmira?

We have already seen that there was a trend to Truman, particularly during the final stage of the campaign. This chapter starts with that fact and consists of three parts:

Who made up the trend?

Why were they Republican at the start of the campaign?

Why were they Democratic at the end of the campaign?

253

COMPONENTS OF THE DEMOCRATIC TREND

The trend to Truman was by no means made up of a random sample of Elmirans. It consisted mainly of two types of voters—one defined by political characteristics and the other by socioeconomic ones.

On the political side the trend was composed primarily of former Democratic voters (and secondarily of former neutrals or new voters). Just two-thirds of those who changed to Truman during the campaign and voted for him on election day were Roosevelt supporters in 1944, and nearly all the rest supported neither side in 1944. Only 5 per cent of the changers to Truman came from 1944 Republicans. In short, there was a rally into the Truman Fair Deal camp of former supporters of the Roosevelt New Deal, plus neutrals and new voters who had hesitated. Those who had voted against Roosevelt in 1944 did not respond to Truman in 1948. His support came from voters with a Democratic voting history, or at least a non-Republican history. The campaign trends, then, were less of a conversion than a rally.[1]

On the socioeconomic side the Truman rally was composed of voters with working-class or ambivalent—but not business-class—sympathies.

Indexes of Elmira data can be formed to represent a variety of concepts that occur in theories about socioeconomic "classes" (e.g., objective socioeconomic position, subjective class identification, class-related ideology of a general sort, and specific reactions to current political symbols in this sphere).[2] No matter which index is used, party preference varies with socioeconomic disposi-

---

1. This can also be shown by the trend during the campaign itself, as follows (mortality eliminated):

	PERCENTAGE DEMOCRATIC OF TWO-PARTY VOTE			TOTAL NO. OF CASES
	June	November	Gain	
1944 Democrats.........	52	63	11	200–217
1944 neither.............	27	37	10	112–183
1944 Republicans........	4	4	0	226–241

2. See Appendix B for construction of these indexes and for their combination into one measure of class predisposition. These measures are largely interchangeable, but they are quite useful in getting at the notion of inconsistency or ambivalence of tendencies. The ambivalent cases are chiefly those with two of four

tions. More than that, when these interrelated class indexes are combined, campaign trends are seen as a function not only of their joint effect but also of *inconsistency* or *ambivalence* among them. About two-thirds of the changers to Truman were either working class or ambivalent in their sympathies (see Chart CXVI). The

CHART CXVI*

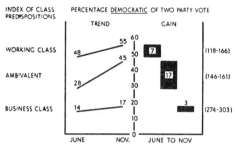

*Sample mortality is eliminated from all these charts, but the number of two-party voters does change within the constant sample.

latter were especially likely to shift to the Democratic side—more even than people with firmer attachments to the class position associated with the Democratic vote.

Now the rallying of earlier political loyalties and of class sentiments were not independent of each other. Each was, in fact, a condition for the operation of the other. Only those former Democrats with tendencies toward the working-class position in socioeconomic affairs responded to Truman's appeal during the campaign proper. And the response to his socioeconomic arguments occurred only among those who had supported or at least had not voted against the Roosevelt New Deal (Chart CXVII). Once the candidates were nominated and the campaign proper was on, the trend to the Democrats was composed of voters without Republican voting histories and without clear business-class sentiments. Almost all the Democratic increase came from the other groups, those with some already-existing affinity for the New Deal party and the socioeconomic interests it represented. Where there were

---

measures indicating positions close to the working class while the other two indicate proximity to the business position. Those with three or four of the measures of class-related dimensions falling on the one side or the other are, of course, the "working-class" or "business-class" cases. Incidentally, in this chapter, where the focus is on the trend to Truman, we use the percentage *Democratic* as the more readable figure.

business-class sympathies or previous Republican voting histories, the response was effectively blocked.

In short, the mere location of 1948 trends suggests (1) the rallying of previously demoralized *party* loyalties through (2) reacti-

CHART CXVII

THE SHIFT TO TRUMAN WAS RELATED TO CLASS DISPOSITIONS
AND POLITICAL LOYALTIES

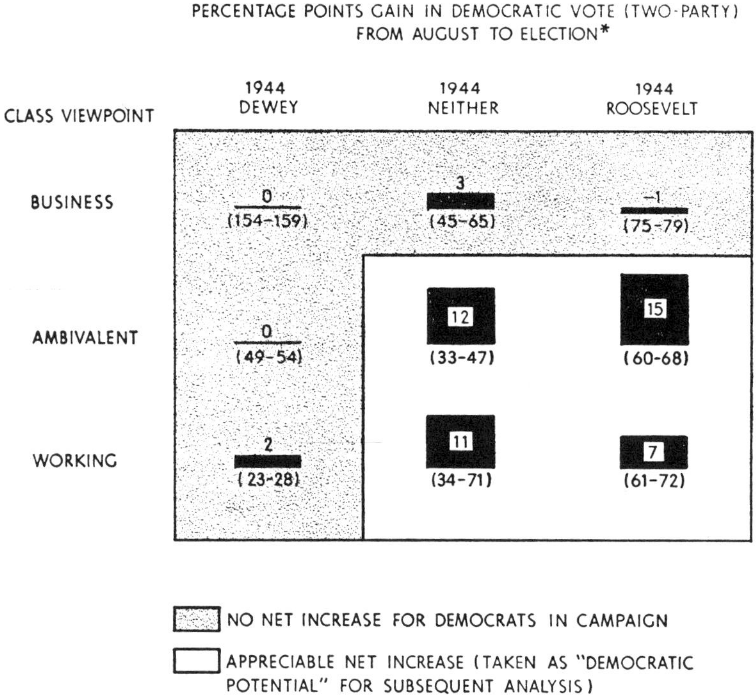

PERCENTAGE POINTS GAIN IN DEMOCRATIC VOTE (TWO-PARTY)
FROM AUGUST TO ELECTION*

CLASS VIEWPOINT	1944 DEWEY	1944 NEITHER	1944 ROOSEVELT
BUSINESS	0 (154-159)	3 (45-65)	−1 (75-79)
AMBIVALENT	0 (49-54)	12 (33-47)	15 (60-68)
WORKING	2 (23-28)	11 (34-71)	7 (61-72)

NO NET INCREASE FOR DEMOCRATS IN CAMPAIGN

APPRECIABLE NET INCREASE (TAKEN AS "DEMOCRATIC POTENTIAL" FOR SUBSEQUENT ANALYSIS)

* Boxed cells, locating the significant Democratic gains in the campaign, define the universe of *"potential Democrats"* or *"Democratic potential"* discussed in the text. The cell entry is, again, the difference in percentage points between the proportion for Truman at the beginning and at the end of his campaign. For reasons that will become clear in the text, the June–August trends at the time of Truman's nomination were confused, and we use August–November data here.

vation of *socioeconomic* interests and sympathies. In the remainder of this analysis of the shift to Truman, we shall deal *only with respondents who could be expected to respond to such a rally* (boxed cells, Chart CXVII). They were "potential Democrats," and our concern is with what happened to them rather than with the quite different situation of the 1944 Republican and/or business classes.[3]

DEMORALIZATION OF THE NEW DEAL MAJORITY

If 1948 was a rally of voters who "should" have been Democratic all along, why had they *left* the party? The potential for change is always present in a two-party democratic system. It is there simply because new events bring new problems and new leaders to deal

CHART CXVIII

PERCENTAGE DEMOCRATIC OF TWO-PARTY VOTE
(1944 Democrats Only)

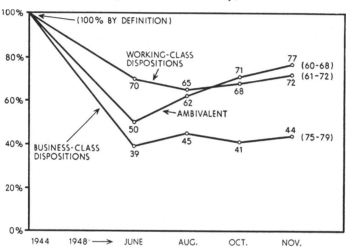

with them. And these were the central conditions explaining the "defection" to the Republicans of potential Democrats at the beginning of the 1948 campaign. First, the Democratic leader was in disfavor (even within his own party) and, second, new issues attracted (the Democrats would say "distracted") the voters. We take up the former problem first.

The Problem of Succession

President Truman's difficulties symbolize the historically significant problem of political succession: how does a political party

3. As indicated in Chart CXVIII, the largest increase came from the 1944 Democrats with ambivalent class positions. They were the fair-weather friends of politics. First they joined the few remaining Roosevelt voters of clearly business sympathies in large-scale defections away from Truman after 1944. Then, in the 1948 campaign, trends among these inconsistent cases were abruptly reversed, and they joined the working-class rally behind Truman.

replace a strong leader? In this instance, after a brief honeymoon period, the replacement of a magnetic leader (President Roosevelt) by the almost necessarily less impressive man who is next in line stimulated party demoralization. This was clearly one of the chief elements in the Democratic situation of 1948. In Elmira the image of Truman was not particularly encouraging; Democrats were much more favorably inclined to Dewey than Republicans to Truman. In fact, twice as many favorable terms as unfavorable

CHART CXIX

THE NATIONAL TREND OF OPINION ON TRUMAN
WAS UNEVEN AND UNFAVORABLE*

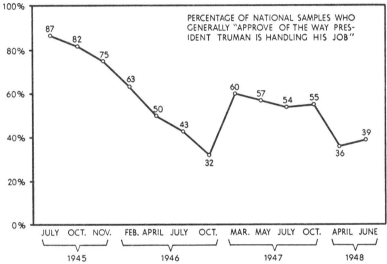

PERCENTAGE OF NATIONAL SAMPLES WHO GENERALLY "APPROVE OF THE WAY PRESIDENT TRUMAN IS HANDLING HIS JOB"

* Percentage of national sample who "approve of the way President Truman is handling his job," from American Institute of Public Opinion, reported in *Public Opinion Quarterly*, XI (1947–48), 494, and XII (1948), 568.

ones were used by Democrats to characterize the opposition candidate after his nomination in August. On the national scene Truman's popularity had fallen regularly for nearly two years following his inauguration, and after a short rise it had gone down again by the summer of 1948 (Chart CXIX).

Among all Elmira voters, and in particular among the potential Democrats (as defined above), there was a marked correlation between the image of Truman and vote. Those with a favorable image of Truman were strong for him; those with an unfavorable image were strong against him (see Chart CXX). And this relationship carried over to *change* in vote. Many potential Democrats were less than happy about Truman's nomination. While most of the defectors had already left the party by June, the very fact of Truman's nomination seemed to repel still more of them between June and August—those who had hoped for other nominations or who had not previously thought much about who would be nominated (Chart CXXI).

Yet, while Truman may have had special troubles of his own, his difficulties were probably typical of political successors who attempt to hold together an already disintegrating majority coalition after the passing of the original leader. Whatever the case, however, part

CHART CXX

PERCENTAGE DEMOCRATIC OF
TWO-PARTY INTENTION (AUGUST)

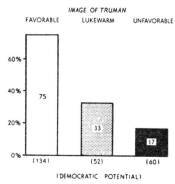

IMAGE OF TRUMAN

FAVORABLE   LUKEWARM   UNFAVORABLE

(DEMOCRATIC POTENTIAL)

* This holds with both 1944 vote and class sympathies controlled.

of the Republican strength at the start of the 1948 campaign was attributable to the dissatisfaction of potential Democrats with Truman the candidate.

The Problem of Distraction

The second major element in the demoralization of the Democratic potential is also an integral part of the rise and fall of political majorities. As the years go by and a political movement like the New Deal matures, new problems (e.g., war and its aftermath) accumulate beyond the set of problems (e.g., socioeconomic reform) that originally characterized the movement. They bring to the fore a new set of issues that often crosscut the original set and hence complicate and disturb the political majority, which in a two-party system is necessarily an alliance of divergent elements.

In Elmira in June, 1948, few voters were concerned with the labor-consumer ("class") issues that had been at the heart of Democratic victories since 1932. When asked about the disagreements

CHART CXXI

CHANGE IN VOTE FROM JUNE TO AUGUST REFLECTED DISSATISFACTION
WITH TRUMAN AS THE CANDIDATE

(Potential Democrats Only)

PERCENTAGE DEMOCRATIC OF TWO-PARTY INTENTIONS IN AUGUST

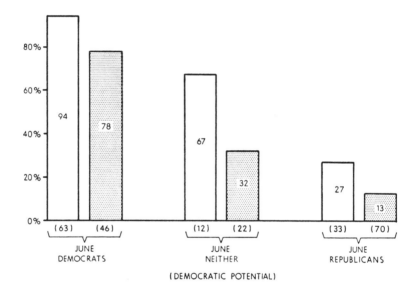

between the two parties, the Democratic potential was either apathetic or concerned with other issues, mainly those dealing with international affairs (see Chart CXXII). As a Democrat might put it, the Democratic potential was "confused" or "led astray" by the day's topical problems.

And such dispersion of attention onto different issues had its effect upon vote intentions. When voters are not attentive to a given set of issues, they tend to overlook their related values and interests. For example, there was a marked difference in Democratic vote between those to whom labor-consumer or "class" issues were salient in June and those to whom they were not (and this result holds with 1944 vote and class position controlled). Thus "distraction" from socioeconomic issues was associated in June, 1948, with defections from the Democratic party among those normally its supporters. With the socioeconomic interests underlying the New

CHART CXXII

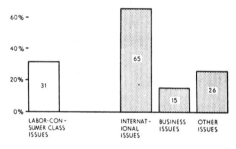

PERCENTAGE MENTIONING ISSUE AS ONE THE TWO
PARTIES "ARE DISAGREEING ABOUT" IN JUNE*

* The Classification of the answers was:

Labor-Consumer Class Issues	Business Issues	International Issues	Other Issues
Cost of living Taft-Hartley Law Rich man–poor man distinctions in general	Taxes Government spending (other than foreign aid)	Foreign policy Foreign aid Communists in U.S. Military strength	Civil rights "Everything" Miscellaneous

Deal majorities in abeyance, at least for the time being, different problems brought different criteria and inclinations into operation on the vote decision (see Chart CXXIII). And again the effect of this "distraction" upon vote carried over from June to August: those to whom class issues were not salient became *less* Democratic by August than those of the same June intention who were conscious of class issues (Chart CXXIV).

In summary, the Democratic potential was (1) vulnerable after the loss of its long-time leader and (2) subject to distraction of attention away from traditional rallying issues and interests of the party. The first difficulty centered around President Truman himself or, more generally, around the problem of effecting a smooth political succession. The second difficulty centered around the loss of socioeconomic class issues or, more generally, around the problem of maintaining the core of a political program or ideology against the pressure of new events. These are interrelated matters, and the Democratic demoralization of mid-summer in 1948 can be summed up in the statement that both the old political loyalties and the socioeconomic interests on which the New Deal had flourished had, under changing conditions, lost their original strength.

CHART CXXIII

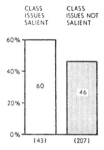

PERCENTAGE DEMOCRATIC OF
TWO-PARTY INTENTIONS IN AUGUST

DEMOCRATIC POTENTIAL*

* The reader is reminded again that the analysis here deals only with the universe of potential Democrats, as defined by the boxed cells on p. 256, among whom the later trends to Truman appeared.

But that demoralization did not continue in force throughout the campaign. The Democrats regained enough of their former support to make the difference between defeat and victory. And that brings us to our third and, of course, most important question.

THE FAIR DEAL RALLY

Why did a sizable portion of the Democratic potential return to the fold? In terms of our previous analysis there are two possibilities. First, it may have been that people came to like President Truman better, thus allowing old Democratic political loyalties to come back into force. He may, so to speak, have "sold himself" as Roosevelt's successor. Or, second, the focus of attention may have changed away from Truman and the distracting issues and back to the socioeconomic class issues of the times, thus enabling the interests, values, and "prejudices" associated with these issues to reassert their force.

To state the alternative hypotheses more generally, voters may have kept the *same standards* of judgment, that is, considering which person they wanted, but adopted a *different evaluation* within

CHART CXXIV

CHANGE IN VOTE FROM JUNE TO AUGUST REFLECTED
"DISTRACTION" FROM CLASS ISSUES

PERCENTAGE DEMOCRATIC OF TWO-PARTY INTENTIONS IN AUGUST

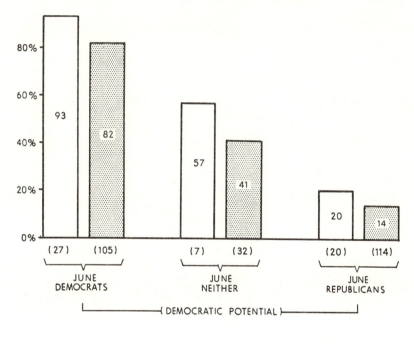

such standards (e.g., they may have come to like Truman better). Or they may have kept the *same evaluation* of the candidates but shifted to *different standards* (e.g., from judging "the man" to judging "the issues"). Was it a change in evaluation or a change in standards?

Image and Saliency

To evaluate the two hypotheses, let us start with the voters' image of Truman. Among Democratic-inclined voters, was there a major change in evaluation of Truman? Actually, from August to October there was almost no change at all in what potential Democrats thought of him as a candidate (see Chart CXXV). The voters' image of the President had been built up over a period of years, including three years as chief executive, and it was not subject to much manipulation during the few months of the campaign. Truman's campaign made no net change in what people thought of him as a candidate. The trend toward Truman in vote intention was

CHART CXXV

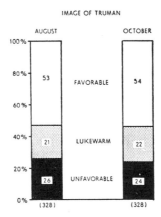

IMAGE OF TRUMAN

AUGUST   OCTOBER

100%

80%   53   FAVORABLE   54

60%

40%   21   LUKEWARM   22

20%

26   UNFAVORABLE   24

0%
(328)   (328)

greater than the trend toward acceptance of Truman personally. People came to vote for Truman faster than they came to like him.

Now, to consider the alternative, there *was* a sharp shift in the saliency of "class" issues for the voters. The campaign was characterized by a resurgence of attention to socioeconomic matters, at the expense of international affairs (see Chart CXXVI). The image of Truman did not change, but the image of what was important in the campaign—and perhaps even the image of what Truman stood for—*did* change to a dominance of socioeconomic issues.[4]

4. The saliency of class issues was brought home through the mass media. Of those to whom such issues were not salient in June, 59 per cent of the highly exposed mentioned them in October as compared to only 38 per cent of the people not closely following the campaign in the newspapers or on the air.

And what of the mutual influence of image of Truman and saliency of class issues? How did they affect one another? In each case, of course, we have two measures—one earlier (June for saliency, August for image) and one later (October for both). By cross-tabulating the four combinations at the earlier period with the four at the later, we can analyze the joint changes through time.[5] We present here a simple measure of mutual effect (Chart CXXVII). But however it is analyzed, saliency of class issues makes more of a difference in the later image of Truman than the other

CHART CXXVI

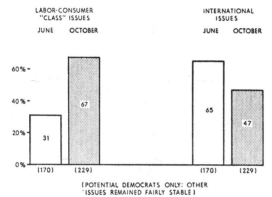

PERCENTAGE MENTIONING EACH TYPE OF ISSUE AS ONE THE PARTIES "ARE DISAGREEING" ABOUT *

(POTENTIAL DEMOCRATS ONLY: OTHER ISSUES REMAINED FAIRLY STABLE)

* "Disagree about nothing" and no opinion eliminated. Percentages add to more than 100 because some people mentioned more than one issue.

way round. A more favorable image of Truman was more likely among those already attentive to class issues; saliency did increase among those favorably inclined to Truman, but not so much.

5. This is the table (potential Democrats only):

	Class Issues Image of Truman		Later Time (October)				
	Class Issues (June)	Image of Truman (Aug.)	Sal. Fav.	Sal. Unfav.	Not Sal. Fav.	Not Sal. Unfav.	Total
Earlier time......	Sal.	Fav.	20	2	8	1	31
	Sal.	Unfav.	6	7	3	6	22
	Not sal.	Fav.	52	14	54	23	143
	Not sal.	Unfav.	16	37	19	60	132
		Total	94	60	84	90	328

CHART CXXVII

Saliency Predicts Image More than the Other Way Round

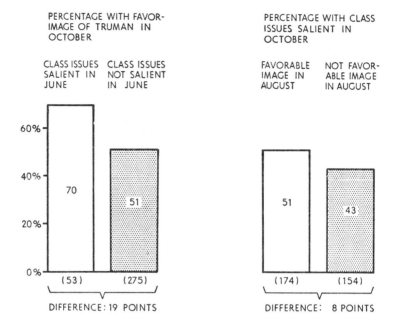

PERCENTAGE WITH FAVOR-IMAGE OF TRUMAN IN OCTOBER

PERCENTAGE WITH CLASS ISSUES SALIENT IN OCTOBER

CLASS ISSUES SALIENT IN JUNE — CLASS ISSUES NOT SALIENT IN JUNE

FAVORABLE IMAGE IN AUGUST — NOT FAVOR-ABLE IMAGE IN AUGUST

70   51   51   43

(53)   (275)   (174)   (154)

DIFFERENCE: 19 POINTS   DIFFERENCE: 8 POINTS

CHART CXXVIII

The Sharpest Increase in Democratic Vote Intentions Came from Those with Unfavorable Image of Truman*
(Potential Democrats Only)

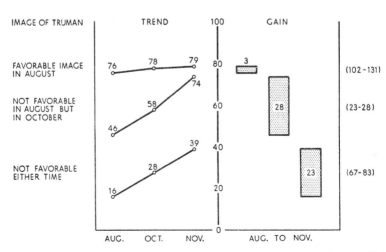

PERCENTAGE DEMOCRATIC OF TWO-PARTY VOTE (INTENTIONS)

IMAGE OF TRUMAN   TREND   100   GAIN

FAVORABLE IMAGE IN AUGUST   76   78   79   80   3   (102-131)

NOT FAVORABLE IN AUGUST BUT IN OCTOBER   46   58   74   60   28   (23-28)

NOT FAVORABLE EITHER TIME   16   28   39   40   23   (67-83)

20

AUG.   OCT.   NOV.   0   AUG. TO NOV.

*Note that size of bars does not indicate *numbers* of changers; for example, most changers to Truman had negative images at *both* times, as roughly indicated by sample sizes.

The trend in vote further clarifies the matter. The voters within the Democratic potential who did *not* have a favorable image of Truman in *either* August or October nevertheless increased in intention to vote for him (Chart CXXVIII). The trend to Truman was concentrated among those who had *not* previously liked him, nor did they like him even when they changed to his side. (While the trend is sharp among those whose image improved, they are few in number.) Improved opinions of Truman were not the dominant feature of the rally; they were less changed than simply overridden. Vote trends were *negatively* related to images of what was being voted for!

CHART CXXIX

THE SHARPEST INCREASE IN DEMOCRATIC VOTE INTENTIONS CAME
FROM THOSE TO WHOM CLASS ISSUES WERE SALIENT*

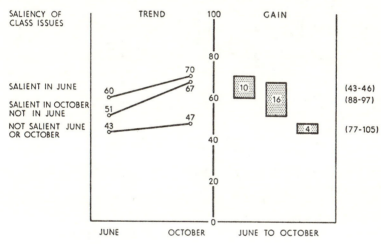

PERCENTAGE DEMOCRATIC OF TWO-PARTY VOTE (INTENTIONS)

*Here the largest number of changers to Truman came from those who increased saliency, as sample sizes indicate.

However, saliency of "class" issues had a *positive* relation to the trend. The increase in Democratic support from June to October came largely in relation to the saliency, and to an *increase* in the saliency, of economic labor-consumer "class" issues (Chart CXXIX). The net trends prior to October were concentrated among the people for whom class issues were or became salient in this period. The voting trends were negligible among the cases who had not focused on them by October. We have here, then, a relationship consisting of *simultaneous* trends in the focus of attention and in the voting rally of potential Democrats.

Now if such simultaneity of change is the case, then those who had *already* made socioeconomic issues their focus of attention at the peak of the campaign would not change their votes further in the final weeks. Instead, the additional net recruitment of Democratic strength might be expected to come from among those who had not previously "got the point" of the Democratic campaign, that is, who had not previously seen these socioeconomic issues as the main point of the argument. Such indeed may have been the case; at least it was the previously "dormant" cases who moved *after* October (see Chart CXXX). The intensifying campaign of the

CHART CXXX

PERCENTAGE DEMOCRATIC OF TWO-PARTY VOTE (INTENTIONS)

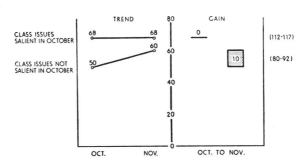

last two weeks presumably brought home to them what was already clear to others.

Reasons for Change

Now these trends summarize many small shifts of a compensating nature. But taken in the aggregate, like time-series data, they indicate a *timing* of the Democratic rally corresponding to the timing of attention to these class issues, perhaps even to the delayed Democratic voting reaction of those who did not recognize such issues to the very end. Thus, one might infer from these data alone that an important role was played by these issues in the Democratic rally, just as their *absence* had evidently played a role in the earlier demoralization of the Democratic party.

Fortunately, we have additional evidence of the role of the issues in the direct reports of the people who changed votes. All those who made some kind of a voting change (either from nonvoting to a party or from one party to the opposition) were especially questioned as to "why" they had done so. A classification of the political content of the reasons given for these changes, made independent of and prior to this analysis, clearly shows the same result: a marked shift in the basis of decision from the matter of personality to that of class issues (Chart CXXXI). In their own reasons for change to

CHART CXXXI

In Reasons for Change to Truman, Class Issues Became
More Important and Personalities Less*

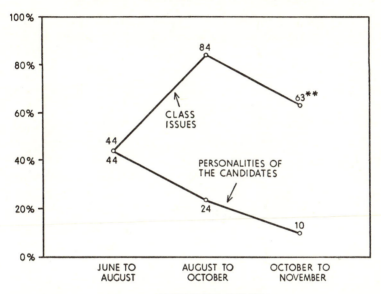

REASONS FOR CHANGE

* These data refer to all respondents, not just potential Democrats; data on latter only are not available Other reasons referred primarily to general political arguments (e.g., need for a change) or to campaign speeches. Class-issue reasons for change are analogous to those in the earlier classification on page 261, with the Taft-Hartley Act and to a lesser extent price controls the central arguments of a specific sort.

** The apparent decline of these socioeconomic or class issues after October is an artifact of interviewing and coding problems. A category of "campaign speeches" greatly increased as a reason given for change (11 to 15 to 44 per cent in the three periods), and the specific issues involved in these speeches were harder to distinguish. If the data were percentaged without the ambiguous replies, they would show a symmetrical increase in socioeconomic issues.

Truman the respondents reveal a marked shift in the standard by which they were judging the campaign.

The comments of the changers give the flavor of the arguments effective at the close of the campaign:

I was waiting for Dewey to give an opinion on the Taft-Hartley Law. I work in a plant, and I am against it. When I heard him in that speech in Pittsburgh, he said that the Taft-Hartley Law was good for both labor and management, but it might have to have some changes. He didn't enumerate those changes, so I went to the other side, because I was dead set against the law . . . and I know Truman will fight against it. [A fifty-year-old tool-and-die maker, Republican in August.]

Truman is the only man for labor. We have had better Presidents than Truman, but he is the best man running now because he is for labor. [A sixty-five-year-old machinist, changing to Truman.]

[I'll vote for Truman] because the Democrats have always been better for the working people. [A secretary, changing to Truman.]

A modern presidential campaign is won or lost on the basis of a multitude of appeals, and a variety of "explanations" can thus be abstracted out of the total phenomenon. But in our data it seems clear that an impending defeat for the Democratic party was staved off by a refocusing of attention on the socioeconomic concerns which had originally played such a large role in building that party's majority in the 1930's. While an improving appreciation of Truman was partly involved in the process, we are led on several grounds to discount this idea as the primary notion explaining the 1948 campaign trends. We are led, rather, to conclude that such a trend was subsidiary to the shift in attention and in standards of judgment, *away* from Truman's personal difficulties and other problems that had inhibited the Democratic vote prior to the campaign and *toward* another focus of attention more favorable to the Democrats, namely, a focus on class issues. The rally was due more to a change in standard than to a change in evaluation.

PSYCHOLOGICAL AND POLITICAL IMPLICATIONS

Such an analysis of a concrete historical phenomenon can be interpreted in a variety of ways. Let us call particular attention to two ideas suggested by these data, the first psychological and the second historical and political.

In connection with attitudinal and perceptual phenomena, social psychologists have for some time been calling attention to "reference" phenomena—"reference frames," "reference groups," "reference points," and the like. If one chose this terminology, the rally of potential Democrats could be described as a "change in the frame of reference."

Unfortunately, the writings of social psychologists on this subject reveal a loose mixture of meanings for the term "frame of reference." But perhaps the primary thread of theoretical reasoning can be put something like this: People can differ from one another, and within themselves from time to time, by emphasizing different dimensions of things they perceive—in this case, for example, one time focusing upon Truman's difficulties or foreign policy but the next time upon the Taft-Hartley Act. An American voter can organize his ideas about the political parties with respect to the statesmanship of their candidates or with respect to the economic interests served by their programs. And, of course, this selection is associated with tendencies to action learned in the past. For example, voters have learned what to do about an "unstatesman-like" candidate as well as what to do about a party that serves the economic interest of "rich people." The theory is that once the perception is clear, proper behavior follows almost automatically.

But what if one party has the "unstatesman-like" candidate but the other serves the interests of "rich people"? Then, the theoretical argument runs, the resulting action would depend on *which* consideration was dominant. To some extent, this depends in turn on the nature of external campaign events. As these change, then, we would expect roughly corresponding changes in behavior like those observable in the 1948 campaign trends.

In the politico-historical realm the development of the 1948 campaign can be seen as a revealing instance in the broad movement of political cycles. How does a major political movement typically rise and fall? Let us try a speculative answer in terms of our whole analysis of the role of issues in Elmira in 1948. The generalized picture might look something like this (and we extrapolate to post-1948 events):

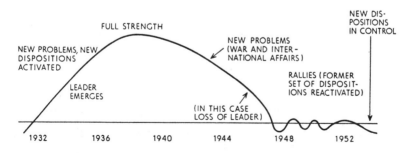

PERCENTAGE VOTING FOR THE MOVEMENT

The depression or the early 1930's raised new problems for the society to solve. They in turn presented new issues at the political gateway and activated new sets of dispositions. New standards or "frames of reference" were brought into play by which political decisions would be made. In this case, the shift of issues was from Style issues (like prohibition) to Position issues (like unemployment). As the movement gained strength, it became symbolized in a leader who (in this case) was successful in assimilating the next big set of issues presented by events on the international front. This held the movement in power through the war, but in the first postwar election the loss of the leader and the complication of new issues of quite different character threatened to defeat the movement. Only the heavy emphasis upon the old Position issues at the core of the movement carried the day. Four years later, in 1952—when, incidentally, the Democratic candidate did not campaign strongly on economic issues—the old concerns appeared to have run their life-history, so to speak, and new Style issues (e.g., communism in government) established themselves. The resulting defeat "ended" the original cycle.[6]

SUMMARY

Components of the Democratic Trend

138. The Democratic trend was composed (*a*) in political terms of former Democrats, neutrals, or new voters and (*b*) in socio-economic terms of voters with working-class and ambivalent class dispositions.

    and: (*a*) About two-thirds of the Democratic trend was made up of voters combining these two characteristics.

    (*b*) The Democratic trend was particularly strong among those of ambivalent class dispositions (who had been most likely to leave the party).

Demoralization of the New Deal Majority

139. Democrats were more favorably inclined toward the image of Dewey as a candidate than Republicans were toward the image of Truman.

6. Our story of the role of issues in Elmira is thus a microcosmic analysis of certain parts of a historical process. This, incidentally, is a primitive example of what we consider a valuable type of analysis that moves toward integration of historical studies, political theory, and empirical social research.

140. Among potential Democrats the image of Truman correlated strongly with vote.

141. Potential Democrats who were not favorably impressed with Truman as the prospective candidate were more likely to shift away from a Democratic vote intention between June and August (the convention period).

142. Among potential Democrats vote intention correlated with the saliency of labor-consumer "class" issues in June.

143. Potential Democrats to whom class issues were not salient in June were more likely to shift away from a Democratic vote intention between June and August.

The Fair Deal Rally

144. There was little change in the image of Truman among potential Democrats from August to October.

145. There was a sharp increase in the saliency of class issues among potential Democrats from June to October.

146. Saliency of class issues affected the image of Truman more than the image affected saliency.

147. The increase in Democratic vote intentions from August to November was sharpest among those who had, at the start, an unfavorable image of Truman.

148. The increase in Democratic vote intention from June to October was sharpest among those to whom class issues were becoming salient.

149. Class issues and the personalities of the candidates were mentioned equally as reasons for change to Truman early in the campaign, but class issues were mentioned much more frequently than personalities later in the campaign.

13 THE SOCIAL PSYCHOLOGY OF THE VOTING DECISION

In our last two chapters we shall relate the findings of this study to some broader problems of the social sciences. In this chapter we deal with some conditions that *determine* the way a man votes and hence with some ideas coming from social psychology and sociology. In the next chapter we discuss the *consequences* for the body politic, and there the frame of reference is political theory.

We do not propose to summarize all the findings in this report that might be of interest to behavioral scientists. Rather, we shall develop the following line of argument. We shall start by locating our main focus of attention as an analysis of the process by which acts are carried out. We shall then describe what it means to analyze a "process": the operations that are involved and the types of findings that result. This will lead to a discussion of two objections to these studies: that they are too gross to contribute to psychological knowledge and, on the other hand, that they are too atomistic to add to sociological theory. In answer to these objections, we shall suggest that the type of study exemplified in this book may very well turn out to be a very appropriate way of analyzing the short-range formation of opinions and decisions.

IMPLEMENTATION—A FORGOTTEN CONCERN

Some psychologists employ the following scheme in approaching a question. An organism is in a certain state, the outside world acts as a stimulus, and the organism responds in a way which is codetermined by its state and by the stimulus. The experiences resulting from this response affect, in turn, the state of the organism. According to this scheme, changes of opinion and final decisions come about through the repeated chain of stimulus-organism-response (Fig. 1).

It has been suggested that one might distinguish psychologists according to which segment of this chain they concern themselves with.[1] If they focus on the state of the organism and its history, then this is called the study of motivation or, to use a more neutral term, of *dispositions;* for, whether we talk about needs or personality traits or attitudes, these are all descriptions of the state of the organism. And these descriptions are analyzed in terms of so-called "state parameters"—those factors which determine variation in re-

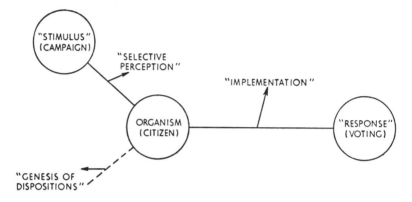

Fig. 1.—A psychologist's view of the vote

sponse to the same objective situation in the environment. Another group of psychologists concern themselves mainly with the first (afferent) half of the arc; they study how the stimulus, in combination with the specific state or disposition in which the person finds himself, affects his *perception* of the outside world.

There is a third portion of the diagram on which attention might center; this is the second (efferent) half of the arc, from the disposition of the individual to his final, manifest response. There is no term in the vocabulary of present-day psychologists to describe this part of the arc. But, in order to locate some of the major problems and findings of this report, we shall use the word *"implementation."* By this term we mean the way in which more or less vague

1. David Krech, "Notes toward a Psychological Theory," in *Perception and Personality: A Symposium* (Durham, N.C.: Duke University Press, 1949–50).

dispositions, intentions, and interests regarding a specific subject matter may lead, finally, to the performance of a specific act like buying a car, going on a trip, or voting for a candidate.

It is not difficult to understand why the study of implementation has received little attention at the same time that the study of perception has flourished so manifestly. Laboratory experiments can be performed more readily on the latter; for the implementation process often goes on over a considerable period of time and easily escapes systematic exploration. But it is an aspect of behavior to which field panel studies call special attention.

There have been periods in the history of psychology when attention was focused on the process of implementation, but, for a variety of reasons, none of these efforts had lasting success. For example, a group of prominent German psychologists studied "the will" in great detail.[2] Experimental subjects were assigned minor tasks and then, in detailed retrospective interviews, were asked to describe how they carried out their instructions. (It was then, incidentally, that the concept of "attitude" was introduced.) These important studies were temporarily engulfed in the onrush of behaviorism, and it is only now that they are receiving renewed recognition. Later on, Kurt Lewin, in his famous studies on the psychology of action, gave focus to implementation, but in a negative sense. He wanted to determine what became of intentions when they were obstructed by outside interruptions, through the intrinsic difficulties of the task, or by some physical barriers. Lewin's notion of "locomotion through psychological space" is very similar to what we, in these pages, have called "implementation."[3]

Much of the material in our election studies clearly falls within this research tradition. When we study the movement of votes during a campaign, we are concerned mainly with individuals who, at the beginning of a campaign, have only a vague notion that they will have to vote sometime in the next few months or with those who have a variety of ideas about the political scene which are not

2. E. Boring, *History of Experimental Psychology* (New York: Appleton-Century-Crofts, 1950), pp. 402 ff.

3. The most important statement of Lewin on this point is only now available in English; see his "Intention, Will and Need," in *Organization and Pathology of Thought: Selected Sources*, ed. D. Rapaport (New York: Columbia University Press, 1951).

yet co-ordinated into a definite or stable vote intention. Our efforts are directed toward finding out "how they make up their minds," or "carry through their intentions," or, to put it in terms of the general scheme of the psychologist, how dispositions in May are finally crystallized or realized or—as we choose to say—"implemented" into a response to the demands of society for a vote in November.

We are aware that few new terms are ever entirely satisfactory. There are a number of alternatives that might have been used; but each has its shortcomings. "Execution" connotes too much rational plan; "realization" has special meaning in the psychology of cognition. "Implementation," in the sense of a vague and general direction which becomes more specific through a step-by-step process, will suffice, provided the reader gives up his personal associations with the word and thinks only of the purpose for which the scheme is introduced here.[4]

Directing attention to a problem area and labeling it with a term is, at best, a first step in any inquiry. The second and more important one is to find the appropriate mode of collecting empirical evidence bearing on the problem. The study of implementation forces one to develop methods for studying *processes* as they take place.

PROCESS ANALYSIS

To the reader of the preceding chapters the mode of data collection employed in this investigation should be entirely clear. The core data of this study, and of its predecessors, were obtained in repeated interviews with the same sample of persons over six months of the political campaign. Each voter was characterized by his responses to a great variety of questions; some of these questions were repeated from one interview to the next, and others were introduced as the changing political situation required.

It might be helpful to point out in this summary that the way

4. The purpose is to locate, relative to each other, the points which various students select out of a broad problem-complex of concern. Thus, Murray speaks of the "regnant function of personality," such as reduction of conflicts by social conformity, scheduling of value priorities, and other processes which clearly fall into that part of our problem area which we have designated as "implementation" (H. A. Murray and C. Kluckhohn, "Outline of a Conception of Personality," in *Personality*, ed. Murray and Kluckhohn [New York: A. A. Knopf, 1949], pp. 12 ff.). Murray's examples, however, pertain to rather purposive and highly motivated activities, to which, we stress, voting often does not belong.

in which we have made use of repeated interviews is very similar to the way in which modern economists use time series in order to study business cycles and economic growth. As a matter of fact, the phrase "process analysis" has achieved some currency among economists, and they have tried to clarify its meaning.[5] One of them, the Dutch economist Tinbergen, has presented an "arrow scheme" which clarifies the basic idea of process analysis (Fig. 2).[6]

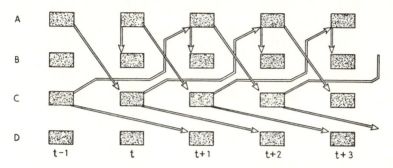

Fig. 2.—A scheme to show the idea of a "process analysis"

On the horizontal axis are charted the successive periods of time at which observations are made. On the vertical axis are letters designating the variables under observation. In political studies these variables might be vote intentions, attitudes toward various issues in the campaign, the opinions of family members, etc. The arrows in the scheme represent the relations between these variables. Some of these arrows have "time lags"; we might want to know, for example, whether an individual's vote intention is affected by what he has read at an earlier time. Others of the arrows relate different variables at the same time period; we might want to find out, for example, whether an individual shares his opinions with his friends. Still other arrows cross several time periods and several variables; for example, exposure to a friend's opinion at time t may be followed by a new way of looking at the campaign at time $t+1$ and, finally, by a changed vote intention at time $t+2$.

5. William J. Baumol, *Economic Dynamics* (New York: Macmillan Co., 1951); and Paul A. Samuelson, "Dynamic Process Analysis," in *A Survey of Contemporary Economics*, ed. Howard S. Ellis (Philadelphia: Blakiston Co., 1948), chap. x, pp. 352–87.

6. Jan Tinbergen, "Econometric Business Cycle Research," *Review of Economic Sudies*, VII (1940), 73–90.

From this kind of process analysis, econometrists derive systems of formal equations which are rooted in a theoretical tradition, prominent in which is a concern for the dynamic interaction of a limited number of key variables. Panel analysis has the same dynamic character, but at the present stage it is more descriptive, less translatable into mathematical models. And, for better or worse, it uses a larger number of variables, chosen more to serve the problem at hand than derived from a basic theoretical system. By culling three examples of increasing complexity from our preceding chapters, the reader might want to review the character of process analysis done through panels.

a) Chapter 7 provided documentation for the following general finding: If the members of a particular social stratum reveal a tendency to vote in the same way, and if, within such a stratum, we compare those who have the "proper" vote intention with those who, in the early stages of the campaign, intend to vote against the prevailing trend, then we find that the deviants have a tendency to return to the fold on election day and to cast their votes in the way which is appropriate to their social group.

This result can be formulated in a variety of ways. We can say that the proper vote intention is stronger and more durable than the deviant one, or we can say that the vote intention which has a smaller probability of finding social support in the environment is more likely to be unstable.

The interesting point to note is that this finding has great generality and turns up in various areas of action. For example, in a study of attitudes regarding the California loyalty oath, Lipset found that Jews were more likely than non-Jews to say that they would refuse to sign the oath.[7] Later on he checked the actions of those who had not intended to take the oath; in line with the findings of our study, he discovered that those with the "proper" social characteristics (in this case, the Jews) were more likely to have carried out this intention than were those whose social characteristics were indicative of less support from their social environment. Again, Rossi found in a study of residential mobility that young people expressed more often than old people the desire to move.[8] A year later he revisited those who had voiced a desire to

7. *Public Opinion Quarterly*, Vol. XVII (1953).

8. *Residential Mobility in Philadelphia* (to be published by the Federal Housing Administration).

find a new residence. The "mobile" group, those who were young, carried out their intentions by and large; the old people included a higher proportion of defectors from the original intention. A third source of corroboration comes from Army studies regarding occupational plans for the postwar period. Clausen found that plans related to previous experiences (return to school by soldiers who already had a considerable amount of education or the purchase of a farm by soldiers who had previously worked on farms) were more often carried through than plans not so founded.[9]

In sum, we have a general finding on implementation. Intentions supported by one's social surroundings are more predictably carried out than are intentions lacking such support. In the field of voting this can be formulated as the "rule of political predisposition." If we find, at the beginning of a political campaign, that certain demographic characteristics are correlated with a particular vote intention, then those who possess these predisposing characteristics are more likely than those without them to carry out this intention on election day.[10]

This first example of process analysis is fairly simple in nature. At the time of one interview we characterize respondents according to their vote intention and certain of their background characteristics. In a later interview we investigate what has become of these original vote intentions. Our second example describes a somewhat more complex process.

b) At several points in our report, and in previous studies as well, we spoke of individuals who were under "cross-pressures." These are combinations of characteristics which, in a given context, would tend to lead the individual to vote on both sides of a contest. A variety of cross-pressures can be distinguished. The probability of a person's vote (we omit here many significant details) is affected, as we have seen, by his position in the social structure, by his former party allegiance, and by the specific appeals of the campaign. Any two of these factors predisposing him in different directions can lead to cross-pressures. In addition, his social posi-

9. *The American Soldier*, Vol. IV, chap. xv.

10. A careless reading of this finding can lead to grievous misunderstandings, as is shown in a paper by Janowitz and Miller on "The Index of Political Predisposition in the 1948 Election" (*Journal of Politics*, Vol. XIV). Their data, on which they base a refutation of the rule, show that, in actuality, it holds quite clearly (*ibid.*, p. 718).

tion alone can create cross-pressure (e.g., in recent elections, a rich Catholic); and so can his stand on various issues (e.g., an isolationist New Dealer). The psychological impact of these various kinds of cross-pressures may be quite different. Some such situations may have *no* subjective reality for the voter himself at the moment; it is merely that we as observers can foresee his future vulnerability by virtue of his location within cross-currents of social influence.

It is easy to see why these combination-variables indicating situations of contradiction and inconsistency should play such a major role in the empirical study of voting decisions in a country which adheres to a two-party system (chap. 9). The large variety of interests and opinions, which are distributed in all sorts of combinations, have to be resolved into a dichotomous vote. Moreover, the distribution of molecular social influences is complicated, and the political stimuli themselves are far from unidimensional. The group of cross-pressure variables locates the respondents, so to speak, in a complicated system of probabilities of which a final vote is the resultant. Their analytical importance is therefore hardly surprising under field conditions.

While theory regarding these cross-pressures is not yet particularly advanced, an impressive series of empirical results has accumulated over the last fifteen years of research. An individual who is characterized by any type of cross-pressure is likely to change his mind in the course of the campaign (chap. 2), to make up his mind late (chap. 7), and, occasionally, to leave the field and not to vote at all.

There is one finding which deserves special attention, because it indicates how material obtained through process analysis can lend support to a position of different origin. Psychologists deriving from the Berlin school have emphasized in many ways that there is a tendency toward a "strong Gestalt." Krech and Crutchfield have made some headway in applying this doctrine to major social issues. We might quote two of the principles which these authors make part of their system: "Other things being equal, a change introduced into the psychological field will be absorbed in such a way as to produce the smallest effect on a strong structure." Or, again: "Objects or events that are close to each other in space or time, or resemble each other, tend to be apprehended as parts of a common structure."[11]

The reader who has followed the development of these studies, especially the one carried out in 1940, will notice an emerging empirical regularity which can well be considered a special case of these general principles. *Under the increased pressures of a campaign, people have an increased tendency toward consistency, in all relevant aspects.* As time goes on, as we compare materials collected early in the campaign with those obtained at later stages, we find that people abandon deviant opinions on specific issues to agree with the position taken by their party (or at least to perceive such agreement); in consequence, inconsistencies on various issues reduce in favor of two major opinion patterns characteristic for each of the two parties. In 1948, focusing on primary groups, we found that disagreements between friends and families disappear and make way for a homogeneity of attitude within various social groups. The tendency toward "strong Gestalt" within individuals —and analogously within groups—certainly receives support in our material.

Two corollaries of this finding deserve special mention. One is of practical importance: individuals who are "inconsistent" at the beginning of the campaign are likely to change their vote intentions; they therefore merit the attention of the practical politician as well as that of the political forecaster. Furthermore, evidence of this "tendency toward consistency" is interesting from a methodological point of view. We know that this tendency is accentuated in the heat of the campaign, when, presumably, people become more involved in the issues under discussion. But, at any given point in time, we can separate our respondents according to the degree of their political interest. If this is done, we find that those who are relatively more involved in the campaign are indeed more consistent in many aspects of their attitude structure (chap. 9). A "strong Gestalt," we might speculate, is increased by external pressures as well as through higher personal motivation.[12]

11. David Krech and Richard S. Crutchfield, *Theory and Problems of Social Psychology* (New York: McGraw-Hill Book Co., 1948), p. 108.

12. Notice the form of this result. We are prone to think in terms of correlation and partial correlation, as the main way in which variables are related. But here is clearly a conditional relation. How two attitudes hang together can

THE SPECIAL SIGNIFICANCE OF PRIORITY VARIABLES

Before turning to our third example, we must deal with a general question. The arrow scheme, presented above, does not specify what kinds of "state parameters" are to be used in characterizing respondents. Some of them derive almost necessarily from the purposes of the study under consideration. For example, in an election study, we shall obviously want to know how the respondent feels about the issues in a campaign, about the candidates, etc. Other variables are included, because they are traditional to all social research: the age and sex of the respondent, his socioeconomic status, etc. From these simple data more complex units are constructed by combining information about the respondent. The cross-pressures which we discussed represent one kind of so-called "combination variable." Another type of combination would result in time patterns. For example, we might consider the previous voting record of the respondent to see whether he should be characterized as a traditional Republican, a traditional Democrat, or as a voter with a mixed record. As we have seen, this kind of characterization played a distinct role when it came to the final voting decision in 1948. Time patterns are of course especially characteristic for panel analysis. Notions like "vacillation" or "strengthening of conviction" require repeated observations in order to be used in empirical research.

Perhaps the most interesting characterization of our respondents is through so-called *priority variables*. The notion that individuals take only selective cognizance of their environment is a familiar one in psychology. Support for this notion usually comes from experiments in which, for example, subjects who have been deprived of food tend to see food objects when they look at clouds or ink blots. But if one wants to describe behavior outside a laboratory, such ideas as "frame of reference" or "reference group" cannot be dealt with only inferentially. One must find what it is a *particular* person selects for special attention, what in his environment or in the organization of his ideas he gives priority to.

---

differ according to whether a third one (here interest) is or is not present. Often in this report such conditional relations prove a forceful tool of analysis. A typical example: If people are interested in the campaign, then demographic characteristics like sex or education make much less difference for their responses than if they are not interested.

Several kinds of priority variables have been used in our study. One pertained to the saliency of issues. Respondents were asked, in a variety of ways, what they considered the crucial topics of the campaign, whether they were more concerned with foreign or domestic affairs, etc. (The way they looked at the campaign had strong bearing on vote intention and its change, as we saw in chaps. 9–12.) A similar approach proved useful in connection with the notion of "reference groups," a concept which so far has been used mainly inferentially by social psychologists. Respondents were asked to indicate which in a list of groups, including church, occupation, social clubs, and the like, were most important for them. Moreover, special questions were asked of particular groups. Thus, for example, Negroes were asked how actively they participated in racial affairs; Jews were asked how seriously they took their religious duties; workers were queried on the extent of their contact with their unions.[13] In this way, individuals could be classified according to the priorities they actually gave to various groups, either habitually or at the time of the interview. In many respects one's involvement in the campaign as a whole is also a matter of assigned priority, and this too can be easily ascertained in an interview. The question, "How interested are you in the campaign?" is understood and readily answered by most respondents.[14] This self-rating turns out to be the core around which a large number of findings can be organized (see chaps. 2 and 11).

Here is the beginning of a program which will require considerable ingenuity. The findings of "cognitive psychology," to be made fruitful in field studies, will have to be translated into instruments of classification; otherwise, they cannot be related to an individual's state of needs or to the specific external influences to which he was exposed. The devices of panel analysis *applied* to these variables

13. In all these cases it was found that (1) the more frequently an individual participated in the social activities characteristic of his demographic stratum, or (2) the greater the psychological meaning of the class or group to him, the more likely he was to share the political preferences prevailing within it (chap. 4). In the present chapter we shall not discuss these static findings, because we want to emphasize the role of priority variables in the analysis of *change*.

14. More complicated indexes have been tried, but they do not affect the basic findings. It is true that factor analysis makes it possible to distinguish different types of interest—for example, spectator versus participant interest. But, at the present stage of work, this distinction has not yet been pursued (W. S. Robinson, *American Sociological Review*, 1950).

will then furnish results which are a needed complement to the findings of the laboratory. Our third type of example should help to clarify this point.

c) As we indicated in chapter 12, we know how each respondent felt about Truman and how important he considered economic issues, both in June and at the height of the campaign in October. In an extended argument centering on Charts CXXV, CXXVI, and CXXVII–CXXXI, we were able to show that the "Truman rally" of the last few weeks of the campaign was due less to improved images of Truman than to increased concern with socioeconomic issues. At this point we want to focus on just one aspect of this complex of data. As Truman became more specific about his platform, there was an interaction between the feelings which voters had toward Truman and the issues which they consider salient. Individuals for whom economic issues were important to begin with developed a more favorable opinion of Truman when he began to focus his campaign on such issues; conversely, individuals who had confidence in Truman started to take economic matters more seriously when their candidate began to stress them.

If we are to analyze a process in all its complexity, we must consider more variables, and we must obtain more observations over a longer period of time. But the basic idea is an important one; it is handled quantitatively in a "sixteen-fold table" of the kind presented on page 265.[15] Without going into details, we can report a number of such interactional processes which have been investigated. For example, it is a well-known fact that the interest which people take in political affairs is correlated with the degree to which they expose themselves to the media of communications in which such topics are discussed. Again, the interaction is a mutual one: interest leads to an increase in newspaper-reading and radio-listening, but greater exposure also leads to an increase in interest.

Our questions on the relative importance of different reference

15. The term "sixteen-fold table" refers to the fact that two dichotomies, measured at two points in time, provide a total of sixteen combinations. Such a table is therefore an extension of a fourfold table, in which two dichotomies are cross-tabulated. For a more detailed discussion see S. Lipset *et al.*, "The Psychology of Voting: An Analysis of Political Behavior," in *Handbook of Social Psychology*, ed. G. Lindzey (Cambridge: Addison-Wesley, 1954). It is unfortunate that, because of limitations in the 1948 data and editorial requirements of a volume of this type, we could not use such analyses more often in this report.

groups were not repeated during the course of the campaign, so no pertinent example can be reported here.[16] But one further application of sixteen-fold-table analysis elucidates a much-discussed problem. Vote intentions are always very highly correlated with expectations as to who will win the election. Two interpretations of this result offer themselves. On the one hand, we might be dealing with a "bandwagon effect"; people may tend to vote for the man whom they expect to be the winner. On the other hand, it might be a matter of projection; people may expect that the candidate toward whom they (and their friends) feel favorably inclined will win. It is safe to assume that both of these interpretations are correct; but how can their relative importance be assessed? If we have repeated observations, we can study how vote intention at Time 1 is related to *changes* in expectation between Time 1 and Time 2; and, conversely, the expectation at Time 1 can be related to changes in the vote intention between the two time periods. When subjected to analysis of this kind, data from the 1940 and the 1948 elections suggest that the bandwagon effect and the projection effect are approximately equal in strength.

These are then the kinds of findings which are most characteristic for panel analysis. Here two or more mutually interacting variables are studied; their relative weight in the whole dynamic process is found by observing their concurrent change over time. It is at this point where one can see best how panel analysis complements laboratory experiments. In an experiment we usually observe the effect of one variable upon another; in a panel study we focus on interaction.[17] But even beyond specific results an

16. The research group from Cornell University which co-operated in the present study remained in Elmira after election day to collect further information regarding ethnic groups. From their data will come reports regarding the interrelations between contact with and attitudes toward minority groups over time.

17. There are many other points of comparison, and designs exist which mediate between panels and experiments; but this is not the place to follow up the comparison in detail.

It would be most instructive, for example, to integrate experimental and field studies on selective perception. In chaps. 4 and 10 of the present book we provide a considerable body of field data as to how the social and political position of our respondents is related to their expectations regarding the way in which other people will vote or the way in which particular candidates will behave. On the other hand, Ernest Hilgard's article on "The Role of Learning in Perception" summarizes many experiments dealing with the way in which past

understanding of empirical process analysis helps to clarify a number of problems which have long been a source of logical difficulty in theoretical discussions. What a person considers important will affect what he notices in his environment. But an environment which impinges forcefully on an individual may very well modify his priorities. The interrelation between "needs" and "valences" (the psychological appeals of the objective environment) has been troublesome ever since Kurt Lewin brought it to the attention of psychologists. The same is true of the corresponding relationship between "attitudes" and "values," which the authors of *The Polish Peasant* attempted to make the cornerstone of a theoretical system. Now how are these problems resolved by the kind of process analysis on which the present study is based? The data which we need for such analysis consist of reports, obtained on at least two occasions, regarding the priorities which each individual assigns to issues or groups and his recent experiences or activities. We then ascertain how priorities at one time affect experiences at a later time; and, conversely, we study how experiences at one time period modify later priorities. Thus we end up with a set of empirical findings rather than a logical puzzle.

But one topic is still unsettled. If we have the right psychological variables and if we use panel analysis skilfully, are we in principle able to cover all essential elements in the course of an implementation? Some writers answer in the negative, because all this does not catch the "psychological mechanisms" which sustain the process. Asch, particularly, has voiced this warning in his critique of *The People's Choice*.[18] According to him, the panel analyst does not clarify "the processes that intervene between conditions and consequences"; nor does he provide the "meaningful nexus between his variables." But the matter is not quite so simple. In order to demonstrate this, we shall consider how one such "psychological mechanism" might be dealt with.

---

experiences affect perception (Hilgard's article appears in *Perception: An Approach to Personality*, eds. Robert R. Blake and Glen V. Ramsey [New York: Ronald Press Co., 1951]). Now the characteristics we used can be thought of as representing stored-up experiences. A comparison of experimental and field results, begun in two chapters here, should be carried out systematically.

18. *Social Psychology* (New York: Prentice-Hall, Inc., 1952), pp. 531 ff.

REACTIVATION—AN EXAMPLE OF A "PSYCHOLOGICAL MECHANISM"

No one, to our knowledge, has clearly defined what is meant by a psychological mechanism or a meaningful nexus. In giving an example, one has to do one's best to stay close to the concern on hand without quibbling about words. We shall offer here a simple mechanism of this kind and consider how it would be approached by various research designs. But first a word is needed on the choice of the example.

To a considerable extent, every presidential campaign provides its own focus for psychological inquiry. During the election of 1884, for example, the moral qualifications of the candidates were much discussed; in such a campaign the question of moral convictions as opposed to economic interests might become the focus of theoretical generalizations. In 1896 a very complicated substantive topic—the gold standard—was the main issue; in that campaign social psychologists might have gained considerable insight into the relation between information and attitudes. It is important to see how this point differs from the objection that, in studies of this kind, we cannot be certain that the results obtained in one community will hold true for all mankind at all times. There is no work in psychology except perhaps that of the strictest physiological kind which is not subject to this limitation. When we carry out experiments on suggestibility with American subjects, we cannot tell whether or not we would find the same results in another society in which conformity with one's fellows is not part of the culture. The difference between such studies and those reported here lies at quite another point. In these studies of suggestibility we determine in advance what it is, precisely, that we want to study. When we follow voters through six months of a political campaign, we focus, in a general way, on decision-making. But *what specific psychological mechanisms will come into play* depends to a considerable extent upon the nature of the campaign; and this can be known surely only after the fact.

In 1948, as the material of chapter 12 has made quite clear, the psychologically most interesting (and, at the same time, the politically most relevant) phenomenon was the last-minute return of many voters to an earlier disposition. These were persons who had voted for Roosevelt in 1944 and often had many demographic characteristics or past political allegiances which would predispose them to a Democratic vote. In June, 1948, however, they expressed little confidence in Truman and intended to vote for Dewey. Yet just before election day they changed in their intentions. Their final Democratic vote was thus the reactivation of a previous tendency.[19]

Detailed case studies might provide an idea of how such reactivation comes about. But some picture of this "mechanism" can be gleaned from materials more easily fitted into a panel study. Following the August wave of the panel, we selected a number of respondents who interested us for any of a number of reasons: some of them were clearly under cross-pressures (e.g., Catholic members of the CIO who intended to vote for Dewey); others had already registered a change in vote intention between two earlier interview waves. These individuals were interviewed in some detail regarding the way in which they then felt about the campaign and the approaching election, and the information from those interviews was combined with other questionnaire data obtained later from the same individuals. Thus, a composite picture of the typical "reactivation" sequence could be drawn.

Often we find that, at the beginning of the sequence, there is "consultation" with a friend, husband, father, brother, or mother who holds a more authoritative position with regard to politics. Some times it is practically an order to change votes. As one young woman reported: "My brother sent word to me to vote for him [Truman]. We just talked about what is going on. I usually take his advice, because he knows."

More often, however, the social contact need not "tell" the voter what to do. The voter tells himself, simply by talking it out. For example, a voter who changed some of his ideas on the Taft-Hartley Law said: "I just figured it out. I talked to the fellows about it.

19. This phenomenon has been observed before, of course. Consider, for example, the increased interest in classical music which developed when radio came on the scene and was able to provide a supply of such music. Very often those who were "influenced" by radio had had some musical education in high school, had negleced this interest later, and had reactivated it when radio provided an opportunity to hear good music (Edward A. Suchman, "Invitation to Music," *Radio Research 1941*, ed. P. F. Lazarsfeld and F. N. Stanton [New York: Duell, Sloan & Pearce, 1941]). In unpublished studies dealing with referenda on liquor and gambling laws, McPhee also found that, under the influence of propaganda, casual early attitudes of prospective voters gradually shifted so that they finally conformed to basic moral attitudes which had been held for a long time. None of these findings precludes the possibility, of course, that in some campaigns genuine conversions to new positions may come about.

We discussed it. Some agreed and some disagreed. We were just talking, and I thought of it." There is a very simple reason why these people turn back in the direction of the party that is *natural* for their type of person. They turn to their social environment for guidance, and that environment tends to support the party that is "right" for them also.

After this consultation with others or with one's self, a next stage sets in—typically in the heat of the campaign itself. Now, the newly formed but "natural" vote begins to be buttressed by changing foci of attention, by changes in subsidiary attitudes, and often by increasing interest. For example, the woman who had got her voting "orders" from her brother had said in June that she did not have time to "pay much attention to politics." In August, after she had heard from her brother and changed her intention to Truman accordingly, she still was lukewarm to Truman, confused his stand on the Taft-Hartley Law with Dewey's, and believed that Truman intended to compromise with Russia. However, her interest had quickened, and her store of supporting information had increased. For example, by October, she believed Truman was being blocked by the Republicans in his efforts to get public housing and that the Taft-Hartley Law was a major issue between the parties, with the Democrats fighting against it. She had now found time to discuss the elections, to read and hear news about them in all major media, and to have more opinions about the election than the people of average interest.

In other cases no direct personal influence can be traced at first. What we find, rather, is a slowly growing feeling of uneasiness which leads to a corrosion of the vote intention, temporarily at variance with one's environment. Quite likely, there are weak points in the attitude structure of these respondents; they like the candidate but disagree on an issue, or the other way around. Slowly, emphasis shifts to the negative element, until the entire deviant vote intention corrodes and crumbles, to be followed by a more "appropriate" one.

A plant worker was interviewed in September, literally in the midst of his shift in focus of attention and basis of decision. Two parts of the same interview with him reveal his earlier focus, and then the later one that was supplanting it: "I thought Dewey was the best man. I thought maybe changing the government would help. *I vote for the man.* . . . *I thought Truman wasn't qualified* to do what he stood for, but now I wonder. . . . Now I don't know. . . . [But] *I'm more for unions.* I don't believe in the Taft-Hartley Law. The Democrats as a whole are more for the middle class and poor. . . ." During his temporary intention to vote for Dewey he stresses the importance of personalities. When he is about to "return to the fold," he begins to advance the arguments which could reunite him with his occupational fellows in a common loyalty.

Sometimes a reactivation spans over quite a long time period. One Catholic family of fairly high income level started the campaign with an almost solid Republican stand on all issues. The entire family had driven to Albany to see Dewey return from the convention! At the start of the campaign their Republican ideas remained firm. But the image of the candidate was disintegrating by mid-September. For example: "Dewey is a snob who rules with his head not his heart. . . . Other people say Dewey is cocky, he lacks humility, can't be humble, is not interested in small people's opinion." The Republican vote remained a while, but by October most of the earlier decision had crumbled, with the solid middle-class Republican stand on issues breaking into indecision and occasional Democratic stands. Shortly thereafter, the party choice and vote followed. The people who made these remarks about Dewey's not being "interested in small people's opinions" were actually quite removed from the small people of Elmira, prosperous themselves and holding firm business-class convictions. But why did they, and not others of the same class, react so strongly to Dewey's lack of humility? The thing that distinguishes them from other Elmirans of their class is that they are Irish Catholics, perhaps with memories of their own or their parents' earlier days as underdogs in the melting pot, and perhaps in small ways still not "belonging" in the upper-middle-class, old-stock Protestant ruling circles of the town. In a curious way Dewey's person and behavior may have evoked old underdog hostilities in a way that Truman did not.

Here, then, is a possible example of what might be meant by a "psychological mechanism" (if we have correctly understood the proponents of this kind of concern): details on the reactivation of an earlier preference which had been dormant but which had regained its role in the course of the implementation process.

At this point the question of reactivation may be turned over to the experimental psychologist. He would raise questions of the following kind: How long can a latent disposition persist and still be reactivated? Obviously, a moment must come when it is so "buried" that no outside influence can revive it. What role is played by the circumstances under which the activity was abandoned in the first place? Which is easier to reactivate: an old interest which was just displaced by another one or an old one which somehow became frustrated and repressed? Are there rules which relate the situations in which a disposition was originally built up and those in which it is being reactivated? What ratio of similarity and difference in these situations is most conducive to reactivation?[20]

Now, what does a panel analyst do with this notion of reactivation? First, it must be remembered,. he identifies the process. He has observed shifting vote intentions for several months during the 1948 campaign and has noted that there were many more "rebels" among the traditional Democrats in early summer than on election day. He then asks himself what characterizes the persons whose Democratic predispositions were finally reactivated; and he finds that it was the people with low political interest, those with conflicting attitude patterns and background characteristics, who strayed from their old vote and returned to the fold in the end. They discussed politics less but were more influenced by discussion when it occurred; they were less active in middle-class organizations and therefore found less support for their temporary Republican vote intention. Interestingly enough, they were not often singled out by party contacts; but, when this happened to them, they were impressed. Furthermore, at the beginning of the campaign they attached little importance to economic matters; but, as election day approached, this issue acquired greater saliency for them.

20. Because modern psychologists exercise such ingenuity in developing experiments, it is sometimes mistakenly assumed that they have been equally successful in developing theoretical systems. This is not always the case. For example, Egon Brunswik, whose experiments during the 1930's were largely responsible for current interest in problems of social perception, reviewed the field recently and stated quite frankly that it "fall[s] just short of a full-fledged consideration of motivational factors . . . our instructions have in most cases endeavored to shift . . . from one cognitive variable to another rather than to modify the strength of intent toward one and the same variable" (*Perception and Personality: A Symposium*, pp. 62 ff.).

Note that, even as we state this summary, we introduce new "mechanisms": support from the primary environment, vulnerability to propaganda, increased saliency, etc. These, too, can be subjected to the same kind of investigation, making use of variables which have been observed repeatedly in time. More generally, we can say that a "psychological mechanism" usually starts out as a qualitative observation. Further investigation of these observations may take the form either of experiments or of field studies making use of panel interviews. In interpreting these empirical data, new "mechanisms" will be called into play. And so the cycle continues.[21]

It seems, then, that the relation between panel studies and psychological analysis is about as follows. The concepts of the systematic psychologist have to be translated into variables so that individual respondents can be identified and classified in regard to their relevant characteristics. Empirical process analysis, then, permits the testing of the relations which are presumed to exist. Usually a great part of a field study, however, is devoted to exploration and comes up with unanticipated findings. As they are interpreted, either existing theories can be drawn upon or the need for new developments is indicated. Here, as elsewhere, theory and empirical work meet and complement each other.

So far we have considered the fear that field studies based on panel data are not "deep" enough in a psychological sense. Now we must turn to another problem. Are these studies "broad" enough, in the sense of giving adequate consideration to social contexts?

THE SOCIOLOGICAL APPROACH

Again, there can hardly be general agreement on what is meant by a sociological approach. But the idea probably covers one or more of the following possibilities:

21. One effort has been made to translate a psychological mechanism into the language of process analysis. This dealt with "value homophily," the tendency of friends to agree with each other on important issues. It was found that a large part of the qualitative content could be translated into relations between variables over time. But there was a residual of expressions, similar to "reactivation," which resisted analysis; further examples would include such concepts as aggression, frustration, repression, and projection. At this moment it is still not clear whether or not the empirical content of these terms can be adequately described by a time-series analysis of carefully selected psychological and sociological variables (see Paul F. Lazarsfeld and Robert K. Merton, "Friendship as Social Process: A Substantive and Methodological Analysis," in *Freedom and Control in Modern Society: Papers in Honor of R. M. MacIver* [New York: D. Van Nostrand Co., 1954]).

1. That the variables of a panel analysis should contain information on primary social contacts; the kinds of friends people have, the frequencies with which they discuss politics, the associations to which they belong, etc.
2. That some other variables should take into account broader institutional positions of the respondents: whether a man works in a small shop or a big plant; whether a lawyer works for a corporation or as a free professional; whether a man grew up on a farm and then moved to the city or is city-born; etc.
3. That by and large we should not be concerned with explaining individual vote decisions but rather with accounting for the difference in voting *rates*, if they show consistent variations between different social groups.
4. That we should relate data collected about individuals to other data collected on changes in the activities of institutions, like the propaganda of parties, the role of labor unions, etc.
5. That we should not confine ourselves to one community but study on a comparative basis several communities which vary in sociologically significant ways.

The first and the last of these requirements we can quickly dispose of: the first because the reader will have noticed how much information we have available on the primary contacts of our respondents, the latter because everyone agrees in principle—as a matter of fact there are comparative data already available, as can be seen from Appendix A. It is only a matter of time when comparative studies will be carried out in a more systematic way. The remaining three requirements do deserve comment, and it seems best to start with the third one, the emphasis on consistent social differences in rates. In principle, the matter can be formulated as follows. Until now we have been focusing on individual voters and studying the influences which impinge upon them. From this perspective, other persons play the role of external stimuli, comparable to the influence of a pamphlet or of the weather. Suppose, however, that we consider *groups* of individuals as our units of study. Then we will be able to analyze the *behavior of collectivities* over time.

In many senses this is a time-honored tradition. More than fifty years ago Durkheim pointed out that the essence of sociological method is its concern with rates;[22] he emphasized that, as a sociologist, he wanted most of all to explain why suicide rates, for example, vary from one group to another. Later on, chiefly under the

22. *The Rules of Sociological Method* (Chicago: University of Chicago Press, 1938), chaps. i and v.

influence of Pareto's American interpreter,[23] a more complex type of sociological analysis evolved: in it the notion of "social system" received emphasis. This idea became more than a figure of speech with the development of mathematical models describing how such systems are maintained. A model of this kind might take the following form: Each individual in a group of people would be characterized by a certain attitude. Two equations might then be set down: one would indicate the probability of contact between people having different attitudes; a second would describe the changes in attitudes which might come about as a result of these contacts. Such a system of equations would then permit us to predict what attitude distribution would evolve in time for the group as a whole; it would also permit us to make quite interesting, and not at all obvious, deductions which could themselves be tested.[24]

A sociological proposition involves properties of groups; a sociological interpretation explains findings in terms which include interactions between group members. In the present study this approach is best exemplified by the material in chapters 6 and 7. We shall summarize these in a simplified form in order to bring out the main lines of thought. First of all, we note that the ratio of Republicans and Democrats in Elmira changes little over many years. This constancy of the net distribution is the result of many compensating shifts and is more surprising than it seems at first glance. In order to come about, it is necessary that—in raw numbers—approximately as many Democratic vote intentions turn Republican as the reverse. But there are many more Republicans than Democrats in Protestant middle-class Elmira. Therefore, the *rate* of defection from the minority party has to be considerably larger than the defection rate in the majority, if the exchanges in raw numbers are to be equal.

How is this to be explained? The answer has to do, crudely, with the number of interactions which come about and the effect they have on people. Merely on the grounds of probability considerations, Democrats are more likely to meet with Republicans than

23. L. J. Henderson, *Pareto's General Sociology: A Physiologist's Interpretation* (Cambridge, Mass.: Harvard University Press, 1937).

24. J. Coleman, "An Expository Analysis of Some of Rashevsky's Social Behavior Models," in *Mathematical Thinking in the Social Sciences* (Glencoe, Ill.: Free Press, 1954), pp. 105–55.

the opposite case; this could account for the larger defection rate of the Democrats. But our findings go a step further. Within various social strata (ethnic, religious, and economic) the political parties maintain fairly constant rates of support which differ markedly from one stratum to the next. In order to account for this, one has to assume that political discussion goes on mainly *within* certain groups and is much less likely to cross social barriers of all kinds. This, too, is corroborated by the empirical findings. Thus, we have here all the elements which are needed for a more complex analysis in terms of a "social system": contact frequencies differentiated according to the attitudes of the group members; effects of contacts at one time on attitudes at a subsequent period; resulting consequences for the attitude equilibrium in the group—which includes net changes for the total system as well as compensating shifts among individuals.

Furthermore, the interaction and conversation rates between people seem to vary with the cycle engendered by the recurrence of elections every fourth year. Under the pressure of presidential campaigns, contacts with political content increase. As a consequence, the difference in defection rates between majority and minority are accentuated, and this, in turn, leads to an increasing polarization of the community. Between elections political conversations are much less frequent, and, as a result, it must be that the primary groups and the demographic strata become less homogeneous.[25] Thus we have made part of our sociological approach the study of contacts and conversations, and at this point our book ties in with a tradition which has been badly neglected for some time.

At about the turn of the century public opinion ceased to be a topic of general speculation and became the object of specific and detailed monographs. Among the earliest of these were a number

25. This political "pulsation" of the community—if, as our data indicate, there *is* such a detectable cycle—is probably different according to different historical conditions. More detailed study is quite feasible with historical data (on voting in small ecological units of a socially homogeneous type). McPhee has found, for example, a detectable pulsation whereby Democratic congressional districts (over 60 per cent) became more Republican between 1948 and 1950 and Republican districts more Democratic (the latter in almost half the cases, despite a nation-wide Republican trend). The matter would have to be checked with much smaller and more homogeneous districts, however, with careful consideration of certain statistical difficulties (e.g., regression phenomena). This will be attempted in the analysis of the 1950 study.

of essays by Gabriel Tarde, the French psychologist. In one, Tarde concerned himself with the effect which outside influences, like newspapers, had in the process of opinion formation. But the analysis he considered central was contained in his paper, "La Conversation."[26] He was convinced that opinions are really formed through the day-to-day exchange of comments and observations which goes on among people. His suggestions came very close to our notion of implementation: by the very process of talking to one another, the vague dispositions which people have are crystallized, step by step, into specific attitudes, acts, or votes. He felt that careful empirical study of conversations was basic to sociology; and he suggested a large number of hypotheses as to who talked to whom about what and how much, all in terms of the social characteristics of the interlocutors and of variations in the historical scene.

When *The People's Choice* was written, this side of Tarde's ideas was not known to the authors. Still, as was pointed out at the time, the role of personal influence impressed itself as crucial. The way the matter was looked at then illustrates the difference between using individual as opposed to collective units of analysis. In that stage whatever findings existed became formulated in what one might call an asymmetric way. Attention was focused upon the individuals in the sample; people outside the sample, with whom conversations were reported, were considered as "influences." Upon subsequent thought, however, it became obvious that there is no difference between people inside or outside the sample. If the latter were interviewed, they would have reported our original respondents as influences. The correct solution is to make the conversation —the pair or group of interlocutors—the unit of analysis. This brings us back, full circle, to thinking which parallels Tarde's ideas and to the material recorded in this report, especially in chapter 6.[27]

26. *L'Opinion et la foule* (Paris, 1901), pp. 82–159.

27. A study carried out in Decatur, Illinois, represents something of a halfway mark between the "asymmetric" position of *The People's Choice* and the "symmetric sociology" toward which chap. 7 of the present report is a beginning (see E. Katz and P. F. Lazarsfeld, *Personal Influence*, to be published by the Free Press, 1954). It is interesting that in the systematic sociology of Leopold von Wiese, which is also based on the analysis of interaction, the notion of conversation hardly appears (see the English ed. by Howard Becker [New York, 1932]). On the other hand, the categories developed by Bales to describe interactions of people during the group discussion very clearly belong in the Tarde tradition.

Our study unquestionably contains data which deal with systems of individuals and, to this extent, fits in with one tradition of sociology. Yet we still must relate data of the kind just considered to sociological contexts which are even broader. It is conventional to distinguish three levels of sociological analysis: that concerned with primary groups like the family and friendship cliques; that dealing with organizations like political parties or unions; and that which considers broad social units like communities, regions, or nations. Clearly, the bulk of our data relate either directly to primary groups or to clusters of them in social strata, with the latter taken, in fact, as indicators of present and past primary contacts. Organizations like the political parties have been described qualitatively, but, as has been mentioned in the Introduction, they are seldom linked systematically with our data. The broad regional and national scene is referred to only occasionally. Still, in one respect, these larger contexts come into the empirical evidence. Social influence is exerted on the individual primarily through his intimate associates, of course. But when these primary groups are not homogeneous politically, the more distant surroundings—here the Republican community—may have especial effect. This is what has been called, in chapter 6, the "breakage" effect, for want of a better term. The context—the climate of opinion, the atmosphere, so to speak—breaks through whenever the primary environment gives it an opening. As fragile as our data are at this point, this result at least illustrates how mechanisms discovered in these "microscopic" studies can be linked to macroscopic sociological and historical concerns.

This question of the importance of context is intimately connected with a matter on which the Elmira study provides little clear knowledge but many intriguing clues. It is a phenomenon that is recurrent in politics, public opinion, and especially in popular culture—the idea of "age generations" with distinctive tastes dating back to the peculiar conditions under which each came of age.[28] In a general way, it is intuitively understandable why we should have "lost generations," "depression generations," and the like, for these people grew up politically in different atmospheres. But what more particular clues can our data provide about the way this comes about?

28. For a review of the major literature see R. Heberle, *Social Movements* (New York, 1951), chap. 6.

For one thing, while it is true that we find generations to exist in politics (those who came of age in the 1920's being more Republican, those in the 1930's more Democratic), actually what is more marked in the data and more interesting is this: that these generations differ markedly in the basis of their voting traditions. The generation of the 1920's splits more on religion, that of the 1930's more on socio-economic class (chap. 4). The changes in national atmosphere which we call "historical eras" must have less permanent effect on the party division on votes than on the *basis* of this division, that is, the kinds of strains, disagreements, conflicts of interest, etc., that are salient in affecting the votes of a given generation. In other words, not only opinions themselves but also the priority variables which we discussed earlier shift rather discontinuously from one generation to the next.[29]

It is commonly assumed (and probably true in Europe) that the break comes early in political life, perhaps in the teens; but our data favor the idea that American generations grow apart in politics at later ages, say, in the late twenties or early thirties. One reason, of course, is the apolitical nature of American youth. But a more compelling consideration arises: It is only in adulthood that most youths in places like Elmira face the problem of adjusting *groups* politically. They are, first of all, rapidly forming *new groups* in the twenties, as they get married, settle down to permanent jobs, take up residence in their neighborhoods, etc. Especially we know that, when kinship groups of differing political beliefs come together in marriage, one or the other of them "loses" a vote and thus loses the continuity of its political tradition. Second, *existing* groups are for the first time "coming alive" politically. We know, for example, that young first voters aged twenty-one to twenty-four have a rather large degree of heterogeneity within their friendship groups. This must be in part because they do not care. But, as these young groups become more interested in politics, between ages twenty and thirty, there must inevitably follow adjustments of conflicting beliefs, selections

---

29. Society may tend to adjust itself to new problems—and thus develop new grounds for political decision—less by individual changes in preferences than by changes *between* generations. A father may not change his mind, nor a son his, but the *society* "changes its mind" when the son differs from the father. It is a familiar idea in history and sociology that, the more rapidly the society changes, the more strains appear between generations.

of compatible friends, and the mutual influence of each member on the others, with respect now to *politics* and other adult concerns (as opposed to popular music or dating, for example). Our data crudely indicate that much of the adjustment takes place by age thirty-five.

Now to return to our itemization of what might be meant by a sociological approach. While not all the elements have been developed in this study, some are very clearly present, others are implied, and for all of them one statement seems justified: In principle they *can* be introduced into this kind of process analysis and there is good reason to hope that this will happen as the methological problems involved become gradually clearer. One possibility deserves special mention. Ample data are available to develop what one might call an "ecological" type of panel study. We could, for example, take the counties within a state and look at their voting record over a period of decades. Technically, this would be equivalent to repeated interviews with the same people. The corresponding variables would be voting rates, economic indexes, population data, etc. Here is a task in which social research could help the historian to enlarge the scope of his work.[30]

CONCLUSION

We have now located the Elmira study in a broader context of inquiry. Its characteristic procedure—the panel technique—mediates between detailed psychological analysis and the tracing-out of broad structural contexts. It emphasizes short-range change but in such a way that its findings can be fitted into longer historical trends.

In his presidential address before the American Psychological Association, one psychologist who had collaborated with a team of sociologists called for a "single behavioral science, with the theoretical structure that will account for the *actions* and the changes of potentialities for action both of *individuals and of groups*."[31] Why we "vote for a congressman" was one example of relevant behavior he felt we should be able to explain. His suggestion was made in ex-

30. As a matter of fact, such studies are now being developed at Columbia University's Bureau of Applied Social Research by S. M. Lipset and Lee Benson.

31. Robert Sears, "Social Behavior and Personality Development," Talcott Parsons and E. A. Shils (eds.), in *Toward a General Theory of Action* (Cambridge: Harvard University Press, 1951), pp. 465 ff.

plicit awareness that we are still very far from this goal and that we are not always precisely sure what direction to follow. Detailed monographic studies on various types of actions are likely to bring us forward a step or two. The present study, we hope, is a useful illustration.

14 DEMOCRATIC PRACTICE AND DEMOCRATIC THEORY[1]

> There is always a terrible gulf between the fine and
> elevating theories about democracy which we read in
> books on political theory and the actual facts of politics.
> LORD LINDSAY

I

What does all this mean for the political theory of democracy? For
we have been studying not how people come to make choices in
general but how they make a political choice, and the political
content of the study has broad ramifications beyond the technical
interests. In the end, of course, we must leave such theoretical questions to the political theorists and the political philosophers. But
the fact that they would not be at home in our empirical material
has encouraged us to speak at least briefly to their concerns. Both
theory and facts are needed. As Schumpeter says in *Capitalism,
Socialism and Democracy*: "The question whether [certain] conditions are fulfilled to the extent required in order to make democracy work should not be answered by reckless assertion or equally
reckless denial. It can be answered only by a laborious appraisal of
a maze of conflicting evidence."

With respect to politics, empirical-analytic theory and normative
theory have only recently become truly separated—and often to their
mutual disadvantage and impoverishment. In a recent essay a
British scholar comments on "The Decline of Political Theory."
That there has been and is now a "decline" seems to be generally
accepted. Why? Because, says Alfred Cobban, the theory of the
great political thinkers of the past was written "with a practical

1. The senior author is particularly indebted to his friend and colleague,
Edward Shils, for stimulation and instruction on this topic in general and for
advice on this chapter in particular.

purpose in mind. Their object was to influence actual political behavior. They wrote to condemn or support existing institutions, to
justify a political system or persuade their fellow citizens to change
it: because, in the last resort, they were concerned with the aims,
the purposes of political society." He points out that John Stuart
Mill tried to reconcile the demands for state action with established
ideals of individual liberty, Bentham to establish a theoretical basis
for the legislative and administrative reforms that were then urgent-
ly needed, Burke to provide an alternative to the new democratic
principle of the sovereignty of the people, Locke to provide a political theory for a generation that had overthrown divine right and
established parliamentary government, Hobbes to maintain the pri-
macy of sovereignty in an age of civil wars, etc. From being "formerly the work of men intently concerned with practical issues," the
study of political theory

has become instead an academic discipline written in various esoteric jar-
gons almost as though for the purpose of preventing it from being understood by those who, if they did understand it, might try to put it into
practice. . . . Political theory has in this way become disengaged from
political facts. Even worse, it has become disengaged on principle, as it
has seldom if ever been in the past.

Here, it seems to us, lies one potential use of our data. If the
political theorists do not engage directly in politics, they might
explore the relevance, the implications, and the meaning of such
empirical facts as are contained in this and similar studies. Political
theory written with reference to practice has the advantage that its
categories are the categories in which political life really occurs.
And, in turn, relating research to problems of normative theory
would make such research more realistic and more pertinent
to the problems of policy. At the same time, empirical research can
help to clarify the standards and correct the empirical presupposi-
tions of normative theory. As a modest illustration, this concluding
chapter of the volume turns to some of the broad normative and
evaluative questions implied in this empirical study.

REQUIREMENTS FOR THE INDIVIDUAL

Perhaps the main impact of realistic research on contemporary
politics has been to temper some of the requirements set by our
traditional normative theory for the typical citizen. "Out of all this

literature of political observation and analysis, which is relatively new," says Max Beloff, "there has come to exist a picture in our minds of the political scene which differs very considerably from that familiar to us from the classical texts of democratic politics."

Experienced observers have long known, of course, that the individual voter was not all that the theory of democracy requires of him. As Bryce put it:

> How little solidity and substance there is in the political or social beliefs of nineteen persons out of every twenty. These beliefs, when examined, mostly resolve themselves into two or three prejudices and aversions, two or three prepossessions for a particular party or section of a party, two or three phrases or catch-words suggesting or embodying arguments which the man who repeats them has not analyzed.

While our data do not support such an extreme statement, they do reveal that certain requirements commonly assumed for the successful operation of democracy are not met by the behavior of the "average" citizen. The requirements, and our conclusions concerning them, are quickly reviewed.[2]

Interest, discussion, motivation.—The democratic citizen is expected to be interested and to participate in political affairs. His interest and participation can take such various forms as reading and listening to campaign materials, working for the candidate or the party, arguing politics, donating money, and voting. In Elmira the majority of the people vote, but in general they do not give evidence of sustained interest. Many vote without real involvement in the election, and even the party workers are not typically motivated by ideological concerns or plain civic duty.

If there is one characteristic for a democratic system (besides the ballot itself) that is theoretically required, it is the capacity for and the practice of discussion. "It is as true of the large as of the small society," says Lindsay, "that its health depends on the mutual understanding which discussion makes possible; and that discussion is the only possible instrument of its democratic government." How much participation in political discussion there is in the community, what it is, and among whom—these questions have been given answers in an earlier chapter. In this instance

2. A somewhat more general statement is contained in Bernard Berelson, "Democratic Theory and Public Opinion," *Public Opinion Quarterly*, XVI (fall, 1952), 313–30.

there was little true discussion between the candidates, little in the newspaper commentary, little between the voters and the official party representatives, some within the electorate. On the grass-roots level there was more talk than debate, and, at least inferentially, the talk had important effects upon voting, in reinforcing or activating the partisans if not in converting the opposition.

An assumption underlying the theory of democracy is that the citizenry has a strong motivation for participation in political life. But it is a curious quality of voting behavior that for large numbers of people motivation is weak if not almost absent. It is assumed that this motivation would gain its strength from the citizen's perception of the difference that alternative decisions made to him. Now when a person buys something or makes other decisions of daily life, there are direct and immediate consequences for him. But for the bulk of the American people the voting decision is not followed by any direct, immediate, visible personal consequences. Most voters, organized or unorganized, are not in a position to foresee the distant and indirect consequences for themselves, let alone the society. The ballot is cast, and for most people that is the end of it. If their side is defeated, "it doesn't really matter."

Knowledge.—The democratic citizen is expected to be well informed about political affairs. He is supposed to know what the issues are, what their history is, what the relevant facts are, what alternatives are proposed, what the party stands for, what the likely consequences are. By such standards the voter falls short. Even when he has the motivation, he finds it difficult to make decisions on the basis of full information when the subject is relatively simple and proximate; how can he do so when it is complex and remote? The citizen is not highly informed on details of the campaign, nor does he avoid a certain misperception of the political situation when it is to his psychological advantage to do so. The electorate's perception of what goes on in the campaign is colored by emotional feeling toward one or the other issue, candidate, party, or social group.

Principle.—The democratic citizen is supposed to cast his vote on the basis of principle—not fortuitously or frivolously or implusively or habitually, but with reference to standards not only of his own interest but of the common good as well. Here, again, if this requirement is pushed at all strongly, it becomes an impossible demand on the democratic electorate.

Many voters vote not for principle in the usual sense but "for" a group to which they are attached—their group. The Catholic vote or the hereditary vote is explainable less as principle than as a traditional social allegiance. The ordinary voter, bewildered by the complexity of modern political problems, unable to determine clearly what the consequences are of alternative lines of action, remote from the arena, and incapable of bringing information to bear on principle, votes the way trusted people around him are voting. A British scholar, Max Beloff, takes as the "chief lesson to be derived" from such studies:

> Election campaigns and the programmes of the different parties have little to do with the ultimate result which is predetermined by influences acting upon groups of voters over a longer period. . . . This view has now become a working hypothesis with which all future thinking on this matter will have to concern itself. But if this is admitted, then obviously the picture of the voter as a person exercising conscious choice between alternative persons and alternative programmes tends to disappear.

On the issues of the campaign there is a considerable amount of "don't know"—sometimes reflecting genuine indecision, more often meaning "don't care." Among those with opinions the partisans *agree* on most issues, criteria, expectations, and rules of the game. The supporters of the different sides disagree on only a few issues. Nor, for that matter, do the candidates themselves always join the issue sharply and clearly. The partisans do not agree overwhelmingly with their own party's position, or, rather, only the small minority of highly partisan do; the rest take a rather moderate position on the political considerations involved in an election.

Rationality.—The democratic citizen is expected to exercise rational judgment in coming to his voting decision. He is expected to have arrived at his principles by reason and to have considered rationally the implications and alleged consequences of the alternative proposals of the contending parties. Political theorists and commentators have always exclaimed over the seeming contrast here between requirement and fulfilment. Even as sensible and hard-minded an observer as Schumpeter was extreme in his view:

Even if there were no political groups trying to influence him, the typical citizen would in political matters tend to yield to extra-rational or irrational prejudice and impulse. The weakness of the rational processes he applies to politics and the absence of effective logical control over the results he arrives at would in themselves suffice to account for that. Moreover, simply because he is not "all there," he will relax his usual moral standards as well and occasionally give in to dark urges which the conditions of private life help him to repress.

Here the problem is first to see just what is meant by rationality. The term, as a recent writer noted, "has enjoyed a long history which has bequeathed to it a legacy of ambiguity and confusion. . . . Any man may be excused when he is puzzled by the question how he ought to use the word and particularly how he ought to use it in relation to human conduct and politics." Several meanings can be differentiated.

It is not for us to certify a meaning. But even without a single meaning—with only the aura of the term—we can make some observations on the basis of our material. In any rigorous or narrow sense the voters are not highly rational; that is, most of them do not ratiocinate on the matter, e.g., to the extent that they do on the purchase of a car or a home. Nor do voters act rationally whose "principles" are held so tenaciously as to blind them to information and persuasion. Nor do they attach efficient means to explicit ends. The fact that some people change their minds during a political campaign shows the existence of that open-mindedness usually considered a component of rationality. But among whom? Primarily among those who can "afford" a change of mind, in the sense that they have ties or attractions on both sides—the cross-pressured voters in the middle where rationality is supposed to take over from the extremes of partisan feeling. But it would hardly be proper to designate the unstable, uninterested, uncaring middle as the sole or the major possessor of rationality among the electorate. As Beloff points out: "It is likely that the marginal voter is someone who is so inadequately identified with one major set of interests or another and so remote, therefore, from the group-thinking out of which political attitudes arise, that his voting record is an illustration, not of superior wisdom, but of greater frivolity."

The upshot of this is that the usual analogy between the voting "decision" and the more or less carefully calculated decisions of consumers or businessmen or courts, incidentally, may be quite incorrect. For many voters political preferences may better be considered analogous to cultural tastes—in music, literature, recreational activities, dress, ethics, speech, social behavior. Consider the parallels between political preferences and general cultural tastes. Both have their origin in ethnic, sectional, class, and family traditions. Both exhibit stability and resistance to change for individuals but flexibility and adjustment over generations for the society as a whole. Both seem to be matters of sentiment and disposition rather than "reasoned preferences." While both are responsive to changed conditions and unusual stimuli, they are relatively invulnerable to direct argumentation and vulnerable to indirect social influences. Both are characterized more by faith than by conviction and by wishful expectation rather than careful prediction of consequences. The preference for one party rather than another must be highly similar to the preference for one kind of literature or music rather than another, and the choice of the same political party every four years may be parallel to the choice of the same old standards of conduct in new social situations. In short, it appears that a sense of fitness is a more striking feature of political preference than reason and calculation.

II

If the democratic system depended solely on the qualifications of the individual voter, then it seems remarkable that democracies have survived through the centuries. After examining the detailed data on how individuals misperceive political reality or respond to irrelevant social influences, one wonders how a democracy ever solves its political problems. But when one considers the data in a broader perspective—how huge segments of the society adapt to political conditions affecting them or how the political system adjusts itself to changing conditions over long periods of time—he cannot fail to be impressed with the total result. Where the rational citizen seems to abdicate, nevertheless angels seem to tread.

The eminent judge, Learned Hand, in a delightful essay on "Democracy: Its Presumptions and Reality," comes to essentially this conclusion.

I do not know how it is with you, but for myself I generally give up at the outset. The simplest problems which come up from day to day seem to me quite unanswerable as soon as I try to get below the surface. . . . My vote is one of the most unimportant acts of my life; if I were to acquaint myself with the matters on which it ought really to depend, if I were to try to get a judgment on which I was willing to risk affairs of even the smallest moment, I should be doing nothing else, and that seems a fatuous conclusion to a fatuous undertaking.

Yet he recognizes the paradox—somehow the system not only works on the most difficult and complex questions but often works with distinction. "For, abuse it as you will, it gives a bloodless measure of social forces—bloodless, have you thought of that?—a means of continuity, a principle of stability, a relief from the paralyzing terror of revolution."

Justice Hand concludes that we have "outgrown" the conditions assumed in traditional democratic theory and that "the theory has ceased to work." And yet, the system that has grown out of classic democratic theory, and, in this country, out of quite different and even elementary social conditions, does continue to work—perhaps even more vigorously and effectively than ever.

That is the paradox. *Individual voters* today seem unable to satisfy the requirements for a democratic system of government outlined by political theorists. But the *system of democracy* does meet certain requirements for a going political organization. The individual members may not meet all the standards, but the whole nevertheless survives and grows. This suggests that where the classic theory is defective is in its concentration on the *individual citizen*. What are undervalued are certain collective properties that reside in the electorate as a whole and in the political and social system in which it functions.

The political philosophy we have inherited, then, has given more consideration to the virtues of the typical citizen of the democracy than to the working of the *system* as a whole. Moreover, when it dealt with the system, it mainly considered the single constitutive institutions of the system, not those general features necessary if the institutions are to work as required. For example, the rule of law, representative government, periodic elections, the party system, and the several freedoms of discussion, press, association, and assembly have all been examined by political philosophers seeking to clarify and to justify the idea of political democracy. But liberal democracy is more than a political system in which individual voters and political institutions operate. For political democracy to survive, other features are required: the intensity of conflict must be limited, the rate of change must be restrained, stability in the social and economic structure must be maintained, a pluralistic social organization must exist, and a basic consensus must bind together the contending parties.

Such features of the system of political democracy belong neither to the constitutive institutions nor to the individual voter. It might be said that they form the atmosphere or the environment in which both operate. In any case, such features have not been carefully considered by political philosophers, and it is on these broader properties of the democratic political system that more reflection and study by political theory is called for. In the most tentative fashion let us explore the values of the political system, as they involve the electorate, in the light of the foregoing considerations.

REQUIREMENTS FOR THE SYSTEM

Underlying the paradox is an assumption that the population is homogeneous socially and should be homogeneous politically: that everybody is about the same in relevant social characteristics; that, if something is a political virtue (like interest in the election), then everyone should have it; that there is such a thing as "the" typical citizen on whom uniform requirements can be imposed. The tendency of classic democratic literature to work with an image of "the" voter was never justified. For, as we will attempt to illustrate here, some of the most important requirements that democratic values impose on a system require a voting population that is not homogeneous but heterogeneous in its political qualities.

The need for heterogeneity arises from the contradictory functions we expect our voting system to serve. We expect the political system to adjust itself and our affairs to changing conditions; yet we demand too that it display a high degree of stability. We expect the contending interests and parties to pursue their ends vigorously and the voters to care; yet, after the election is over, we expect reconciliation. We expect the voting outcome to serve what is best for the community; yet we do not want disinterested voting unattached to the purposes and interests of different segments of that community. We want voters to express their own free and self-determined choices; yet, for the good of the community, we would like voters to avail themselves of the best information and guidance available from the groups and leaders around them. We expect a high degree of rationality to prevail in the decision; but were all irrationality and mythology absent, and all ends pursued by the most coldly rational selection of political means, it is doubtful if the system would hold together.

In short, our electoral system calls for apparently incompatible properties—which, although they cannot all reside in each individual voter, can (and do) reside in a heterogeneous electorate. What seems to be required of the electorate as a whole is a *distribution* of qualities along important dimensions. We need some people who are active in a certain respect, others in the middle, and still others passive. The contradictory things we want from the total require that the parts be different. This can be illustrated by taking up a number of important dimensions by which an electorate might be characterized.

Involvement and Indifference

How could a mass democracy work if all the people were deeply involved in politics? Lack of interest by some people is not without its benefits, too. True, the highly interested voters vote more, and know more about the campaign, and read and listen more, and participate more; however, they are also less open to persuasion and less likely to change. Extreme interest goes with extreme partisanship and might culminate in rigid fanaticism that could destroy democratic processes if generalized throughout the community. Low affect toward the election—not caring much—underlies the resolution of many political problems; votes can be resolved into a two-party split instead of fragmented into many parties (the splinter parties of the left, for example, splinter because their advocates are *too* interested in politics). Low interest provides maneuvering room for political shifts necessary for a complex society in a period of rapid change. Compromise might be based upon sophisticated awareness of costs and returns—perhaps impossible to demand of a mass society—but it is more often induced by indifference. Some people are and should be highly interested in politics, but not everyone is or needs to be. Only the doctrinaire would deprecate the moderate indifference that facilitates compromise.

Hence, an important balance between action motivated by strong sentiments and action with little passion behind it is obtained by heterogeneity within the electorate. Balance of this sort is, in practice, met by a distribution of voters rather than by a homogeneous collection of "ideal" citizens.

Stability and Flexibility

A similar dimension along which an electorate might be characterized is stability-flexibility. The need for change and adaptation is clear, and the need for stability ought equally to be (especially from observation of current democratic practice in, say, certain Latin-American countries).

How is political stability achieved? There are a number of social sources of political stability: the training of the younger generation before it is old enough to care much about the matter, the natural selection that surrounds the individual voter with families and friends who reinforce his own inclinations, the tendency to adjust in favor of the majority of the group, the self-perpetuating tendency of political traditions among ethnic and class and regional strata where like-minded people find themselves socially together. Political stability is based upon social stability. Family traditions, personal associations, status-related organizational memberships, ethnic affiliations, socioeconomic strata—such ties for the individual do not change rapidly or sharply, and since his vote is so importantly a product of them, neither does it. In effect, a large part of the study of voting deals not with why votes change but rather with why they do not.

In addition, the varying conditions facing the country, the varying political appeals made to the electorate, and the varying dispositions of the voters activated by these stimuli—these, combined with the long-lasting nature of the political loyalties they instil, produce an important cohesion within the system. For example, the tendencies operating in 1948 electoral decisions not only were built up in the New Deal and Fair Deal era but also dated back to parental and grandparental loyalties, to religious and ethnic cleavages of a past era, and to moribund sectional and community conflicts. Thus, in a very real sense any particular election is a composite of various elections and various political and social events. People vote for a President on a given November day, but their choice is made not simply on the basis of what has happened in the preceding months or even four years; in 1948 some people were in effect voting on the internationalism issue of 1940, others on the depression issues of 1932, and some, indeed, on the slavery issues of 1860.

The vote is thus a kind of "moving average" of reactions to the political past. Voters carry over to each new election remnants of issues raised in previous elections—and so there is always an overlapping of old and new decisions that give a cohesion in time to the political system. Hence the composite decision "smooths out" political change. The people vote *in* the same election, but not all of them vote *on* it.

What of flexibility? Curiously, the voters least admirable when measured against individual requirements contribute most when measured against the aggregate requirement for flexibility. For those who change political preferences most readily are those who are least interested, who are subject to conflicting social pressures, who have inconsistent beliefs and erratic voting histories. Without them—if the decision were left only to the deeply concerned, well-integrated, consistently-principled ideal citizens—the political system might easily prove too rigid to adapt to changing domestic and international conditions.

In fact, it may be that the very people who are most sensitive to changing social conditions are those most susceptible to political change. For, in either case, the people exposed to membership in overlapping strata, those whose former life-patterns are being broken up, those who are moving about socially or physically, those who are forming new families and new friendships—it is they who are open to adjustments of attitudes and tastes. They may be the least partisan and the least interested voters, but they perform a valuable function for the entire system. Here again is an instance in which an individual "inadequacy" provides a positive service for the society: The campaign can be a reaffirming force for the settled majority and a creative force for the unsettled minority. There is stability on both sides and flexibility in the middle.

Progress and Conservation

Closely related to the question of stability is the question of past versus future orientation of the system. In America a progressive outlook is highly valued, but, at the same time, so is a conservative one. Here a balance between the two is easily found in the party system and in the distribution of voters themselves from extreme conservatives to extreme liberals. But a balance between the two is also achieved by a distribution of political dispositions through time. There are periods of great political agitation (i.e., campaigns) alternating with periods of political dormancy. Paradoxically, the former—the campaign period—is likely to be an instrument of conservatism, often even of historical regression.

Many contemporary campaigns (not, however, 1952) must be stabilizing forces that activated past tendencies in individuals and reasserted past patterns of group voting. In 1948, for example, the middle-class Protestants reaffirmed their traditional Republican position, the working-class Protestants reverted toward their position of the 1930's and the working-class Catholics toward their position not only of the 1930's but of a generation or more earlier. In this sense the campaign was a retreat away from new issues back toward old positions.

Political campaigns tend to make people more consistent both socially and psychologically; they vote more with their social groups and agree more with their own prior ideas on the issues. But new ideas and new alignments are in their infancy manifested by inconsistency psychologically and heterogeneity socially; they are almost by definition deviant and minority points of view. To the extent that they are inhibited by pressure or simply by knowledge of what is the proper (i.e., majority) point of view in a particular group, then the campaign period is not a time to look for the growth of important new trends.

This "regressive tendency" may appear as a reaction to intense propaganda during decisive times. The term "regressive" need not imply a reversion to less-developed, less-adaptive behavior; in fact, one might argue that the revival of a Democratic vote among workers was functional for their interests. What it refers to is simply the reactivation of prior dispositions—dispositions in politics that date back years and decades, often to a prior political era.

Its counterpart, of course, is what we believe to be an important potential for progress during the periods of relaxed tension and low-pressure political and social stimuli that are especially characteristic of America between political campaigns. The very tendency for Americans to neglect their political system most of the time—to be "campaign citizens" in the sense that many are "Sunday church-goers"—is not without its values. Change may come best from relaxation.

Again, then, a balance (between preservation of the past and receptivity to the future) seems to be required of a democratic electorate. The heterogeneous electorate in itself provides a balance between liberalism and conservatism; and so does the sequence of political events from periods of drifting change to abrupt rallies back to the loyalties of earlier years.

Consensus and Cleavage

We have talked much in the text, and perhaps implied more, about consensus and cleavage. Although there were certain clusters of political opinion in Elmira, at the same time there were a number of opinions that did not break along class or party lines. American opinion on public issues is much too complex to be designated by such simple, single-minded labels as *the* housewife opinion or *the* young people's opinion or even *the* workers' opinion. If one uses as a base the central Republican-Democratic cleavage, then one finds numerous "contradictions" within individuals, within strata and groups, and within party supporters themselves. There are many issues presented, cafeteria-style, for the voter to choose from, and there are overlaps in opinion in every direction.

Similarly there are required *social* consensus and cleavage—in effect, pluralism—in politics. Such pluralism makes for enough consensus to hold the system together and enough cleavage to make it move. Too much consensus would be deadening and restrictive of liberty; too much cleavage would be destructive of the society as a whole.

Consider the pictures of the hypothetical relationships between political preference (e.g., party support) and a social characteristic as presented in this chart:

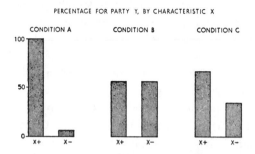

PERCENTAGE FOR PARTY Y, BY CHARACTERISTIC X

In Condition A there is virtual identity between the characteristic and political preference; all the people of type $X+$ vote one way, and all the people of $X-$ vote the other way. In Condition B the opposite is the case, and there is no relationship between vote and the characteristic; both parties are supported equally by people of the two types. In Condition C there is neither a complete relationship nor a complete absence; more $X+$'s than $X-$'s are partisans of a given side, but there are some members of each type in each political camp.

Now a democratic society in which Condition A was intensified would probably be in danger of its existence. The issues of politics would cut so deeply, be so keenly felt, and, especially, be so fully reinforced by other social identifications of the electorate as to threaten the basic consensus itself. This might be called "total politics"—a conception of politics, incidentally, advanced by such leading theorists of National Socialism and communism as Carl Schmitt and Lenin. This involves the mutual reinforcement of political differences and other social distinctions meaningful to the citizen. The multiplication of Condition B, on the other hand, would suggest a community in which politics was of no "real" importance to the community, in which it was not associated with special interests. Condition C is a combination of Conditions A and B—that is, a situation in which special interests are of some but not of overriding importance. It portrays neither the extremist or fanatical community like A nor the "pure" or utopian community like B.

There is nothing in Elmira that represents Condition A; the

closest approximation would be the relationship between vote and religion or minority ethnic status, and even here there are group overlaps in vote amounting to from a quarter to a third of the members. The nearest approximation to Condition B is the relationship between vote and sex, which is another way of saying that there is little relevance of this characteristic to political matters, at least so far as party preference is concerned. The relationships between vote and socioeconomic status or vote and occupation are examples of Condition C.

The social and political correlations we find in places like Elmira (that are not a priori meaningless) are of the C type to a greater or less extent. What this means is that there is a good deal of cross-group and cross-party identification and affiliation within the community. The political lines are drawn in meaningful ways but are not identical with the lines of social groupings. The same social heterogeneity that produces self-interest also produces a cross-cutting and harmonious community interest.

Thus again a requirement we might place on an electoral system—balance between total political war between segments of the society and total political indifference to group interests of that society—translates into varied requirements for different individuals. With respect to group or bloc voting, as with other aspects of political behavior, it is perhaps not unfortunate that "some do and some do not."

Individualism and Collectivism

Lord Bryce pointed out the difficulties in a theory of democracy that assumes that each citizen must himself be capable of voting intelligently:

> Orthodox democratic theory assumes that every citizen has, or ought to have, thought out for himself certain opinions, i.e., ought to have a definite view, defensible by argument, of what the country needs, of what principles ought to be applied in governing it, of the man to whose hands the government ought to be entrusted. There are persons who talk, though certainly very few who act, as if they believed this theory, which may be compared to the theory of some ultra-Protestants that every good Christian has or ought to have . . . worked out for himself from the Bible a system of theology.

In the first place, however, the information available to the individual voter is not limited to that directly possessed by him. True, the individual casts his own personal ballot. But, as we have tried to indicate throughout this volume, that is perhaps the most individualized action he takes in an election. His vote is formed in the midst of his fellows in a sort of group decision—if, indeed, it may be called a decision at all—and the total information and knowledge possessed in the group's present and past generations can be made available for the group's choice. Here is where opinion-leading relationships, for example, play an active role.

Second, and probably more important, the individual voter may not have a great deal of detailed information, but he usually has picked up the crucial *general* information as part of his social learning itself. He may not know the parties' positions on the tariff, or who is for reciprocal trade treaties, or what are the differences on Asiatic policy, or how the parties split on civil rights, or how many security risks were exposed by whom. But he cannot live in an American community without knowing broadly where the parties stand. He has learned that the Republicans are more conservative and the Democrats more liberal—and he can locate his own sentiments and cast his vote accordingly. After all, he must vote for one or the other party, and, if he knows the big thing about the parties, he does not need to know all the little things. The basic role a party plays as an institution in American life is more important to his voting than a particular stand on a particular issue.

It would be unthinkable to try to maintain our present economic style of life without a complex system of delegating to others what we are not competent to do ourselves, without accepting and giving training to each other about what each is expected to do, without accepting our dependence on others in many spheres and taking responsibility for their dependence on us in some spheres. And, like it or not, to maintain our present political style of life, we may have to accept much the same interdependence with others in collective behavior. We have learned slowly in economic life that it is useful not to have everyone a butcher or a baker, any more than it is useful to have no one skilled in such activities. The same kind of division of labor—as repugnant as it may be in some respects to our individualistic tradition—is serving us well today in mass politics. There is an implicit division of political labor within the electorate.

CONCLUSION

In short, when we turn from requirements for "average" citizens to requirements for the survival of the total democratic system, we find it unnecessary for the individual voter to be an "average citizen" cast in the classic or any other single mold. With our increasingly complex and differentiated citizenry has grown up an equally complex political system, and it is perhaps not simply a fortunate accident that they have grown and prospered together.

But it is a dangerous act of mental complacency to assume that conditions found surviving together are, therefore, positively "functional" for each other. The apathetic segment of America probably has helped to hold the system together and cushioned the shock of disagreement, adjustment, and change. But that is not to say that we can stand apathy without limit. Similarly, there must be some limit to the degree of stability or nonadaptation that a political society can maintain and still survive in a changing world. And surely the quality and amount of conformity that is necessary and desirable can be exceeded, as it has been in times of war and in the present Communist scare, to the damage of the society itself and of the other societies with which it must survive in the world.

How can our analysis be reconciled with the classical theory of liberal political democracy? Is the theory "wrong"? Must it be discarded in favor of empirical political sociology? Must its ethical or normative content be dismissed as incompatible with the nature of modern man or of mass society? That is not our view. Rather, it seems to us that modern political theory of democracy stands in need of revision and not replacement by empirical sociology. The classical political philosophers were right in the direction of their assessment of the virtues of the citizen. But they demanded those virtues in too extreme or doctrinal a form. The voter does have some principles, he does have information and rationality, he does have interest—but he does not have them in the extreme, elaborate, comprehensive, or detailed form in which they were uniformly recommended by political philosophers. Like Justice Hand, the typical citizen has other interests in life, and it is good, even for the political system, that he pursues them. The classical requirements are more appropriate for the opinion leaders in the society, but even they do not meet them directly. Happily for the system, voters distribute themselves along a continuum:

SOCIABLE MAN	POLITICAL MAN	IDEOLOGICAL MAN
(Indifferent to public affairs, nonpartisan, flexible . . .)		(Absorbed in public affairs, highly partisan, rigid . . .)

And it turns out that this distribution itself, with its internal checks and balances, can perform the functions and incorporate the same values ascribed by some theorists to each individual in the system as well as to the constitutive political institutions!

Twentieth-century political theory—both analytic and normative—will arise only from hard and long observation of the actual world of politics, closely identified with the deeper problems of practical politics. Values and the behavior they are meant to guide are not distinctly separate or separable parts of life as it is lived; and how Elmirans choose their governors is not completely unrelated to the considerations of how they are *supposed* to choose them. We disagree equally with those who believe that normative theory about the proper health of a democracy has nothing to gain from analytic studies like ours; with those who believe that the whole political tradition from Mill to Locke is irrelevant to our realistic understanding and assessment of modern democracy; or with those like Harold Laski who believe that "the decisions of men, when they come to choose their governors, are influenced by considerations which escape all scientific analysis."

We agree with Cobban: "For a century and a half the Western democracies have been living on the stock of basic political ideas that were last restated toward the end of the eighteenth century. That is a long time. . . . The gap thus formed between political facts and political ideas has steadily widened. It has taken a long time for the results to become evident; but now that we have seen what politics devoid of a contemporary moral and political theory means, it is possible that something may be done about it."

To that end we hope this book will contribute.

Appendixes ☒

Summary of Findings from Similar Election Studies

The Preface to the second edition of *The People's Choice* remarked on the tendency in parts of the social sciences not to repeat studies of the same phenomena. "Until recently the social sciences exhibited an unfortunate tendency to conduct a survey here and an experiment there, and to let it go at that. . . . Actually, the opposite trend should prevail. Results should be checked and rechecked under both identical and varying conditions. The complexity of social life requires that the same problems be studied many times before basic uniformities can be differentiated from transitory social occurrences."

In certain parts of the social sciences (e.g., learning theory in psychology or the analysis of the business cycle in economics), a number of replications of earlier studies have been made, and from such studies has gradually emerged a body of verified knowledge about the subject. Learning situations can be set up experimentally and can thus be repeated a number of times under controlled conditions. But, even in real life, opportunities for approximated replications are available: the course of economic affairs has its recurrent ups and downs, and the study of them leads to generalizations about the business cycle.

The situation in our case is somewhere between the other two: we cannot call for an election whenever we would like one and on whatever terms; but, on the other hand, we do not have to wait upon the irregular shift in the business cycle. A presidential election is held every four years, and we can study the process of opinion formation at least that often. In addition, there are opportunities for study of congressional, state, and local elections (and, indeed, such studies have been carried out—most notably, the 1950 studies of congressional and gubernatorial elections now under analysis). Since the original Erie County study in 1940, every presidential election in this country has been studied in this fashion to a greater or lesser degree;

and that study also inspired two studies of general elections in Britain, one in 1950 and one in 1951. In all, there have been five major studies here and two abroad in this period. Not all have been fully analyzed, but to date a total of fourteen publications or manuscripts have appeared to our knowledge.

The following pages contain a list of findings from such studies of electorate behavior, organized by subject matter. With certain exceptions noted below, the list attempts to include all the generalizations on political opinion—their causes, their conditions, and their consequences—that have appeared in panel studies of major elections in this country and in England since the initial Erie County study of 1940. Studies are arranged in order of completion of analysis (and, in most cases, of publication). The generalizations are of two kinds: (1) statements of incidence, e.g., the amount of change in opinion that is found during a political campaign, and (2) statements of relationships, e.g., correlation between personal characteristics and party preference or vote.

There are a number of exclusions from this "replication table." First, the table includes only findings reported from *panel* studies (i.e., studies with repeated interviews of the same people), although, as will be noted below, by no means all the findings are based upon panel data. A number of other studies, from earlier ecological analyses to recent polls, could contribute further evidence on a number of the generalizations, but such studies were not examined largely through lack of time and resources. An inventory of generalizations on political behavior is now being prepared by a group at Columbia University, and it is expected that their study will cover the field more adequately. Second, the list does not contain findings in the studies of a methodological character, e.g., of the relation of interviewer ratings and occupation (Benney & Geiss) or on the relation between intention to vote and actual turnout (Ziff). Third, the list does not contain a number of findings of a purely topical nature, e.g., relations between vote and opinion on particular issues like price control or labor-management.[1] Fourth, in some cases the list does not include certain technical refinements or elaborations of particular generalizations, e.g., the testing of a finding with additional controls.

---

1. For example, the recent study by Louis Harris, *Is There a Republican Majority?* (New York: Harper & Bros., 1954), is not included because of its focus on topical commentary.

Fifth, the list does not contain findings that do not refer directly to electorate behavior, e.g., results in *The People's Choice* of a content analysis of the treatment of the campaign in communication media. Sixth, the list does not contain a few findings in these studies that seemed on first inspection to be tautological, to be based upon dubious evidence, or to be otherwise suspect.

Any classification of such a wide range of material is bound to be arbitrary, and it is not unlikely that some injustices have been perpetrated upon the materials in the course of this analysis. We hope that the injustices have been minor and few, we bespeak the sympathy of the various authors, and we encourage someone to do an improved and extended version.[2]

Some brief comments may be made about this list. In the first place, although these are all panel studies, there is relatively little use of data on the stability or instability of opinions over time as revealed by repeated interviews of the same respondents. It is impossible to measure this directly, but certainly not as much as a quarter of the findings have any reference whatever to the time dimension in opinion formation—and this despite the general acknowledgment that opinion formation cannot satisfactorily be studied through simple correlational techniques and the deliberate design of these studies to that end. This deficiency tends to make these studies more "descriptive" than "analytic," more studies of conditions than of processes. In this connection it is worth noting that only the Erie County and the Elmira studies had more than two interviews with the same respondents (seven in the one case and four in the other), except for a subsample given a third interview in the Benney & Geiss study. In short, the time dimension seems not to be efficiently or effectively utilized in most of these studies.

Second, the decade since *The People's Choice* has produced a large number of hypotheses that can be used in subsequent studies and in the construction of a theory of political behavior. But in its present unfinished state the inventory varies in the degree to which

2. Four notes on the table: (1) if the same finding from a single set of data is included in two or more reports, it is noted here only for the major report; (2) in the British studies, for "Republican" in the generalization read "Conservative" and for "Democratic" read "Labour"; (3) in many cases, from our private knowledge of Elmira data, findings are supported by *unreported* data, and this is undoubtedly true of other studies as well; but such confirmations are *not* included; and (4) the numbers in the table do *not* correspond to those in the chapter summaries.

the propositions are *verified*. But it does seem useful to indicate the scope of empirical relationships *asserted* to this point.

Accompanying this rapid development of more or less tested generalizations—perhaps because of its rapidity—is a striking lack of cumulation. Despite the fact that this is a relatively limited field, especially when it is limited to panel studies of major elections, only a few of the generalizations have been tested in more than one study. Almost three-fourths of the generalizations appear in only a single study, less than a fifth in two, and only about a tenth in three or more, out of a possible total of eight separate studies. No finding appears in more than five of the eight, and only one in that many. (At the same time in only a very few cases do the data from one study contradict the findings from another.) In only two of the subjects—the relations of personal characteristics to vote and to turnout —do the multiple confirmations equal or exceed the single ones; and these, of course, are the most elementary matters extensively documented in other studies as well. In short, there is relatively little cumulation in these studies, much less than "the field" might have a right to expect under the circumstances.

Finally, for the most part these findings are generalizations of a relatively low order. The characteristic finding tells who (in terms of such personal characteristics as age or occupation) does what (in terms of voting or preferring one party over another or having interest in the election or reading and listening to campaign communications). For the most part they represent simple correlations between such factors. "Synthesis"—when it appears at all—does so in the form of an index in which several personal characteristics are put together in order to maximize the correlation with the dependent variable. Generalizations of greater stature appear only infrequently.

It may be, of course, that this is the nature of scientific work and that the history of the attack upon other problems would reveal much the same thing, namely, a series of collections of data dealing with relatively simple descriptive matters that only after a period of time are built into a more imposing structure of generalizations. In any case, the unevenness of the propositions—in generality, in importance, in verification—is a sign of the present stage of development in this field of empirical work. And by the same token it represents a rare opportunity for theoretical synthesis in the presence rather than the absence of empirical evidence.

Time	Place	Nature of Study	Report	Symbol
1940	Erie County, Ohio	Original sample of 3,000 classified into panel of 600 and three control groups of 600 each. All respondents interviewed in May; the panel interviewed in June, July, August, September, October, and November; one control group interviewed again in July, one in August, and one in October	Paul F. Lazarsfeld, Bernard Berelson, and Hazel Gaudet, *The People's Choice* (1st ed.; New York: Duell, Sloan & Pearce, 1944; 2d ed.; New York: Columbia University Press, 1948)	PC (1)
		Special interviews of two groups—182 respondents of higher education from an earlier control group, and 497 of October control group	Bernard Berelson, "Content Emphasis, Recognition, and Agreement: An Analysis of the Role of Communications in Determining Public Opinion" (Doctoral dissertation, University of of Chicago, 1941)	BB (2)
1944	Nationwide	Interviews by National Opinion Research Center of 2,564 respondents in last week of October and re-interviews with 2,030 after the election	Sheldon J. Korchin, "Psychological Variables in the Behavior of Voters" (Doctoral dissertation, Harvard University, 1946)	Kor (3)
			Ruth Ziff, "The Effect of the Last Three Weeks of a Presidential Campaign on the Electorate" (Master's thesis, Columbia University, 1948)	Ziff (4)
1948	Nationwide	Interviews by Survey Research Center, University of Michigan: 610 respondents in October and 662 in November, with 577 respondents in both waves	Angus Campbell and Robert L. Kahn, with the editorial assistance of Sylvia Eberhart, *The People Elect a President* (Survey Research Center, Institute for Social Research, University of Michigan, 1952)	C & K (5)
			Substantially same data as above issued in mimeographed form: "A Study of the Presidential Vote: November 1948," by the Survey Research Center, April, 1949	
			Morris Janowitz and Warren E. Miller, "The Index of Political Predisposition in the 1948 Election," *Journal of Politics*, XIV (1952), 710–27	Jan-Mill (6)

Time	Place	Nature of Study	Report	Symbol
1950	Greenwich, England	First interview with 856 respondents in December, 1949, ten weeks before election; subsample of 363 respondents re-interviewed during the two weeks before the election; final interview of 839 immediately after election day. 444 respondents interviewed in first and third waves; 337 in first, second, and third; 133 other—a total of 914 persons	Mark Benney and Phyllis Geiss, "Social Class and Politics in Greenwich," *British Journal of Sociology*, I (1950), 310–27	B & G (7)
1951	Bristol, England	One sample with 428 interviews two weeks before election and 403 interviews after the election	R. S. Milne and H. C. Mackenzie, "A Study of Voting Behaviour in the Constituency of Bristol North-East at the General Election, 1951" (manuscript, 1953) (London: Hansard Society, 1954).	Milne Mack (8)
1952	Nation-wide	Interviews by the Survey Research Center of 2,021 respondents in October (including 222 "loading" in the Far West) and 1,614 re-interviews after the election	Angus Campbell, Gerald Gurin, and Warren E. Miller, "Political Issues and the Vote: November 1952," *American Political Science Review*, XLVII (June, 1953), 359–85	CGM (9)
			Morris Janowitz and Dwaine Marvick, "Campaign Pressure and Political Consent in the 1952 Presidential Election" (mimeographed manuscript, 1953)	Jan-Marv (10)
			Angus Campbell, Gerald Gurin, and Warren E. Miller, with the assistance of Sylvia Eberhart and Robert O. McWilliams, *The Voter Decides* (Chicago: Row-Peterson, 1954)	Vot. Dec. (11)
1948	Elmira, New York	Four waves of interviews: 1,029 in June, 881 re-interviews in August, 814 re-interviews in October, and 944 re-interviews in November	Helen Dinerman, "1948 Votes in the Making," *Public Opinion Quarterly*, XII (winter, 1948–49), 585–98	Din (12)
			Alice Kitt and David B. Gleicher, "Determinants of Voting Behavior," *Public Opinion Quarterly*, XIV (fall, 1950), 393–412	K & G (13)
			Bernard R. Berelson, Paul F. Lazarsfeld, and William N. McPhee, *Voting* (Chicago: University of Chicago press, 1954)	Voting (14)

Finding or Generalization	Erie County, Ohio, 1940		Nation-wide Study, NORC, 1944		Nation-wide Study, Survey Research Center, 1948		Greenwich, England, 1950	Bristol, England, 1951	Nation-wide Study, Survey Research Center, 1952			Elmira, New York, 1948		
	PC (1)	BB (2)	Kor (3)	Ziff (4)	C & K (5)	Jan-Mill (6)	B & G (7)	Milne Mack (8)	CGM (9)	Jan-Marv (10)	Vot. Dec. (11)	Din (12)	K & G (13)	Voting (14)
SOCIAL CHARACTERISTICS AND THE VOTE DECISION														
Socioeconomic Status														
(1) *Class status (SES level):* The higher the status, the more Republican (or analogous Conservative vote, in Britain).	X			X										X
(2) *Income:* The higher the income, the more Republican.	X									X				
(3) *Occupation:* The "higher" the occupation, the more Republican.			X X		X X		X	X X	X		X X			X X
but: (a) With SES controlled, occupation does not correlate with vote.														
and: (b) White-collar and business groups have greater political solidarity than workers, as indicated by party preference.														
(4) *Subjective class identification:* The higher the identification, the more Republican.	X						X	X						X
and: (a) With SES controlled, subjective class identification correlates more highly with vote than does objective occupation.	X													
(b) The vote of lower-middle-class people (by objective classification) especially correlates with their subjective class identification.														
(c) Contemporary American workers are not particularly "class conscious" in their reaction to symbols, their aspirations, and their political militancy.														
Religion														
(5) Catholics vote more Democratic than Protestants (in some studies: regardless of social factors controlled)	X				X									X
and: (a) Catholics vote more Democratic than Protestants regardless of their "liberalism" or "conservatism" in attitudes on political issues			X	X					X					X
(6) Catholics closely identified with their religion vote more Democratic than Catholics not so identified.														X
(7) Catholics personally involved in political affairs follow the religious lead in voting less than Catholics not so involved.														X
(8) Jews vote more Democratic than Protestants or Catholics.			X		X						X			X
and: (a) Younger Jews vote more Democratic than older Jews														X
(9) Young people are more likely to resolve the cross-pressures of religion and SES in favor of class (in the contemporary era).														X
Residence														
(10) *Size of Community:* Urban residents vote more Democratic than rural residents	X										X			X
but: (a) Residents of metropolitan areas and open country vote more Democratic than residents of middle-size towns and cities.									X					
Region														
(11) There are no appreciable differences among broad census-type regions except for the Democratic vote of the South.				X							X			X

Finding or Generalization	Erie County, Ohio, 1940		Nation-wide Study, NORC, 1944		Nation-wide Study, Survey Research Center, 1948		Greenwich, England, 1950	Bristol, England, 1951	Nation-wide Study, Survey Research Center, 1952			Elmira, New York, 1948		
	PC (1)	BB (2)	Kor (3)	Ziff (4)	C & K (5)	Jan-Mill (6)	B & G (7)	Milne Mack (8)	CGM (9)	Jan-Marv (10)	Vot. Dec. (11)	Din (12)	K. & G. (13)	Voting (14)
SOCIAL CHARACTERISTICS AND THE VOTE DECISION—*Continued*														
Age														
(12) Younger people vote more Democratic than older people.	X		X	X	X			X	X		X			X
but: (a) With SES controlled, there is no age difference.														
(b) The age-vote relationship is different in different religious groups: younger people follow the political tendency of their religion less—i.e., younger Catholics vote more Republican than older Catholics, and younger Protestants vote more Republican than older Protestants.														
(c) The difference by age is explained partly by differential death rates in classes and partly by recency in rise of labor party and its image.														
Education														
(13) The higher the educational level, the more Republican.	X			X	X			X	X		X			X
but: (a) With SES controlled, there is no relationship between education and vote.														
Sex														
(14) Women vote more Republican than men.			No	X	X			X	X		X			X
(15) Women—less politicized than men—follow the class lead in voting less than men.														
Race														
(16) Negroes vote more Democratic than white people.					X				X					X
and: (a) Younger Negroes vote more Democratic than older Negroes.														X
Ethnic Background														
(17) White, native-born Protestants vote Republican more than minority ethnic groups, specifically Catholics, Italian-Americans, Jews, and Negroes.											X			X
(18) Voters of Scandinavian, German, and Scotch-English origins were more Republican than voters of Irish-Catholic, Italian, and Polish origins.											X			X
but: (a) Irish-Protestants were strongly Republican.														
(19) The more closely that members of ethnic minorities identify with their ethnic group, the more Democratic their vote.														X
SOCIAL GROUPS AND THE VOTE DECISION														
Organizational membership														
(20) People belong to organizations perceived as politically congenial.	X													
(21) Organizational membership brings out latent political predispositions (e.g., class effects on vote), especially for the less interested.														
and: (a) Members of social organizations vote more Republican than non-members.	X													X

Finding or Generalization	Erie County, Ohio, 1940		Nation-wide Study, NORC, 1944		Nation-wide Study, Survey Research Center, 1948		Greenwich, England, 1950	Bristol, England, 1951	Nation-wide Study, Survey Research Center, 1952			Elmira, New York, 1948		
	PC (1)	BB (2)	Kor (3)	Ziff (4)	C & K (5)	Jan-Mill (6)	B & G (7)	Milne Mack (8)	CGM (9)	Jan-Marv (10)	Vot. Dec. (11)	Din (12)	K & G (13)	Voting (14)
SOCIAL GROUPS AND THE VOTE DECISION—*Continued* *Organizational Membership*—*Continued*														
(22) Membership in labor unions, by self or breadwinner, is correlated with Democratic vote (in some studies with other factors controlled)					X			X	X		X			X
and: (a) The more that union members are committed to unionism in general or particular, the more Democratic their vote														X
(b) The more interaction with other union members (within a single plant), the more Democratic vote, especially among (less interested) women														XX
(c) Integration in the plant makes nonunion workers more Democratic														
(23) Membership in co-operative societies is correlated with labor vote														
Family														
(24) In the overwhelming majority of cases (from 80 per cent up) the respondent and his immediate family agree in the vote			X					X		X	X			X
and: (a) The influence toward family homogeneity in vote runs from husbands to wives	X	X					X	X			X			
(b) Family homogeneity in vote is least strong in the lower middle class	X						X	X			X			X
(25) The vote of the present generation is correlated with the vote of the parents, although less so when in conflict with class or religion														X
and: (a) Children who have achieved social mobility over their parents vote more Republican														XX
(b) The new generation is politically trained in a politically homogeneous family										X	X			X
(c) The new generation is at first only superficially involved in politics														
Personal Associations (Friends and Co-workers)														
(26) People generally agree in vote with their friends and co-workers														XX
and: (a) Such homogeneity is slightly higher for friends (who are self-chosen) than for co-workers														X
(b) Political homogeneity among friends increases with age														XX
(27) Voters predisposed to the Republican position by class or religion have more Republican friends														X
(28) The more homogeneous the personal associates, the stronger the conviction in support of a candidate														X
(29) When the voter's immediate personal environment is split in political preference, he is more likely to vote in line with the majority of the larger community														X

Finding or Generalization	Erie County, Ohio, 1940		Nation-wide Study, NORC, 1944		Nation-wide Study, Survey Research Center, 1948		Greenwich, England, 1950	Bristol, England, 1951	Nation-wide Study, Survey Research Center, 1952			Elmira, New York, 1948		
	PC (1)	BB (2)	Kor (3)	Ziff (4)	C & K (5)	Jan-Mill (6)	B & G (7)	Milne Mack (8)	CGM (9)	Jan-Marv (10)	Vot. Dec. (11)	Din (12)	K & G (13)	Voting (14)
TIME OF VOTE DECISION														
(30) Low degree of interest in the election delays the final vote decision	X													X
(31) The more cross-pressures the voter is subject to, the later his final vote decision (cross-pressures, e.g., between religion and SES, the voter and his family, attitudes on different issues, etc.)	X				X									X
and: (a) Low interest and cross-pressures are about equally strong in delaying decision and their joint effect is quite powerful														
(32) Voters in families whose other members have no vote intentions decide later than voters in families whose other members do have vote intentions	X				X	X								X
(33) Democratic voters decide later than Republican voters	XX													
(34) Voters constant between two elections (1948 and 1952) decide earlier than new or shifting voters	XX				X									X
(35) The weaker the voter's partisanship, the later his final decision														
(36) There is no difference in time of decision by educational level of the voters														
(37) Voters who decide late in the campaign are more influenced by personal contact than early deciders					X									
(38) Late deciders are more likely to split their vote between parties than early deciders	X													
TURNOUT (i.e., casting a vote)														
(39) The higher the political interest, the greater the turnout	XX				X					X	X			X
(40) Men vote more than women	XX		X		X									
but: (a) If women say they intend to vote, they are more apt than men actually to do so														
(41) The higher the educational level, the more the turnout				X	X									
but: (a) With economic status controlled, education does not correlate with turnout			X		X									
(b) With interest controlled, education does not correlate with turnout	X		X								No		X	
(42) The older, the more turnout			XX								XX			
but: (a) There is a reversal toward less turnout among people over fifty-five														
(43) The higher the economic status, the greater the turnout			X		X									
(44) The higher the occupation, the greater the turnout			X		X									
(45) Jews vote more than Catholics, and Protestants slightly less than Catholics			X		X									
(46) Residents of metropolitan areas vote more than residents of towns and cities, and they, in turn, more than rural residents			X		X						X		X	
and: (a) People who like living in a particular community are more likely to vote (and to vote for the dominant party there) than people who do not like to live in the community (or who like to live there less)														

Finding or Generalization	Erie County, Ohio, 1940		Nation-wide Study, NORC, 1944		Nation-wide Study, Survey Research Center, 1948		Greenwich, England, 1950	Bristol, England, 1951	Nation-wide Study, Survey Research Center, 1952			Elmira, New York, 1948		
	PC (1)	BB (2)	Kor (3)	Ziff (4)	C & K (5)	Jan-Mill (6)	B & G (7)	Milne Mack (8)	CGM (9)	Jan-Marv (10)	Vot. Dec. (11)	Din (12)	K & G (13)	Voting (14)
Turnout—*Continued*														
(47) Members of labor unions turn out more than nonmembers in the same occupations														X
(48) People whose primary groups (family, friends, co-workers) do not vote tend not to vote themselves														XX
(49) The higher the level of political information, the more turnout			X		X									X
(50) The less firm the position on issues (i.e., the more indecision), the less turnout					X						X			
(51) The stronger the partisanship and identification with the party, the more turnout														
(52) Constants in vote intention vote more than party changers or crystallizers				X										
(53) In this period people with a Republican vote intention turn out more than people with a Democratic vote intention				XX	X			X						X
(54) Contact by party representatives increases turnout, especially among the less interested										XX	XX			
(55) The more communication exposure, the more turnout														
(56) More people actually vote on election day than are interested in the election or than express their interest in political activity of any other kind											X			XX
Political Interest and Activity														
Amount														
(57) About a third of the electorate is greatly interested in the election. *and:* (a) About a fifth think it makes "a good deal" of difference who wins	X													No
(58) About one-fourth of the electorate do anything to get their candidate elected (including attempts at persuasion of others)														X
(59) Interest increases slightly during campaign. *but:* (a) Although there is little net change in interest during the campaign there is a considerable amount of gross turnover	X													
Sources of Political Interest														
(60) The higher the educational level, the greater the interest	XX						XX							XX
(61) The higher the socioeconomic status, the greater the interest. *and:* (a) In this period Republicans are more interested than Democrats, and they care more who wins							X				X			XX
(62) Men have more interest than women	XXX													XXX
(63) Older people have greater interest than younger														
(64) The more cross-pressures, the lower the interest														
(65) People who think that they can have some effect upon governmental policy or that governmental policy can have some effect on events are more likely to be interested than those who do not think so														XX
(66) The greater the partisanship, the greater the interest														
(67) As the campaign goes on, political factors come to influence interest more and social factors less														X

Table of findings (rotated landscape table). Column group headings, left to right:

- **Erie County, Ohio, 1940** — PC (1), BB (2)
- **Nation-wide Study, NORC, 1944** — Kor (3), Ziff (4)
- **Nation-wide Study, Survey Research Center, 1948** — C & K (5), Jan-Mill (6)
- **Greenwich, England, 1950** — B & G (7)
- **Bristol, England, 1951** — Mlne Mack (8)
- **Nation-wide Study, Survey Research Center, 1952** — CGM (9), Jan-Marv (10), Vot. Dec. (11)
- **Elmira, New York, 1948** — Din (12), K & G (13), Voting (14)

Finding or Generalization	PC (1)	BB (2)	Kor (3)	Ziff (4)	C & K (5)	Jan-Mill (6)	B & G (7)	Mlne Mack (8)	CGM (9)	Jan-Marv (10)	Vot. Dec. (11)	Din (12)	K & G (13)	Voting (14)
Political Interest and Activity—*Continued*														
Consequences of Political Interest														
(68) Interested or active voters have more opinions on political issues than un-interested or inactive voters	× ×													×
(69) Interested voters participate more in the campaign than uninterested	× ×										×			
(70) Interested voters read and listen more to campaign communications than un-interested	×													
(71) The more interested voters support their own candidate more fully on the subsidiary issues of campaign		×												
(72) The more interested voters are more likely to think that their own candidate will win			×											
(73) Interested voters follow their own class dispositions less strongly than the un-interested			×											×
(74) Although the voters' estimate of their political interest does not change on the average during the campaign, certain types of behavior that manifest political interest increase (e.g., political discussion)							×							×
Opinion leadership														
(75) Opinion leaders exist in all strata and groups	×													×
(76) Opinion leaders are characterized by their greater interest and competence in politics and by their greater activity in social affairs *and:* (a) Within broad strata opinion leaders are slightly higher in occupational and educational status than others							×							×
(77) Opinion leaders support their own party position more strongly on the subsidiary issues than do others														×
Sources of Political Activity														
(78) The more extreme the partisan position on issues, the more political activity											×			
(79) The more concern with issues, the more political activity											×			
(80) The stronger the feelings about the candidate as a personality, the more political activity											×			
(81) The stronger the feelings about one's capacity to influence political affairs, the more political activity											×			
(82) The stronger the feelings about the duties of citizenship, the more political activity														×
(83) Of many types of party workers, few seemed primarily motivated by ideological concerns or civic duty														
Communication and Contact														
Amount														
(84) During the last two weeks of the campaign, about half the population read newspaper items on the election or listened to radio speeches, and one-fourth read magazine items	×													
(85) About one-fourth of the people were contacted by one or the other party by the last few weeks of the campaign (more by mail than in person) and about one-third knew a party worker														×

COMMUNICATION AND CONTACT—*Continued*

Distribution

By Volume

Finding or Generalization	Erie County, Ohio, 1940		Nation-wide Study, NORC, 1944		Nation-wide Study, Survey Research Center, 1948		Greenwich, England, 1950	Bristol, England, 1951	Nation-wide Study, Survey Research Center, 1952			Elmira, New York, 1948		
	PC (1)	BB (2)	Kor (3)	Ziff (4)	C & K (5)	Jan-Mill (6)	B & G (7)	Milne Mack (8)	CGM (9)	Jan-Marv (10)	Vot. Dec. (11)	Din (12)	K & G (13)	Voting (14)
(86) Campaign exposure generates more of the same, e.g., exposure at an earlier time increases exposure at a later time.	X													X
(87) The higher the educational level, the more exposure to campaign communications.	X													X
(88) The higher the SES level, the more exposure to campaign communications.	X													X
(89) Older people expose to campaign communications more than younger.	X													X
(90) Men expose to campaign communications more than women.	X													
(91) Urban residents expose to campaign communications more than rural residents.	X													
(92) Opinion leaders expose to campaign communications more than nonleaders.	X													X
(93) Exposure to *political* materials in the mass media is higher for people who give more *general* attention to the media.														
(94) People already decided on their vote intention expose to campaign communication more than the undecided, the changers, or the nonvoters.	X													
(95) Recognition of campaign arguments corresponds to their emphasis in the content of the public media.		X						X						X
(96) The people who expose more to campaign communications at one period of the campaign also tend to do so at another period.	X													X
(97) People who tend to expose more to campaign communications in one medium tend to do so in other media.	X													
By Partisanship														
(98) The stronger the partisanship, the more exposure to campaign communications	X			X										
(99) People tend to expose to their own (partisan) side of campaign communications (rather than to the other side or to a random selection).	X													
and: (a) The constants particularly expose to their own partisan communications, as compared with changers.	X													
(b) This self-selective exposure is especially strong in the case of political meetings														
(c) People are more likely to know party workers from their own side than from the other side.														
(d) The greater the total amount of campaign exposure, the higher the proportion of exposure to one's own side.								X						
(100) Party workers are more likely to contact people favorable to their own side in attitude or in predisposition.	X	X												
(101) Those undecided in vote intention tend to expose to campaign communications favoring the side associated with their own predispositions.	X							X						X

339

FINDING OR GENERALIZATION	ERIE COUNTY, OHIO, 1940		NATION-WIDE STUDY, NORC, 1944		NATION-WIDE STUDY, SURVEY RESEARCH CENTER, 1948		GREENWICH, ENGLAND, 1950	BRISTOL, ENGLAND, 1951	NATION-WIDE STUDY, SURVEY RESEARCH CENTER, 1952			ELMIRA, NEW YORK, 1948		
	PC (1)	BB (2)	Kor (3)	Ziff (4)	C & K (5)	Jan-Mill (6)	B & G (7)	Milne Mack (8)	CGM (9)	Jan-Marv (10)	Vot. Dec. (11)	Din (12)	K & G (13)	Voting (14)
COMMUNICATION AND CONTACT—*Continued* *Distribution*—*Continued* *By Channels*														
(102) There is a differential use of newspapers and radio by Republicans and Democrats: Republicans expose more to newspapers, and Democrats to radio; Republicans generally prefer newspapers, and Democrats radio as sources of information about the campaign; Democrats consider the radio relatively more accurate; and Republicans mention the newspaper more in connection with reasons for a change in vote intention, and Democrats mention the radio more	X		X (in part)											
(103) Much political talk is centered in the family; and married women report discussing politics in the family more than married men, especially in quiet times														X
(104) Much political discussion goes on among people of like characteristics—like in friendship, in age, and in occupation.														X
and: (a) When characteristics are unlike, the lower (in age or occupation) report talking to the higher.														X
(105) Political discussions are made up much more of mutual agreement than of disagreement														X
and: (a) Voters are more likely to agree with someone of higher occupational status than themselves		X												X
(b) Voters are more likely to agree if they have initiated the discussion themselves														X
(106) Voters who talk politics the least are most likely to agree in vote with their friends	X													X
(107) The frequency of the discussion of political arguments in private conversation corresponds to the frequency with which they appear in the mass media														X
(108) Private conversation is used more than the media as a source of political arguments by those undecided in vote intention.														
(109) Those interested in politics are more likely to know party workers														X
(110) Those better integrated into the community are more likely to know party workers														X
By Consequences														
(111) The more communication exposure, the less indecision on political issues.	X													
(112) Communication exposure to campaign material increases interest in the election	X													X
(113) The more exposure to the campaign in the mass media, the more strongly voters come to feel about their candidate.														X
(114) The more exposure to the campaign in the mass media, the more correct information the voters have about the campaign and the more correct their perception of where the candidates stand on the issues														X

Finding or Generalization	Erie County, Ohio, 1940		Nation-wide Study, NORC, 1944		Nation-wide Study, Survey Research Center, 1948		Greenwich, Eng., 1950	Bristol, Eng., 1951	Nation-wide Study, Survey Research Center, 1952			Elmira, New York, 1948		
	PC (1)	BB (2)	Kor (3)	Ziff (4)	C & K (5)	Jan-Mill (6)	B & G (7)	Milne Mack (8)	CGM (9)	Jan-Marv (10)	Vot. Dec. (11)	Din (12)	K & G (13)	Voting (14)
COMMUNICATION AND CONTACT—*Continued*														
By Consequences—*Continued*														
(115) Campaign exposure converts a small minority of voters against predisposition	X			X										X
(116) The more exposure to the campaign in the mass media, the less voters change their positions and the more they turn out on election day		X												X
(117) Within the effect of predispositions, communication exposure tends to regulate relative agreement with campaign arguments			X											
and: (a) Campaign communications influence judgments on which issues are important.														
(118) Campaign arguments have a better chance of acceptance if they are (a) old, (b) associated with a prominent current event, (c) "crucial" to the central vote decision, and (d) highly supported by either side.		X						X						
(119) There are fewer "boomerang" effects from private conversations about politics than from the mass media.	X													
(120) Individual items of campaign communication do not have much effect in isolation.								X						
(121) Party contact increases turnout most among those least likely to vote.														X
and: (a) Party contact increases turnout most among people of long residence in the community.														
(122) Party contact is not particularly effective in converting voters from one party to the other														X
but: (a) Acquaintance with party workers is correlated with change in voting.													X	X
(123) Party contact increases the level of interest in the campaign.														X
ISSUES														
Agreement on Issues														
(124) Only a small minority of the voters in a party agree with their candidate on "all" the important issues	X							X	No	X				X
and: (a) There is little difference between Republicans and Democrats in voting a straight or split ticket.														
(b) Conservatives support their own side more strongly than laborites support theirs.														
(125) Partisan disagreement on the issues is sharpest for those issues in the "political gateway" at a given time; there is relatively little disagreement on those issues that have passed through the "gateway," or those not yet there.								X			X			X
(126) Republicans and Democrats hold different opinions on a variety of particular issues (e.g., rich-man/poor-man issues, foreign affairs).					X						X			X
(127) When partisans agree on the ends of political policy (e.g., firmness toward Russia), they disagree on which candidate will better realize the end.	X													X

ISSUES—Continued

Agreement on Issues—Continued

Finding or Generalization	Erie County, Ohio, 1940		Nation-wide Study, NORC, 1944		Nation-wide Study, Survey Research Center, 1948		Greenwich, England, 1950	Bristol, England, 1951	Nation-wide Study, Research Center, 1952			Elmira, New York, 1948		
	PC (1)	BB (2)	Kor (3)	Ziff (4)	C & K (5)	Jan-Mill (6)	B & G (7)	Milne Mack (8)	CGM (9)	Jan-Marv (10)	Vot. Dec. (11)	Din (12)	K & G (13)	Voting (14)
(128) People in different class positions hold different opinions on political issues *and:* (a) On most issues the lower middle class is more in agreement with the middle class than with the working class							X							X
(129) Vote differs more by the voters' stand on domestic-economic (Position) issues than by international-ethnic (Style) issues							X							X
(130) There is no correlation between "liberalism" on domestic-economic (Position) issues and "liberalism" on international-ethnic (Style) issues														X
(131) Both Conservative and Labour voters are more favorable to socialist goals than to socialist means; and there is greater difference between them on means than on goals							X							
(132) "New" Republicans in 1952 supported the party position on a variety of political issues less strongly than did regular Republicans; but "new" Democrats supported the party position as strongly as regular Democrats									X					X
(133) Regular Republicans hold substantially the same opinions on political issues regardless of their occupational, educational, union, or religious characteristics; the same for regular Democrats									X					
(134) Issues dealing with the personalities of the candidates are agreed to across party lines more than issues dealing with political policy *and:* (a) In 1952 Republicans voted more for "the man" and Democrats more for "the party". (b) In 1952 "new" Republicans most strongly favored the Republican candidate, only partly favored Republican issues, and least strongly favored the Republican party		X								X				
(135) Saliency of class issues predicted the image of the candidate more than the image predicted saliency											X			X
(136) The stronger the partisan position on the parties, the issues, or the candidates, the stronger the support given the candidates *and:* (a) The stronger the partisan position on the parties, the issues, or the candidates, the more straight-ticket voting (b) The stronger the partisan position on the parties, the issues, or the candidates, the less consideration given the opposing candidate											X			
(137) The greater the interest in the election, the sharper the differences between partisans on the issues								X						X
(138) The maximum proportion whose vote is primarily decided by an issue or issues is small (not over 10 per cent)														X
(139) The party choice of cross-pressured voters tends to follow the priorities assigned to different subjects or issues *and:* (a) Shifts in vote among such people also correspond to the priorities assigned to the issues														X

Finding or Generalization	Erie County, Ohio, 1940		Nation-wide Study, NORC, 1944		Nation-wide Study, Survey Research Center, 1948		Greenwich, England, 1950	Bristol, England, 1951	Nation-wide Study, Survey Research Center, 1952			Elmira, New York, 1948		
	PC (1)	BB (2)	Kor (3)	Ziff (4)	C & K (5)	Jan-Mill (6)	B & G (7)	Milne Mack (8)	CGM (9)	Jan-Marv (10)	Vot. Dec. (11)	Din (12)	K & G (13)	Voting (14)
ISSUES—Continued														
Agreement on Issues—Continued														
(140) Issue cross-pressures are most often resolved in favor of past vote history....														X
Expectation of Winner														
(141) There is a correlation between expectation of winner and vote intention....														
but: (a) There are different explanations of that fact:														
(1) bandwagon effect....	X		X											
(2) projection	X		X											
(142) The greater the interest in the election, the closer the relationship between expectation of winner and vote intention.	X													
(143) The greater the interest in the election, the less change in expectation of winner	X													
(144) Expectation of winner is more variable than vote intention	X													
Postelection Opinions														
(145) There was less anxiety about result of election after it was over than there was anxiety about its possible result before.				X										
(146) After the election the partisans of the winning side were more likely than those of the losing side to feel that the campaign clarified rather than confused issues			X											
(147) Voters believe more strongly after the election that their own party is generally superior on the issues than before (i.e., opinions within a party "harden" during the campaign)														
POLITICAL PERCEPTION														
Perception of Issues														
(148) The partisans generally agree on what are the important issues of the campaign (including criteria for selection of candidates and expectations of future events)														X
(149) Party preference alone does not particularly affect the aggregate of voters' perceptions of where the candidates stand on major issues controversial at the time.								X						X
(150) The less ambiguous the objective situation, the more agreement in perception between the two sides on where the candidates stand on the issues								X						X
(151) Voters with opinions on particular issues are likely to feel their candidates hold the same opinion on the issues, especially if their candidate's position is ambiguous														X
(152) Voters tend not to perceive differences with their own candidate or similarities to the opposition candidate.														X
(153) Voters who feel strongly about their candidate are more likely to perceive the candidate's stand on the issues as favorable to their own.														X
(154) If the "reality" of objective events favors the opponent on a particular issue, the supporters of a candidate are more likely to think there is no difference between the candidates or to be undecided on the issue.			X											
(155) Social differences in voting are still apparent regardless of perceived agreement with the candidates.														X

Finding or Generalization	PC (1)	BB (2)	Kor (3)	Ziff (4)	C & K (5)	Jan-Mill (6)	B & G (7)	Milne Mack (8)	CGM (9)	Jan-Marv (10)	Vot. Dec. (11)	Din (12)	K & G (13)	Voting (14)
POLITICAL PERCEPTION—*Continued*														
Perception of Issues—*Continued*														
(156) Voters who *disagree* with both candidates' stands, as perceived, support their own candidate more strongly than those who *agree* with both														X
(157) Only about one-third of the voters are highly accurate in their perception of where the candidates stand on the issues														X
(158) Accuracy of perception is related to communication exposure, education, interest, organization, membership, and "neuroticism"—with communication exposure probably the strongest influence														
Perception of Parties														
(159) About three-fourths of the voters usually think of themselves as Republicans or Democrats (party identification)														X
(160) The degree of party identification does not vary by broad region, except for fewer "independents" in the South			X								X			
(161) The stronger the party identification, the more likely is support of the party regardless of the candidate.											X			
and: (a) The stronger the party identification, the more constant is support of the party in different elections											X			
(b) The stronger the party identification, the more likely is straight ticket voting							X				X			
(162) Both Republicans and Democrats perceive that the parties disagree on certain issues (e.g., rich-man/poor-man issues)	X				X		X				X			
(163) Republicans consider that their party would be better for their whole community, and Democrats consider that their party would be better for everyone except the rich														
(164) Party policy is less important as a determinant of party preference than the class character of the party's public image.														X
(165) In their public image, parties are believed to serve class rather than national interests														
Perception of Groups														
(166) About one-third of the electorate profess not to know how each of the major socioeconomic and ethnic groups will vote														
(167) Of those with opinions very few deny the existence of bloc voting, and, in general, people are correct in their estimates, e.g., the working class is generally perceived as voting Democratic, business as voting Republican, and the middle class roughly even							X				X			X
(168) The working class is more likely than the middle or the upper class to feel that people like them ought to vote the same way														X
(169) Perception of the voting of larger groups (e.g., unions) is affected by the voting of small samples of one's intimates (e.g., co-workers) in those groups														X

Finding or Generalization	ERIE COUNTY, OHIO, 1940		NATION-WIDE STUDY, NORC, 1944		NATION-WIDE STUDY, SURVEY RESEARCH CENTER, 1948		GREENWICH, ENGLAND, 1950	BRISTOL, ENGLAND, 1951	NATION-WIDE STUDY, SURVEY RESEARCH CENTER, 1952			ELMIRA, NEW YORK, 1948		
	PC (1)	BB (2)	Kor (3)	Ziff (4)	C & K (5)	Jan-Mill (6)	B & G (7)	Milne Mack (8)	CGM (9)	Jan-Marv (10)	Vot. Dec. (11)	Din (12)	K & G (13)	Voting (14)
POLITICAL PERCEPTION—*Continued* *Perception of Groups*—*Continued*														
(170) Partisans tend to exaggerate the support of socioeconomic groups for their own party *and:* (a) The closer the voter is to the perceived groups in socioeconomic status or past experience (e.g., farm origin), the more likely he is to perceive them as voting his way	X													X
(171) Socioeconomic groups (like farmers, working class, unions, middle class, etc.) are perceived as supporting one or the other party more than are religious or ethnic groups, and more often for group-based reasons	X													X
(172) Members of social and religious groups are more likely than nonmembers to know how their group is voting and to claim split voting by the group	X													
(173) People hostile to religious and ethnic minorities are more likely to assign them to the opposition party	X													X
(174) Members of religious and ethnic minorities tend to see them as voting their own way	X													X
CHANGE IN POLITICAL POSITION *Amount of Change*														
(175) From one election to the next, over three-fourths of the voters in both do not change party position										X	X			
(176) From two-thirds to three-fourths of the voters settle on their final vote by the time the political conventions are over	X	X			X			X			X			X
(177) Changes in party position during the campaign are fewer than changes between campaigns				X	X									X
(178) From late October to election day there is from five to ten times more gross turnover than net change in party support, i.e., the shifts are compensatory	X	X						X			X			
(179) In over half the cases the over-all effect of the campaign is to reinforce an existing party position: in about one-sixth of the cases the campaign has no effect; for another one-sixth it has an activating effect; and for the final one-sixth it has a converting effect	X	X												
(180) Only a small proportion (under 10 per cent) of the changers during a campaign move from one party to the other	X	X												
(181) Partisanship in political support increases during the campaign	X	X						X						X
Direction of Change														
(182) The over-all effect of the campaign was to speed up the between-campaign trend of vote movement	X													No
(183) During a campaign, when voters hold opinions on particular issues contrary to the position of the party they support, there is a tendency for them to change such "inconsistent" opinions to fit their vote intention *and:* (a) Hence the campaign results in increased consistency within individuals and groups and increased polarization between groups within the society	X													X

Finding or Generalization	Erie County, Ohio, 1940		Nation-wide Study, NORC, 1944		Nation-wide Study, Survey Research Center, 1948		Greenwich, Eng-land, 1950	Bris-tol, Eng-land, 1951	Nation-wide Study, Survey Research Center, 1952			Elmira, New York, 1948		
	PC (1)	BB (2)	Kor (3)	Ziff (4)	C & K (5)	Jan-Mill (6)	B & G (7)	Milne Mack (8)	CGM (9)	Jan-Marv (10)	Vot. Dec. (11)	Din (12)	K & G (13)	Vot-ing (14)
CHANGE IN POLITICAL POSITION—*Continued*														
Direction of Change—*Continued*														
(184) The majority of voters who change their vote intention change it in the direction of the prevailing vote of their social group.	X													
(185) In 1948 the Democratic trend was essentially a rally composed (a), in political terms, of former Democrats, neutrals, or new voters and (b), in socioeconomic terms, of voters with working-class and ambivalent dispositions.				X	X					X				X
(186) Demoralization of Democratic voting strength prior to the 1948 campaign was related (a) to unfavorable reception for Roosevelt's successor, Truman, and (b) to focus of attention on new problems unrelated to the socioeconomic "class" issues on which the party majority had been built.														X
(187) A change in the focus of attention, with renewed saliency of socioeconomic issues, was the primary feature of the Democratic rally in Elmira in 1948.	X													X
(188) Voters with ambivalent class dispositions displayed these fluctuations most.														XX
(189) The people who do not expect to vote during the campaign but then actually do vote on election day tend to follow the predominant party pressure in their locale.			X											
(190) Most of the voters who leave their party position for indecision later return to their original party position; most of those who leave for the other party do not return.	X													
(191) Change in party position from the 1948 to the 1952 election cannot be attributed to any single issue or located predominantly in any single group.											X			
(192) Most conversion in vote during the campaign is composed of movement between moderate positions on the two sides.	X													
Conditions of Change														
(193) Voting changes between generations are affected by the political preferences of social strata: among Catholics, Republican fathers "lose" more children to the opposition; among Protestants, Democratic fathers "lose" more (and similarly for occupational groups). *and:* (*a*) Between generations—and especially in homogeneous social strata—it is the group tradition in voting that survives better than individual father-to-son preferences.							X	X						X
(194) Turnover in opinion on campaign issues is correlated with the (presumed) influence of the events of the time.														X
(195) Turnover in vote during the campaign is not so great as turnover in opinion on issues														X
(196) The less homogeneous the family in its political position, the more change among its members.	X													X

CHANGE IN POLITICAL POSITION—*Continued*

Conditions of Change—Continued

Finding or Generalization	Erie County, Ohio, 1940		Nation-wide Study, NORC, 1944		Nation-wide Study, Survey Research Center, 1948		Greenwich, England, 1950	Bristol, England, 1951	Nation-wide Study, Survey Research Center, 1952			Elmira, New York, 1948		
	PC (1)	BB (2)	Kor (3)	Ziff (4)	C & K (5)	Jan-Mill (6)	B & G (7)	Milne Mack (8)	CGM (9)	Jan-Marv (10)	Vot. Dec. (11)	Din (12)	K & G (13)	Voting (14)
(197) The less homogeneous one's friends and co-workers in political position, the more change. *and:* (a) Shifts in a vote are related to the political inclination of one's friends (i.e., those with Republican friends shift more toward the Republicans, and those with Democratic friends shift more toward the Democrats)														
(198) The less interested the voter is in the election, the more likely he is to change his vote preference during the campaign, in any direction	X			X									X	X
(199) The more cross-pressures and inconsistencies the voter is subject to, the more change in his vote preference	X			X				X		X				X
(200) People who do not discuss politics much are relatively unstable in their voting *and:* (a) People who do not discuss politics much are more likely to follow the secular trend of the times														X X
(201) Voters who have previously changed their party position are more likely to change again than those who had not previously changed	X			X										X
(202) The changers who moved from one party to the other during the campaign were (a) least interested in the election; (b) least concerned about the outcome; (c) least attentive to campaign communications; (d) last to decide on their vote decision; and (e) most likely to be influenced by personal persuasion rather than political issues	X													X
(203) Voters who change from one party to the other support their initial candidate on the issues less strongly than the nonchangers								X						(in part)
(204) Voting changes within the campaign are affected by the partisan character of political discussion engaged in (e.g., the more talk with members of the opposition party, the more likely a change in vote to that party)														
(205) Voters who change from one election to another (1948–52) hold opinions on a variety of political issues in between the opinions of regular Republicans and regular Democrats									X					X
(206) Deviation from group norms in voting (for religious and class groups) is stronger between campaigns than during campaigns														
(207) Voters who change parties occupy an intermediate position in social class between the nonchangers														X
(208) Within social strata with unambiguous political preferences, the political majority is more stable than the political minority								X						X
(209) The cycle of greater and lesser discussion of politics produces a pulsating system, with greater polarization between dissimilar social groups in periods of greater political discussion														X

Questionnaires and Indexes
THE 1948 VOTING STUDY

FIRST QUESTIONNAIRE   **JUNE, 1948**

1. Where do you get most of your news about things like the coming Presidential election—from the radio, from the newspapers, from magazines, from talking to people, or where?

Radio	5–1
Newspapers	2
Magazines	3
Talking to people	4
Other (specify)	5–
Don't know	X

2. As you read or listen to the news these days, do you find you are paying a great deal of attention to things about the election, only a little attention, or no attention at all?

Great deal	6–1
Only a little	2
None at all	3
Don't know	4

3. Well, how much <u>interest</u> would you say you have in this year's Presidential election—a great deal, quite a lot, not very much, or none at all?

A great deal	7–1
Quite a lot	2
Not very much	3
None at all	4
Don't know	5

4. Would you say that you are <u>more</u> interested or <u>less</u> interested in this year's election that you were in the last Presidential election?

More	8–1
Less	2
Same	3
Don't know	4

a. *(Unless "Same" or "Don't know")* Why do you feel this way?

....

.... 9–

5. Do you ever get as worked up about something that happens in politics or public affairs as you do about something that happens in your personal life?

Yes 10–1   No 2   Don't know 3

6. Regardless of who you think might be nominated, which of the Republican candidates for the Presidential nomination do you think would make the best President?

Dewey	11–1
Stassen	2
Taft	3
Vandenberg	4
Martin	5
Warren	6
MacArthur	7
Eisenhower	8
Other (specify)	11–
None	0
Don't know	X
Don't know candidates	Y

7. Regardless of who you think might be nominated, which of the Democrats do you think would make the best President?

Truman	12–1
Eisenhower	2
Douglas	3
Other (specify)	12–
None	0
Don't know	X
Don't know candidates	Y

8. What do you think are the major issues between the Republicans and Democrats in this year's Presidential election—that is, what things do you think the two parties will be disagreeing about?

....

....

.... 13–

9. How about the Wallace Third Party? What do you think are the main points on which the Third Party will be disagreeing with the other two parties?

....

.... 14–

10a. In this election year, here are some important problems facing the country. Would you please read through them and tell me which two of the problems are the most important to you personally in making up your mind how to vote? *(Hand Respondent Card).*

b. Which two seem to you to be the least important compared with the others?

	a. Most Important	b. Least Important
1. How our relations with Russia should be handled	15–1	16–1
2. How the relations between Labor and Management should be handled	2	2
3. How the cost of living can be kept from rising further	3	3
4. Whether there should be more or less government controls over Big Business	4	4
5. How to strengthen the United Nations	5	5
6. How we should deal with the Communist party in the United States	6	6
Don't know most important	7	
Don't know least important		7

11. Do you think whoever is elected President this year will affect how our relations with Russia are handled, or won't it make any difference?

Affect	17–1
No difference	2
Don't know	3

12. Do you think whoever is elected President will affect how the relations between Labor and Management are handled, or won't it make any difference?

Affect 18–1

No difference..............2

Don't know 3

13. How about keeping living costs from rising further—will whoever is elected President affect this, or won't it make any difference?

Affect 19–1

No difference..............2

Don't know 3

14. On the whole, would you say it is more important this year to elect a president who can handle domestic affairs here at home or one who can handle international affairs and foreign relations?

Domestic 20–1

International 2

Both 3

Don't know 4

15. On the whole would you say it is more important this year to elect a president who has had experience in government, or one who has had experience in business?

Government 21–1

Business 2

Both 3

Don't know 4

16. As things look now, for which party do you think you will vote in the presidential election?

Republican 22–1

Democratic 2

Third (Wallace) 3

Other 4

Don't know 5

Do not intend to vote 6

Qualified answer (write in specific details)

....

....22–

....

a. *(If a definite party choice)* Right now, how strongly do you feel about your choice—very strongly, only fairly strongly, or not very strongly at all?

Very strongly 23–1

Fairly strongly 2

Not strongly 3

Don't know 4

b. *(If a party choice or qualified answer to 16)* Are you personally doing anything to help your party win the Presidential election this year?

Yes.............. No..............24–2

1. *(If "Yes")* What sort of thing are you doing?

....

....24–

c. *(If no party choice or no qualified answer)* Well, even though you don't know for sure how you will vote, which party are you leaning toward now—the Republican, Democratic, or Wallace Third Party?

Republican 25–1

Democratic 2

Third (Wallace) 3

Other 25–

None 0

Don't know X

1. *(If no party choice and "Don't know")* What would you say is the reason you haven't made up your mind?

....

....26–

17. Nobody knows for sure, of course, who the candidates will be. But if the candidates were Truman, Vandenberg and Wallace, for whom do you think you would vote?

Truman 27–1

Vandenberg 2

Wallace 3

Don't know 4

18. What if the candidates were Truman, Dewey and Wallace—which of these three do you think you would vote for?

Truman 28–1

Dewey 2

Wallace 3

Don't know 4

19. Regardless of which party you yourself might vote for, which party do you think is actually going to win the presidential election?

Republican 29–1

Democratic 2

Third (Wallace) 3

Don't know 4

Depends on who runs 5

20. Do you remember for certain whether you voted in the 1944 Presidential election (between Roosevelt and Dewey)?

Voted ....

Didn't vote 30–7

Too young to vote 30–8

Don't remember 9

a. *(If voted)* For whom did you vote?

Roosevelt............30–1 Dewey 30–2

Other ....30– Don't remember 30–5

21. How about the Presidential election of 1940, between Roosevelt and Willkie—did you vote then?

Voted ....

Didn't vote 31–7

Too young to vote 31–8

Don't remember 9

a. *(If voted)* For whom did you vote then?

Roosevelt............31–1 Willkie 31–2

Other ....31– Don't remember............31–5

349

22. Do you remember for certain whether you voted in the Congressional elections of 1946?

Yes............ No.............32-5

Too young...........32-6 Don't know...........32-7

a. (If voted) In the Senate race did you vote for Ives or Lehman?

Ives............32-1 Lehman ....2 Don't know...........3

b. (If voted in answer to 22) In the election for Representative from this district did you vote for W. Sterling Cole or for William Heidt, Jr.?

Cole 33-1

Heidt 2

Other (write in) 33-

Don't remember 6

23. As you remember it, for which party did your father usually vote in Presidential elections when you were too young to vote?

Republican 34-1

Democratic 2

Sometimes one, sometimes other...........3

Other party (specify)...........34-

Father couldn't vote 0

Don't know X

24. Do you think most .... around here would be more likely to vote for the Republican, Democratic or Wallace Third party?

	Rep.	Dem.	Third	Don't Know	Won't Vote as Bloc
Factory workers	37-1	2	3	4	5
Communists	38-1	2	3	4	5
Poor people	39-1	2	3	4	5
Rich people	40-1	2	3	4	5
Catholics	41-1	2	3	4	5
Negroes	42-1	2	3	4	5
Farmers	43-1	2	3	4	5
College people	44-1	2	3	4	5
Jews	45-1	2	3	4	5

25. How do you feel about our present relations with Russia? Do you feel the United States should be more willing to compromise, or is our present policy about right, or should we be firmer than we are today?

More willing to compromise 46-1

About right 2

Firmer 3

Don't know 4

26. With which of these four statements do you come closest to agreeing? (Hand Respondent Card)

1. Labor unions in this country are doing a fine job...........47-1

2. While they do make some mistakes, on the whole labor unions are doing more good than harm 2

3. Although we need labor unions in his country, they do more harm than good the way they are run now 3

4. This country would be better off without any labor unions at all 4

Don't know...........5

27. Do you think it would be better to put price controls back on some things, or to let things work out as they are now without price controls.

Controls ....5-5 No controls...........6 Don't know...........7

28. During the past ten years there have been a number of corporations that sold one billion dollars or more of goods each year. Which of these four statements comes closest to describing your feeling about a corporation that does this much business? (Hand respondent card)

a. It is dangerous for the welfare of the country for any companies to be this big and they should be broken up into smaller companies. 6-7

b. While it may be necessary to have some very large companies, we should watch their activities very closely and discourage their growth as much as possible. 8

c. There may be some drawbacks to having such large companies, but on the whole they do more good than harm to the country. 9

d. It is foolish to worry about a company just because it is big; large companies have made America the kind of country it is today. 0

e. Don't know X

29. Do you personally expect that we will have a depression in this country within the next five years or so, or do you think there is a good chance of avoiding it?

Expects depression 7-1

Expects recession 2

Doesn't expect depression 3

Depends (on what)...........7-

Don't know 6

30. Do you personally expect that this country will be in another great war within the next ten years or so, or do you think there is a good chance of avoiding it?

Expects war 8-8

Doesn't expect war 9

Depends (on what)...........0

Don't know X

350

31. Do you think that people like you have a lot of influence on how the government runs things, some influence, or not much influence at all?

Lot of influence	9–8
Some	9
Not much	0
Don't know	X

32. Can you tell me any job each of the persons on this list has held? *(Hand respondent card)*

	Correct Identification	Incorrect Identification	Don't Know
a. Glen Taylor	10–7	8	9
b. Harold Stassen	11–7	8	9
c. Abdullah	12–7	8	9
d. David E. Lilienthal	13–7	8	9
e. Robert F. Wagner	14–7	8	9
f. Winston Churchill	15–7	8	9
g. W. Averill Harriman	16–7	8	9
h. Alcides de Gasperi	17–7	8	9
j. Trygve Lie	18–7	8	9

33. Do you think any of these groups are getting more power anywhere in the United States than is good for the country? *(Hand Respondent card)* How about in Elmira?

	U.S.A.	Elmira
Protestants	19–1	20–1
Catholics	2	2
Jews	3	3
Negroes	4	4
Labor unions	5	5
Business men	6	6
Foreign born	7	7
None	8	8

34. From what you know about it, do you feel the Jews or the Arabs are more in the right in the present trouble in Palestine?

Jews	22–5	Arabs	6
Both	7	Don't know	8

35. Which of these groups do you consider yourself a member of? By and large do you think of yourself as being in the upper class, the upper middle, the middle, the lower middle, or the lower class?

Upper	23–7
Upper middle	8
Middle	9
Lower middle	0
Lower	X

36. In general, how do you feel about living in this community— would you say it's a very good community to live in, only fairly good, or not good at all?

Very good	24–1
Only fairly good	2
Not good	3
Don't know	4

a. *(If only fairly good, or not at all good)* Why do you feel this way?

....

....

....24–

37. Here in this town, what clubs and organizations such as, social, business or political, do you belong to? (Are there any others?)
a. About how often do you attend their meetings—would you say usually, only occasionally, or almost never?
b. Are you, or were you ever, an officer or committee member of the club?

Organization	Meeting Attendance			Officer or Committee Member
	Always or Usually	Occasionally	Never or Almost Never	
....	....	....	....	....
....	....	....	....	....
....	....	....	....	....
....	....	....	....	....
....	....	....	....	....
			Belong to no clubs	....

c. Are there any other groups that you meet with pretty regularly, like card clubs or neighborhood groups or discussion clubs or anything like that?

Yes............... No...............

1) *(If "Yes")* What are they?

.... 25–
26–
.... 27–

351

38. Do any of your closest friends disagree with your political opinions?

Yes ....
No 28–6
Don't know 7

a. *(If "Yes")* Would you say most of your closest friends disagree with you, some of them, or only a few of them?

Most 28–1
Some 2
Only few 3
Don't know 4

39. Do you know anybody personally who is an active member or worker for the Republican party here in Elmira?

Yes................29–1 No................2

a. *(If "Yes")* Who is that? (relation to respondent)

....29–

b. *(If "Yes")* What does he do for the party?

....30–

40. How about the Democratic party here in town—do you know anybody personally who is an active member or worker for that party?

Yes................31–1 No................2

a. *(If "Yes")* Who is that? (relation to respondent)

....31–

b. *(If "Yes")* What does he do for the party?

....32–

41. Finally, do you know anybody personally who is an active member or worker for the Wallace third party?

Yes................33–1 No................2

a. *(If "Yes")* Who is that? (relation to respondent)

....33–

b. *(If "Yes")* What does he do for the party?

....34–

42. So far as you know, how are the people in your family living here going to vote in the Presidential election this year?

	Relationship	Rep.	Dem.	Wallace	Other (Specify)	Don't know	DEV
1.							
2.							
3.							
4.							
5.							
6.							

35–
36–

43. Compared with the people you know, are you more or less likely than any of them to be asked your views about politics?

More 37–8   Less 9
Same 0   Don't know X

44. Have you talked politics with anyone recently?

Yes............38–5 No .... 6 Don't know............7

(If "Yes" Ask "A" through "G")

a. Do you talk politics with people often or only rarely?........

....

b. Who did you talk with last? (relation to respondent)

....

c. What was his (her) occupation?..

....

d. What did you talk about?..

....

e. Where and when did it happen?..

....

f. How did the discussion start? Did the other person ask your views? ....

....

g. Did you generally agree or disagree?..

....

39–
40–

352

45. Suppose you had some question in connection with the Presidential campaign and wanted to discuss it with someone — is there any one person among the people you know and associate with to whom you would be most likely to go? Anyone else?

(1) _____   (2) _____
         Name   Name

_____   _____
Specify Relationship   Specify Relationship

_____   _____
Occupation   Occupation

Sex: Sex:
   Male_____   Male_____
   Female_____   Female_____
          Age_____   Age_____
                                         41—
                                         42—

46. About how many hours a day, on the average, do you listen to the radio?

Don't listen	........43—1
Less than an hour	2
1-2 hours	3
From 2 to 4 hours	4
From 4 to 6 hours	5
Over 6 hours	6
Don't know	7

47. Which of the local newspapers here in Elmira do you read more or less regularly?

Star Gazette	........44—1
Telegram	2
Advertiser	3
Other (specify)	........44—
None	0

48. Do you read any out-of-town newspapers?

Yes........   No........45—1

(If "Yes") Which ones?

New York Times	........45—3
Herald Tribune	4
Daily News	5
Mirror	6
Journal American	7
PM	8
New York Sun	9
New York Post	0
World-Telegram	X

_____........45—

49. What magazines do you read more or less regularly? (Are there any others?)

Time	........46—1
Life	2
Sat. Eve. Post	3
Good Housekeeping	4
Ladies' Home Journal	5
McCall's	6
Woman's Home Companion	7
Reader's Digest	8
Collier's	9
Look	0

All others (Specify) _____

_____........46—
                              47—

50. About how many times do you go to the movies in the average month?

Don't go	........48—6
Once	7
Two or three times	8
Four or five times	9
Six or more times	0
Don't know	X

51. About how many books do you read in the average month?

None	........49—6
One	7
Two	8
Three	9
Four or more	0
Don't know	X

52. Do you use the public library here in Elmira regularly, once in a while, or not at all?

Regularly	........50—7
Once in a while	8
Not at all	9
Don't know	0

FACTUAL

Sex:

Male	........51—0
Female	X

Age:

Up to 25	........52—6
26 - 34	7
35 - 44	8
45 - 54	9
55 - 64	0
65 and over	X

Economic Level:

A	........53—8
B	9
C	0
D	X

Telephone:

Yes	........54—7
No	8

Automobile:

Yes	........54—0
No	X

Marital Status:

Single	........55—6
Married	7
Other	........55—

Race:

White	........56—9
Negro	0
Other	X

Education: What was the last school you attended?

None	........57—6
Some grammar school	7
Grammar school graduate	8
Some high school	9
High school graduate	0
College	X

Religion:

Catholic	........58—1
Protestant (which denomination?)	
_____	........58—
Jewish	3
None	4
Other	5

353

Occupation: (Job and Industry)

(If housewife, note occupation of breadwinner. If housewife who works part-time, note occupation of breadwinner and circle X here)

(Occupation of breadwinner)

59–

A. Do you (your husband) work for yourself or for someone else?

Self ....

Someone else ....

B. By and large, are you (your husband) satisfied with his present job or not?

Satisfied 60–9

Not satisfied 0

Don't know X

C. Are you (your husband) a member of a labor union?

Yes .... No .... 61–0 Don't know X

(If "Yes") Which one?

AFL .... 61–5 CIO .... 6 Other 7

D. Are you yourself a veteran of the last war?

Yes .... 62–1 No ....

a. *(If "No")* Was anyone in your immediate family in the last war?

Yes .... 62–2 No 3

1. *(If "Yes")* Who?

Veteran is respondent's 62–

E. What was the occupation of your father when you were in your teens?

....63–

F. Did he work for himself or for someone else?

Self ....

Someone else ....

G. How long have you lived in this town?.... 64–

H. How long have you lived in this neighborhood?.... ....

I. How long have you lived here in this house where you are now? 65–

J. Do you own your home here, or do you rent?

Own..................66–5 Rent..............6

K. What country were you born in?.................................. 66–

L. Were you born on a farm, in a small town, in a suburb of a big city, or in a big city?

Farm 67–9

Small town 0

Suburb X

Big city .... Y

M. In what country was your father born?........................... 68–

N. In what country was your mother born?.......................69–

Name of respondent...

Address ....

Segment No. ....

Name of Interviewer...

....70–

Date of Interview...

1. I'd like to ask you how closely you followed the news about the conventions. How about the Republican convention — did you follow it very closely, only fairly closely, or not closely at all.

Very closely 5–1
Only fairly closely................2
Not closely at all.................3
Don't know...........4

2. And the Democratic convention — did you follow it very closely, only fairly closely, or not closely at all?

Very closely 6–1
Only fairly closely................2
Not closely at all.................3
Don't know...........4

3. And finally the Wallace Third Party convention — did you follow it very closely, only fairly closely, or not closely at all?

Very closely 7–1
Only fairly closely................2
Not closely at all.................3
Don't know...........4

4. Do you intend to vote in the presidential election in November?

Yes 8–1
No 2
Don't know 3

(a) *(If "No")* Why not?..............

.................................9–

(b) *(If "Don't know")* Why might you not vote?..............

....

(c) *(If "No" or "Don't know")* Even though you might not vote, which candidate would you prefer?

Dewey 10–1
Truman 2
Wallace 3
Other 4
Don't know 5

IF RESPONDENT DOES NOT PLAN TO VOTE, SKIP TO QUESTION 20.

5. *(If plan to vote)* As things look now, which candidate do you think you will vote for in the presidential election?

Dewey 11–1
Truman 2
Wallace 3
Other 4
Don't know 5

Qualified Answer ....

(Write in details)

(a) *(If a definite choice)* Right now, how strongly do you feel about your choice — very strongly, only fairly strongly, or not very strongly at all?

Very strongly 12–1
Only fairly strongly.............2
Not strongly 3
Don't know 4

(b) *(If no definite party choice)* Well, even though you don't know for sure how you will vote, which candidate are you leaning toward now — Dewey, Truman or Wallace?

Dewey 13–1
Truman 2
Wallace 3
Other 4
Don't know 5

RECORD FROM JUNE INTERVIEW:

IF NO CHANGE FROM JUNE, SKIP TO QUESTION 20.

CRYSTALLIZERS
(No definite vote intention in June but definite vote intention now)

6. In June you hadn't decided for whom you would vote. Now you are planning to vote for .... What is the reason you decided to vote for him?

.................................14–

7. Are there any other reasons for your deciding to vote for him? What are they?

.................................15–

8. *(If more than one reason mentioned in answer to Questions 6 and 7)* Which of these reasons *(mention all named in Questions 6 and 7)* is most important to you in making up your mind?

.................................16–

NOW SKIP TO QUESTION 16.

DISINTEGRATERS
(Definite vote intention in June but no definite vote intention now)

9. In June you planned to vote for.............................. Now you no longer plan to vote for him. What made you decide not to vote for him?

.................................14–

10. Are there any other reasons for your deciding not to vote for him? What are they?

.................................15–

11. *(If more than one reason mentioned in answer to Questions 9 and 10)* Which of these reasons *(mention all named in Questions 9 and 10)* is most important to you in making you decide not to vote for him?

.................................16–

NOW SKIP TO QUESTION 16.

CONVERTERS
(Definite vote intention in June and a different definite vote intention now)

12. In June you planned to vote for.............................. Now you plan to vote for................ What made you change your mind?

.................................14–

13. What made you decide not to vote for..............................?

.................................15–

14. What made you decide to vote for..............................?

.................................16–

15. *(If more than one reason mentioned in Questions 12, 13 and 14)* Which of these reasons *(mention all named in Questions 12, 13 and 14)* was most important to you in making up your mind?

.................................17–

NOW GO TO QUESTION 16.

16. *(Ask All Changers)* Did any of your reading or listening or talking to people help you make up your mind?

Yes 18–1

No 2

(a) *(If "Yes")* What was that? *(Get specific details)* ....

....

............18–

17. *(Ask All Changers)* (You've just told me .... helped you make up your mind). Please tell me if any of these (others) helped convince you to make up your mind this way. Which? (USE CARD)

a. Radio news broadcast 19–1
b. Radio news commentator 2
c. Political speeches on radio 3
d. Article in newspaper 4
e. Editorial in newspaper 5
f. Picture in the newspaper 6
g. Magazine article 7
h. Book 8
i. Somebody I talked with 9
j. Someone I overheard 0
k. Speaker I heard in person X
l. Newsreel ....Y

m. Other (specify details) ....

............20–

18. *(If i. or j. is checked in Question 17)* Who is that?

Mentioned in "i":

Relationship to respondent: ....

Name: ....

Address: ....

Occupation: ....

Occupation of head of family (if not employed) ....

Mentioned in "j":

Relationship to respondent: ....

Name: ....

Address: ....

Occupation: ....

Occupation of head of family (if not employed) ....

............21–

............22–

19. *(Ask only if more than one source is mentioned in Questions 16 and 17)* Which of all these things you mentioned *(INTERVIEWER: Name all mentioned in Questions 16 and 17)* was most important to you in making up your mind?

............23–

20. *(Ask Everybody)* Regardless of which candidate you yourself might vote for, which one do you think is actually going to win the presidential election?

Dewey 24–1

Truman 2

Wallace 3

Other 4

Don't know 5

21. (a) Which of these words comes closest to describing the idea you have of President Truman? Choose as many words as you think describe him. (USE CARD)

(b) Which of these words comes closest to describing the idea you have of Dewey? Choose as many words as you think describe him. (USE CARD)

	(a) Truman	(b) Dewey
Courageous	25–1	26–1
Conservative	2	2
Weak	3	3
Honest	4	4
Inadequate	5	5
Sound	6	6
Confused	7	7
Efficient	8	8
Cold	9	9
Well-meaning	0	0
Thrifty	x	x
Opportunist	y	y

22. Have you heard or read anything about President Truman's Civil Rights Program?

Yes 27–1

No 2

(a) *(If "Yes")* As far as you know, is the Democratic Party united in support of this program?

United 28–1

Not united 2

Don't know 3

23. (a) How much need would you say there is for a program to improve the position of Negroes and other minority groups in this country? Would you say there's a very great need, some need but not very great, or practically no need?

(b) How about in Elmira, how much need is there for such a program here? Would you say there's a very great need, some need but not very great, or practically no need?

	(a) Country	(b) Elmira
Very great need	29–1	30–1
Some need	2	2
Practically no need	3	3
Don't know	4	4

Depends (write in) ....

24. (a) From what you know, does Truman favor compromising with the Russians or taking a firm stand with them?

(b) How about Dewey—do you think he favors compromising with the Russians or taking a firm stand with them?

	(a) Truman	(b) Dewey
Compromise	31–1	32–1
Firm stand	2	2
No stand	3	3
Don't know	4	4

25. (a) Do you think Truman is in favor of putting back price controls on some things or of leaving prices without controls the way they are now?

(b) Do you think Dewey is in favor of putting back price controls on some things or of leaving prices without controls the way they are now?

(c) How do you personally feel about this—are you in favor of putting back price controls on some things or of leaving prices without controls as they are now?

	(a) Truman	(b) Dewey	(c) Respondent
Put back controls	33–1	34–1	35–1
Leave off controls	2	2	2
No stand	3	3	3
Don't know	4	4	4

26. Have you heard of the Taft-Hartley law which regulates labor unions?

Yes 36–1
No 2

IF "YES" ASK a, b and c

(a) From what you know, is Truman for the Taft-Hartley law or against it?

(b) How about Dewey—is he for it or against it?

(c) And you personally—are you for the Taft-Hartley law or against it?

	(a) Truman	(b) Dewey	(c) Respondent
For it	37–1	38–1	39–1
Against it	2	2	2
No stand	3	3	3
Don't know	4	4	4

27. Which of these two statements comes closer to your own feelings?

It doesn't matter how long a party is in power, providing it is doing a good job 40–1

When any party, whether it's Republican or Democratic, has been in power for a long time, it's a good thing for the country to have a change 2

Don't know 3

28. If you were asked to use one of these four names for your social group, which would you say you belonged in: the middle class, lower class, working class, or upper class?

Upper class 41–1
Middle class 2
Working class 3
Lower class 4

29. From what you know, which of the parties—the Republican, Democratic, or Wallace Third Party—would do the best job for the upper class? How about the middle class? the working class? How about the lower class?

	Republican	Democratic	Wallace Third	Don't know
Upper class	42–1	42–2	42–3	42–4
Middle class	43–1	43–2	43–3	43–4
Working class	44–1	44–2	44–3	44–4
Lower class	45–1	45–2	45–3	45–4

30. How would you say most people like you—that is, people who work and live the way you do—how would you say most of them are going to vote?

............5–

31. A number of community organizations in Elmira would like to know what you think Elmira is most in need of? How much need would you say there is for a public swimming pool? A very great need? Some need but not great? Or practically no need? How about better street repair service? (ASK FOR EACH)

	Very Great Need	Some need But Not very Great	Practically No Need	No Opinion
A public swimming pool?	6–7	6–8	6–9	6–0
Better street repair service?	7–7	7–8	7–9	7–0
A new YWCA residence hall for young women?	8–7	8–8	8–9	8–0
A non-profit cafeteria run by a community organization	9–7	9–8	9–9	9–0
More public housing projects	10–7	10–8	10–9	10–0

32. Taking into account changes in income and also changes in the cost of living, would you say that you and your family are better off financially than you were in 1944, or less well off?

Better off 11–7
Less well off 8
About the same 9
Don't know 0

33. Here is a list of statements that people have different opinions about. Please tell me whether you agree or disagree with each statement.

	Agree	Disagree	Can't decide
(a) I have to struggle for everything I get in life	12–9	12–0	12–x
(b) Prison is too good for sex criminals: they should be publicly whipped or worse	13–9	13–0	13–x
(c) A lot of people around here ought to be put in their place	14–9	14–0	14–x
(d) I often find myself worrying about the future	15–9	15–0	15–x

34. Do you think there are any groups or kinds of people in this country who are trying to get ahead at the expense of people like you?

Yes 16–1
No 2

(a) (If "Yes") Which group or groups?

............16–

35. Some say that you can't be too careful in your dealings with people, while others say that most people can be trusted. From your own experience, which would you agree with more?

You can't be too careful 17–9
People can be trusted 0
Don't know x

36. Now to get back to politics: when you and your friends discuss political questions, what part do you usually take? (USE CARD)

Even though I may have strong opinions, I usually just listen 18–7

I listen a lot, but once in a while I express my opinion 8

I take an equal share in the conversation 9

I have definite ideas and try to convince the others 0

Don't know x

Comments: ....

37. Have you been reading or listening to news about the Communist spy hearings in Washington?

Yes 19–R
No 1

(a) (If "Yes") Which of these statements comes closest to your own feelings about this: (USE CARD)

(1) These spies are a serious threat to our country and the hearings deserve all the attention they are getting 19–2

(2) These spies are a threat to our country but they are getting all this attention only because the political parties are playing politics in an election year 3

(3) The spies are not a very serious threat but it is a good idea to give the hearings a lot of publicity in order to keep the spies from becoming more dangerous 4

(4) The spies are not a very serious threat now and all this publicity is just because the political parties are playing politics in an election year 5

(5) Don't know 6

38. How much interest would you say have in this year's Presidential election—a great deal, quite a lot, not very much, or none at all?

A great deal 21–7
Quite a lot 8
Not very much 9
None at all 0
Don't know x

39. By the way, are you employed now or not?

Employed 22–0
Not employed x

IF EMPLOYED, SKIP TO QUESTION 41.

40. (If employed) Think now of three persons with whom you work most closely at your job. How is each of these persons going to vote?

	Republican	Democratic	Wallace	Other	Co-worker hasn't decided	Respondent doesn't know
First co-worker						
Second co-worker						
Third co-worker						23–

41. Think of your three closest friends (outside of work). How is each of them going to vote?

	Republican	Democratic	Wallace	Other	Friend hasn't decided	Respondent doesn't know
First friend						
Second friend						
Third friend						24–

42. (If employed) Do you yourself belong to a union?

Yes 25–0

No x

IF "YES" ASK A AND B

(a) (If "Yes") Which local is it? ....

............26–

(INTERVIEWER: Get name of local and number of local)

(b) (If "Yes") For which candidate do you think most of the people in your union will vote?

Dewey 27–7

Truman 8

Wallace 9

Other 0

Split x

Don't know............y

43. (For each group affiliation of respondent) You told us you belong to the............. As far as you can tell, which candidate will receive the support of most members of this group?

(RECORD ANSWER BELOW)

	Group Affiliation	Truman	Most Members Dewey	Wallace	Split	Respondent doesn't know
(1)						
(2)						
(3)						
(4)						28– 29–

44. Which of these are most important to you? Choose as many as you feel are very important to you (USE CARD)

Your union 30–4

Your religious group 5

Your political party 6

Your social group 7

Your lodge 8

Your work group (profession) 9

Your race 0

Your nationality x

45. Have you lived in Elmira all your life?

Yes ....

No ....

(a) (If "No") Where did you live just before you came to Elmira? ....

(city and state or country)

....

46. (If Before August 24) Do you intend to vote in the primary on August 24?

Yes 31–7

No 8

(a) (If "Yes") For whom do you intend to vote?

............31–

47. (If on or After August 24) Did you vote in the primary on August 24?

Yes 31–7

No 8

(a) (If "Yes") Who did you vote for?

............31–

48. Has any of your family in this household changed his mind about how he was going to vote since the nominations of Truman and Dewey?

Yes 32–1

No 2

(a) (If "Yes") Who?

(b) (If "Yes") What was the change?

Relationship to respondent: ....

Change: 32–

49. Do you (or any member of your family in the household) own a phonograph?

Yes 33–0

No x

(a) (If "Yes") With or without a radio combination?

With 34–9

Without 0

Don't know x

50. Do you (or any member of your family in the household) own an electric mixer?

Yes 35–0

No x

51. Do you (or any member of your family in the household) own an automatic pop-up toaster?

Yes 36–0

No x

INTERVIEWER: JUST CHECK APPROPRIATE CATE-GORIES

52. Interviewer's rating of socio-economic level:

A 37–8

B 9

C 0

D x

53. Interviewer's rating of respondent's cooperation:

Cordial all the way through 38–8

Cordial at first, reluctant toward end 9

Reluctant at first, cordial at end 0

Reluctant all the way through x

RESPONDENT'S VOTING RECORD: June:

August:

*1. Do you intend to vote in the presidential election in November?

Yes 7–1
No 2
Don't know 3

(a) (If "No") Why not?

....

....

....

(b) (If "Don't know") Why might you not vote?...........8–

....

....

(c) (If "No" or Don't know" because not registered) Why didn't you register?

....

....

(d) (If "No" or "Don't know") Even though you might not vote, which candidate would you prefer?

Dewey 9–1
Truman 2
Wallace 3
Other 4
None 5
Don't know 6

(e) (If "Yes") Have you registered to vote?

Yes 10–1
No 2

IF RESPONDENT DOES NOT PLAN TO VOTE AND DIDN'T PLAN TO VOTE IN AUGUST EITHER, SKIP TO QUESTION 17. IF RESPONDENT DOES NOT PLAN TO VOTE BUT DID PLAN TO VOTE IN AUGUST, SKIP TO QUESTION 6.

IF PLANS TO VOTE

*2. As things look now, which candidate do you think you will vote for in the presidential election?

Dewey 11–1
Truman 2
Wallace 3
Other 4
Don't know 5
Qualified answer
(write in) 6

(a) (If a definite choice) Right now, how strongly do you feel about your choice—very strongly, only fairly strongly, or not very strongly at all?

Very strongly 12–1
Only fairly strongly 2
Not strongly 3
Don't know 4

(b) (If no definite choice) Well, even though you don't know for sure how you will vote, which candidate are you leaning toward now—Dewey, Truman or Wallace?

Dewey 13–1
Truman 2
Wallace 3
Other 4
Don't know 5

IF NO CHANGE FROM AUGUST VOTE INTENTION, SKIP TO QUESTION 17.

CRYSTALLIZER TYPE
(Definite choice now but didn't know in August or surer now than was in August)

*3. In August you hadn't decided (weren't sure, etc.) for whom you would vote. Now you are planning to vote for...................... . What is the reason you decided to vote for him?

....14–

*4. Are there any other reasons for your deciding to vote for him? What are they?

....15–

*5. (If more than one reason mentioned in answer to questions 3 and 4) Which of these reasons (mention all named) is most important to you in making up your mind?

....16–

NOW SKIP TO QUESTION 13.

DISINTEGRATOR TYPE
(Definite vote choice in August but none now or less definite about choice now than was in August)

*6. In August you planned to vote for (were sure you would vote for) .... Now you no longer plan to vote for him (are not so sure you will vote for him). What made you feel you would not (might not) vote for him?

....14–

*7. Any other reasons?

....15–

*8. (If more than one reason mentioned in answer to 6 and 7) Which of these reasons (mention all named) is most important to you in making you decide not to vote for him?

....16–

NOW SKIP TO QUESTION 13.

CONVERTER TYPE
(Planned to vote for or leaned toward one candidate in August and now plans to vote for or leans toward a different candidate)

*9. In August you planned to vote for (were leaning toward)...................... . Now you are planning to vote for (leaning toward) .... What made you change your mind?

....14–

*10. What made you decide not to vote for ....?

....15–

*11. What made you decide to vote for ....?

....16–

*12. (If more than one reason mentioned in 9, 10, 11) Which of these reasons (mention all named) was most important to you in making up your mind?

....17–

NOW GO ON TO QUESTION 13.

*13. *(Ask all changers)* Did any of your reading or listening or talking to people help you make up your mind?

Yes 18–1

No 2

(a) *(If "Yes")* What was that? *(Get specific details)*

*14. *(Ask all changers)* *(You've just told me ....* *helped you make up your mind).* Please tell me if any of these *(others)* helped convince you to make up your mind this way? (USE CARD)

a. Radio broadcast 19–1
b. Radio news commentator 2
c. Political speeches on the radio 3
d. Article in newspaper 4
e. Editorial in newspaper 5
f. Picture in the newspaper 6
g. Magazine article 7
h. Book 8
i. Somebody I talked with 9
j. Someone I overheard 0
k. Speaker I heard in person X
l. Newsreel .... Y
m. Other 20–

*15. *(If i. or j. is checked or if "talking to people" mentioned in 13)*

	Mentioned in "i"	Mentioned in "j"	Question 13
Relationship to respondent:			
Name:			
Address:			
Occupation:			
Occupation of head of family (if person unemployed):		 21–	 22–

*16. *(Ask only if more than one source is mentioned in Questions 13 and 14)* Which of all these things you mentioned *(name all mentioned)* was most important to you in making up your mind?

.... 23–

*17. *(Ask everybody)* Regardless of which candidate you yourself might vote for, which one do you think is actually going to win the presidential election?

Dewey 24–1

Truman 2

Wallace 3

Other 4

Don't know 5

*18. (a) Which of these words comes closest to describing the idea you have of President Truman? Choose as many words as you think describe him. (USE CARD)

(b) Which of these words comes closest to describing the idea you have of Dewey? Choose as many words as you think describe him. (USE CARD)

	(a) Truman	(b) Dewey
Courageous	25–1	26–1
Conservative	2	2
Weak	3	3
Honest	4	4
Inadequate	5	5
Sound	6	6
Confused	7	7
Efficient	8	8
Cold	9	9
Well-meaning	0	0
Thrifty	X	X
Opportunist	Y	Y

19. If Eisenhower were running on the Republican ticket against Truman, which one would you vote for?

Eisenhower 27–1

Truman 2

Other 3

Don't know 4

Depends 5

Neither 6

20. If Eisenhower were running on the Democratic ticket against Dewey, which one would you vote for?

Eisenhower 28–1

Dewey 2

Other 3

Don't know 4

Depends 5

Neither 6

*21. What do you think are the major issues between the Republicans and the Democrats in this year's presidential election—that is, what things do you think the two parties will be disagreeing about?

.... 29–

*22. With which of these four statements do you come closest to agreeing? (USE CARD)

a. Labor unions in this country are doing a fine job 30–1

b. While they do make some mistakes, on the whole labor unions are doing more good than harm 2

c. Although we need labor unions in this country, they do more harm than good the way they are run now 3

d. This country would be better off without any labor unions at all 4

Don't know 5

23. Now we would like to know your opinion about several business concerns. For example, would you describe your feelings about Remington Rand as on the friendly side, not so friendly, or completely neutral? How about General Motors? (ASK ABOUT EACH COMPANY)

	Friendly	Not so Friendly	Neutral or Don't Know
Remington Rand	31–1	31–2	31–3
General Motors	32–1	32–2	32–3
U. S. Steel	33–1	33–2	33–3
General Electric	34–1	34–2	34–3
Standard Oil of N. J.	35–1	35–2	35–3
Bendix	36–1	36–2	36–3

24. By the way, you probably know there are several Standard Oil companies—to name a few, Standard Oil of Indiana, Standard Oil of California, etc. Do you think of them as all one company, or each as an entirely separate company?

Entirely separate 37–1

Separate companies with some tie-up (only if volunteered) 2

All one 3

Don't know 4

*25. Do you personally expect that this country will be in another great war within the next ten years or so, or do you think there is a good chance of avoiding it?

Expects war 38–1

Doesn't expect war 2

Depends (on what?) 3

Don't know 4

(a) *(If "Expects war")* How soon do you think the next war will come?

.... 38–

*26. From what you know about it, do you feel the Jews or the Arabs are more in the right in the present trouble in Palestine?

Jews 39–1
Arabs 2
Both 3
Don't know 4

(a) *(Unless "Don't know")* What makes you feel that way?

....39–

*27. How much interest would you say you have in this year's presidential election—a great deal, quite a lot, not very much, or none at all?

A great deal 40–1
Quite a lot 2
Not very much 3
None at all 4
Don't know 5

*28. As you read or listen to the news these days, do you find you are paying a great deal of attention to things about the election, only a little attention, or no attention at all?

A great deal 41–1
Only a little 2
Not at all 3
Don't know 4

29. Can you remember the last two items you read in the newspaper about the election? What were they about?

....42–

30. Can you remember the last two speeches or programs you heard on the radio about the election? What were they about?

....43–

31. Can you remember the last two stories about the election which you have seen in magazines? What were they about?

....44–

32. Please look at this list of things and tell me which of these you remember reading about or listening to: (HAND RESPONDENT CARD)

....

....

33. Who was the last person you discussed the election or the candidates with? (NOTE RELATIONSHIP) Who was he going to vote for? What did he say about it?

Relationship: 7–

Vote: 8–

Conversation: ....

34. As far as you know, how are the people in your family living here going to vote in the Presidential election this year?

Relationship	Rep.	Dem.	Wallace	Other	D.K.	DEV	Resp. D.K.
....	....	....	....	....	....	....	....
....	....	....	....	....	....	....	....
....	....	....	....	....	....	....	....
....	....	....	....	....	....	....	9–
....	....	....	....	....	....	....	10–

35. (a) What do you think of Truman's campaign? Which of these words describe it? (USE CARD)

(b) What do you think of Dewey's campaign? Which of these words describe it? (USE CARD)

	(a) Truman	(b) Dewey
Undignified	11–1	12–1
Hard-hitting	2	2
Lofty	3	3
Unfair	4	4
Vague	5	5
Honest	6	6
Good-natured	7	7
Double-talk	8	8
Confident	9	9
Dignified	0	0
Mud-slinging	X	X

36. In the last three or four weeks has anyone from any of the parties seen or 'phoned you in regard to the election campaign?

Yes 13–7
No 8

(a) *(If "Yes")* From what party?

Republican 14–7
Democratic 8
Wallace 9
Other 0
Don't know X

(b) *(If "Yes")* Did he try to get you to register, try to convince you about how to vote, did he take you to the polls, or what?

Tried to get you to register 15–7
Tried to convince how to vote 8
Took to polling place 9
Other (what?) ....

....0

37. Did you receive any postcards, pamphlets or other literature about the election?

Yes 16–8
No 9

(a) *(If "Yes")* From what party?

Republican 17–7
Democratic 8
Wallace 9
Other 0
Don't know X

(b) *(If "Yes")* How did you get it?

In the mail 18–7
Someone left it 8
Other (what?)

....9

38. Regardless of how you may vote in the coming election, how have you usually thought of yourself—as a Republican, Democrat, Socialist, or what?

Republican 19–1
Democratic 2
Socialist 3
Independent Voter 4
Other specific party 5
Sometimes one, sometimes other 6
Don't know 7

(a) *(Unless names specific party)* Have you ever considered yourself a Republican or Democrat?

Yes 20–R
No 7

(1) *(If "Yes")* Which?

Republican 20–8
Democrat 9
Both at different times 0

39a. From what you know, is Truman for or against having the government sponsor more public housing projects? (RECORD BELOW)

b. How about Dewey — is he for or against having the government sponsor more public housing projects? (RECORD BELOW)

c. How do you personally feel about this — are you for or against having the government sponsor more public housing projects?

	(a) Truman	(b) Dewey	(c) Respondent
For	21–8	22–8	23–8
Against	9	9	9
No stand	0	0	0
Don't know	X	X	X

40. (TO BE ASKED ONLY IF CHECKED IN MARGIN AS PERSON WHO THINKS DEMOCRATS WOULD DO THE BEST JOB FOR HIS CLASS BUT IS VOTING FOR DEWEY) You told us last time you felt the Democrats would do the best job for the .... class and that you felt you were a part of the .... class. Yet you are planning to vote for Dewey. How is that?

(BE SURE TO NOTE RESPONDENT'S REACTION TO THIS QUESTION:) 24–

....25–

Seems never to have thought of this contradiction ....

Seems to have thought of the contradiction and to have decided nonetheless to vote for Dewey ....

Embarrassed ....

Annoyed ....

Pretty matter of fact ("Sure that's the way politics goes") .....

Other interviewer comments...

....

361

41. (TO BE ASKED ONLY IF CHECKED IN MARGIN AS PERSON WHO IS CATHOLIC AND THINKS MOST CATHOLICS WILL VOTE FOR ONE PARTY WHEREAS HE HIMSELF PLANS TO VOTE FOR THE OTHER PARTY) You told us last time you thought most Catholics would vote for the .... And yet you are planning to vote for the .... How does that happen?

....

....

(Interviewer: Note reaction of respondent at being asked about contradiction) 22–

*42. Do you think any of these groups are getting more power anywhere in the United States than is good for the country? (HAND RESPONDENT CARD) How about in Elmira?

	U.S.A.	Elmira
a. Protestants	26–5	27–5
b. Catholics	6	6
c. Jews	7	7
d. Negroes	8	8
e. Labor unions	9	9
f. Business men	0	0
g. Foreign born	X	X
h. None	Y	Y

JUNE RECORD:

....

(If change from June) Last time you felt the .... (or none) were getting too much power. Will you tell me how you happened to change your mind?

43. Congress has passed a bill to admit 200,000 refugees to the United States in the next few years. Do you approve or disapprove this?

Approve 28–9

Disapprove 0

Don't know X

Comment: ....

44. Suppose a family from any of these American groups were about to move next door. Are there any of them you would prefer not to have as neighbors? (USE CARD AND RECORD ANSWERS IN FIRST COLUMN BELOW)

　a) (IF ANY NAMED) Are there any others? (RECORD IN FIRST COLUMN BELOW)

45. Do you have any friends among members of these groups with whom you exchange visits? (RECORD IN SECOND COLUMN BELOW)

　a) (IF ANY NAMED) Are there any others? (RECORD IN SECOND COLUMN BELOW)

46. During the last month, did you personally come into contact with any of these groups? (RECORD IN THIRD COLUMN)

	44. Keep Out	45. Friends	46. Contact
a. American Protestants	29–5	30–5	31–5
b. American Catholics	6	6	6
c. American Jews	7	7	7
d. American Negroes	8	8	8
e. Italian-Americans	9	9	9
f. Irish-Americans	0	0	0
None	X	X	X
All	Y	Y	Y

47. All of us have our own opinions about different groups and kinds of people. Here are some statements that people make about other people. Please tell me if you agree or disagree:

	Agree	Disagree	Can't Decide	Not Asked
This country would be better off if there were not so many foreigners here	32–9	32–0	32–X	32–Y
Generally speaking Negroes are lazy and ignorant	33–9	33–0	33–X	33–Y
Although some Jews are honest, in general Jews are dishonest in their business dealings	34–9	34–0	34–X	34–Y
Americans must be on guard against the power of the Catholic Church	35–9	35–0	35–X	35–Y

48. As far as you know, do any of these magazines show any favoritism for one or the other candidate? (USE CARD AND RECORD BELOW)

　a) (If "Yes") Which magazines? (RECORD BELOW)

　　(1) (ASK FOR EACH MAGAZINE MENTIONED) For whom does it show favoritism — for Dewey or for Truman? (RECORD BELOW)

49. Incidentally, which of these magazines have you read in the past six months or so? (USE CARD AND RECORD BELOW)

50. (FOR EACH MAGAZINE MENTIONED IN ANSWER TO 48) Do you read................................regularly, occasionally or seldom?

	Ques. 48a Favoritism	Ques. 48a (1) For Dewey	For Truman	Ques. 49 Read past six months	Ques. 50 Regularly	Occasionally	Seldom
Reader's Digest	36–4	37–0	37–X	44–4	45–9	45–0	45–X
Life	5	38–0	38–X	5	46–9	46–0	46–X
Satevepost	6	39–0	39–X	6	47–9	47–0	47–X
Colliers'	7	40–0	40–X	7	48–9	48–0	48–X
Time	8	41–0	41–X	8	49–9	49–0	49–X
Look	9	42–0	42–X	9	50–9	50–0	50–X
Newsweek	0	43–0	43–X	0	51–9	51–0	51–X
None	X			X			

51. Which of these magazines do you like best?

....52–

52. (If names specific magazine in question 51) Which one do you like next best?

....53–

53. We'd like to know whether or not you ever listened to certain radio programs last winter. (October through May) Did you ever listen to Telephone Hour on Monday evening? How about the New York Philharmonic on Sunday afternoon? And the Theatre Guild of the Air on Sunday evening?

　a) (ASK FOR EACH LISTENED TO) About how often did you listen to .... last winter — three or four times a month, once or twice a month, or less often than that?

	Telephone Hour on Monday Evening	N. Y. Philharmonic Symphony on Sunday Afternoon	Theatre Guild on the Air on Sunday Evening
a. Ever Listened:			
Yes	54–R	55–R	56–R
No	7	7	7
b. How Often:			
3-4 times mo.	8	8	8
1-2 times mo.	9	9	9
Less Often	0	0	0

54. From which of the following sources do you and your family receive the major part of your family income:

Fixed salaries 57–1

Wages (hourly or piece-work) 2

Profits or fees, self-employed 3

Savings 4

Interest on savings or investments 5

Private or public help 6

Pensions 7

55. Education: What was the last school you attended?

None 58–6

Some grammar school 7

Grammar school graduate 8

Some high school 9

High school graduate 0

College or University..........................X

56. During the last year, have you made any contributions of money to any political party?

Yes 59–X

No ....Y

362

THE 1948 VOTING STUDY

QUESTIONNAIRE

FOURTH WAVE* (NOVEMBER)

1. Did you vote on November 2? Yes_____

    No_____

VOTERS

2. Whom did you vote for?

    Dewey _____

    Truman _____

    Wallace _____

    Other _____

3. How about the election for congressman—which candidate did you vote for?

    Cole (Rep) _____

    O'Connor (Dem) _____

    Other _____

4. If you knew it was going to be such a close race between Truman and Dewey, would you have voted any differently?

    Yes _____

    No _____

  (a) (If "Yes") For whom would you have voted?

    Dewey _____

    Truman _____

    Other _____

NONVOTERS

2. Why didn't you vote?

    _____

    _____

    _____

3. If you had known it was going to be such a close race between Dewey and Truman, would you have voted (registered)?

    Yes _____

    No _____

  (a) (If "Yes") For whom would you have voted?

    Dewey _____

    Truman _____

    Other _____

* Questions 1–4 were sent by mail to all respondents in the original design. Questions 5–15 were asked by phone or by personal interview of all appropriate respondents.

FOR ALL WHO CHANGED, VOTERS *AND* NONVOTERS

5. (*a*) Did you listen to or read any of Truman's speeches in the last few days before the election?

        Yes _____

        No _____

(*b*) Did you listen to or read any of Dewey's speeches in the last few days before the election?

        Yes _____

        No _____

(*c*) Did you hear the broadcast by the Republicans, with all the movie stars, on the night before the election?

        Yes _____

        No _____

(If "Yes") Did you like it?

        Yes _____

        No _____

(*d*) Did you hear the broadcast by the Democrats, with Barkley and Truman, on the night before the election?

        Yes _____

        No _____

        Not sure _____

(If "Yes") Did you like it?

        Yes _____

        No _____

6. Before election day, what did you really think of the way Dewey ran his campaign? _____

_____

_____

7. Before election day, what did you really think of the way Truman ran his campaign? _____

_____

_____

8. Did anyone in your family or any of your friends change their minds about how to vote in the last week or so before the election?

        Yes _____

        No _____

(If "Yes") (*a*) Whom did they finally vote for?

>Dewey ——

>Truman ——

(*b*) What made them change their minds?

_____

9. Did anyone in your family or any of your friends not vote, **even though** they had intended to vote before the election?

>Yes ——

>No ——

(If "Yes") (*a*) Which candidate did they favor?

>Dewey ——

>Truman ——

(*b*) Why didn't they vote? _____

CHANGERS WHO VOTED	CHANGERS WHO DIDN'T VOTE
CONVERTER 10. (*a*) A few weeks ago you were leaning toward ——, yet you actually voted for ——. What made you change your mind? *or:* CRYSTALLIZER ON CANDIDATE 10. (*c*) You hadn't decided whom to vote for when we spoke to you a few weeks ago. What made you decide to vote for ——? *or:* CRYSTALLIZER ON INTENTION TO VOTE 10. (*d*) You weren't planning to vote when we spoke to you a few weeks ago. What made you change your mind and vote for —— after all?	10. (*b*) When we spoke to you a few weeks ago, you were planning to vote for ——. What happened to make you change your mind and **not** vote after all? 11. (*a*) When was it that you definitely decided not to vote for ——? 12. (*a*) What happened at that time to make you decide that way? *(END OF QUESTIONNAIRE FOR CHANGERS WHO DIDN'T VOTE.)*

CHANGERS WHO VOTED

11. (*b*) When was it that you definitely made up your mind to vote for _____?

12. (*b*) What happened at that time to make you decide that way?

13. Please tell me if any of these were particularly important in influencing you to make up your mind that way. (*USE CARD.*)

(*a*) Radio broadcast

(*b*) Radio news commentator

(*c*) Political speeches on radio

(*d*) Articles in newspaper

(*e*) Editorial in newspaper

(*f*) Pictures in newspaper

(*g*) Magazine article

(*h*) Book

(*i*) Somebody I talked with

(*j*) Someone I overheard

(*k*) Speaker I heard in person

(*l*) Newsreel

(*m*) Other

(If any) What was it specifically?

14. (*a*) Which of these were the two most important factors in making you decide to vote as you did? (*USE CARD.*)

(*b*) Which two do you think were the most important factors for most Democrats? (*USE CARD.*)

(*c*) Which two for Republicans? (*USE CARD.*)

(1) Dewey's stand on the issues

(2) Truman's stand of the issues

(3) What the Eightieth Congress accomplished

(4) Dewey's personality and ability

(5) Truman's personality and ability

(6) What the Republican party stands for

(7) What the Democratic party stands for

(8) Dewey's chances to win

(9) Truman's chances to win

(10) The way Dewey campaigned

(11) The way Truman campaigned

15. Did you go to the election place with anyone, or did you go alone?

With someone _____

Alone _____

(If with someone) (*a*) With whom? _____

(*b*) How did they vote? _____

SUPPLEMENTARY MAIL QUESTIONNAIRE[1]

During the last ten years there have been a number of corporations that sold one billion dollars or more of goods each year. Which of these four statements comes closest to describing your feeling about a corporation that does this much business?

1) It is dangerous for the welfare of this country for any companies to be this big, and they should be broken up into small companies.
2) While it may be necessary to have some very large companies, we should watch their activities closely and discourage their growth as much as possible.
3) There may be some drawbacks to having such large companies, but on the whole they do more good than harm to the country.
4) It is foolish to worry about a company just because it is big; large companies have made America the kind of country it is today.

With which of these four statements do you come closest to agreeing?

1) Labor unions in this country are doing a fine job.
2) While they do make some mistakes, on the whole labor unions are doing more good than harm.
3) Although we need labor unions in this country, they do more harm than good in the way they are run now.
4) This country would be better off without any labor unions at all.

Which of the following statements comes closer to your own opinion?

1) Most city governments are controlled by businessmen in their own interests.
2) Most city governments make the welfare of all citizens their main concern.

Which of the following would you say is the reason most people who are successful have gotten ahead?

1) Because of their ability.
2) Because of their luck.
3) Because they have had pull.
4) Because of the better opportunities their families have given them.

Do you prefer to belong to organizations (such as bowling clubs, bridge clubs, baseball teams, lodges, and so on) whose members are all of your own social class, or ones whose members are persons of various classes?

1) All of my own social class.
2) Mixed classes.

1. Referred to in chap. 4. Field work in March and July, 1950.

Do you like to read or hear stories about any of the following? Please check as many as apply: Working people, Business people, Doctors, Lawyers, Movie stars, Explorers.

If you had a son who studied law, whom would you rather have him work for? (*Check the one you favor most*) The government, A business corporation, A union, Himself, A law firm.

How about medicine? If you had a son who studied medicine would you prefer him to eventually become: (*Check one*) A specialist with a private practice, Head of a government medical service, Head of a private hospital.

Do you think it would be good for the country as a whole if the labor unions had a political party of their own? Yes, No.

INDEXES

Socioeconomic Status (*SES*)

This index was constructed from three items:

Education
(Breadwinner's) occupation
Interviewer rating of economic level

The scoring:

INTERVIEWER RATING*	PROFESSIONAL, SEMI-PROFESSIONAL, MANAGERIAL, EXECUTIVE, AND CLERICAL-SALES		SKILLED LABOR, SEMI-SKILLED, UNSKILLED, AND SERVICE WORKERS	
	High-School Graduates and Above	Some High School and Below	High-School Graduates and Above	Some High School and Below
(High) A, B	5	4	4	3
C+	4	4	3	3
C−	4	3	3	2
(Low) D	3	3	2	1

* The "C's" were broken into two groups on the basis of ownership of common household utilities.

Distribution of cases:

High (score 5) 79
High middle (score 4) 128
Middle (score 3) 290
Low middle (score 2) 394
Low (score 1) 138

Total no. of cases 1,029

In the text this distribution is collapsed into two or three groupings:

Two		Three	
Middle and above	497	High middle and high	207
Low middle and low	532	Middle	290
		Low middle and low	532

Incidentally this combination of variables correlates highly with the respondent's subjective class identification:

Interviewer Rating	Percentage with Middle- or Upper-Class Identification			
	Professional, Semiprofessional, Managerial, Executive, and Clerical-Sales		Skilled, Semiskilled, Unskilled, and Service Workers	
	High-School Graduates and Above	Some High School and Below	High-School Graduates and Above	Some High School and Below
A, B...........	85	72	58	50
C+............	77	61	52	43
C−............	60	32	48	23
D.............	67	32	32	18

Media Exposure

This index was constructed from answers to the questions about campaign items seen in newspapers and magazines and heard over the radio during the last few weeks of the campaign. Three were recall questions (October Questions 29–31), and another was a recognition-from-check list (October Question 32). They are highly interrelated, as the following table shows; the index they form is interchangeable with other exposure questions.

RECALLED FOLLOWING NUMBER OF ITEMS OUT OF POSSIBLE SIX	RECOGNIZED FOLLOWING PERCENTAGES OF CHECK-LIST ITEMS OUT OF TOTAL POSSIBLE			
	30 Per Cent or More	20–29 Per Cent	10–19 Per Cent	Less than 10 Per Cent
Three or more..........	62	50	34	13
Two.................	20	25	27	24
One.................	9	18	22	19
None................	9	7	17	44
Total no. of cases....	160	126	183	345

The scoring:

RECALLED FOLLOWING NUMBER OF ITEMS OUT OF POSSIBLE SIX	PERCENTAGE WHO RECOGNIZED FOLLOWING PERCENTAGES OF CHECK-LIST ITEMS OUT OF TOTAL POSSIBLE			
	30 Per Cent or More	20–29 Per Cent	10–19 Per Cent	Less than 10 Per Cent
Three or more..........	6	5	4	3
Two.................	5	4	3	2
One.................	4	3	2	1
None................	3	2	1	0

Distribution of cases:

High (score 6 and 5)	196
High middle (score 4 and 3) ...	236
Low middle (score 2 and 1)	227
Low (score 0)	155
Total no. of cases (October) ..	814

The distribution is presented in two groups:

High and high middle	432
Low middle and low	382

Internationalism

This index was constructed from four questions:

October Question 43: "Congress has passed a bill to admit 200,000 refugees to the United States in the next few years. Do you approve or disapprove of this?"

Score: "Approve" = plus. All other answers = minus.

October Question 47: "All of us have our own opinion about different groups and kinds of people. Here are some statements that people make about other people. Please tell me if you agree or disagree. (1) This country would be better off if there were not so many foreigners here."

Score: "Disagree" = plus.   All other answers = minus.

June Question 10a: "In this election there are some important problems facing this country. Would you please read through them and tell me which two of the problems are the most important to you personally in making up your mind how to vote?"

Score: "How to strengthen the United Nations" = plus.

All other answers = minus.

June Question 14: "On the whole, would you say it is more important this year to elect a President who can handle domestic affairs here at home or one who can handle international affairs and foreign relations?"

Score: "International" or "both" = plus. All other answers = minus.

The scoring:

	DP+ Foreign.+	DP+ Foreign.−	DP− Foreign.+	DP− Foreign.−
UN+ Intl. Pres.+..	5	5	4	3
UN+ Intl. Pres.−..	5	4	3	2
UN− Intl. Pres.+..	4	3	2	1
UN− Intl. Pres.−..	3	2	1	0

Distribution of cases:

International Liberals	score 5	77
	score 4	140
	score 3	129
	score 2	123
	score 1	205
International Conservatives	score 0	138
	Unknown	2
Total no. of cases (October)		814

This distribution is collapsed into two or three groupings:

Two		Three	
Score 3 and above	346	Score 4 and 5	217
Score 2 and below	466	Score 2 and 3	252
		Score 0 and 1	343

(*Economic*) *Liberalism*

This index was constructed from three questions:

June Question 27: "How do you personally feel about this—are you in favor of putting back price controls on some things or of leaving prices without controls as they are now?"

June Question 28: "During the last ten years there have been a number of corporations that sold one billion dollars or more of goods each year. Which of these four statements comes closest to describing your feeling about a corporation that does this much business?"

(*a*) It is dangerous for the welfare of the country for any companies to be this big, and they should be broken up into small companies.

(*b*) While it may be necessary to have some very large companies, we should watch their activities very closely and discourage their activities as much as possible.

(*c*) There may be some drawbacks to having such large companies, but on the whole they do more good than harm to the country.

(*d*) It is foolish to worry about a company just because it is big; large companies have made America the kind of country it is today."

June Question 26: "With which of these four statements do you come closest to agreeing?

(1) Labor unions in this country are doing a fine job.

(2) While they do make some mistakes, on the whole labor unions are doing more good than harm.

(3) Although we need labor unionism in this country, they do more harm than good the way they are run now.

(4) This country would be better off without any labor unions at all."

The scoring:

Responses "for" price controls, "unfavorable" to big business (*a* and *b*) and "favorable" to unions (1 and 2) were scored +1; responses "against" price controls, "favorable" to big business and "unfavorable" to unions were scored —1. All other answers were scored 0.

Distribution of cases:

Liberal	+3	84
	+2	52
	+1	302
	0	118
	—1	287
	—2	66
Conservative	—3	118
Unknown	....	2
	Total no. of cases	1,029

The distribution is presented in two groupings:

Liberals	438		Liberals	136
Conservatives	471		Middle-of-the-road	707
(Score 0 omitted)	(118)		Conservatives	184

Voting History

This index was constructed from three questions:

June Question 20: "Do you remember for certain whether you voted in the 1944 presidential election (between Roosevelt and Dewey)?
"*a*) (If voted) For whom did you vote?"

June Question 21: "How about the presidential election of 1940, between Roosevelt and Willkie—did you vote then?
"*a*) (If voted) For whom did you vote then?"

June Question 22: "Do you remember for certain whether you voted in the congressional elections of 1946?
"*a*) (If voted) In the Senate race did you vote for Ives or Lehman?"

The scoring:

In each case, a vote for the Democratic candidate $= -1$,
a vote for the Republican candidate $= +1$
other responses (other candidates,
did not vote, too young to vote,
does not recall, etc.) $= 0$

Distribution of cases:

All Republican (+2 and +3)	228
More Republican (+1)	117
Neutral (0)	287
More Democratic (−1)	131
All Democratic (−2 and −3)	266
Total no. of cases	1,029

"Neuroticism"

This index (admittedly a crude and inadequate measure of "neuroticism") was constructed from one question in four parts:

August Question 33: "Here is a list of statements that people have different opinions about. Please tell me whether you agree or disagree with each statement:

I have to struggle for everything I get in life.
Prison is too good for sex criminals: they should be publicly whipped.
A lot of people around here ought to be put in their place.
I often find myself worrying about the future."

The scoring:

"Agree" with each statement $= +1$
Other responses $= 0$

Distribution of cases:

Low (non-"neurotic")	115
Low middle	251
High middle	281
High	234
Total no. of cases (August)	881

The groups used in the text are:

Low	115		Lower	366
Middle	532		Higher	515
High	234			

Accurate Perception of Candidates' Stands

This index was constructed from two questions:

August Question 25: "(a) Do you think Truman is in favor of putting back price controls on some things or of leaving prices without controls the way they are now?
(b) Do you think Dewey is in favor of putting back price controls on some things or of leaving prices without controls the way they are now?"

August Question 26: "Have you heard of the Taft-Hartley Law which regulates labor unions?
　If 'yes': *a*) From what you know, is Truman for the Taft-Hartley Law or against it?
　　　b) How about Dewey—is he for it or against it?"

Total scores were:

All 4 accurate	138
Three accurate	183
Two accurate	239
One accurate	224
None accurate	94
No answer	3
Total no. of cases (August) ...	881

Groupings used in the text are indicated there (e.g., 3 or 4 accurate).

(An Index of Accuracy of Perception of Groups, e.g., rich people, Catholics, etc., was constructed analogously, by cumulating the number of correct perceptions, but is used only as a control variable in one table in this volume.)

Image of Truman

This index was constructed from two questions:

August Question 21a: "Which of these words comes closest to describing the idea you have of President Truman? Choose as many words as you think describe him." (The respondent was handed a list.)

October Question 18: Same as above.

The scoring:

Responses "efficient," "courageous," "honest," and "sound" = A (high)
Responses "well-meaning," "thrifty," and "conservative" = B (middle)
Responses "weak," "inadequate," and "confused" = C (low)

Distribution of cases:

	August	October
A only.............	64	61
AB.................	209	200
B only.............	53	37
ABC, AC, none.......	265	220
BC.................	123	115
C only.............	167	181
Total no. of cases	881	814

The distribution is presented in three groups:

	August	October
Favorable (A, AB, B)........	326	298
Lukewarm (ABC, AC, none)..	265	220
Unfavorable (BC, C)........	290	296

Political Involvement

This index was constructed from three questions:

June Question 31: "Do you think that people like you have a lot of influence on how the government runs things, some influence, or not much influence at all?"

June Question 5: "Do you ever get as worked up about something that happens in politics or public affairs as you do about something that happens in your personal life?"

June Question 44: "Have you talked politics with anyone recently?"

The scoring:

Responses "lots of influence" or "some influence," "get worked up," and "talked politics recently" were scored +1. All other responses were scored 0.

Distribution of cases:

High (+3)	70
High middle (+2)	199
Low middle (+1)	377
Low (0)	383
Total no. of cases	1,029

The distribution is presented in three groups:

Highly involved	269
Moderately involved ...	377
Not at all involved	383

Objective Agreement with Candidate

This index was constructed from three questions:

August Question 25c: "How do you personally feel about this—are you in favor of putting back price controls on some things or of leaving prices without controls as they are now?"

August Question 26: "Have you heard of the Taft-Hartley Law which regulates labor unions?
If 'yes': *c*) And you personally—are you for the Taft-Hartley Law or against it?"

October Question 39c: "How do you personally feel about this—are you for or against having the government sponsor more public housing projects?"

The scoring:

> Agree with Truman: "For price control," "against Taft-Hartley," and "for government sponsorship of more public housing" = +1. All other responses = 0.
>
> Agree with Dewey is scored analogously.

Distribution of cases:

Agree with Truman	on all three (+3)	......	110
	on two (+2)	....	334
	on one (+1)	....	237
	on none (0)	....	79
	Total (Aug. & Oct.)	...	760
Agree with Dewey	on all three (+3)	......	39
	on two (+2)	....	136
	on one (+1)	....	288
	on none (0)	....	297
	Total (Aug. & Oct.)	...	760

Groupings used are indicated in text.

Political Discussion

This index was constructed from two questions:

June Question 44: "Have you talked politics with anyone recently?"

October Question 33: "Who was the last person you discussed the election or the candidates with?"

The scoring:

> "Have talked politics" and "can name last person" = +1. All other responses = 0.

Distribution of cases:

Talk politics regularly (+2)	....	241
Intermittently (+1)	....	454
Talk politics seldom (0)	....	119
Total no. of cases (October)	..	814

Information

This index was constructed from one question:

June Question 32: "Can you tell me any job each of the persons on the list has held? Glenn Taylor, Harold Stassen, Abdullah, David E. Lilienthal, Robert F. Wagner, Winston Churchill, W. A. Harriman, Alcide de Gasperi, Trygve Lie."

The scoring:

> Correct identification of each was scored +1.

Distribution of cases:

High (+4 or more) ...	347
Middle (+2 and +3) ..	285
Low (+1 and 0)	397
Total no. of cases	1,029

Opinion Leader

This index was constructed from two questions:

June Question 43: "Compared with people you know, are you more or less likely than any of them to be asked your views about politics?"

June Question 44: "Have you talked politics with anyone recently?"

The scoring:

"Opinion leaders" were defined as (1) all respondents who answered that they were "more" likely to be asked their views on politics plus (2) all those who answered "same" *and* had talked politics recently.

Distribution of cases:

Opinion leaders	234
Non-opinion leaders	795
Total no. of cases	1,029

Effect of Election

This index was constructed from two questions:

June Question 11: "Do you think whoever is elected President this year will affect how our relations with Russia are handled, or won't it make any difference?"

June Question 12: "Do you think whoever is elected President will affect how the relations between labor and management are handled, or won't it make any difference?"

The scoring:

Domestic more relevant: Response that election will affect labor-management relations but not relations with Russia.

International more relevant: Response that election will affect relations with Russia but not labor-management relations.

Mixed: Other responses, e.g., think election will affect both or neither.

Distribution of cases:

	All Cases	Cross-Pressured Cases Used in Text
Domestic more relevant.........	160	36
Mixed.......................	721	192
International more relevant......	148	46
Total no. of cases..........	1,029	274

Most Important Problems

This index was constructed from two questions:

June Question 10a: "In this election year here are some important problems facing the country. Would you please read through them and tell me which two of the problems are the *most* important to you personally in making up your mind how to vote?"

June Question 10b: "Which two seem to you the *least* important compared with the others?"

The domestic problems were:

How the relations between labor and management should be handled.
How the cost of living can be kept from rising further.
Whether there should be more or less government control over big business.

The international problems were:

How our relations with Russia should be handled.
How to strengthen the United Nations.
How we should deal with the Communist party in the United States.

The scoring:

Domestic problems more important. was defined as follows: All responses that mentioned domestic issues as the *most* important problems but did *not* mention international, plus those who mentioned both kinds of problems or none as most important problems and consider international problems the *least* important.

International problems more important: Responses mentioning international issues as the *most* important problems, plus all those mentioning both kinds of problems or none as the most important problems but consider domestic problems the *least* important.

Mixed: All other cases.

Distribution of cases:

	All Cases	Cross-Pressured Cases Used in Text
Domestic most important........	280	70
Mixed.......................	436	109
International most important.....	313	95
Total no. of cases...........	1,029	274

Agreement between Candidates' Stand and Respondents' Perception of Candidates' Stand

This index was constructed from five questions covering four topics:

June Question 25: "How do you feel about our present relations with Russia? Do you feel the United States should be more willing to compromise, or is our present policy about right, or should we be firmer than we are today?"

August Question 24: a) "From what you know, does Truman favor compromising with the Russians or taking a firm stand with them?"
b) How about Dewey—do you think he favors compromising with the Russians or taking a firm stand with them?"

August Question 25: a) "Do you think Truman is in favor of putting back price controls on some things or of leaving prices without controls the way they are now?
b) Do you think Dewey is in favor of putting back price controls on some things or of leaving prices without controls the way they are now?
c) How do you personally feel about this—are you in favor of putting back price controls on some things or of leaving prices without controls as they are now?"

August Question 26: "Have you heard of the Taft-Hartley Law which regulates labor unions?
If 'yes' ask *a, b,* and *c:*
a) From what you know, is Truman for the Taft-Hartley Law or against it?
b) How about Dewey—is he for it or against it?
c) And you personally—are you for the Taft-Hartley Law or against it?"

October Question 39: a) "From what you know is Truman for or against having the government sponsor more public housing projects?
b) How about Dewey—is he for or against having the government sponsor more public housing projects?
c) How do you personally feel about this—are you for or against having the government sponsor more public housing projects?"

The scoring and distribution of cases:

Agreement between respondent's opinion and his conception of *Truman's* stand:

On all four issues	57
On three	135
On two	210
On one	228
On none	130
Total no. of cases ..	760

Agreement between respondent's opinion and his conception of *Dewey's* stand:

On all four issues	58
On three	165
On two	214
On one	226
On none	97
Total no. of cases ..	760

Index of Class Predispositions

This index is a combination of other indexes. It was constructed as part of an attempt to develop various measures of stratification or "class" concepts. The four measures used in the final index, in their essential details for present purposes, were:

Objective Class Position:

> The SES index used in this volume, with low and low-middle scored as "working class" (June).

Subjective Class Identification:

> Those who identify themselves as lower or working class (August Question 28) were (with a few exceptions irrelevant to the present analysis) taken as "working class."

General Worker-Management Sympathies:

> Constructed from questions asking about: attitudes to unions (June Question 26) and large corporations (June Question 28); unions or corporations "getting too much power" (June Question 33); and attitude to local corporation involved in 1947 strike (October Question 23). Those who sided with workers on three or more of the four, plus those who, while friendly to corporations, sided with labor on both union questions, were scored as "working class."

Reaction to Political Symbols:

> Those for price control (August Question 25) and *not* for Taft-Hartley (August Question 26) were scored "working class."

Each of the above was cut into working-class versus all others. The resulting four dichotomies, taken as single items (similar to what Stouffer calls "contrived items"), were then treated by the method of scaling known as latent structure analysis. The resulting distribution of cases was:

Working-class dispositions ($p_w = .80$ or more)*	209
Ambivalent ($p_w = .20$ to .79)	208
Business class dispositions ($p_w = .19$ or less)	343
Total no. of cases	760

* The notation p_w is the probability that a person giving a particular pattern of responses is "of the working class" (see Stouffer *et al.*, *Measurement and Prediction* [Princeton: Princeton University Press, 1950], p. 429).

The Sample of the Study

The Sample Design

The so-called "area" method of probability sampling was used. This is the method introduced in the decade preceding the Elmira study to overcome certain systematic biases of previous methods; it is now in general use. The aim is to assure stricter randomness of selection. The application in Elmira and its suburbs for this study are described in more detail by McCarthy[1] (who designed the sample) and by Williams.[2]

With the use of detailed maps the survey area was divided into 816 small segments, typically city blocks, of roughly comparable size. They were numbered in serpentine fashion, and every third was chosen for the sample. All the dwelling units exclusive of institutions, dormitories, and large rooming-houses—roughly excluding the institutional and the transient population—were then listed by field interviewers. Of the six-thousand-odd dwelling units so listed, 1,267 households were chosen on a systematic basis (every 5%). We attempted to interview one adult[3] in each, in anticipation that, after inevitable losses, a panel sample of about one thousand would remain. Results of the June interview attempts were as follows:

	Number	Percentage
Total attempts................	1,267	100
Interview completed and respondent recruited into panel.......	1,029	81
Interview not completed and respondent dropped from panel...	238	19

1. Philip J. McCarthy, "Sampling Procedure for the 1948 Voting Study" (New York State School of Industrial and Labor Relations, Cornell University, 1948). (Mimeographed.)

2. Robert Williams, "Probability Sampling in the Field," *Public Opinion Quarterly*, summer 1950, pp. 316–30.

3. A test to see if weighting by size of household would improve representativeness produced only negligible differences.

Of the 238 cases omitted in the June interview and thereafter not included as part of the panel waves in August or October, about equal numbers were "unobtainable" (90 cases not at home after several calls, out of town, etc.) and "refusals" (92 cases who would not participate). The remaining losses were because of illness (33), non-English-speaking (12), and miscellaneous reasons (11). With the original exclusion by definition of the transient and institutional population, and these omissions, it is likely that the Elmira panel of 1,029 cases is representative of the accessible, permanent part of the population.

After the election, vigorous follow-up provided interviews with 181 of the 238 cases so omitted. Following are certain comparisons between the panel sample of 1,029 and the 181 follow-up cases (of June omissions) on various items of the November interview on which differences were found. The combined sample of the two is also shown at the right to indicate the weight of the omitted cases in the total.

	PERCENTAGES		
	Interviewed in June	Omitted in June	Combined Total
Voted in November............	72	64	71
Voted for:			
Dewey......................	61	44	59
Truman.....................	33	43	34
Minor parties...............	1–	0	1–
No answer..................	5	13	6
Less than age sixty-five*........	88	80	86
At least grammar-school graduate	90	79	88
Married now or before..........	88	81	87
Protestant....................	67	50	65
Automobile owner.............	62	54	61
No. of cases.................	1,029—683	181—116	1,210—799

* Glock has found in examining six panel studies that younger adults were more likely to participate *initially* in all six. Thereafter, however, age is not consistently related to panel mortality (C. Y. Glock, "Participation Bias and Re-interview Effect in Panel Studies" [Doctoral dissertation, Faculty of Political Science, Columbia University, 1950]). The interested reader should consult this work and a forthcoming volume on panel analysis edited by Lazarsfeld and Wiggins for a more extensive treatment of experience with panel studies.

The differences were negligible in sex, age, race, and telephone ownership. But on the above items the differences are noticeable—especially on party preference—and only the relatively small size of the omitted cases within the total hold down their effect on the panel data. The direction of the omissions is toward underrepresentation of the marginal or unintegrated elements in the community—the very old, the poorly educated, the unmarried, the ethnic minorities, and the political minorities.[4] How the latter omission would have affected the accuracy of the Elmira panel, had it been used for prediction, is as follows:

	PERCENTAGE		
	Panel Alone	Omissions Plus Panel	Official Vote
Dewey..............	64.8	62.8	60.3
Truman.............	34.5	36.5	38.1
Minor parties.......	0.7	0.6	1.6
Total no. of cases..	683	799	....

The Panel Mortality

That is the story on the omissions prior to the establishment of the June panel of 1,029 cases. We now turn to what are called mortality losses in subsequent interviews with the established panel of 1,029 cases. The other interview waves consisted of 814 cases in August, 881 in October, and 944 in November.[5] The following table illustrates typical turnover, for the two waves with *most* mortality:

	OF THE JUNE PANEL OF 1,029 CASES		
	Interviewed in August	Mortality in August	Totals
Interviewed in October	760	54	814
Mortality in October..	121	94*	215
Total.............	881	148	1,029

* No attempt made for 50 of these 94 cases.

4. The data and the interpretations of this section are drawn from McCarthy, *op. cit.*, and from Wagner Thielens, "The Elmira Mortality" (typed manuscript on file at the Bureau of Applied Social Research, Columbia University).

5. In addition, a subsample of about 100 respondents who had changed their minds or had not decided were interviewed intensively for an average of several hours each in September.

Below is a summary of the entire four-wave panel operation. About 28 per cent of the cases missed one or more waves, but only about 12 per cent were lost in two or more waves.

Interviewed in:	No. of Cases	Percentage
All four waves........................	746	72
Three of the four.....................	161	16
Mortality in August............53		
In October....................94		
In November..................14		
Two of the four......................	79	8
Mortality in August–October.... 51		
In August–November.......... 1		
In October–November.......... 27		
Only one (June)......................	43	4
Total...........................	1,029	100

In his analysis of the mortality in the regular panel, Thielens found that the cases who missed one or more waves are characterized by:

1. Somewhat less interest and involvement in the subject matter. The mortality cases are less informed, have less communication exposure, and discuss the subject of politics somewhat less than those who participate more regularly. While the differences are seldom striking,[6] this is a characteristic tendency in panel operation, as found by Glock in several studies.

2. Lesser integration into the settled community than the regularly accessible respondents. These differences are of the same order as, and serve to intensify the effect of, the original sample bias toward the "settled community" as opposed to the total census population.[7]

If any one statement can summarize the general nature of the panel nonparticipants, then, it would be that they are somewhat more often nonparticipants *generally* in community life as in politics.

6. The largest difference was in discussion of politics. In June, 33 per cent of those who subsequently were regular participants in the panel had discussed the election, while only 22 per cent of those who subsequently missed one or more waves did so.

7. Perhaps the most striking differences are those that occur in organization membership. About 58 per cent of the regularly available respondents belonged to community organizations, while only 46 per cent of the people who were not at home and only 39 per cent of those who refused on one or more waves were organization members. The regular participants belonged to more organizations also.

Thus, the general bias of figures from this study is somewhat to exaggerate the degree of interest and participation (of the total census population). Since the customary point at which such estimates are introduced into the text deals with the *low* participation, information, and involvement of Americans in politics, the fact that such estimates represent the more settled, integrated, interested part of the population simply reinforces the generalization.

Actually, Thielens found that there are at least *two* distinctively different kinds of mortality (and sample loss generally). Classifying the bulk of the lost cases from the panel as to whether they were primarily "refusals" or primarily "unavailables," it is found that the two contribute quite different—and in part canceling—kinds of distortions.

Here is a comparison of certain characteristics of the two types of mortality with the regular participants in the panel:

	PERCENTAGE		
	---	---	---
	Participated in All Four Waves	Missed One or More Waves	
		Primarily Refusal	Primarily Unavailable*
Characteristics high among refusals:			
Women..................	56	64	48
Catholic..................	27	45	30
Grammar-school education...	24	37	25
No organization memberships.	42	61	54
Characteristics high among unavailables:			
Under forty-five in age.......	55	42	67
Newcomer:			
To Elmira..............	15	7	31
To neighborhood..........	40	28	58
Home renter..............	42	48	61
No telephone..............	26	25	45
Income level rated D........	18	14	27
Total no. of cases........	746	109	144

* "Unavailable" means not home on repeated visits or out of town. Thirty cases, primarily those sick, are not used here.

The pattern seems rather clear in these data: those lost by refusals are more often isolated from participation in public affairs, being members of minority ethnic groups, the "second sex," uneducated, and nonjoiners. In contrast, those lost because they could not be found at home are, obviously, the opposite of stay-at-homes: the young, newcomers, renters, and people of marginal or not-yet-established incomes. If an immigrant grandmother is taken as the prototype of the refuser, a young itinerant worker might be taken as the prototype of the unavailable respondent.

However, these are only tendencies, and the mortality could be further subdivided into still different types. In the end, the reasons for mortality must be as varied as the reasons for missing appointments or failing to register. This heterogeneity, plus the small weight or moment of the mortality in the totals for a single month, keeps the total distortion within reasonable bounds. With appropriate caution about the inadvisability of making absolute estimates for the *census* population, we take our data to be typical of the settled, well-integrated adult residents of an American community.

Index ☒

☒ INDEX